Revolutionary Outlaws

*Ethan Allen and the Struggle for Independence
on the Early American Frontier*

Ethan Allen Homestead, 1787 – Burlington, Vermont

Revolutionary Outlaws

Ethan Allen and the Struggle for
Independence on the
Early American Frontier

Michael A. Bellesiles

UNIVERSITY PRESS OF VIRGINIA
Charlottesville and London

THE UNIVERSITY PRESS OF VIRGINIA
Copyright © 1993 by the Rector and Visitors
of the University of Virginia

First published 1993
First paperback edition 1995

Line drawing of Ethan Allen Homestead,
Burlington, Vermont,
by Charles S. Bergen

Library of Congress Cataloging-in-Publication Data

Bellesiles, Michael A.
    Revolutionary outlaws : Ethan Allen and the struggle for
independence on the early American frontier / Michael A. Bellesiles.
        p.   cm.
    Includes bibliographical references and index.
    ISBN 0-8139-1419-1 (cloth). ISBN 0-8139-1603-8 (paper)
    1. Allen, Ethan, 1738–1789.   2. Revolutionaries—United States—
Biography.   3. Vermont—History—Revolution, 1775–1783.   I. Title.
E207.A4B44   1993
974.3'03—dc20   92-31324
                                                                     CIP

Printed in the United States of America

E
202
A4
.B44
1996

This work is gratefully dedicated
to the three great teachers of my life:
Paul Liley, Christine Heyrman, and Kate Dornhuber.
Their wisdom fills my days.

WITHDRAWN
KELLY LIBRARY
Emory & Henry College
Emory, VA 24327

Contents

Acknowledgments

THE best part of writing this book has been the friends I have made along the way. Almost everywhere I turned, I discovered kindness and generosity. It is a great pleasure for me to acknowledge all those who have given so much of their time to help me with this work.

In the early stages of this project Jack Diggins, Karl Hufbauer, Jon Dewald, Ted Koditschek, and James Kettner offered encouragement and numerous intelligent ideas. I am especially grateful for having made the acquaintance of Michael Johnson while working on my dissertation at the University of California, Irvine. A thorough editor, a wise counselor, a fine scholar, and a great teacher, Professor Johnson enriched the lives of all those he taught. He is a rare and wonderful man.

Grants from the American Antiquarian Society, the Henry C. Huntington Library, and the National Endowment for the Humanities brought me into contact with a number of scholars who have since become friends. Mary Beth Norton, Jean Friedman, John Hench, Bob Dykstra, and JoAnne Manfra made the Antiquarian Society a second home. John Phillip Reid and Bob and Pat Smith made lunch at the Huntington Library an intellectual treat. Gregory Nobles gave freely of his time and knowledge, deepening my understanding of New England rural society. Don Higginbotham offered an insightful and extremely helpful reading of this work, one which I believe has improved the book considerably. My gratitude to them all.

Portions of chapter 7 appeared in the *Journal of American History* 73 (1987): 895–915. My thanks to that journal for awarding this article the Louis Pelzer Memorial Award and for their kind permission to reprint that material here.

My colleagues at Emory University have created the perfect working environment, one which meets the finest ideals of an academic community. My deepest thanks to Jon Prude, Jim Roark, James Melton, Margot Finn, Stephen White, Sharon Strocchia, John Juricek, Tom Burns, and Sheila Cavanagh. My appreciation also to the university itself for its institutional support—and for the job.

Peter Onuf deserves pages of praise from me. I regret that I cannot list all the assistance he has proferred over the last several years. Professor Onuf has proven generous with his time, materials from his own research, intelligent commentary, and companionship. Our rather extended coffee breaks at the Antiquarian Society were high points of my academic career. His willingness to read successive drafts of this book bears credit to his scholarly commitment and goes beyond the call of friendship. He has earned my sincerest admiration.

My thanks to the people of Vermont. My research took me all over the state to a score of repositories. The people who worked in them were almost always dedicated and interested. There are dozens of individuals I would like to thank, but I will limit myself to Ruth Levin of the Bennington Museum and Gregory Sanford, the State Archivist. Their devotion to the documents in their care is appreciated by all who have encountered them. In Greg Sanford, Vermont has probably the finest archivist in the Union; no one works harder at preserving crumbling documents for the use of scholars.

Though they never understood why I quit a respectable career as a bartender to become a professor, my family has remained supportive and amazed. My thanks to them all—and they are too numerous to list. Two of them, Mark Bellesiles and Marjorie Jayne, put me up in their house on the Hudson while I was conducting my research and put up with hours of Ethan Allen stories. My daughter Lilith had the consideration to wait to be born until two days after I finished my dissertation. She has been a glorious distraction and good-humored companion as we traveled to Ireland, England, France, and Germany for my research and teaching. Thanks also to my other good friends who demonstrated heroic patience and good humor: Paul and Arline Liley, Kate Dornhuber, Chris Davis, Janet Ruprecht, Paul Roach, Diana Cammack, and the late Lutz Peter.

And finally, for all it is worth, this book would not exist but for my adviser, Christine Heyrman. Every step of the way she has been a model of a great mentor: she pushed when necessary and left me to figure it out for myself when appropriate; her suggestions were always helpful, her criticisms always correct—which can get a bit annoying at times—and her reading of my work is consistently sensitive and insightful. Professor Heyrman always knew what I was trying to say, even when I was not very certain myself. She has become a valued friend and admired colleague. I hope that the finished book can offer some small recompense for all she and my other friends have given of themselves.

Revolutionary Outlaws

Ethan Allen and the Struggle for Independence
on the Early American Frontier

State Formation on the Early American Frontier

One story is good till another is told.

Ethan Allen, 1775

S URVEYING the northern frontier of the new United States, the Loyalist Peter Oliver could only shake his head in disbelief. Here, it seemed, stood absolute proof of the dissipated nature of the Americans and the dangerous consequence of unchecked democracy. The region to the east of Lake Champlain, recently labeled Vermont by its inhabitants, produced only discord and conflict, disrupting first the British Empire and then the United States. Vermont seemed home to chaos but was no worse than any other frontier region, except in one particular: it was led by a "brave, but unprincipled . . . Rebel," Ethan Allen. Oliver thought Allen was "of a bad Character, & had been guilty of Actions bad enough to forfeit even a good one." With such a leader, there could be no hope for Vermont. But such was the nature of democratic leadership. "This Man seems to be so overstocked with Honor, that there will never be an End to its Dissipation." [1]

Oliver captured precisely one view of New York's northeastern frontier. This region, also known as the New Hampshire Grants, appeared to all respectable people a den of "outlaws." A mob of land thieves and banditti—as the government called them—not content with breaking the law, desired to reject it entirely. According to the government of New York, the worst of the rioters was their leader, Ethan Allen: a thug, a bully, a loudmouthed terrorist—and an atheist!—with a £100 reward on his head. Admittedly charismatic, Allen had succeeded in uniting his neighbors—a motley and volatile collection of ethnic and religious groups who could agree only on hating Yorkers—in the cause of extra-

I

legal resistance to proper authority. On these points every New York government of the 1770s and 1780s agreed, as each was equally certain that it could defeat this mob with the force of law.

Today the history of North America's eighteenth-century frontier is being told again. Historians recently have focused their attention on the western portions of Pennsylvania, the Carolinas, Virginia, and Georgia, as well as the European-American settlements west of the Appalachians. Most of these studies indicate that all these regions exhibited similar patterns of chronic instability and sporadic violence. Economic hardship and cultural differences fueled frontier frictions and ignited into conflict when settlers rejected efforts by eastern elites to dominate the land and political structures of these western territories. Frontier settlers fought back by banding into paramilitary organizations led by local warlords, attacking representatives of the wealthy, politically powerful eastern elites who threatened local autonomy and economic independence.[2]

Where historians once worked under the spell of Frederick Jackson Turner—seeing the eighteenth-century frontier as the preserve of egalitarianism, the seedbed of democracy, and a "safety valve" for diffusing social and political tensions[3]—most modern historians now perceive an embattled borderland afflicted with the social tensions of inequality, autocracy, and even militarism.[4] The very definition of *frontier* currently favored by historians implies confrontations born of diverse cultural contacts and structural developments.[5] Where historians once conceived of the frontier as little more than a region on the "fringes of civilization," it is now seen largely as an area where diverse cultures meet and interact and as a region not yet consolidated into a larger political unit.[6]

The Green Mountain frontier in the years from 1760 to 1789 matches in many particulars the histories of a half dozen other eighteenth-century frontier regions. This northern frontier shares many of the characteristics of the backcountry of Pennsylvania, Maine, and the southern states. All were settled by families devoted to subsistence farming and activated primarily by concerns for economic security rather than profit. The settlers of each region were divided among themselves by religious and ethnic differences and became embroiled in controversies over land titles and political jurisdiction, all of which were complicated by the American Revolution. And in all their controversies with seaboard elites, the frontier settlers believed their resistance animated by a desire to respect traditional understandings of the law.

Students of Frederick Jackson Turner speak of the availability of "free land" on the American frontier. Certainly not free, it was almost always stolen. The native inhabitants rarely considered the seizure of their land an exercise in governmental charity, while most land held under European and European-American title passed first through the hands of wealthy land speculators. Such was the case on the northern New England frontier in the eighteenth century. What makes this frontier interesting, though, and perhaps unique, was the ability of the region's settlers not only to steal the land away from these elites but also to appropriate the era's great political struggle to their own purposes, creating their own state as a way of validating their theft. In this fashion, the settlers of the Green Mountains were both outlaws and revolutionaries.

The northern frontier of New England, at least as embodied in the Grants, differed in several ways from other colonial frontiers. Those who settled in the Green Mountains encountered very little resistance from native Americans. While many Dutch, Germans, Scots, and Irish did settle in the Grants, the vast majority of the population originated in New England. Likewise, despite religious diversity, the religious ethos of most settlers derived from a traditional New England Puritanism. There were a few African-Americans in the region, but only a handful arrived as slaves, unlike most on the southern frontiers. And, most curiously, a single family, the Allens, dominated the political life of the Grants region. Perhaps that unity of leadership explains why the Revolution, which produced bitter civil wars in the southern backcountry, actually enhanced local solidarity in the Green Mountains and allowed these frontier settlers to carry the words of the Declaration of Independence to their logical conclusion. All these characteristics which distinguished the Grants from other colonial frontiers shaped its distinctive insurgency against the legitimate jurisdiction of, first, the royal province and, later, the state of New York. These same social distinctions led the Grants settlers to discover the reasonableness of forming their own state, Vermont, based on their own political logic rather than abstract philosophical premises.

Their success explains a final peculiarity: the persistence of the region's population. Unlike so many other frontiers which served largely as way stations on the search for a better life, Vermont kept its settlers. The majority of families in the New Hampshire Grants in 1775 stayed in their original town of settlement through the Revolutionary period, while a remarkable 95 percent remained in the state at least until 1791, when Vermont entered the union. But then they had no need to move on, for they had constructed a state to meet the architecture of their desires.[7]

What follows is the story of a singular, and singularly neglected, colonial frontier. As early Vermont's fortunes were inextricably bound up with one leading family, the Allens, and its most celebrated representative, Ethan Allen, it is almost impossible to separate the family's story, and his, from the history of this region and these people. In the same fashion, it would be meaningless to speak of Ethan Allen's life without placing his experience firmly within his social context. For Allen, self, family, and community formed a unified whole. Often, as Ethan's brothers Levi and Ira so keenly understood, this self-perception grew from vanity—what we would perhaps call an overactive ego. But, as his brothers also admitted, Ethan held passionately to his loyalties, even to the point of irrationality.

Allen deserved his reputation as a scoundrel, a charismatic charlatan of enormous strength and courage, and a braggart of almost mythical proportions. In short, Allen was the ideal of the frontier redneck, Davy Crockett in a tricorne. Yet Allen also wrote several books, including a very popular narrative of his captivity by the British, liked to be called "the Philosopher," numbered St. John de Crevecoeur and George Washington among his admirers, and wrote the first deistic work in America. This book seeks to study both Allen and his community, to present the story of Ethan Allen as the charismatic organizer of disparate communities into a single political unit and as an eternal outsider.

Ethan Allen was not one of the traditional great men born with all the advantages, like Jefferson or Washington, but a leader who rose from the people. Historians often ignore people like Allen as secondary figures in the American Revolution, but the patriots of the late eighteenth century would have repudiated such a view as limiting one's understanding of the Revolution. To supporters of American independence— from George Washington and John Adams to an artisan in a Philadelphia crowd or a minuteman at Concord—the Revolution expressed a collective endeavor. These patriots thought that no one individual made the Revolution and that none embodied its character and goals. If the American people had relied on a few "Great Men" for direction and leadership, their Revolution would have been stillborn. Widespread involvement and commitment made the Revolution a success as a struggle for political independence and led to the creation of a single American nation.

Ethan Allen stands out as simply the most vocal of thousands of poorly educated but committed people. They left their record, and they speak for themselves. To his opponents Allen seemed the result and the servitor of disorder. Yet rather than disrupting, he drew these communities together through his skill as a communicator and his status as a symbol. In his pamphlets and speeches, Allen gave voice and structure to the feelings of the Grants settlers. Like Patrick Henry and Sam Adams, Allen used his oratorical skill to link local concerns and cultural values to larger translocal issues, making the Green Mountains conflict part of a general revolutionary and democratic movement. For poor settlers suffering from the attention of the rich and the powerful, Allen was a potent weapon in an otherwise hopeless situation. He came to represent the resistance of independent agricultural communities against the machinations of distant governments under the control of wealthy speculators intent on stealing the land of the poor. Allen symbolized Vermont, the one great victory of the powerless against vested interest.

In their turn, the settlers of the northern frontier represent America's commoners. Only 5 percent of colonial America lived in an urban environment; most of the rest lived in agrarian communities and relied on agriculture for survival. Allen spoke for a generation of proud commoners who demanded that the theoreticians, whether Blackstone or Calvin, just "let us clodhoppers alone to our own manner of existence."[8]

Taken together, the Allens and Vermont offer a unique opportunity to reevaluate the complexity of the frontier experience in revolutionary America. Together they showed what a simple and poor people in the eighteenth century might hope to create if given the chance, if freed from traditional bounds. The message of their story is found in what they made together: the independent state of Vermont and the most democratic constitution of its time.

CHAPTER ONE

Legacies

Was ever stable joy yet found below,
Or perfect bliss without mixture of woe? . . .
Like as a bubble, or the brittle glass,
Or like a shadow turning as it was.
More fool then I to look on that was lent,
As if mine own, when thus impermanent.

Anne Bradstreet

THEY found him at their father's grave. Just an hour earlier the family had buried Joseph Allen in the fields behind their house and then gone inside to receive the condolences of the community. His brothers noticed Ethan Allen's absence and went in search of him. They discovered him next to the mound of earth covering the new grave, appealing to his father to return and tell him if there really was an afterlife.

As in a Greek drama, good fortune preludes disaster. In 1755 the family of Joseph and Mary Allen of Cornwall, Connecticut, seemed particularly blessed. All eight of their children, ranging in age from four to seventeen, enjoyed good health and faced a prosperous future. The eldest child, Ethan, showed promise and was preparing, at considerable sacrifice to his family, to attend Yale. At the beginning of that hopeful year, Ethan went to study with a relative, a minister of a nearby town. But the Reverend Jonathan Lee did not have time to prepare Ethan for the unexpected burdens ahead. In April 1755 Joseph Allen died suddenly at the age of forty-six. Buried with him were the hopes and certainties of seventeen-year-old Ethan. Even as his brothers led him away, Ethan continued to demand of his father an answer to a question most people held not open to debate: Was there an afterlife? This question would haunt Allen his whole life.

But for the moment more practical problems confronted Ethan. He abandoned his plans to attend Yale, staying in Cornwall to take his father's place. Like most New Englanders, Allen subordinated personal desires to the family's security. Yet his family realized, as brother Ira later reported, that their father's death affected Ethan deeply, accentuating his earlier erratic behavior and religious doubts. Unable to accept his father's death, Ethan became disturbed by fears of his own mortality.[1] Life on the New England frontier seemed, as Anne Bradstreet wrote upon the death of her granddaughter, "like as a bubble, or the brittle glass," yet the constancy of death did not inure New Englanders to the loss of a parent, sibling, or child.[2] Family bonds retained their centrality on the northern frontier, passing communal values and Puritan legacies from one generation to another. The experiences of one generation replicated those of the parents.

I

We may with rational certainty conclude, that moral goodness and happiness will ultimately be victorious over sin and misery.

—Ethan Allen

Some responsibilities went unquestioned. His community expected Ethan Allen, as the eldest son, to administer his father's estate, care for his mother, and see his siblings into adulthood and "a fair sustenance." He had little with which to work. In a more established, longer-settled New England community, the Allens' seventy-two acres would have been sufficient for a generation. But Cornwall lay on Connecticut's northwestern frontier. Ethan's father, among the founders of the town in 1741, had not made a very good choice. As Timothy Dwight said of the place:

> The God of Nature, from his boundless store,
> Threw Cornwall into heaps, and did no more.

Cornwall, Dwight noted, "is generally considered as the roughest township" in Connecticut. In the first winters livestock froze, planting had to be delayed a dangerously long time, and children died of starvation.

Minister Solomon Palmer later wrote, "So great was the expense, fatigue and hardship that I endured for the first three years, that I would not suffer them again for the whole township."[3]

In 1742 Joseph Allen, serving as Cornwall's tax collector, rated the town's fifty-two households for future assessment. The average Cornwall household had just one cow and a horse, and maybe an ox and some swine. The average rating stood at £27.10; neighboring Woodbury's average assessment was £80. Cornwall's newness, its poor soil, and its lack of good grazing land limited the town's involvement in any wider market economy while making for a relatively even distribution of wealth, as elsewhere on the New England frontier. Early town leaders often died insolvent, as did George Holloway, the first town clerk and the wealthiest man in Cornwall's first assessment. The distance between the highest and lowest remained minimal.[4]

Since nearly every family owned lots of undeveloped land, livestock tended to determine wealth differentials. At the bottom of the wealthiest quartile, Joseph Allen owned two oxen, two cows, two horses, and one pig, with a net rated worth, excluding the poll rating, of £21. Yet only two oxen and a pig separated Allen from the median; and had he lived in Woodbury, Allen would have fallen into the poorest quartile.[5]

This small gap widened with time, as oxen helped to clear fields and plant crops. It took only an accident for a family to lose its grip on subsistence, as happened when Ethan Allen's uncle, Remember Baker, died at the age of twenty-six. In this instance the only child, also named Remember, lived for a time with different family members before being apprenticed out as a joiner.[6]

In the first decade of settlement, economic differences remained unimportant. An equality of hardship made the frontier a relatively open society. In Litchfield, Joseph Allen had been a farmer of no real consequence in the town's government. Civic responsibility and status came with age, and then primarily to members of a very few families.[7] In Cornwall's first decade, every one of its forty adult males held some town office. Though only thirty-one when he moved to Cornwall, Allen was elected the town meeting's first moderator and then a selectman, tax collector, and chair of the land division and ministerial search committees. But the relative economic equality and political openness of Cornwall diminished with time. The first twelve years that Cornwall sent representatives to the General Assembly, 1761 to 1773, seven men shared fifty terms between them, with four men serving forty-seven of these terms, and the other three each serving only once. With the near monopolization of power by an emerging political elite, someone from the middle of the social scale, like one of selectman Joseph Allen's sons, could no longer hope to rise to a position of authority.[8]

The social organization of colonial New England rested on the family. In 1737 Joseph Allen married Mary Baker of nearby Woodbury. Ten months later, on 10 January 1738, Mary Allen gave birth to her first child. As did most New Englanders, the Allens turned to the Old Testament for a name: Ethan, denoting strength and firmness. He was followed in the next fourteen years by seven siblings: Heman, Lydia, Heber, Levi, Lucy, Zimri, and Ira. These seven children became Ethan's primary responsibility in 1755. As the eldest son, he inherited a double portion of what was left after the widow's third. His father left deeds to just over five hundred acres, but plowland constituted only thirteen acres. Ethan inherited fifty-four unimproved acres, mostly uncleared forest. But he never made any effort to break up the family farm, to distinguish his lands from those of his brothers and mother.[9]

Instead, Ethan attempted to step into his father's place by seeing to the details of the family economy: apportioning work, planting crops, laboring in the fields, bargaining with and suing neighbors, and slowly paying off Joseph Allen's £224 debt. After two years of ineffectually asking one of his father's debtors to pay up, Ethan went to court for the first time, acting in his mother's name, and won his case, collecting £9.13. The success of the family remained a joint effort, with the nine Allens working together for their collective prosperity. Marriages and migrations did not break this chain of responsibility. The Allens were known for an individualism of character which bordered on eccentricity. Yet such personal traits did not impede family solidarity. The eighteenth-century economy allowed more room for individual thought than for individual action.[10]

None of the Allens ventured forth alone. Only the French and Indian War drew Ethan away from his family, and then for only a brief stint in the community's militia. When the French threatened Fort William Henry in the summer of 1757, the inhabitants of Cornwall encountered the outside world for the first time. A recruiter, one of the few sojourners to Cornwall in its first quarter century, persuaded the town meeting to send some of their youths to the defense of the fort. Relying on his siblings to see to the farm, Ethan joined a company from Cornwall marching north. But they arrived too late, for the French had already seized the fort, and the Cornwall volunteers returned home after two weeks of service. Eighteen years passed before the future commanding general of the armies of independent Vermont undertook his next tour of duty.[11]

After this brief flurry of activity, Ethan settled back into the quiet life of Cornwall and the heavy work of running the family farm. In 1761, when Elihu Allen needed £50 to buy a farm in Cornwall, he went to his cousin Ethan for help. Ethan gladly aided another Allen to settle in the area, writing Elihu a note for £50.[12] The Allens' farm supported the family but did not advance them. Ethan saw that as his siblings became adults and sought to establish their own families, their collective resources would be exhausted quickly. In 1762 Ethan thought he discovered a solution to this problem. Rumor held a hill in nearby Salisbury to be composed of iron ore. Winter was a time for deals, and while in Salisbury in January 1762, Ethan met his friend Paul Hazeltine's brother John. Ethan convinced the older man to join him in entering a partnership with the Forbes brothers, who owned the iron hill. Allen put up the note from his cousin as his share of the capital. The four men, joined by Heman Allen, then purchased water and timber rights on Tohconnick Mountain from the Owen brothers for £20, completing the prerequisites for their operation. Family networks, notes, and labor made up the complex and fragile economic relations in eighteenth-century New England.[13]

To undertake an endeavor this tenuous—one requiring the steady application of hard physical labor, a careful balancing of limited capital, and a great deal of luck in a very chancy new industry and market—demanded enormous self-confidence, if not bravado. On the other hand, a small preindustrial forge was easily shut down and restarted, and thus capable of adjusting production to demand. Such flexibility allowed Allen to solve the classic problem of these early forges: labor. He continued to farm and draw upon his family's labor as necessary. Inefficient enterprises, these early iron forges burned up many acres of forest a year, but they were not capital-intensive, making family partnerships sufficient. Allen thrived on the challenge but was dependent on the pooling of his family's and friends' resources. Without their help, Ethan's confidence would have been insufficient.[14]

Allen lived at the site and did most of the work. Within a year he had built the first major iron furnace in Connecticut. An increase in demand for potash kettles made the enterprise profitable for several decades. In 1763 Ethan and his partners expanded their enterprise by purchasing the Owens' forge and its land for £430. By the mid-1760s the forge employed fifty men and had a furnace capable of producing two tons of molten iron at a time. Known in later years as the "Ethan Allen Forge," it provided muskets for the Continental army and cannon for the USS *Constellation*. But by that time, Allen was long gone from Connecticut.[15]

In 1763 Elihu Allen paid Ethan the £50 he owed him. Ethan and his brother Heman immediately used the money as down payment on a large and expensive (£500) house overlooking the furnace in Salisbury, mortgaging the family farm to the seller for the remaining amount. Expanding his operations, Ethan purchased the mineral rights to twenty-one acres in Woodbury. His reasoning was sound and his confidence justified; Salisbury stood amidst fertile rolling land, more easily farmed than rocky Cornwall. His evaluation on the Salisbury Grand List increased in a single year from £42 to £125, placing him solidly in the middle of that town's economic order.[16]

Ethan Allen had another reason for buying a large house. As a good New Englander, he prudently postponed marriage until he was established economically. By 1762 he thought himself secure enough to wed. His choice for a wife appeared unusual for the time and, in some ways, for his personality. As an adolescent, Ethan had made trips to the gristmill at Woodbury, where he befriended Remember Baker, Benjamin Stiles, and Mary Brownson, friendships that continued for the rest of their lives.[17]

When Allen turned twenty-four in 1762, Mary Brownson was thirty, and illiterate—she signed her name with a shaky cross. Her father was a prosperous farmer and millowner in Woodbury, and she eventually inherited some of his property.[18] But Ethan Allen did not wed Mary Brownson for her modest dowry. Allen showed little inclination in his life for taking the easy and safe path to money, and the age difference did not trouble him. He and Brownson had been friends for several years by the time of their engagement and evidently saw something in each other's company, getting married on 23 June 1762.[19]

Even while creating his own family, Allen never separated from the one into which he had been born. Ethan Allen wanted to be like his father, and now his father was dead. For many young men, the patriarch's death can be liberating. Ethan could have taken the opportunity and left home to seek adventure in one of New England's port towns. But he chose instead to act on his father's terms, to take on the responsibilities of a large family and the steady hard work of farm and mine. Ethan's wife bore the same name as his mother, and they named their first son Joseph, in honor of his father.[20]

Ethan based his success as a young patriarch on his family's legacies, exchanging the land he inherited to create greater economic opportunities.[21] But he drew also on the less tangible legacy of Allen family traditions. The Allens' goal remained consistent, generation to generation: securing the continuity of the lineal family. Ethan did not have to look far for an example of such focused dedication. His father left Litchfield in 1741 seeking economic security for his family and played a major role in the founding of Cornwall. While this move demonstrated boldness, it paled before the courage of Joseph's mother, Mercy Wright Allen.

Marriage generally constituted the most important decision of a woman's life in colonial America. If she misjudged, a young wife could find herself facing a life of misery without recourse, as society offered little sympathy to the victim of a bad marriage.[22] Mercy Wright's choice of a husband proved, at least in economic terms, an error in judgment. Her cousin Samuel Allen made a career of losing the family's resources. In 1699 he tried his hand at land speculation, a disastrous mistake which wiped out his inheritance except a portion of the family farm in Northampton. Selling this land to his brother, Samuel Allen sought cheaper land for the steadier certainties of farming. In 1705 he found inexpensive land on the frontier, in Deerfield, Massachusetts. Deerfield was a rugged little town sitting in the fertile Connecticut River valley. With sufficient labor a family could survive and maybe prosper, assuming the Indians did not come back. Land was cheap in Deerfield because the previous year, 1704, the Abenaki Indians had attacked, killing thirty-eight people and carrying off more than a hundred in the "Great Deerfield Raid." Few people wanted to live on this particular frontier, including, eventually, Samuel Allen. After eight years he and his family sought security in the central Connecticut town of Coventry, a river town enjoying the benefits of commercial agriculture—benefits largely limited to those who already owned land there, which the Allens did not.[23]

When Samuel Allen died in 1718, he left his seven children a far smaller estate than his father had willed him. More importantly, Samuel had not seen to his children's economic future while he was alive. Where his father had worked to ensure his eldest son's place in society by providing him with a farm, Samuel failed to make the same provisions for any of his children, leaving them wholly dependent on their mother, Mercy Allen. Fortunately for the Allen children, they had a remarkable mother.[24]

Mercy Allen could have done as many others in Coventry did and apprenticed her children out as artisans, a common strategy for families facing economic decline. But such a approach often led to the disintegration of the family. So Allen decided to barter her small holdings in Coventry for a much larger land right on Connecticut's northwest frontier. In 1715 a group of speculators paid the Pootatuck Indians £15 for an area they named Litchfield. Five years later the "Widow Allen" bought into the Litchfield proprietorship, becoming the only woman proprietor in a rare violation of form attributable solely to her strength of character and persuasive skills.

In moving to Litchfield, the Allens reversed direction, returning to the frontier and gambling that the low cost of land would compensate for their lack of capital. Over the next five years several inhabitants of Litchfield had violent encounters with Indians, and one settler was scalped in 1723. The work required to clear the land—removing forests, clearing fields of stumps and rocks, pushing archaic plows through reluctant soil, setting out pastures for livestock, and building a home— was rough and difficult. These seemed unnecessary hardships to Mercy Allen's only adult son, Nehemiah, who fled back east during the Indian alarm of 1723. Not every Allen felt the force of family bonds.[25]

Mercy Allen was made of tougher material, and she hung on with her five younger children. She drew for a house lot in the town's first land division in 1721, took responsibility for building Litchfield's south garrison during the Indian scare that drove her son away, and directed the family in clearing their farm. Widow Allen made the necessary economic negotiations for her young family in a doubly hostile world—a wilderness adverse to settlement and a male-dominated society suspicious of women. In an age when women generally acted only with male guidance, Mercy Allen held her own on the frontier.[26]

Before her death in 1728, Mercy Allen did her best to correct for the errors of her husband, establishing the older children on farms of their own or in secure marriages. Her youngest son, Joseph, received one-third of her estate, most of it uncleared land.[27] It may have been a small stake with which to start, but he owned land in a community well situated to develop into the trading center of Connecticut's northwest frontier. Litchfield land was still inexpensive compared to the more settled regions of the province, and the Allen family was just large enough to help each other in their mutual struggle to attain economic sufficiency.

Ethan Allen grew up on tales of Mercy Allen's courage. He also learned how the Allens came to Massachusetts from England with Thomas Hooker in 1632, following him three years later to help found the colony of Connecticut.[28] For more than a hundred years, the Allens struggled to ensure their collective survival, relying on one another, exploiting every resource for the benefit of the lineal family. Like a great many early New Englanders, and like the peasantry of contemporary Europe, the Allens found economic security best served by geographic mobility. In this sense the popular image of the Puritan village is often misleading in its emphasis on stability and sedentary families. By focusing solely on the families who stayed put for several generations, one misses the fluidity of a society which, in its insistence on family continuity, required movement.[29]

Ethan Allen adhered to his family's heritage. Like four generations of Allens, he abandoned a community which did not seem to offer a stable economic future to a growing family. While more adventurous than his ancestors in moving from farming to an iron forge, Ethan shared success with his family, using his profits to add to the Allens' landholdings. Working long days at his forge, Allen lived up to his legacies.

II

Nor is it reconcilable to the exalted character that we ought to ascribe to God, to suppose that he has implanted such strong desires and expectations in our souls of surviveing the grave for no purpose . . . . we can ha{r}dly imagine that {God} . . . would by the stroke of death frustrate our expectations by a cruel annihilation.—Ethan Allen

14

As a child of New England, Ethan Allen could not see solely to the needs of this world. With his iron forge, Allen sought a definitive solution to his family's economic security. He desired the same certainty in religious matters.

Standing by his father's grave, demanding an answer, Ethan sought a shortcut around the pervasive uncertainty of Puritanism. According to his brother Ira, Ethan had been obsessed with religion even before the wrenching crisis of his father's death. Like his father, "Ethan began early in life to dispute and argue on religious matters." Allen constantly jotted down whatever occurred to him, attempting to improve his skill and his understanding of the world. In a land where Indians still terrorized white settlements and where bounties were offered on wolves and rattlesnakes, Ethan Allen studied logic.[30]

This driving intellectual desire convinced Joseph Allen to send Ethan to Yale. In a society where labor was scarce, it is a testament to Joseph's confidence in his son that he agreed to lose Ethan's labor for the years of study it would take to prepare for Yale. But considerable returns awaited the Allens if Ethan became a lawyer, merchant, or minister. When Joseph Allen sent Ethan to prepare for college with their relative the Reverend Jonathan Lee, Ethan found himself living with one of Connecticut's more prominent Separates, a dedicated Calvinist who led his congregation into revolt against the standing order.[31]

His studies with Lee did nothing to assuage Ethan's early religious doubts, a crisis of faith brought to a boil by his father's death. Over the following few years, Allen found the answers he demanded in the cool rationalism of the deistic Enlightenment. In 1761 Allen met Thomas Young, an itinerant, self-educated doctor, often labeled a quack. Young finished the religious education Ethan's father began, bringing to the task the formidable prestige of the age's great minds—albeit in a popularized form. An avowed deist, Young believed in a Newtonian world and its great clockmaker god. He despised Calvinism's grim—and in his view, irrational and vindictive—deity, preferring the comprehensible, mechanical order of the deistic universe. Young shared his knowledge, opinions, and books with Allen. Charles Blount and John Locke, a debunker of myths and an epistemologist, especially impressed young Allen. Young and Allen worked together to gain the liberal education they could not afford.

Young helped to resolve Allen's doubts and placed his father firmly in heaven. Compassionate and benevolent, the deist god would allow none of its creation to burn for eternity. Locke's logic invigorated Allen, while the positive hopes for an afterlife he discovered in Blount comforted him. If a letter that Allen wrote twenty years later is to be trusted, Jonathan Lee became concerned when he heard that Allen denied the doctrine of original sin, telling Allen that without original sin there would be no need for atonement, or Christ, or, indeed, Christianity. After several months of reflection, Allen decided that Lee was right: there was no need for Christianity. Allen told Lee he could not accept that just because Adam and Eve ate an apple, their "un-offending offspring" should earn "the eternal displeasure of God." Could a just god "sentence the human progeny to the latest posterity to everlasting destruction?" Allen argued that this false representation of the deity's nature was "the very basis on which christianity is founded, and is announced in the New-Testament to be the very cause why Jesus Christ came into this world." This was not the conclusion desired by the Reverend Lee.[32]

As in his economic conduct, Allen found precedent for his religious views within his own family. The religious rationalism Allen embraced in the 1760s, especially his rejection of original sin and predestination, was a reasonable extension of another Allen legacy: religious liberalism.

In the 1730s Jonathan Edwards of Northampton, Massachusetts, became concerned about the spread of an Enlightenment faith in the effectualness of the human will. He found in what he called Arminianism an increased worldliness which would destroy Puritanism with its heresy that man could save himself, placing human agency on a par with God's will. Edwards launched a crusade to defend Puritanism and its doctrine of man's total dependence on God.[33] In 1734 this message, and Edwards's compelling preaching, bore fruit in Northampton. Under Edwards's careful guidance, a series of emotional conversion experiences, primarily among young people, revivified religious life in the Connecticut River valley. Expectations of great things, perhaps even of the millennium, animated New England. The fires of religious passion burned brighter still in 1739 with George Whitefield's arrival in America.[34]

Whitefield, an Anglican minister, galvanized America, becoming its first national figure, known in every colony. In a triumphal procession from Savannah to Boston, Whitefield drew crowds beyond anyone's anticipation. Witnesses, even the cynical Benjamin Franklin, reported on the majestic power of Whitefield's voice and the succinctness of his message as waves of passion and longing swept through his audiences. Whitefield echoed Edwards in proclaiming the necessity of a church of the truly converted under a converted minister. The message was traditional Calvinism, but the presentation was entirely unique. With thousands of people throughout America feeling the urgency of his call, Whitefield went beyond preaching and initiated a movement, the Great Awakening.[35]

Those converted by Whitefield felt the power of their individual religious passions. They sought others who shared their feelings, and ministers who could continue to stoke the flames of religious enthusiasm. Lay exhorters rose in Whitefield's footsteps, claiming the sufficiency of grace and questioning the authority of ministers. Religious and political authorities moved to control what they saw as a movement bent on radical social change. By 1742 New England was divided between supporters of the revivals, generally called New Lights, and their opponents, labeled Old Lights. To Edwards, writing in that year, it seemed that a "great war" rent New England, with two armies battling for its soul.[36]

Edwards had not wanted to start a social revolution; he had only wanted to arouse the sentiments of his people. Edwards highlighted the same core theological issues as the original American Puritans: the relationship of the individual with God, of the congregation with its minister, and of church and state. Edwards did shift the psychology, holding that each of these relationships should be spiritual; to his opponents he made them merely "enthusiastic." Edwards found New England's religious life too passive: his congregants awaited salvation rather than seeking it. Edwards' ideas may have been traditional in intent, but their impact was revolutionary; he may have hoped for a simple revival of religious sentiment, but he, and America, got much more. Nearly every town in New England divided over the Great Awakening, including Litchfield, Connecticut.[37]

The Great Awakening hit Litchfield hard. The whole town shared Calvinist beliefs; but the majority of church members, inspired by Whitefield, insisted on the public relation of a "second birth" for participation in communion and attacked liberals like Joseph Allen for taking too favorable a view of human ability, playing down original sin and undermining the church of visible saints that had long been the Puritan ideal. On the other hand, Allen and a substantial number of his fellow church members suspected the enthusiasm and self-righteousness of the evangelicals. The salvation of the individual appeared more important to the evangelicals than the harmony of the community; the New Lights' censoriousness and demands for more exclusive churches threatened to divide the congregation, the community, and Puritan Christianity itself. Each side of the dispute in Litchfield put on the mantle of Puritanism; it fit them both.

The conflict between the two factions intensified as evangelicals declared their minister "unconverted" and the town meeting became a battleground. These events replicated events in many New England towns. When in the minority, New Lights separated from those "holding to, and practicing upon, the principle of graceless communion," to organize a purer, uncontaminated church. Occasionally, as in Litchfield, the evangelicals constituted the majority of a church's membership. Those within the congregation who disagreed with the evangelicals, whether members or not, faced the uncomfortable choice of accepting their spiritual inferiority at every church meeting or of separating themselves. The Allens and other Litchfield liberals chose to leave both the church and the town, purchasing rights to the new town of Cornwall, twenty rugged miles northwest, over the hills in the Housatonic Valley. All but a few of the first fifty families which moved to Cornwall between 1740 and 1744 came in family groups from the Litchfield area. Again, this pattern typified New England frontier towns and would be repeated a generation later when Joseph Allen's sons joined an even larger migration north.[38]

These settlers did not perceive themselves redefining their society by moving to the frontier but rather upholding traditional standards under attack by the excesses of the Great Awakening. In their own eyes they remained simple Puritans trying to hold their community together in the face of radical social changes. Cornwall stuck with their old Litchfield covenant, including the Half-Way Covenant which, in their reading, allowed all into communion while limiting membership to those who had conversion experiences.[39] Seeking to accentuate their continuity with the past, they even attempted to lure their former minister, Timothy Collins, to Cornwall. But Collins felt responsible for his Litchfield congregation and still hoped to resolve the crisis there.[40] Turned down by Collins, the town meeting appointed a committee of three men, including Joseph Allen, which chose Solomon Palmer.[41]

Well satisfied with its minister, Cornwall voted Palmer a salary comparable to that paid in more settled communities and, unlike most New Englanders, gave their minister little grief over its payment. But this carefully constructed consensus did not last. In March 1754, shortly after the Litchfield church dismissed Collins as unregenerate, Palmer resigned his ministry, announcing his intention of becoming an Episcopalian.[42]

Suddenly it became very clear that theological attitudes had undergone a number of changes over the previous decade. During that period Joseph and Mary Allen and several of their neighbors had ceased being Calvinists. Many in town joined Joseph Allen in support of Palmer: the congregation voted not to dismiss him and urged that he continue as the town's minister even if he joined the Church of England. But the Litchfield Consociation of Churches, to which the Cornwall church belonged, furiously declared the Cornwall pulpit vacant, and Palmer left for England.[43]

The Great Awakening established a pattern repeated in dozens of towns for half a century. The Old Lights left Litchfield in 1741 to establish a church which included all the townspeople within its covenant; by 1775 Cornwall had evangelical Congregational, liberal Congregational, Episcopalian, Presbyterian, and Baptist meetings. Religious controversy may not have always created new church members, but it certainly produced new churches.[44]

Ethan Allen learned his religious rationalism at home. In colonial New England, religion was the core of community life, essential to any town's cohesion. Joseph Allen insisted on the importance of religious experience, on the need to strive for the sensation of grace and full membership in the community's church. But he objected to the evangelicals' limitation on human agency, which held those who had not yet felt the power of conversion hopeless before an angry god. As Ethan Allen later recalled, his father had taught him "to reject the doctrine of original sin." Original sin condemned without compassion or justice the mass of humanity, including Ethan's father, to eternal damnation. Joseph Allen taught Ethan that the Calvinists failed to consider "that if it was consistent with the perfection of God to save them, his salvation could not fail to have been uniformly extended to all others" equally deserving. In short, justice demanded an equality of salvation. The Allens' concept of a just god demanded theological equity, implying the possibility of universal salvation.[45]

Ethan Allen's denial of original sin grew from personal need. Death exists because of original sin, so rejecting original sin denies the existence of death. As Allen pointed out to Lee, removing original sin from the equation of life removed the need for Jesus Christ as a redeemer. Through a logistical trick, Allen gave his father immortality. Having made this discovery, Allen clung to it the rest of his life. The starting point of all his later religious discussions would be the invalidity of original sin in a universe created by a benevolent deity.

As the young Ethan Allen developed these ideas, he insisted that the needs of an interdependent frontier community required an open communion, for exclusivity promised the sort of divisions which isolated neighbor from neighbor. Allen later concluded his attack on New England's Calvinists with a critique of their social failures: "As they exclude reason and justice from their imaginary notions of religion," so they excluded both from their government of society. Drawing upon his father's views, Allen faulted the evangelicals for their theological differentiation and individualism. The New Lights made some people better than others in the eyes of God, separating them from the community. Allen rejected all religious hierarchy, whether ministerial or sacramental.[46] It is impossible to know if Joseph Allen would have accepted his son's views, but these opinions reconciled Ethan to his father's death and his own mortality. Ethan Allen found rationalism very comforting.

III

By Jesus Christ, I wish I may be Bound Down in Hell with old Belzabub a Thousand years in the Lowest Pitt in Hell and that Every Little Insippid Devil should come along by and ask the Reason of Allens Lying there, {if} it Should be said {that} he made a promise . . . that he would have satisfaction of Lee and Stoddard and Did Not fulfill it.—Ethan Allen, 1764

By 1765 Ethan Allen apparently had resolved his two primary crises: the family economy and his own psychic security, both of which had been threatened by the death of his father. His iron forge increased the family's capital, allowing Ethan to purchase more farmland; while his friendship with Thomas Young clarified his father's teachings. Yet Ethan's efforts to build upon each of these foundations backfired, bringing his hard-won security crashing down around him, and threatening the very unity of his family and community.

The problem for Allen was that he found it difficult to reconcile the social need to get along, upon which economic success so often hinged, with his inner striving for intellectual understanding. For instance, Connecticut outlawed inoculation; but those who believed in enlightened scientific methodology dismissed the fears of inoculation as rank superstition. Linking himself with the great modern thinkers, Allen was inoculated with smallpox in 1764 by Thomas Young, in front of the Salisbury meetinghouse, on Sunday. Threatened with prosecution by his cousin the Reverend Lee, Allen made several unpleasant references to Jesus Christ, Beelzebub, hell, and "every little insipid Devil" and was tried for blasphemy. The outcome of this trial is unknown, but the results were clear: social ostracism.[47] Despite his economic success, Allen became increasingly unpopular in Salisbury. It did not do for an upcoming young citizen, a man who showed potential of becoming a town leader, to walk around denying the divinity of Christ. To further aggravate the community, Allen had a habit of solving his contentions on the spot, relying on his own physical strength—which was legendary—rather than the solemn judgment of the town assembled in meeting.

The great political issue of eighteenth-century New England was pigs. Those who raised large numbers of the beasts constantly lobbied for the pigs' right to roam freely. The majority, including the Allens, consistently voted to require that they remain properly penned. One day, finding eight of Samuel Tousley's pigs in his garden, Ethan and his brother Heman seized the swine and locked them in a friend's pen. Rather than simply getting his pigs and taking them home, Tousley took the Allens to court, charging that the animals had not been placed in a legally defined pound, which was the case. Appearing before Justice of the Peace John Hutchinson, Ethan argued that one pen was as good as another. Hutchinson upheld the point of law and ordered the Allens to pay Tousley a ten-shilling fine plus five shillings in costs, a valuable lesson in legal formalism.[48]

Ethan then demanded immediate payment of a note for £2 owed him by Samuel's brother John Tousley, who refused to pay. A week later Allen was in court, allowing Justice Hutchinson to even the score by ordering Tousley to make good on his note. If one could not get back at an individual with whom one had a dispute, a relative would suffice.[49]

In October 1765 Ethan and Heman Allen made the serious financial error of selling their interests in the iron forge to George Caldwell for £500 and their house to Oliver Millard. Both deals brought only the barest profit, with which the Allens opened a general store in Salisbury.[50] But there was disagreement over the terms of the sale, Ethan expecting more cash up front, and he was again hauled before Justice Hutchinson, charged with assault upon the new owner of the forge. The court records described Allen's method of conflict resolution: "Ethan Allen did, in a tumultuous and offensive manner, with threatening words and angry looks, strip himself even to his naked body, and with force and arms, without law or right, did assail and actually strike the person of George Caldwell of Salisbury, aforesaid, in the presence and to the disturbance of His Majesty's good subjects." Allen was fined ten shillings.[51]

A month later Allen encountered Caldwell and Robert Branthwaite on a road outside Salisbury. Words were exchanged, and Allen "stripped off his clothes to his naked body" and beat up both men. Appearing before the justice, Allen again exposed "his naked body and in a threatening manner with his fist lifted up repeated these malicious words three times [to Caldwell]: 'You lie you dog,' and also did with a loud voice say that he would spill the blood of any that opposed him." Hutchinson dismissed charges when Allen agreed to leave town.[52]

Leaving Heman in Salisbury to operate the general store, Ethan took his family—which included his newborn son, Joseph—to Northampton, where his grandfather had died eighty years before. Using the capital left from the sale of the Salisbury mine, Ethan bought a lead mine in Northampton with his in-laws Abraham and Israel Brownson and Benjamin Stiles. Ethan, whose investment was smallest, acted as overseer, managing the daily operation of the mine. Unlike his earlier mining effort in Salisbury, this one was not a success, and Allen quickly found himself in debt and subject to several lawsuits.[53]

His cousin Joseph Allen, a man of some consequence in Northampton, came to Ethan's aid on several occasions, despite deep religious differences. One of Jonathan Edwards's strongest advocates in the controversy which had driven that esteemed minister out of town, Joseph Allen hoped, like the Reverend Lee, to save Ethan's soul. Toward this end he loaned Ethan the collected sermons of Edwards. Again, the effect was not that intended. While sharing Edwards's fascination with and respect for nature, as well as his concern with epistemology, Ethan was stunned by the dark pessimism of Edwards's vision, with his portraits of an angry and vindictive God and the torments of damnation which seemed to await the majority of humanity. Ethan quickly became the village scoffer, a tavern debater of some forcefulness. But while he derided Edwards mercilessly, Allen also defended Edwards's right to state his views publicly and criticized the town of Northampton for driving its brilliant minister into exile.[54]

The citizens of Northampton, still sensitive about the entire Edwards incident, objected to Allen's conduct. The Reverend Jonathan Judd visited Allen's mine several times to speak with Ethan of his dangerous errors and to entreat him not to corrupt his peers. These gentle rebukes failed to move Allen. In July 1767 Northampton's town meeting ordered Ethan Allen and his family to leave town. The exact reason is not recorded, but one can safely assume that this warning out was in response to Allen's general disruptiveness.[55]

Allen returned to Salisbury in low spirits and moved in with Heman. The Allen family showed ominous signs of collapsing under the pressures of economic setbacks. The lead mine had been such a disaster that the Brownsons were unable to pay Ethan his wages, so Ethan sued them. They sued in return for some personal possessions which Ethan had kept. Allen then paid off another debt by acting as attorney for the plaintiff in a suit against Israel Brownson. At one point Mary Allen drove her brothers off with an axe when they came to seize some of Ethan's property. The entire affair was a mass of confusion which the courts could not unravel. In the midst of it all, in the summer of 1768, Israel Brownson packed up and moved north to the Green Mountains, leaving his debts behind.[56]

It was a dismal time for thirty-year-old Ethan Allen. To his community, and probably to himself, he appeared a failure. On the verge of securing prosperity for his family, Allen's desires and beliefs came into conflict with social norms and led to his expulsion from two towns. At the end of 1769 Ethan's sister Lydia, with whom he was very close, became seriously ill. The entire family rushed to Goshen, where she lived with her new husband, bringing doctors, medicines, folk remedies, anything that would halt her slow decline. But all to no purpose: Lydia died early in 1770. Immediately after Lydia's funeral, Ethan's mother, Mary

Allen, had a stroke, and Ethan literally carried her back to Heman's house in Salisbury. His world slipping from his grasp, Ethan resented his inability to control events.[57]

There is a story which Ira Allen later told about this period, one which is perhaps too appropriate. While admitting to an admiration for his oversized brother, Ira displayed a tinge of contempt in his memory of Ethan's failures in these years. Attempting to demonstrate his greater craftiness, Ira bet Ethan that he could beat him to a hickory tree that lay on the other side of a bog behind the family's farm. In Ira's telling, Ethan went straight for it, crashing through the underbrush and splashing noisily in the stagnant water. Meanwhile Ira took a path around the swamp that he knew led to the tree. The two Allens arrived at the tree at the same time, reaching the goal by different means, though Ethan was a lot dirtier.[58]

Either way, the point was to avoid vanishing in the bog. Even in his darkest times in 1768 and 1769, Ethan Allen never abandoned his search for an alternative, some route that would allow him his autonomy even while holding the family together. He would find his answer in seeming to thrash through the swamp while actually employing all his brothers' skills to sneak around the morass of social conflict. That route led him into the Green Mountains of northern New England.

CHAPTER TWO

"No Change Was to Be Expected"

F RAUD often breeds opportunity. Nowhere were those opportunities spread more widely than on the empire's frontiers, where land titles were sometimes more a matter of assertion than deed. But those assertions could compete with one another and clash with the aspirations of settlers who lacked respect for legal technicalities and proper authority. The vagueness of colonial borders and the process of settlement brought serious social conflict to most of Britain's North American frontiers. As Gregory Nobles has written, seaboard elites "sought to shape the frontier to fit their social vision and economic interests," but not without opposition.[1]

Whether in the Carolinas or New York, elites sought not just profit from the frontier but continued social and political power. Toward that end they attempted to control settlement, to "plant" properly deferential individuals who would make profits for the elite while respecting their leadership. Yet time and again landlords found even the settlers they had planted going their own way without regard to their betters. The elite despised these settlers, dismissing them as wild growths of the frontier, as savage as their Indian neighbors and therefore due the same violent treatment. But despite the supposed tendency of the frontier to breed barbarians, land speculators could not resist the temptation to profit from cheap wilderness lands.[2]

Ethan Allen joined this search for opportunity, benefiting often from the greed of others. But his motivations appear slightly different from those of the major speculators who sought profit on the muddled edges of the British Empire. Perhaps Ethan Allen first came to the Green Mountains in search of a quick pound note. He stayed to found a state.

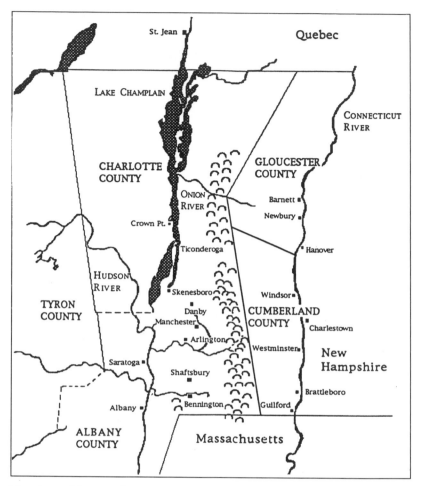

Northeast New York, 1774

I

But what chiefly operated to embroil our ancestors with these strange folks was an unwarrantable liberty which they occasionally took of entering in hordes into {our} territories . . . and settling themselves down, without leave or licence, to improve the land. . . . This unceremonious mode of taking possession of new land was technically termed squatting.—Washington Irving

In early 1769 Allen decided to leave the scene of his failures and humiliations. Together with his brother Levi, he headed north by foot through the Berkshires, a region claimed by both New York and Massachusetts, and then wandered the old trails leading toward Canada. From the hills above Pownal the Allens looked out over a long narrow valley, bounded on the east by the high rugged Green Mountains and on the west by the Taconic hills. Within this valley, which stretched up to Lake Champlain, lived fewer than two thousand people, farmers clearing a wilderness of seemingly endless trees to allow room for their poor homesteads.[3]

The Allens showed no interest in these pathetic frontier farms, seeking instead fur for brother Heman's store. The family's timing in opening the Salisbury store and Heman's management were excellent, taking advantage of the needs of the new settlers in the Berkshires and Green Mountains. While Mary, Zimri, Heber, and Ira Allen saw to the family farm in Cornwall, Heman accumulated capital, and Ethan and Levi became classic frontier entrepreneurs—collecting and trading pelts, befriending the Indians, and looking over the region's various speculative prospects. Both Allens enjoyed the work, despite the hardships they suffered. As Ira Allen wrote, Ethan preferred hunting to all other activities, amusing himself by "killing deer."[4]

Though he continued to enjoy killing deer, Ethan Allen soon discovered the limitations of hunting as a profession. Hunters, having brought the beaver to near extinction in the southern part of the Green Mountains by 1770, had to go further afield with each new year, coming into occasionally violent competition with other trappers and merchants and finding their profits unreliable. But other sources of economic advancement beckoned. As Levi wrote, Joseph Allen had taught his children that "next to religion landed Property was the most Substantial" commodity. Through the winter of 1770, the Allens discussed the possibility of investing in the Green Mountains.[5]

There was only one problem. The Green Mountains belonged to the royal province of New York, and its government and elite families—essentially one and the same—controlled the region's development. Worse, the great New York landowners intended to implement a tenancy system in the Green Mountains. There would be no room in this region for smallholders or small investors like the Allens. Or at least that would have been the case had not one royal governor been moved by such greed as shocked even the British government.[6]

The English thought the region of little value. Largely uninhabited since the beginning of the century when disease had decimated the native population, the Green Mountains attracted few visitors—except during war—and fewer settlers. Native Americans hunted and planted crops along the Connecticut River, but they preferred to live in the north, as far from the aggressive English as they could get.[7]

The woods of the Green Mountains stood quiet until 1741. In that year George II appointed an American, Benning Wentworth, the first governor of New Hampshire. Born to wealth and an expectation of power, educated at Harvard, ambitious, pompous, and as crafty a manipulator of vague charter rights as ever disrupted the British Empire, Wentworth possessed that most essential native characteristic, an eye for the main chance. Examining New Hampshire's charter, Wentworth noted that his border ran west with Massachusetts's until "it meets with our other Governments." One would assume that "other Governments" referred to New York, its eastern boundary fixed at the Connecticut River. Yet both Connecticut and Massachusetts extended their jurisdictions well beyond the Connecticut River, and New York had not established any government in the Green Mountains. In addition, the king ordered Wentworth to plant settlers in his western territories and to maintain a garrison at Fort Dummer, on the Connecticut River's west bank. Obviously, Wentworth reasoned, His Majesty meant for him to extend New Hampshire's rule into this undeveloped region.[8]

Governor Wentworth had cause, beyond personal greed, for assuming rights to the west bank of the Connecticut River. The region's status had long been shrouded in confusion because the royal charters for all the northern provinces overlapped and primitive surveying methods left every border subject to dispute. Efforts to resolve these uncertainties led to first Connecticut, then Massachusetts, and finally New Hampshire gaining control of thousands of acres claimed by New York.[9]

In the 1740s Great Britain's Royal Council, royal attorney, and solicitor general reinforced Wentworth's claims to land west of the Connecticut River by declaring the territory to be part of New Hampshire, though always in the context of that colony's responsibility to maintain Fort Dummer. Thus supported by the crown, Wentworth issued his first grant on 3 January 1749, creating the town of Bennington. Wentworth sited this township as far west as he could without running into any already settled New York towns, a direct and bold challenge to New York's authority.[10]

Much to Wentworth's surprise, New York did not respond to his open provocation. So he wrote New York's Governor George Clinton, telling him that the king had determined New Hampshire's boundary to lie twenty miles east of the Hudson, inducing New Hampshire to issue grants "which will fall in the Neighbourhood of your Government." Wentworth troubled Clinton with this information, he said, only to discover how far north New York extended. Clinton issued a terse response: he ordered Wentworth to cease and desist immediately, as the land Wentworth intended granting belonged to New York. If New Hampshire persisted, Clinton warned, he would be compelled to report Wentworth to the king.[11]

Wentworth's manipulation of the empire's contradictions, combined with the government's inefficiency, postponed a resolution of the dispute between New Hampshire and New York until 1764. By then a royal order could resolve nothing. For fifteen years Wentworth stalled the British government, largely because of the validity of his central point: the borders of all the British North American colonies were extraordinarily vague.[12]

Throughout his dispute with New York, Wentworth played the injured party. He could hardly vacate his grants, Wentworth told Clinton, as so many livelihoods depended on them, but he would gladly submit the whole matter to the king's pleasure. Clinton erred fatally in thinking Wentworth sincere. New York's governor not only agreed to arbitration by the Privy Council, he even offered to exchange pleas with New Hampshire. Wentworth approved, telling Clinton that he hoped for a "speedy settlement" and promising to send a copy of New Hampshire's statement as soon as it was "perfected." In March 1751 Wentworth sent his petition to London, neglecting to reciprocate with a copy to New York.[13]

A brilliant twisting of the facts, New Hampshire's representation anticipated New York's case, putting it in the worst possible light before the Privy Council saw it. Connecticut and Massachusetts had "allowed the Government of New York to extend their Claim" to a line twenty miles east of the Hudson (a reversal of the actual events); New Hampshire would allow the same border. Wentworth went on the offensive by asking the king to set New York's northern boundary, insisting that the duke of York's charter ran only sixty miles north of the sea. Such an interpretation placed Albany well outside New York's jurisdiction.[14]

Meanwhile New York's attorney general, Richard Bradley, spent a year preparing his case. Since Bradley based his argument solely on the duke of York's 1664 charter, it is difficult to understand this delay. Lieutenant Governor Cadwallader Colden fumed to the New York council that he found little worth in either Bradley's presentation or royal charters. As "the Soil of both the provinces of New York and New Hampshire is now vested in the Crown," Colden observed, "the King may fix the boundary between these his two Governments at his pleasure." Colden felt that New York should base its case on more practical grounds: Albany's superior situation as a trade center for the region; New York's ability to protect the inhabitants of the contested area, which fell within the traditional invasion route down the Champlain Valley; and most significantly, the greater profits that New York's quitrents offered the crown.[15]

Despite Colden's forcefulness, the New York government did not send its representation to its London agent until November 1753, two and a half years after the Privy Council received New Hampshire's petition. Meanwhile Wentworth busily issued charters to the disputed land.[16]

The French and Indian War bought Wentworth further time, the Privy Council facing more pressing issues than remote border disputes. At the war's end, divisions within New York aided Wentworth. In 1763 five council members petitioned Governor Robert Monckton to end the dispute by handing the Green Mountains over to New Hampshire on condition that already-issued New York titles be respected. The governor forwarded this document to London, inspiring an angry rebuttal from Colden, who bypassed the governor and council to write the Board of Trade directly. Colden reminded the board of New York's high quitrents and libeled New Hampshire's government as operating under "Republican Principles" contrary to the highest ideals "of the Constitution of Great Britain." In addition, Colden wrote, a number of former British soldiers had appealed to him for land grants in the area.[17]

Colden barraged the Board of Trade with letters and the border region with proclamations. He informed the board that New Hampshire had issued grants to another thirty townships "at such low rates, as evince the claimants had no Intention of becoming Settlers." One man, "in appearance no better than a Pedlar," traveled the North selling land grants for "trifling considerations." Colden ordered the Albany County sheriff to send him a list "of all and every Person" who attempted to settle the region under false titles "that they may be proceeded against according to the law."[18]

Wentworth replied to Colden with a proclamation of his own, warning that Colden's proclamation, "carrying an air of Government in it, may possibly affect & retard the Settlement of His Majesty's Lands." Wentworth summarized his differences with Colden: New York's quitrents might be higher, but that hardly mattered as that province settled no one in the contested area; New Hampshire did.[19]

Angered by Wentworth's challenge, Colden fired off another salvo to the Board of Trade. His single peddler became a troop "hawking & selling their pretended rights to great numbers of ignorant people at low rates and defrauding them of large sums of money." No one intended settling or improving the land, seeking only "to put large sums of money in their pockets" by trading the rights. In contrast, Colden wrote, hundreds of former soldiers clamored at his gate for land.[20]

Colden finally activated the Board of Trade. When the board at last made its recommendation to the king in July 1764, it quoted extensively from Colden's letters and echoed his insistence that deciding in New York's favor reflected the crown's best interest. The board reprimanded Wentworth for selling grants "with a view more to private interest than public advantage" and questioned if "this Gentleman [is] a proper person to be entrusted with Your Majesty's Interests in this Important Station," avoiding reference to its own earlier decisions placing New Hampshire's border somewhere to the west of the Connecticut River.[21]

The king responded to the board's recommendation with the Royal Proclamation of 20 July 1764. The Connecticut River, the king proclaimed, marked the eastern border of New York "from where it enters the Province of the Massachusetts Bay" on the Connecticut border north to the 45th parallel.[22] Not just the governments of New Hampshire and Massachusetts felt the sting of this edict; anyone living west of the river under what they assumed to be a New England government faced serious problems.

What many thought the final clarification of New York's eastern border produced some dramatic effects. Wentworth resigned as governor, passing the office on to his nephew John Wentworth, and retired to enjoy the fruits of his labor, leaving those who had purchased grants from him with worthless titles. New York began issuing land patents in the Green Mountains in earnest. Between 1765 and 1775 three New York governors granted more than two million acres in the New Hampshire Grants, collecting £76,373 in fees, and approved an additional 300,000 acres in military grants. Yet during that entire period, few people settled under these grants and those scattered settlers established no towns.[23]

New York's failure to occupy the lands it had so recently won proved its most serious error. The future political composition of the Grants would be decided by New Englanders living in New England towns, operating with New England structures and New England expectations. New Yorkers remained few and isolated, easily identifiable as outsiders seeking their own ends rather than the well-being and security of their communities. Even those towns which later supported New York's authority were settled under New Hampshire grants.

The English crown assumed it had resolved this petty feud. But as was so often the case with British colonial rule in North America, the crown made little effort to enforce its policy. Within one month of the 1764 royal proclamation settling the boundary, the New Hampshire grantees launched their first act of resistance against New York's authority, beginning a long conflict in which Ethan Allen would play the leading role.[24]

II

Every planter went upon his farm {in the Grants} with a full conviction that no change was to be expected in his civil concerns. —Timothy Dwight

Benning Wentworth had been a persuasive man. People believed Wentworth because they deeply wanted what he offered. Thousands of New Englanders and even many New Yorkers bought into his fraud. Many did so as part of what amounted to a pyramid scheme, hoping to sucker in others and then unload their shares before the law caught on. But the great majority of those who bought New Hampshire grants did so with conviction, heading north to settle on the lands that Wentworth's documents said they owned.

The first New Englanders to settle the region often held older titles from Massachusetts which Wentworth gladly confirmed for a small fee and a piece of the township. By 1755 a scattering of settlements clustered around the blockhouses at Fort Dummer, Rockingham, Westminster, and Putney, in addition to some squatters across the river from Fort Number Four (Charlestown, New Hampshire) and a few Dutch in West Hoosic. But most settlers evacuated the northern frontier during the French and Indian War as the Abenakis attacked every European community in the region.[25]

The Treaty of Paris in 1763 changed everything. With the war over, a large number of New Englanders, including Ethan Allen, turned Wentworth's speculation into settlement. Over the next dozen years approximately twelve thousand people settled in the area known as the New Hampshire Grants, with another four thousand born there in those years.[26]

While hunting in the Green Mountains, Allen encountered his brother-in-law Israel Brownson and reconciled their past differences. Brownson started Ethan thinking about some advice Thomas Young had passed on, that land speculation was far preferable to hard work. In 1764 Young had become involved with an Indian trader, Colonel John Henry Lydius, in the purchase of questionable land grants in the Green Mountains. Young wrote a spirited defense of the right of possession and improvement to land on the frontier, invoking "Liberty and Property (the Household Gods of Englishmen)" to support the claims of untitled settlers. Young's example, though, proved a poor one, as he lost his investment and became an itinerant doctor.[27]

Nonetheless, visions of fast, easy gains danced in Ethan Allen's head. In 1763 Allen paid £500 for 95 acres in Salisbury, a good farming area. The next year he sold 72 acres of farmland in Cornwall for £450— cleared land, but not as rich as in Salisbury. Allen speculated in the volatile Connecticut land market over the next six years but ended up losing equity.[28]

Wentworth's machinations presented Allen with the opportunity to start over despite a paucity of capital. On 29 May 1770 Ethan Allen, "yeoman," bought one right to land in the Grants town of Poultney, representing at least 400 acres, from Daniel Warner, a Portsmouth merchant, for £4. A week later, Allen purchased a right to Castleton, also in the Grants, from Zenas Person, a Springfield bricklayer, for £6. These two sellers represent different types of speculators in frontier land. Warner, one of the premier investors in Grants land, an original proprietor in fifty-one different townships, hoped that his minimal investment would bring a quick return. Person could only afford a single right to land, which he purchased from the original proprietor. Both investments paid off, in their minor way. Warner made an impressive 300 percent profit, or £3; Person pulled in a 200 percent profit, or £4. Allen became a third kind of land speculator, the sort who settled the frontier. He bought into this corrupt land system and used it for his own purposes.[29]

Thomas Young had been right: selling land was easier than most other forms of work. Allen began buying as much Grants land as his credit allowed. In March 1771 he made his first sale, transferring his Castleton right to Israel Holmes of Salisbury for £24, or a 300 percent profit. Though his only sale of the year, it provided the capital Ethan and Ira needed to buy thirty-two rights in Hubbardton for £60. And in January 1772 Ethan sold off the last of his father's Cornwall estate for £23. In exchange for those eighty-seven acres, Ethan bought rights in Castleton equal to at least five times as much land. Though not approaching the grandeur of Benning Wentworth, Ethan Allen did his best to cash in the opportunities presented by the confusion of the northern frontier.[30]

Yet there is a curious complication in Ethan Allen's motivations. As his brother Levi put it, Ethan tended to act as "dictator of the younger brethren," constantly arranging their lives for them. One of the most "arbitrary" exercises of this authority came in 1770, when Ethan decided to move his entire extended family to the New Hampshire Grants.[31]

Thomas Young had boosted speculation, missing a deeper potential which Allen grasped. The northern frontier offered opportunities for the creation of new towns, new communities, a new New England. Like so many Americans who project their fantasies onto the frontier, Allen saw a chance to make over his world. As his father had been instrumental in the migration to Cornwall, so Ethan might lead his family and neighbors again into the wilderness to create a community.

Through 1770 and 1771 Ethan set aside his best land for his family. In 1770 he persuaded Ira to sell his share of "the estate of my honored Father" for £48 in order to purchase several rights of land in Poultney. Ethan then bought a house for brother Heber, who moved up the next year. They were soon joined by several other Allens and cousins Remember Baker and Seth Warner.[32]

The gathering of the Allen clan in the Grants is not in itself remarkable. Yet this family migration indicates that Ethan Allen's interests were not narrowly entrepreneurial but encompassed as well a concern for family security and unity, and perhaps even a desire to retrieve his position as family patriarch. On all these points Levi and Ira Allen agree in their autobiographies. Levi admitted that his "arbitrary brother" had learned much from his early mistakes and "misfortune," and his decision to move them all north in 1770 proved "advantagious to others of the family." Ethan may have begun with exclusively entrepreneurial ambitions and then glimpsed other possibilities as he wandered the wilderness, discerning the chance to achieve wider, culturally approved goals. It seems evident that by 1770 he had concluded that the easy availability of land under New Hampshire title gave the Allens a chance to regroup, under his "dictatorial" control of course.[33]

Certainly, Ethan Allen would have been a very unusual New Englander had the well-being of his family not figured as a prominent motivation. One of the few aspects of colonial New England upon which historians agree is the social primacy of the family. The pressure of a rapidly growing population threatened the family's centrality in the mid-eighteenth century. A township's first generation had more land at its disposal than it could use, but the size of individual landholdings usually decreased with each division by successive generations. If the second generation consisted of the average of five to seven children, and if the third followed suit, an original family farm of one hundred acres might shrink in a generation or two to diminutive personal farms of ten to twenty acres, barely enough to support a family, especially yet another large brood.[34] Moreover, married adult children did not expect to stay long on their parents' farm; few households in the Connecticut River valley had more than a single adult male. For example, at the time of his birth, Ethan Allen's hometown of Cornwall had only three households with more than one adult male. Adult children, once they wed, were expected to start their own families on separate farms—nearby and in close contact with their parents, but on their own.[35] Yet what happened when surplus land within the original township ran out? Joseph Allen's family encountered that crisis.

New England families had strategies for dealing with these crises. Many parents apprenticed sons to artisans in hopes that they might learn a trade. But most New England towns could not support more than a blacksmith and a few part-time artisans, resulting in a significant migration of young men to the cities of the northern colonies. Most often, a family raised the capital to establish one of their number in a new community, usually on the frontier. Perceived necessity, not a spirit of adventure, moved young couples to abandon their childhood homes and expose themselves to the hardships of frontier life. Yet they did so in enormous numbers.[36]

These New Englanders fanned out to the northern frontiers. The Iroquois and Abenakis made migrants hesitant to settle in western New York, along the Susquehanna, or in Maine, while its tenant land system made upstate New York unattractive. The relatively few Indians living in the Grants made that area a far safer frontier than others; Wentworth's cheap titles made it seem perfect.[37]

Like Allen, most Grants settlers shared a commitment to providing for the future economic security of the lineal family. Mostly mature men and women in their late twenties and thirties, they faced a future of limited opportunity, not just for themselves but for their families. If their inheritance seemed small, that of their children would be even smaller. Allen spent the years before 1770 caring for—and bossing around— his family: he helped establish his brothers and sisters and provided for their mother; aided cousins and in-laws with loans and labor; worked the farm; and tried his hand at new enterprises which might guarantee the future prosperity of the Allens. Mary Allen gave birth to her third child in 1768. What could they expect? What would Ethan and Mary Allen leave to them? How could they help their children in a society of shrinking opportunities?

When New Englanders thought of prosperity, of opportunity, of survival, they thought of land. Wentworth made titles to land readily available in the Green Mountains, with inexpensive deeds that could ensure the continued well-being of the Allens for at least another two generations, if not longer. If Ethan Allen journeyed north into the Green Mountains as a rugged individualist seeking wilderness to claim, he was also an advance scout for his family, seeking new lands to settle upon. Many historians of the frontier depict pioneers eyeing the horizon, longing to go over one more hill, seeking a little elbowroom far from the smoke of a neighbor's cabin. The reality of the pioneers' search demonstrates a different passion. They looked to their families and risked a great deal to win security and a moderate prosperity for them within communities of like-minded people.

These settlers cannot be called restless youths, coming as they did in family groups.[38] In 1764 Bennington formed a militia company including every able-bodied adult male between the ages of sixteen and sixty. The sixty-six men who reported for service, with a median age of thirty-three, included seven Scots, five Robinsons and Clarks, four Fassetts and related Smiths, and seven other families with multiple membership in the militia. All but a few of these men were directly related to at least one other member of the militia.[39] Of the eighty-one adult males settled in Bennington in 1765, thirty-two came from Hardwick, seventeen from Newent, and fourteen from Sunderland. Looked at another way, at least sixty-three of these eighty-one men came to Bennington as members of organized migrations, and more settlers from these three towns followed in the next few years.[40] One Hardwick migrant, Thomas Freeman, journeyed to the frontier with his wife and four sons, his daughter and son-in-law, his brother and a cousin, two brothers-in-law, and six nephews. All together there were twenty adult males in this one extended family—a migration unto itself. Most of Bennington's first settlers knew each other before they moved, and very few newcomers could not point to some connection with those already settled.[41]

The same configuration appears elsewhere in the Green Mountains. In 1764 a group of twelve families from Newtown, Connecticut, settled in Arlington, instantly constituting a majority of the population. Those who followed came from Newtown and three neighboring towns in northwest Connecticut. Between Bennington and Arlington lay the towns of Sunderland and Shaftsbury. The first settlers of Sunderland were Ethan Allen's in-laws, Timothy Brownson, from Salisbury, and Gideon Brownson, from Guilford, who arrived in 1766. Over the succeeding few years, Sunderland greeted an influx of families from both of these Connecticut towns, mostly people encouraged to move by the Brownsons. Similarly, Shaftsbury drew its settlers from two towns, Norwich, Connecticut, and Bristol, Rhode Island. This distinctive pattern of migration, a few large groups from one or two New England towns buying proprietors' shares in a Grants township, held to the north of Arlington in Manchester, Clarendon, Dorset, and Danby.[42] And also like Bennington, these new Grants towns grew quickly. Clarendon, for example, first settled in 1769, claimed fifty-seven households by 1770. Forty-six of these households included a total of eighty-eight children, indicating the high concentration of families among the first settlers of the frontier. At the same time, the relatively low number of children per household underscores the youthfulness of pioneer parents.[43]

Similar patterns of settlement obtained on the other side of the Green Mountains. All of New Pomfret's first settlers came from Pomfret, Connecticut, and neighboring Woodstock. The pioneers of Windsor comprised two interrelated groups from Petersham, Massachusetts, and Charlestown, New Hampshire; Sudbury and Shrewsbury in Worcester County, Massachusetts, supplied the first settlers of Newfane; while all of Norwich's first two hundred settlers originated in Mansfield, Connecticut.[44]

The same motivations moved even Scottish migrants to the New Hampshire Grants. Although the economic hardships and religious persecution pushing the Scots out of their homes exceeded the pressures faced by New Englanders, the Scots also desired to maintain a community of shared cultural values and provide their families with freeholds. The Grants' pattern of interconnected migration held even when crossing the Atlantic.

In 1774 a group of farmers in Rippen parish, Scotland, formed a company with the stated goal of settling in America. They had two strikes against them from the perspective of the British government: they were Presbyterian and poor. Worse than Presbyterians, these farmers belonged to the Reformed Presbyterian Church, founded by the notorious Covenanters who rejected British control of their church.[45] Subject to fines and other civil penalties for professing the Reformed Covenant, the Rippen farmers faced a choice of becoming landless agricultural laborers or urban poor as their small holdings reverted to the region's great landlords. Not willing to remain victims of British persecution or economic change, this group of farmers decided, despite the costs and risks, on emigration as the only way to avoid the destruction of their way of life. The group selected twenty-seven-year-old Alexander Harvey to search out suitable and affordable land. A thorough man, Harvey kept a journal of his expenses and his travels that affords a rare glimpse of the process of land purchase and settlement in the Green Mountains.[46]

Harvey and John Clark, another member of the "United Company of farmers," arrived in New York in the summer of 1774. Harvey spent his first week counting religious buildings—sixteen churches and one synagogue—and visiting Scots, who supplied him with introductions to reputable men selling land. Traveling first through upstate New York, Harvey doubted that his Scots neighbors would be pleased to join the ranks of Isaac Low's tenants, especially on such small plots of land. Proceeding to Cambridge, New York, Harvey found "the people are mostly Sober and Religious." But while he approved of the inhabitants, Harvey was discouraged by the rocky soil. He discovered that landlords owned New York's best land. Harvey and his fellow Scots did not intend to settle land no better than that they left or to live under a tenancy system similar to that which exploited them in Scotland; the Highland Clearances remained too vivid in their memories to put their trust again in the goodwill of some powerful landlord.

Harvey headed into the New Hampshire Grants, impressed by the quality of the crops and the pious New England settlers. Learning that the Reverend John Witherspoon, the Scottish president of Princeton, owned land in the area, Harvey hiked to Ryegate on the northern edge of the Grants settlements. But another group of Scot farmers had already bought the best land. While in Ryegate, Harvey met Willard Stevens, a proprietor of the adjacent town of Barnet. Stevens, as agent for the other proprietors, offered Harvey half of the township, 7,000 acres in all. The fertile soil, fine stands of oak and maple, and "a very Beautyfull Lake" attracted Harvey, but he hesitated at Stevens's price of a shilling and a half an acre.

Harvey tested his options on another frontier, the Susquehanna Valley of northern Pennsylvania. He found this region inhabited by "manie of all kinds of people" who would make the Scots uncomfortable. Pennsylvania politics appeared equally objectionable, with an inspector who established the right to vote based on a £50 freehold. Further, "there is no minister nor any publick worship and I Believe very little privet. The Method they take to supply this Defect is they meet in the taverns and spend the former part of the Day (viz the Sabath) in Drinking, wrestling and swearing and on the afternoon they betake themselves to the more sober exercise of vomiting and Sleeping. Then in the Evening, they appear Cloathed with the Garment of paleness. They Conclude the Excercise of the Day with a Nip of todie and prayer, the substance of which is that the Lord may Damme their soul." Their grain was good, but for Harvey, not good enough.

Disenchanted with both Pennsylvania and New York, Harvey sought out Willard Stevens's brother and partner, Samuel. After much haggling over prices and payment schedules, the Scots acquired 7,000 acres of Barnet for £408 on 23 November. Clark returned to Bristol to arrange for the transportation of the company of farmers to America, while Harvey spent the rest of the winter in New York City preparing for the move northward by purchasing stocks of axes, nails, sugar, rum, and a compass. Harvey arrived in Barnet on 20 April, two weeks after leaving Hartford.[47] Despite harsh weather, Harvey and his companions built a camp, cut trees down, and planted their first crop within two weeks. To get through these hard times, Harvey bought food from local farmers and enlisted the labor of his fellow Scots from Ryegate. Several families arrived in the New Hampshire Grants from Scotland early in 1776.[48]

As Harvey's experience indicates, those who purchased illegal land grants in the Green Mountains took into account the land tenure systems and cultures operating elsewhere. Harvey, Allen, and many others linked the two considerations: free title to land and agreeable social arrangements constituted requisites for settlement. Neither upstate New York nor northern Pennsylvania offered both of these conditions. By contrast, Harvey found Barnet's soil fertile and New England's laws and society acceptable. More importantly, the Scots farmers would be free to create the kind of community they wanted. They shared the town of Barnet with a group from Hardwick, Massachusetts, but the Scots comprised half of the new town, holding an equal share in forming its future. Such an opportunity exceeded anything available in Scotland. Harvey and his neighbors settled in the Green Mountains for reasons akin to those of Bennington's first inhabitants: they hoped to replicate their familial and communal structures in a favorable environment.

In a society in which land represented a family's livelihood and future security, the Grants speculators aided New England's poorer farmers, albeit unintentionally. Wentworth committed fraud knowingly, not caring whether the land-poor benefited from his land grab. To those with little capital, whether a minor speculator like the bricklayer Zenas Person or a settler like Ethan Allen, the frontier represented one likely avenue to economic security. Government officials and other speculators sought immediate profits; settlers sought farms and communities.[49]

In the fifteen years following Wolfe's victory at Quebec in 1759, the region west of New Hampshire's White Mountains became the locus of New England migration. From the Berkshires in western Massachusetts north to Lake Champlain, and on both sides of the Connecticut River, settlers from southern New England laid claim to tens of thousands of acres. And with one exception, the Grants towns replicated Bennington's settlement pattern of cohesive groups heading north to settle together.[50] What did not exist was any sort of freewheeling grab-bag frontier town of rugged and exclusive individuals from the four corners of the world, or even New England. Instead there was concentrated, focused, purposeful migration. As the example of Ethan Allen suggests, entrepreneurial ambition and a dedication to family interests can coexist.

III

Having buried himself in the wilderness, he builds himself a log hut, clears away a cornfield and potatoe-patch, and, Providence smiling on his labors, is soon surrounded by a snug farm and some half score of flaxen-headed urchins, who, by their size, seem to have sprung all at once out of the earth, like a crop of toadstools. —Washington Irving

Many factors contributed to social conflict on the early American frontier. For instance, in the southern backcountry the wide dispersion of the population and absence of towns hindered the development of social institutions. But land speculation and absentee proprietors most impeded, disrupted, and disordered the development of frontier communities. At first the Green Mountains seemed exceptional. Benning Wentworth did not have the slightest interest in the future shape of the Grants; he just wanted a quick profit. It required the active interest of New York's major land speculators to bring conflict to this frontier.[51]

There was nothing exceptional in Wentworth's avaricious land grants. Like most other colonial governors, including New York's George Clinton, Wentworth attempted to enrich himself at the expense of his province and the British Empire. Wentworth just demonstrated greater ambition and audacity, aiming to appropriate as much of the northern frontier as possible and granting more townships than any other colonial governor.[52] Between 1749 and 1764 he sold grants to 129 townships between the Connecticut River and his claimed border roughly twenty miles east of the Hudson River, running north 130 miles from the Massachusetts border to the shores of Lake Champlain.[53]

In the other New England provinces the legislature issued land grants; in New Hampshire the governor made all his grants under the authority of his council. But Wentworth thought this authority, once given, immutable. Oliver Willard received two townships over a glass of madeira with Wentworth. The governor saw no need to consult the council in whose name he chartered the land "as he had obtained about the Close of the last War their general advice for granting the Lands on Connecticut River." The governor's secretary issued the unsurveyed patents immediately. Willard then went in search of the necessary grantees to fill out the form.[54]

The New Hampshire Grants constituted a fringe benefit of government service. Ten members of the governor's council owned 276 shares. Wentworth usually gave himself 500 acres per town, amassing a total of 65,320 acres. Benning's brother Mark Hunking Wentworth, a member of the council, became a proprietor in thirty-seven townships from 1760 to 1764; he was one of thirteen Wentworths who held grants in the Green Mountains. The two Theodore Atkinsons, senior and junior, secretaries and in-laws to the governor, held seventy-three proprietorships between them. The grants extended outward from Wentworth to include his family and friends, and from thence to anyone willing to pay the money.[55]

To avoid the royal proscription against multiple holdings in one township by a single person, Wentworth made grants to nonexistent people. For example, four Hudsons appear on the Pownal grant: the counterfeiter Seth Hudson, his sons Ezra and Seth, Jr., and Seth III. The latter two sons never existed.[56] In all, 766 real people held rights in at least two townships, 306 of these in three or four, and 151 in five or more.[57]

This dispersion of land titles among a colony's elite was indeed typical, but it did not produce the conflict usually generated by absentee proprietors. The reason was fairly simple: most of the initial proprietors understood the fraud inherent in Wentworth's grants and therefore held their shares for just a brief period, having no interest in settling or controlling the land which they acquired so easily. Rather, they sent agents, Colden's peddlers, through New England selling these rights. The New Hampshire elite made a brisk, though not very substantial, profit off these land titles. Their greed had important consequences.[58]

New Hampshire grants required every proprietor to cultivate five acres for every fifty granted within five years or face forfeiture. Proprietors ignored this aspect of the warrants, and most towns remained unsettled until ten to twenty years after the initial grants. Wentworth reserved all large white pines for the Royal Navy unless he issued a special license, a restriction allowing for abundant earnings. Before any other land division could be effected, the grants required that the actual township and one-acre home lots be laid out and allotted. Proprietors ignored this clause. Each hundred acres carried an annual quitrent of one ear of corn, rising to one shilling after ten years. In fact, New Hampshire never collected any quitrents, in coin or corn.[59]

Governor Wentworth understood that his grants stood on the shakiest legal foundation. He expressed his uncertainty in the low prices he asked for his grants, selling entire townships of 23,500 acres for £20 to £40. New York demanded six different fees for its individual patents, amounting to £36 per one thousand acres. New Hampshire's grants, being issued to groups of forty to fifty proprietors, usually cost the individual speculator less than £1 for a share equaling four hundred acres. Some paid nothing, as Wentworth included many prominent New Englanders and government officials on the list of shareholders at no charge. Without asking, the Society for the Propagation of the Gospel in Foreign Parts (SPG) and the Church of England each received a share in every township. By including the SPG and the Church of England in his grants and by naming townships for prominent British politicians, Wentworth hoped to gain support in England for his land grab.[60]

The second sale of these New Hampshire rights tended to be from one speculator to another. The first owner usually sought a speedy return from the resale, while the second waited for someone who actually wanted to settle the land and thus would pay more. As a result many early grantees quickly expanded their single right into multiple holdings, while others washed their hands of the whole affair for a few pounds. In only one instance, Newbury, did the initial grantees have any intention of settling the township themselves. Insisting that his friends also receive shares, Wentworth expanded the township to accommodate both his associates and the intended settlers.[61]

The price of New Hampshire land titles fluctuated widely, as with any futures market. For instance, all of Bennington's original proprietors had sold their holdings for an average of £4 per share by 1762, the price having peaked in 1761 at £16. But the whole enterprise remained so uncertain that an active market in Wentworth's land grants did not develop until the late 1760s. Speculators who held on to their shares until then sold off portions of their rights, a far more lucrative enterprise. For example, Josiah Willard paid £1 in 1761 for a share of the Windsor proprietary. Over the next six years he purchased another thirteen shares for £42, with prices ranging from £1 to £15. In 1767 he sold the lot of them to Israel Curtis for £200, making £160 profit. Curtis settled in Windsor and sold off his holdings in pieces over the next several years, using the profit from his sales to build a mill and expand his farm. By the mid-1770s he was one of the most prosperous men in the region, though still an insignificant farmer by seaboard standards. But Curtis's relative success depended on Benning Wentworth's stalling techniques to keep New York out while drawing new settlers in.[62]

Within six years of settlement, few townships had more than one or two absentee landholders, and these usually ended bending to pressure from the towns to sell. When absentee proprietors would not sell at the offered price, towns auctioned off all but one hundred acres for failure to pay assessments, as stipulated in Wentworth's grants, setting aside the absentee's remaining acreage in the most undesirable part of town. In 1764 Chester eliminated all its absentee proprietors by means of such expropriation. The following year Arlington sent Jehiel Hawley to Boston and Portsmouth to deal with its absentee proprietors. Hawley pointed to the example of Chester as an oblique threat and purchased all the remaining shares for the town's use.[63] In Connecticut and Massachusetts absentee proprietors retained their lands despite opposition from settlers. But the Green Mountains lacked extralocal structures which could defend the proprietors' interests. As a consequence, the speculators and settlers of the New Hampshire Grants never found themselves at sharp variance. Proprietors became settlers, or they ceased to be proprietors.[64]

The very structure of proprietors' operations ensured the insignificance of absentee owners. A proprietors' meeting required a quorum of only one-sixteenth of the total shares, generally four in number. Most speculators preferred this system, content to leave the organizational work to those so inclined, while they sat back to see if their pound investment would amount to anything. In the case of Windsor, seven of the original fifty-nine proprietors took care of the initial surveying.

By 1764 three brothers—Zedekiah, David, and Samuel Stone—constituted themselves the proprietors' meeting of Windsor and made all the decisions. By 1767 none of the original proprietors except the Stones, who settled in Windsor, owned any shares. These holdings served as a form of disposable capital, useful in a growing but poor town. Selling to newcomers, while a form of speculation, indicates interest in the development of a community. All but three of Windsor's 1767 proprietors lived in town; Dudley, Samuel, and Moses Chase lived directly across the river in Cornish and farmed their Windsor lands into the late 1780s. Like most of the secondary purchasers of New Hampshire grants, they had every intention of using their rights.[65]

If absentee proprietors did not initiate conflict in the Grants, the settlers themselves certainly had the capacity to do so. From a distance, there appeared few differences between the settlers, the majority coming from New England. But this similarity of origin disguised several significant points of contention.

Most of the first inhabitants of the Grants did not feel excessively remote from their former homes, and many maintained contacts with their old neighbors. They followed four main routes into the Grants: due north up the Connecticut River; up the Deerfield River to its origins in the Green Mountains and then down to the west side; along the Housatonic from western Connecticut, through the Berkshires, and into the southwest of the Grants (Ethan Allen's route); and the Crown Point road from New Hampshire's Fort Number Four across the Green Mountains, which also served east-west travel. The Crown Point road had introduced many soldiers from New England to the region during the French and Indian War, some of whom founded Pittsfield and Springfield where the road forded rivers.[66]

Though trips from the Grants down into central New England took many days and much energy, the region was not cut off from communication. Streams and lakes were like pathways in the winter when they froze over, easing travel considerably. Even the Green Mountains did not form a formidable barrier to the experienced traveler; Ethan Allen could cross the mountains in a single day.[67]

This relatively close connection of frontier with points of origin fostered an impression of the Grants as an extension of traditional New England, "New Connecticut" as many called it. Such an identification made New York seem all the more remote. With its alienating economic

policies, centralized political and legal systems, tenancy, absentee landlords, and great landed estates, New York appeared a distant land, one
with which few Grants settlers had connections. The few Yorkers in the
region—obnoxious officials and annoying attorneys—added to the sense
of alienation. A few dozen former soldiers, almost all Scottish, settled as
tenants in the region south of Lake Champlain. The only other Yorkers
in the area were Quakers, who struck New England's Calvinists as a sort
of spiritual plague. New England had a long history of treating Quakers
roughly, and most Grants settlers took their presence in New York as a
sign of that colony's deep failure to maintain proper order.[68]

Given the similarities and shared animosities among the Grants' New
England settlers, the creation of a collective identity would seem a fairly
simple matter. But unity among the settlers of the Green Mountains was
not a foregone conclusion. The Grants constituted a crazy-quilt pattern
of settlement. In addition to the Yorker Scots in the west, the eastside had its Scots in Ryegate and Barnet, representatives of a strange
culture in the eyes of proper New Englanders. The New Englanders
themselves came from a variety of social milieus: bustling seaports like
Ipswich, Massachusetts, and Guilford, Connecticut; hardscrabble hill
hamlets like Allen's own Cornwall; booming communities devoted to
commercial agriculture like Northampton and Windham. Used to different ways of farming, of work cycles determined by specific crops, they
had different ways of conducting business and trade. Commercial towns
like Northampton had bylaws for the regulation of livestock, a practice
unknown in many poor hill towns. In most agricultural towns, erecting
and maintaining fences remained a public affair determined by the town
meeting; in seaports, it had become entirely a private matter. Settlers
from Farmington, Connecticut, or Deerfield, Massachusetts, thought
common fields the norm; those from Kent, Connecticut, or Concord,
Massachusetts, thought them archaic.[69]

People used to one kind of farming and soil settled on unknown land
in the Green Mountains. Farms in Massachusetts's eastern counties devoted more than half the land to pasture and generally only 10 percent
to plowland. Farms in the Connecticut River valley reversed these figures. It was not tradition which determined farming practices, but soil
and growing seasons. Settlers arriving from Litchfield had planted their
crops in Charlton-Paxton soil, though they did not have such names
for it, while those from the Connecticut River valley below Massachu-

setts's northern border knew Weatherfield-Cheshire, and those from the eastern part of New England mostly had experience with Gloucester-Plymouth. They did not find these soils in the Grants. Bennington had Pittsfield soil, the Connecticut River valley Hollis, and the Champlain region Merrimac. The soil in the Grants remains perfectly suited for meadow and pasture grass, which is to say the raising of livestock. Corn, oats, and barley grow best in these soils, except in the Champlain area where potatoes and vegetables flourish. But most settlers brought few cattle with them and knew nothing of sheep raising. Worse still, the soil of the Green Mountains is unsuited for what most settlers knew best: wheat.[70]

In addition to significant differences in economic behavior and expectations, the Grants settlers came from towns with varied traditions of civic and ecclesiastical government. In Cornwall the town meeting selected the minister; full church members made that decision in Litchfield. New Hampshire did not allow indentured servants or foreigners to vote; Connecticut did. New Hampshire had no residence qualifications; Connecticut did. The property qualification for the right to vote ran from Rhode Island's vague persons of "competent estates" to New Hampshire's estate rated at £40. Massachusetts employed different qualifications for local and provincial elections. About half the adult males in Massachusetts's coastal towns met the franchise requirement, 70 percent in Connecticut farm towns, and 75 percent in Providence, Rhode Island.[71] Salisbury, Connecticut, tended to hold one town meeting a year, while Norwich averaged five. Woodbury, Connecticut, attempted to resolve its disputes in the church, nearby Cornwall in the town meeting, while Litchfield's ended up in court. Windham, Connecticut, had twelve taverns; Westborough, Massachusetts, had none.[72]

Ethan Allen had run up against some of these distinctions when he moved from Cornwall to Salisbury, a distance of only ten miles. When he insisted on resolving problems as he had in Cornwall—seizing and holding stray pigs himself—the formal structures of Salisbury fined him for his failure to adhere to local standards and eventually ordered Allen out.

All of these differences were intensified by the wide variety of religious opinions held by Grants settlers. Many came from towns which had experienced deep divisions during the Great Awakening, and they brought a wide range of religious beliefs and practices with them, from Ethan Allen's stark rationalism to the primitive piety of the Separates.

There were Old Lights from Litchfield and New Lights from Windsor, Anglicans from New Haven and Baptists from Rhode Island, Quakers from New York and Presbyterians from Scotland.

What made the attainment of unity all the more unlikely is that while people from the same hometown in New England, or the same parish in Scotland, and even entire Quaker meetings settled in their own quiet and private enclaves in the Grants, they did so adjacent to one another, within the borders of a single town. None of these cohesive groups succeeded in transforming their community into a hermetic enclave of purity. With the exception of Norwich, settled entirely by residents of Mansfield, Connecticut, no Grants town ended its first decade the isolated possession of a single social or religious group.[73] Danby had Baptists, Quakers, and Old Lights; Separates, New Lights, and Baptists settled Shaftsbury; Presbyterians and New Lights divided Barnet; Anglicans, New Lights, and deists competed in Arlington. The differences seemed vital at the time.

For example, Bennington owed its settlement to George Whitefield, by way of Samuel Robinson.[74] Robinson, a deacon of the church in Hardwick, Massachusetts, heard and accepted Whitefield's evangelical message, rejecting what he saw as his own minister's liberal theology. In 1749 Robinson joined several other members of his church in forming a separate congregation, attempting to detach the visible saints who shared the experience of conversion from the corruption of the unregenerate. These Separates were mostly long-settled inhabitants of Hardwick, including several prominent families. They did not seek to save a few pounds by avoiding the ministerial tax, nor did they protest the dominance of an entrenched oligarchy. Rather they seem to have acted from a deep religious conviction that they could not belong to or support a church which included those who had not felt personal regeneration.[75]

But the Hardwick town meeting felt otherwise. The meeting ordered the Separates to pay the ministerial tax while entreating them to return to the fold of the town's one true church. Massachusetts' General Court, which the Separates petitioned, agreed with the Hardwick town meeting. Several times in the 1750s the church and the town meeting censured the Separates for disrupting the harmony of the community, but without visible effect. It was within this polarized atmosphere that Robinson made his decision to move to the frontier and began buying as many shares in the Bennington grant as possible. The frontier provided those dissatisfied with the religious life of southern New England the chance to follow Paul's injunction to the Corinthians: "Be not yoked unequally with unbelievers. . . . Come out from their midst and be separate, says the Lord, and do not touch anything unclean."

In 1761 the first three families, totaling twenty-two people, went north to prepare the site for settlement. Eleazar Harwood's wife made the journey north despite her advanced pregnancy and soon gave birth to the young community's first child. Together these three families cleared some small fields and planted corn in preparation for the arrival of the rest of their party, who left shortly after the fall harvest.[76]

Many other religious dissidents spawned by the Great Awakening congregated in Bennington in the early 1760s. At Robinson's urging, the members of two other Separate churches, from neighboring Sunderland and Newent, Connecticut, also settled in Bennington. Each of the three groups had been through a bitter and divisive separation from their town's church and numbered among "the most zealous of the Separatists." Conflict between the Sunderland church and the Separates lasted four years before the church excommunicated fifteen dissenters in 1753 for "renouncing our communion, and thereby [making] it manifest they do not belong to us." The church further voted "that we judge it to be unlawful and dangerous for persons to frequent . . . the meetings of the Separates." Sunderland's church tried to sever the Separates from the life of the community; instead they drove the dissenters to the frontier.[77]

The Newent Separates provide an even more dramatic example of the revival's disruptive effects. Norwich, of which Newent was a parish, gained five new churches as a result of the Great Awakening, including a Church of England and a freewill Murrayite congregation. At the other end of the New England theological spectrum, the Newent Separates defined membership so strictly that initially only seven of their number qualified for full communion.[78] As did Hardwick, Norwich tried to force all its inhabitants to support a single church. Despite its censure by a parliamentary committee, Connecticut jailed Separates who failed to pay their ministerial tax. At the height of this controversy, the lay minister of the Newent Separates, Bliss Willoughby, met Samuel Robinson in Portsmouth. Robinson persuaded Willoughby that the Green Mountains beckoned as the New Israel for these latter-day Puritans.[79] Religion served as the key force motivating migration to at least six other new Grants towns—Shaftsbury, Windsor, Ferrisburg, Guilford,

Wallingford, and Rutland—and probably was important in a number of other migrations.[80]

Even when a particular religious orientation predominated, as did Bennington's Separates, shared beliefs and values did not guarantee social harmony. Not only did Bennington's Separates come from three different towns with distinct patterns of social organization, but their theology demonstrated little unity. Bennington's other settlers were shocked to discover that the Newent Separates had a history of bitter divisions over sexual and theological issues, and that some of them believed in such radical doctrines as spiritual wifery. At one time or another the Newent congregation admonished nearly everyone for violating one rule of the covenant or another, from "carnal singing" and excess laughter to fornication and undue secularism—"living in friendship with this world." Most shocking of all, it turned out that the church's minister, the adulterer Bliss Willoughby, had secretly converted to the Baptists.[81]

As the inhabitants of Bennington learned, Separate congregations possessed an inherent instability. Groups which invested the individual conscience with ultimate authority yet held to a standard of religious purity splintered from within. Separate congregations in the Grants developed into temporary refuges for true believers who spent much of their energy purging their congregations of the latest revisionists or revanchists. Such weak organizations provided plenty of opportunities for disagreement and undermined social stability.

Lacking legitimate land titles, settled in a rough and uncertain environment, facing a dozen sources of conflict as they attempted to structure their communities, and wanting internal coherence, the settlers of the New Hampshire Grants faced a formidable task. Contests over land distribution, political power, and domination of the church re-created old divisions while fueling new ones. Somehow they needed to apportion the common land, lay out their farms, plan roads, select a site for the meetinghouse, appoint a minister, grant exclusive mill rights, elect town officers, and maintain social harmony. Every decision promised further dispute; their new communities would certainly fracture into a myriad of hostile and competing factions.[82]

While the Grants settlers had much in common, primarily owing to their New England background, powerful social, economic, and political forces were arrayed against them. By 1770 the formation of some sort of common identity seemed highly unlikely. And as if these communities did not have enough to contend with, in that year Ethan Allen arrived in the Grants looking for a new home. Allen already had disrupted and been expelled from two stable New England towns, had a history of personal violence and erratic behavior, and had proclaimed himself a deist. What would such a man do to an unformed frontier society struggling against all odds to survive?

CHAPTER THREE

"The Fatigues of Settlement"

CULTURES meet and interact in frontier regions, often violently but not necessarily so. On most of the frontiers of British North America, European settlers came into conflict with the native populations. The Green Mountain frontier proved a major exception to this rule, not only because few Indians lived in the southern part of this region but also because the Allens worked deliberately to avoid conflict with the Indians living to the north—as when Ira Allen convinced one group of Mohawks to desert their New York allies by telling them that the whites were just fighting over land again.[1]

The settlers' cultural diversity produced a fairly contentious civic life and impeded the formation of any sort of collective identity. Religious and political differences generated their share of friction, though by 1770 no single issue proved sufficiently divisive to create serious breaches within any Grants town. Settlers shared enough culturally, and local government provided sufficient opportunities for participation, to preclude outbreaks of lawlessness; without any sort of police to enforce unpopular decisions, political consensus appeared requisite. But the absence of violence is not equivalent to the presence of a communal spirit and group identity.

The deeper problem for the Grants, the source of its most debilitating and destabilizing conflict, came not from within but from without. The claims of New York's government to the region and its efforts to establish and enforce its authority and apportion land as it saw fit endangered every settlement in the Green Mountains. The Grants settlers did not come into conflict with absentee proprietors or internal elites but with the would-be absentee landlords of New York.

I

But it is not the nature of this most indefatigable of speculators to rest contented with any state of sublunary enjoyment: improvement *is his darling passion.*——Washington Irving

Benning Wentworth's fraudulent machinations may have made cheap lands available, but most New Englanders demonstrated an understandable reluctance to move to the frontier. People did not just pack up and leave their hometowns in the eighteenth century without suffering a traumatic sense of dislocation and loss, and a natural fear of the unknown. In addition, not only did Wentworth's titles appear of dubious long-term value, but everyone appreciated that a frontier existence offered little beyond toil, uncertainty, and probable poverty.

Once migrants had made the daunting journey into the Green Mountains, the hard work began in earnest. Large tracts of deep forest covered the region, and first priority went to clearing and preparing the land for crops. A typical farm family cleared one to three acres a year, exploiting every shortcut possible, seeking whatever already-cleared land they could find.[2] In practice, that meant the sites of beaver dams; intervales (lush riverfront meadows); and as on other frontiers, abandoned Indian village sites. Settlers planted their first crop of corn in such open spaces without regard to land title before beginning to level the surrounding forests.[3]

The settlers saw too many trees to bother about the conservation of resources. Rather than maximizing the use of wood, Grants settlers employed one of two methods to clear the land: girding and burning. Girding involved stripping a section of bark from around the trunk in order to kill the tree quickly; but dead branches from girded trees could crash down on livestock and farmers for several years until the trunk itself fell. Burning was far quicker and left the settlers with piles of ash convertible into potash, their first, and usually only, cash crop. Potash, used in the production of metal items, was in sufficient demand in Albany to justify its transport across the Hoosic swamps.[4]

Traveling through the Green Mountains in the 1790s, the Reverend Timothy Dwight expressed disgust at the wastefulness of the pioneers. The people "appear to have cut down their forest with an improvident hand: an evil but too common in most parts of this country." Everyone complained of this "imprudence," according to Dwight, "and yet not a single efficacious nor helpful measure is adopted to lessen or even to check it."[5] Dwight, who never faced the problems of growing food among forests, would have found it difficult to convince a frontier family that it should preserve some of the thousands of surrounding trees. Far wiser, it seemed to settlers, to clear the land as quickly as possible and plant corn, which thrived among the stumps of felled trees.[6]

Corn ensured survival on the frontier. Settlers who planted corn in mid-June had ears ready for roasting by mid-August. No wonder it was often the only crop grown for the first few years, until settlers could clear fields of stumps and rocks and plant grains. Women—for a gender division of labor existed on the frontier, as elsewhere—roasted and dried corn, pounded it, and made the meal into a pudding served with milk and maple sugar or baked a bread popularly called johnnycake. A few acres of corn, followed by wheat and rye, supplied a family with the barest necessities. With survival, not profit, the goal, farmers across the northern frontier cultivated a diversity of grain and vegetable crops, being ever fearful that one of them might fail through some blight. Settlers' diets remained plain and meager, barely supplying caloric needs and heightening their susceptibility to a long list of diseases. Dietary deficiencies added to the difficulties of settlement but also forced settlers to rely on one another during times of shortages.[7]

The labor-intensive agricultural methods of the Grants settlers would have been familiar to a Massachusetts farmer of the 1640s. They used little fertilizer, and that usually unintentionally, employed clumsy, handmade implements, allowed livestock to roam at will, and planted their land with the same crops until the soil was exhausted. Most frontier farmers had only a hoe and a wooden plow for planting. The plating on iron plows tended to be so uneven that the user had to bear down while guiding the plow, a laborious process. With an ox, a single plow could furrow an acre a day; without oxen, it took three to four days to work an acre. Families winnowed by hand, throwing the grain into the wind and sifting it through sieves. There were generally no mills for the first decade of settlement, making it necessary to grind grain by using a mortar and pestle, tedious and time-consuming work. In all of these tasks, frontier settlers could rely for help only on their families and neighbors.[8]

The poverty of the frontier necessitated cooperative efforts. For instance, saw and grist mills made life easier for those already settled and brought a town to a level of self-sufficiency which would attract hesitant migrants. These considerations prompted every Grants town to offer land and water rights to anyone who would build the first mill; but despite incentives, most towns had difficulty locating prospective millers. They had abundant sources of waterpower and all the wood anyone could possibly need, but all metal parts had to be imported. Faced with the need to travel seventy miles downriver to Charlestown in order to grind their corn, the people of Newbury granted not just more land to their first miller but also the use of everyone's labor. The town sent a committee to purchase and haul a saw and crank by sled over the ice from Concord, New Hampshire—an enormous expenditure of time and effort, but well worth it.[9]

As Timothy Dwight summarized the process, the "foresters" selected a piece of land, often without proper title, "cut down some trees and girdle others; they furnish themselves with an ill-built log house and a worse barn, and reduce a part of the forest into fields. . . . On this scanty provision they feed a few cattle, and with these and the penurious products of their labor . . . they keep their families alive." Another observer found the whole frontier repugnant: the settlers built "dark, dirty and dismal" little shacks with small openings in the ceiling for smoke to escape and lived lives that matched their homes. Clearly, rational human beings would not subject themselves to such conditions.[10]

Indeed, Grants homesteads were modest affairs. The possessions of most early Grants settlers included deeds to many undeveloped acres of land, some pots and tools, cows and some seed, beds and books, and often a prized possession of more emotional than intrinsic value, such as a pair of silver spoons or "my father's fancy vest." Probate inventories of those who died suddenly in the prime of life reveal just how little aside from land titles the average settler in the Green Mountains owned. For instance, Aguila Cleaveland of Guilford left an estate valued at £121, with more than half of that value based on his fifty acres, eighteen of them under improvement at the time of his death. After land, farmers valued tools most highly. Cleaveland had been fortunate in owning an iron plow and the necessary yoke, irons, and team of oxen. With a woolen wheel he and his wife could produce clothing for home use and barter. Cleaveland owned a few cooper's tools, two axes (the settlers' favorite tool), some household goods, a few books, one cow, ten sheep, and an old saddle—though not a horse. Nor did he own a gun; most frontier settlers did not. Unfortunately for his family, Cleaveland also had debts up to ten years old totaling more than £23. As a consequence he died insolvent, and his young widow, Marcy, spent the next several years struggling to hold her family together. But her debtors were also her neighbors and demonstrated sympathy for her plight. One settled for two-thirds of what was owed him as "I have taken the oppinion of some of the Neighbours who think with me that its as much as she can afford to give." [11]

If personal possessions were few, land ownership was common. Of the adult male heads of household in the Green Mountains, 80 percent owned land, and land titles comprised just over half the wealth of most families. These landholdings were roughly equal: few landowners living in the Grants claimed more than three hundred acres, while one-third owned less than one hundred acres. The landless generally held that position temporarily; two-thirds of the discoverable landless adult males in the Grants eventually either inherited or traded their labor for a title to property. [12] In the Green Mountains almost every head of household in the years before 1790 ultimately owned land. Landlessness was a consequence of age rather than a permanent social state. [13]

Such rates of landownership and economic equality surpass anything known in early America's coastal regions. The nearby Hudson River districts of New York demonstrated far greater polarization. In 1779 about one-seventh of those assessed in that area owned real estate worth more than £500, with many estates valued at above £1,000, wealth unknown on the northern frontier where the highest tax assessments did not exceed £150. The wealthiest decile in these New York districts held 40 percent of all taxable property compared with one-quarter in the Grants towns. New England matched New York's economic inequality, with the top decile holding 46 percent of the real estate and nearly one-fourth of the taxpayers in 1771 worth more than £500. In contrast, the Green Mountains appeared a region of rough equality, where most heads of households owned land, and where the middle three-quarters held 70 percent of the wealth, a figure commensurate with their numbers. [14]

The gap between rich and poor narrowed on the northern frontier, but toward the bottom end of the scale. Even extensive landownership did not confer prosperity, for most of the land remained undeveloped, affording little more than claims to uncleared forests. Frontier farms could provide only a precarious, rugged, often hand-to-mouth subsistence. In comparison with the coastal areas of the northern colonies, these frontier families just got by. Excluding their titles to uncultivated land puts these settlers in the bottom tenth of New England's social scale. Still, a substantial difference exists between the successfully subsisting majority and the few families which suffered true destitution. Such unfortunates roamed the frontier; lacking the tools to work the land, they owned too little to become even squatters.

Frontier communities agonized over caring for the destitute. Those unable to support themselves could become serious burdens, confronting a community with a crisis it had few resources to meet. Towns cared for those with some family connection to the community, appointing guardians to manage the assets of an adult while offering remuneration to volunteers who took in orphans. If no one stepped forward to serve as adoptive parents, children faced the unpleasant choice of either leaving or signing papers of indenture, which at least ensured continued survival within the community and the promise of some recompense at the end of the assigned period. In any instance, the town taxed itself to aid those it determined to be truly poor.[15]

For example, Bennington spent several town meetings in 1769 deciding the fate of an extremely ill new arrival, Joseph Bingham, and his children. The town voted to warn out the Binghams "so that they become not town Inhabitants." A traditional New England practice, "warning out" denied inhabitant status to those too poor to care for themselves—a harsh casting out of the indigent. But Bennington also voted to care for Bingham, allocating £50 toward that end, and to meet the expenses of Bersheba Story over the next eight years for taking in Bingham's children. Rather than leaving it to individuals to care for Bingham out of a sense of charity, the town voted unanimously that everyone bore responsibility.[16]

Least fortunate were those wandering poor who had no link to any community. The same year that Bennington spent £70 for the care of the Bingham family, the town meeting voted without dissent to warn out the Horsford family, who could claim no relations in Bennington, and ordered them to leave without allowing the usual two-week grace period. Likewise, in 1779 Danby ordered out several recent arrivals whose poverty exposed the town to future expense. Nonetheless, warning out remained rare. Very few people wandered the frontier without family or regional connections to someone in a settled community.[17]

The rough economic equality of the early Grants did not exclude differences. Subtle gradations of wealth and status persisted, eventually leading certain families to relative wealth and prominence and others to poverty and dependence. On the frontier a shopkeeper, doctor, or minister could, over a twenty-year period, emerge as a community's most prosperous citizen, especially if he had access to credit in Boston or Northampton. Those who held onto land deeds into the 1790s often found themselves among the wealthiest men in the state.

The frontier retained an equitable distribution of property for several decades, largely because few wealthy or destitute people risked the journey north. The rich stayed home to enjoy their property in comfort, content to speculate occasionally in frontier land. The very poor also stayed in the established communities of New England, where their hometowns and families could care for them. Artisans, equally rare on the frontier, stayed where they drew good wages rather than foolishly trying their luck where no markets existed and the wages accrued in commodities. Only amateurs supplementing their farming practiced whatever artisan skills existed in the Green Mountains. Likewise, the few shopkeepers and professional people who did settle in the Grants relied on farming; not until the 1790s would any of them earn a livelihood from their trade.[18]

The combination of scarce labor and primitive technology, as well as the short growing season, eliminated opportunities for attaining wealth in the Grants. With no basis for developing commercial agriculture, most families took part in a subsistence economy, growing what they could and exchanging crops or family possessions for what they needed. Few individuals possessed the requisite equipment, labor, and cleared land to attain self-sufficiency, but in combination with their neighbors, every Grants town managed to survive.[19]

The economy of the New England frontier formed within a web of family connections, community responsibilities, and mutual dependence. Settlers understood wealth in family terms. They assigned values in pounds and shillings but in the absence of currency used such monetary terms as signs of convenience, of economic rationality, not of a market economy. These mechanisms of exchange, recorded in each family's account book, clarified relative indebtedness rather than profits made.[20] For instance, in 1768 Israel Curtis "agreed upon" a price of £3. 10 with his fellow Windsor proprietors for an acre of meadowland, a purchase that did not involve an exchange of currency. Instead, the two parties assigned a value to a blank book that Curtis owned which the town could use for its records and affixed another value on some work Curtis promised to do sometime in the next year on a certain stretch of road. The book and the labor would equal the £3. 10 Curtis owed the town.[21]

Until the 1820s farm commodities remained the standard of value in the Green Mountains; settlers paid taxes, ministers' salaries, and debts of all kind with crops. The more exact and rationalized structure of a cash economy did not appear until half a century after the first settlements in the Green Mountains and did not monopolize exchange until the Civil War. Settlers had no cash but dozens of notes of credit and debt tracing the outlines of a network of interdependence. Prosperity was potential; an equality of poverty, hard work, and hope determined the present.[22]

The distribution of wealth in the Grants did not prove a fundamental source of social and political cleavage. People felt the pressure of knowing that only a bad harvest separated them from disaster. The uncertainties surrounding subsistence created tensions, but not the sort that set one group against another. Neighbors often had no choice but to work together. But such economic interdependence did not prevent many settlers from distrusting and even despising one other. The cooperation mandated by economic exigency did not forge a collective identity, and the Grants remained throughout the 1760s and 1770s a region of often hostile diversity.

II

Hence arises the numerous sectaries and party disputes, which to a person of good understanding, are almost equally nonsensical. Probably we are the most selfish, oddest, and cunningest medley of beings, of our size, in the universe.—Ethan Allen

The tasks of settlement invited dispute, starting with the survey fixing personal and community boundaries. The vagueness and inaccuracy of Wentworth's grants compromised town lines, a problem further complicated by the inferior quality of surveying instruments and the fact that most surveyors in the Grants, such as Ethan Allen's brother Ira, were self-taught and generally incompetent. Parallel lines often met in the Green Mountains, and lots of supposedly equal size were seldom so. Confusion accompanied town planning.

The process of land division reflects the potential for conflicts in the Grants and the ways in which settlers tried to avoid these battles. Proprietors initiated the process by setting aside lands reserved for Wentworth, the Church of England, the Society for the Propagation of the Gospel, the first minister, and a school—shrewdly placing the first three of these grants in the most undesirable locales. Rockingham's proprietors located Wentworth's five hundred acres in a marsh while the SPG and church lands ended up on top of Mount Kilburn. In Guilford, Wentworth received Governor's Mountain, the name it still bears.[23]

Having appeased the formalities, the proprietors undertook the important division, with each proprietor drawing for a farm lot from the best land. Charters required settlers to assign one-acre town plots before proceeding to the division of the rest of the grant, but few proprietors adhered to this obligation. People moved to a township, cleared some land, and dealt with the divisions later, trusting that the necessary allowances would be made: if one drew lot 12 and lived on lot 41, the family who drew lot 41 might trade. Not all did, though, and town meetings worked patiently to resolve the numerous ensuing disputes, freely ignoring the instructions contained in their town charters.[24]

Proprietors also violated the letter of their charters by making town lots larger than the single acre stipulated. Most towns awarded five-acre town lots, though some, such as Windsor, went as high as forty acres. These large house lots altered the physical character of the close, cohesive New England village, with towns scattered over a square mile and more. But the first settlers cheated for a sound economic reason: the early pioneers had a relatively certain source of capital once settlement picked up, as they could sell off half-acre divisions of these town lots to later arrivals.[25]

Future divisions, usually covering a fifteen- to thirty-year period, moved successively outward to the less desirable lands. Settlers drew pastures in a third division and woodlands fourth, and most towns held fifth and sixth divisions as poor surveying left large areas undivided.[26] The resulting pattern of scattered landownership produced an active intratown trade in land rights as families sought to consolidate their holdings. Since only a few acres could be cleared a year, the initial location of a family's lands seemed irrelevant, and the youthfulness of Grants' families allowed many years to elapse before they claimed all their land for use by their children. There seemed plenty of time to arrange the necessary purchases and trades, or to sue.[27]

But lawsuits between individuals remained rare.[28] Dissatisfied settlers could appeal any draw of land to the proprietors' or town meeting. In most cases, these meetings resolved complaints, and those denied an appeal rarely pressed the matter. While someone might object to the quality of a particular portion of their holdings, the quantity more than made up for such disappointments. Each share in a New Hampshire Grant led to the ownership of, on average, just over 350 acres, three to four times what most of the settlers had owned back in Connecticut or Massachusetts. But few settlers held on to all these acres for long.[29]

The quantity of land available in the Green Mountains was the settlers' wild card. Land titles constituted the only form of liquid capital in the Grants, and the first settlers quickly sold to any interested newcomers at almost any rate of exchange. Such sales not only brought credit to the original owner but had the added advantage of bringing more settlers into the area, enhancing the value of everyone's holdings. Simply settling the land immediately increased its value. "Every good planter who seats himself in a new township," Timothy Dwight wrote at the end of the century, "increases the value of every acre which it contains, because he induces other men to settle around him. . . . every stroke of the ax leaves behind it more than the value of the labor." Towns did all they could to encourage settlement, hoping that the labor of these families might transform the forests into valuable farmland, securing the future of the entire community.[30]

But the actual process of building communities evoked conflict more often than consensus. Roads, for instance, remained a particularly sensitive issue. Roads integrated a town into larger economic networks and determined the development of a community for years to come, yet contention surrounded the collective decision of a highway's route. The committees chosen for that crucial task grew larger with each meeting, reflecting efforts to placate all areas of a town. Frustrated by their lack of capital, town meetings levied taxes, required labor from every adult male, and cut corners wherever possible, making broad detours to the farms of those willing to work extra for this convenience.[31]

More significantly, every Grants town broke quickly into factions competing for control of local government. Settlers from Sunderland, Massachusetts, and Salisbury, Connecticut, found it difficult to establish a new identity as residents of Sunderland, New Hampshire Grants. In the absence of any translocal political organization, and given that newcomers tended to live among former neighbors, often literally transplanting neighborhoods to the Green Mountains, it is little wonder that the settlers' primary loyalty remained with their town of origin and those who journeyed with them from that spot. The predilection of the first group that arrived to regard the new community as their town, with those who came later, if only by a matter of months, as interlopers, intensified disputes.[32]

This bias for point of origin is evident in the election of town officers. In Bennington settlers from Hardwick, Massachusetts, held a monopoly on the important town offices throughout the 1760s. Those from outside that founding group held only the unpopular offices, such as hogreave—responsible for chasing and catching stray pigs. Settlers from Sunderland and Newent challenged the dominance of the Hardwick clique, finally uniting into a majority in 1770 and instituting a period of office rotation which lasted into the 1790s. Though belonging to the same church, these settlers could not agree on the local leadership's composition; and in those towns without a single church, the pattern was more pronounced. Even in a small town like Shaftsbury, which barely had enough males to fill all its offices, the majority group from Rhode Island controlled the more significant positions for most of the town's first decade, though not without a battle which also ended in office rotation.[33]

The rapid turnover of town officials suggests a contentious civic climate. In the rest of New England, town officers held their positions for years, often decades, free from serious opposition. Deferential politics allowed local elites to share the prestigious offices of selectman, treasurer, and town clerk among themselves for generations. In the Grants few individuals held one of these offices for more than four years, and rarely for more than two consecutive terms. For instance, Danby's Rhode Island Baptists and New York Quakers contested every election, with the smaller contingent of Connecticut Congregationalists holding the swing votes. Elections often took two and three meetings to resolve, and incumbents rarely were re-elected. Of the thirty-three men who served as selectmen in Danby's first twenty years, one-third held that office just once in their lives, thirteen twice, six served three times, two four times, and only one man held the office five times. The same pattern held for the other offices, and in other towns, with a steady stream of names appearing and vanishing from year to year.[34]

The sheer number of times town meetings met points to the difficulty of resolving local disputes. Meetings addressed agendas crowded with an average of fifteen to twenty items, any of which could arouse the passions of a sizable proportion of the community and take five to ten separate gatherings to resolve. Occasionally dissatisfied citizens walked out of a town meeting and organized a competing assembly.[35]

Pigs, for instance, provoked continuous public debate. Every year in almost every town, inhabitants debated whether pigs should be allowed to run free. Voting, as Bennington did in 1762, "that every man's hogs shall be shut upon his land," obviated the need to elect a hogreave—an office no one ever wanted—and to build a pound. Poorer farmers who had no livestock except pigs favored letting them run free to root in someone else's garden, while those who built fences for their cattle supported pig control. In most Grants towns the antipig faction constituted a majority, but their numerical superiority did not prevent the opposing side from raising the issue for a vote once a year. And despite efforts to avoid the expense, most towns had to build pounds by the 1770s.[36]

Towns also regularly, and vigorously, debated the advantages and dangers of smallpox inoculation; the wisdom and cost of sending for itinerant ministers, and of what denomination; the amount and control of aid for the poor; the propriety and use of public stocks; the need for a freemen's list; the regulation of prices; and what goods and labor would be accepted in payment of taxes by the town. Any expenditure of the town's resources aroused bitter contention which could easily last for several years.

Few battles generated greater heat than those over the location of the meetinghouse. A typical controversy of this kind disrupted Norwich for several years, inhabitants of each section of town insisting upon siting the meetinghouse in their neighborhood. In an effort to resolve the dispute, the town meeting appointed a committee of outsiders, which selected a tract near the Connecticut River. Most of Norwich's forty families, who lived near the river and had migrated together from Mans-field and Hebron, Connecticut, accepted this site. But residents in the west part of town, who all came from Preston, Connecticut, perceived bias in the selection and effectively blocked a tax to fund construc-tion, preventing completion of the meetinghouse for twelve years. Other towns took longer: Danby did not finish its meetinghouse until 1801, after thirty-seven years of contention.[37]

As though such civil matters were not enough to disrupt a town's peace, religious fervor, brought to a white heat by the Great Awakening, threatened to tear them apart. The lack of religious consensus within the Grants towns created two problems. First, settlers disagreed widely on the proper relationship between the church and community. In the absence of courts to resolve disputes and of laws to enforce public wor-ship on the Sabbath—as existed in Connecticut and Massachusetts—debates developed over the proper agency for maintaining moral norms, some arguing for the town, others for the church. The general result was inaction: if the town won, meetings dragged on endlessly; if a church as-sumed responsibility, it proved impossible to adjudicate disputes which involved those of a different denomination.[38]

A second hurdle arose when it came time to hire a settled minister. Obviously a town with some mixture of Separates, New Light Congrega-tionalists, Anglicans, Presbyterians, Quakers, and Baptists would have difficulty agreeing on the merits of any single clergyman, while no one denomination had the numbers or resources to fund its own minister. Complicating matters further, most settlers mistrusted a learned, settled clergy, preferring lay exhorters or itinerants, and the Quakers rejected ministers entirely.[39]

Even when a town or church agreed on and could afford a ministerial candidate, it proved difficult to attract him to the frontier. In 1765 New-bury hired a minister named Moody for six months. At the end of this trial period the town expressed its satisfaction, but Moody did not, and left. The town continued its search but could not find a minister "willing to venture so far out of the world." No Harvard or Yale graduate would follow the call to New England's rugged frontier. As a consequence, the Grants lacked the continuous clerical leadership that so often lent stability to older New England communities.[40]

While Separates predominated among the first Grants settlers—though many Separates took to calling themselves Baptists—sharing supposedly similar theological views did not guarantee agreement. In fact, Separatism's chief characteristics contributed to social fragmentation and conflict by fostering opportunities for division and inhibiting the development of strong institutions. The Separate and Baptist emphasis on lay authority ensured that most of their churches experienced long periods of strife between clergymen and congregations. Wallingford's Baptists decided to select a lay minister, only to find themselves with four candidates from within the church. After two years of praying over the problem and letting the four alternate as readers, the church decided to select an outsider. But this minister held only a brief, stormy tenure and then left. The vacuum at the top of the ecclesiastical hierarchy created ceaseless schism among the laity.[41]

Separates demonstrated a second notable characteristic in the surprising diversity of theological opinion within their ranks. No more a monolith than orthodox Congregationalism, Separatism encompassed a wide range of beliefs, and many who called themselves Separates were just passing through on their way to a completely different religious outlook. At the first meeting of Shaftsbury's Separate church in 1768, "a number of christians, . . . had much labour about the Doctrins of Christ and the form of his house. Some of us hold that the Doctrin of laying on of hands is to be Imposed on Common believers, others hold not." Finally the majority agreed "that Laying on of hands Should not hinder Our building Together" a church. After they agreed to disagree on this issue, there followed "a dispute about Telling Experiences"— relating conversions to the congregation. These efforts to find some common ground, or at least to arrive at a position where differences would not destroy their nascent church community, occurred among only seven people. It was a small beginning to a lengthy history of dissent and division aggravated by the spiritual vagrancy of the church's elders, who moved to opposite ends of the theological spectrum. By 1775 the church contained almost as many theologies as members.[42]

The Separates' endemic theological diversity derived from a third characteristic, the key to their persuasion: their quest for pure churches. Separates saw themselves as the true descendants of New England's Puritans, returning to stricter scriptural rules of behavior. Exalting an earlier, purer age, Separates lamented society's decline into secularism. They hoped to reestablish Winthrop's "city on the hill" in the Green Mountains but could not agree on what shape that city should take.[43]

The decisive religious issue, as during the Great Awakening, remained the determination of church membership. The relation of a conversion experience remained requisite for becoming a church member. Although church elders judged the validity of an applicant's conversion experience, the membership verified, or often rejected, that judgment. And debates over the adequacy of confessions of faith often spilled over into town meetings.[44]

The Separate concern that nothing violate the purity of their congregations led to extreme watchfulness over one another's private lives. As many as one-third of a congregation's members might find their sanctity questioned in the first few years of a church's history, leading to schism upon schism. Shaftsbury's Separate church spun off three progeny, while some churches purified themselves right out of existence—the Halifax Separate Church expelled all but eight of its original forty members, leaving too few to support its continuance.[45]

The nature of Separatism inspired ceaseless controversy, ensuring that only a few Grants towns could unite on the selection of a minister. "For all protestant churches the appeal to conscience, to the inner voice, conflicted with the necessity of organization and discipline."[46] In fact, Separate discipline maintained neither social harmony nor control. The efforts of the Reverend Jedediah Dewey of Bennington to formulate a more inclusive church polity and get a regular salary in the process illustrates the problems facing Separate congregations on the frontier, where every exigency called for merging the church with the community, while every article of faith argued against such a compromise with reality.

Lacking legal power to coerce attendance, the Bennington church could rely only on persuasion to maintain unity. In 1765 the church admonished Bythiah Burnham "for her unscriptural withdrawal from the church," but she seemed not to care. The following year the church sent a committee to speak with those brethren who shunned Sunday services and the Reverend Dewey's salary. Again and again the church ordered its members to "settle with Mr. Dewey," even voting to forgive those behind in their payments if they would pay something, anything. But the "Delinquent Brethren" ignored these suggestions. The church remained unsuccessful in its efforts because far more was at issue than ministerial support.[47]

Dewey aimed to merge church and community, to attain unity in each by making them one and the same. He also saw some advantage in abandoning voluntary support of the minister in favor of mandatory contributions. To attain these goals, Dewey, supported by the majority of church members, expanded voting rights to include the entire church. The new electorate then selected the church's five officers, including two nonmembers, and set Dewey's salary at £50 a year.[48]

This sacred democracy violated the sensibilities of a minority calling themselves the "aggrieved Brethren." What distinction remained, they asked, to being a member of the church? The majority of the membership thought themselves practical. They made a deal with the larger community, which included their own families, allowing partial participation in church affairs in return for support, harmony, and, they hoped, future members. In response, the nine aggrieved brethren charged Dewey with violating the covenant and letting "church and society" stand in equality. The majority appeared dangerously close to establishing on the frontier precisely what they had fled, theological liberalism.[49]

The conflict flowed outward from the church, disrupting twenty-seven town meetings between June 1768 and January 1772. A Separate Ecclesiastical Council held in 1770 supported the minority view that authority rested solely with those who could relate a conversion experience. But the majority of the church members voted themselves guiltless of "Moral Evil" and rejected the council's findings. Through three years of bitter dispute each side threatened to leave, expel one another, and call a church council. Some of the minority confessed their error, with the qualification that they were still right, were welcomed back, and immediately returned to disrupting the meetings. The church verged on collapse.[50]

Resolution came only with the departure of the minority at the end of 1771. Dewey dreaded this rejection of communal unity and labored to recover "those Brethren that have Deserted from us," but without effect. The separating Separates established themselves in a small cabin on the side of Mount Anthony, recruiting a minister to their liking. The Grants' first church had not lasted its first decade as a unified society. Dewey and his congregation now had to deal with another church in the small confines of Bennington.[51]

During their four-year internal conflict, Bennington's warring Separates debated some of the paramount intellectual issues of the day: individual freedom of conscience, the nature of church membership and the relation of the church to society, and the right of a minority to object to majority decisions. The minority felt themselves true to the spirit of Separatism and the Great Awakening, and so they were. The majority saw themselves reacting in a serious and pious manner to the problems of a frontier church, and so they were. Unfortunately for the unity of Vermont's first church, these two forms of piety could not be reconciled.

In many ways, the Grants settlers replicated the experiences of New England's seventeenth-century Puritans, with one key difference. New England's older communities struggled with the questions of church membership and polity, producing a high degree of religious controversy. But the Puritans had arrested the Separatist impulse early, freely using ministerial authority and, when necessary, the courts to keep a tight rein on forces of theological dissolution. And they always had Rhode Island as a convenient dump for the irreconcilable.

The frontier communities of the Green Mountains had none of these advantages, lacking influential ministers, a civil code to enforce adherence to the Congregational way, and courts to punish those who transgressed moral norms. Though the settlers did not know it, they formed the new outcasts of New England—each town was like a little Rhode Island. Unable to continue in obedience to New England's standing order, they fled north with expectations of recreating an imagined past. The problem remained: within any given Grants community a wide variety of imagined pasts contended for primacy. As a result, not only did the Grants settlers enjoy little religious consensus, they suffered from chronic theological contention. Given the extent of diversity and the absence of civil constraints on dissent, religion could not develop as the basis for any kind of collective identity, as it had in the seventeenth century. If deciding issues of the community's relation to the church was difficult in a town with an established minister and basic consensus on theology, it verged on the impossible in the majority of Grants towns, which lacked both.[52]

Ethan Allen and his contentious family settled among these pious people. Ethan, twice exiled from New England towns and an outspoken deist, came to Bennington, the preserve of Separates. Other Allens had also run into trouble for their religious views: Ira Allen had been imprisoned in 1770 for traveling on the Sabbath, and Zimri Allen and Remember Baker were arrested for blasphemy in 1773. The latter two insisted that, being antitrinitarians, "we spake nothing irreverantly." In contrast, the arresting constable held only "such principles as his nurses and ghostly teachers have beat into his head . . . and being sparingly stocked with intelligence . . . over balanced his noodle." Here was some spice for the Grant's theological stew.[53]

Religious disputes vexed these communities, yet the preponderance of Separates and their obsession with purity and exclusivity directed attention inward on fellow congregants. Preoccupied with intrachurch squabbles, the Separates had less energy to invest in battles with Baptists, Anglicans, and Quakers. Yet even if rival sectarians in the Grants did not tear each other apart, religious diversity remained a serious impediment to the emergence of any sense of common identity. The real source of conflict in the Grants, and the ultimate threat to the stability of these frontier communities, came not from internal disputes but from outside.

In 1765 Major Walter Rutherford and the powerful New York attorney James Duane set off from Albany to inspect their Princetown Patent. Their immense tracts overlapped not only the New Hampshire towns of Arlington, Dorset, Sunderland, Manchester, and Pownal but also an Albany land patent and a New York military grant. Rutherford and Duane ignored these contradictions, assuming the land theirs. The whole region from Bennington north, Rutherford wrote, consisted of "very fine Land . . . the Timothy Meadows quite the best I ever saw." The two New Yorkers appreciated the work of Sunderland's settlers in unknowingly preparing the soil for their future landlords. After only three years the settlers already had cleared hundreds of acres and "judiciously laid out" their towns, which "will save us considerable Expense and prevent confusion." Rutherford and Duane spoke at length with two brothers from Connecticut, Gideon and Timothy Brownson. The New Yorkers could not suspect that when the time to evict these troublesome New Englanders arrived, the Brownsons would call upon their brother-in-law, Ethan Allen, for help. Only when New York attempted to enforce its legal structures and land titles did the frontier explode.[54]

III

Can the New York scribblers . . . alter wrong into right, or make any person of good sense believe that a great number of hard labouring peasants, going through the fatigues of settlement, and

cultivation of a howling wilderness, are a community of riotous,
disorderly, licentious, treasonable persons?—Ethan Allen

Anne Grant did not think highly of her new neighbors. Grant, who
lived in Stillwater, New York, found the "rapid and astonishing change
of manners and sentiments" disturbing. The period after the Peace
of Paris dawned full of promise, but, as Grant wrote, "this sunshine
was transient." The older residents "were soon succeeded by Obadiah
or Zephaniah from Hampshire or Connecticut, who came in without
knocking; sat down without invitation; and lighted their pipe without
ceremony; then talked of buying land; and, finally, began a discourse
on politics." The New Englanders "came over foaming with religion and
political fury." Grant compared them to lava "discharged by the fury of
internal combustion, from the bosom of the commonwealth," slow to
cool and turning into "a substance hard and barren, that long resists the
kindly influence of the elements." [55]

The New Englanders' passions heated with visions of owning their
own land. They discovered, "or rather had a revelation," that the New
Hampshire border extended almost to the Hudson. Thus "swarms of
petulent half-educated" New Englanders came into conflict with the
"ephemeral adventurers" of New York, mostly lawyers, "who multiplied
so fast that one would think they rose like mushrooms from the earth."

The whole business seemed cloudy and mysterious. Every deed appeared dubious and indeterminable, its borders set by Indian marks and
stacks of rocks. "The uncertainty of the law was very glorious indeed"
and created numerous opportunities for the clever and patient. Grant's
aunt "sought refuge in the peaceable precincts of the gospel," only to
find her minister more interested in land than in the Good Book. Grant
took refuge in cynicism, noting that the "fierce republicans" of New
England could not match the corruption and chicanery of the Yorkers.
"It was particularly hard for people who acknowledged no superior," she
wrote with some sympathy, "to hold their lands from such people as
my father and others, of 'King George's Red Coats,' as they elegantly
styled them." [56]

Anne Grant saw all New Englanders as alike, but they certainly were
not. By the same token not all New Yorkers shared similar goals and
aspirations. The northern frontier stretched across the unspecified ter-

ritories of New York, Massachusetts, New Hampshire, and Quebec. Around the northern reaches of the Hudson River, in New York's Albany County, a number of great landlords, members of the province's ruling hierarchy, established giant plantations with hundreds of tenant farmers drawn from New York, New England, Scotland, and Germany—each group adhering to a different branch of Christianity. Mixed in with this population, especially in Albany, lived a number of merchants and entrepreneurs, indentured servants and slaves. To the east, in the Grants, hundreds of families settled into a patchwork of small farming communities. These settlers lacked a mutual identity but gloried in a single vital difference from their western neighbors: they owned their land.

In 1764 this whole vast region, incorporating two distinctive patterns of landholding, fell within the jurisdiction of New York by order of the king. And New York intended to enforce that jurisdiction to the exclusion of all alien land titles. Settlers on the west side of the New Hampshire Grants resisted New York's rule from the start, yet their rebellion seemed stillborn. In 1767 the Bennington town meeting sent Samuel Robinson to London, where he lobbied for secure titles regardless of jurisdiction. Robinson found allies in the SPG, which would win thousands of acres if the king confirmed the New Hampshire grants. Responding to an SPG petition, the Board of Trade ordered New York to "desist from making any grant whatever of any part of those lands, until His Majesty's further pleasure shall be known." [57]

But New York's ruling council violated the Board of Trade's orders, granting itself and its associates immense tracks of land. Governor William Tryon awarded himself 32,000 acres in the region and proved most obliging to friends and supporters. Even William Smith, the only member of the council to oppose these actions, obtained 100,000 acres in the northeast. Lord Hillsborough, the secretary of state for the colonies, ordered Tryon to obey the king's instructions. The New York council responded by accelerating its granting of lands. [58]

If New York could ignore the king, then the Grants settlers could ignore New York. The Privy Council ordered the settlers to follow New York laws. Governor John Wentworth advised them "to regulate themselves according to their Grants from New Hampshire" despite the Privy Council's decision. The settlers listened to Wentworth, looking to New Hampshire for their laws and to themselves for the settlement of disputes. In 1768 the proprietors of Windsor, frustrated with their "delinquent proprietors," chose "a committe to Sell Said lands according to the Laws of the Province" of New Hampshire.[59]

But when New York pressed its authority, the Grants resistance folded. When three Dutch families settled in Pownal under New York's Hoosic patent, New Hampshire justice of the peace Samuel Robinson ordered Sheriff Samuel Ashley to evict them. Albany's Sheriff Philip Schuyler arrested Robinson and Ashley in return, confining them in jail for two months. Bennington's first direct resistance ended a humiliating failure, particularly for Samuel Robinson, who regarded himself as the region's patriarch.[60]

Every factor seemed weighted against the New Hampshire claimants: the crown supported New York's jurisdiction; New York's new governor, fresh from crushing the Regulator movement in North Carolina, demonstrated a willingness to employ British troops against dissident farmers; the Grants, divided by the Green Mountains, lacked geographical unity; the settlers offered no sustained justification for their claims; and their only recognized leader, Samuel Robinson, died in 1767.[61] It should have been abundantly clear that New York would succeed in enforcing its authority. But as Ethan Allen noted, claiming and exercising jurisdiction are not the same thing. Even though many settlers in the eastern Grants welcomed New York's authority, that government seemed incapable of overcoming its own ineptness and confusion, as is evident in its efforts to establish courts in the Grants.

Contemporary observers recognized New York's colonial courts as tools of the rich. One 1768 pamphlet charged that the courts were closed to the common man; there simply was "no Law for poor Men." Lieutenant Governor Colden, who often attempted to use the courts for personal advantage, found the entire New York judiciary dominated by the province's largest landowners. Colden condemned the "dilatory Proceedings in the Courts of Law" and "the heavy Expence in obtaining Justice" and demanded that the legislature investigate, something that self-interested party would not do.[62] Nonetheless, scores of inhabitants in the eastern Grants found advantage in having any sort of stable government and formed a powerful faction supporting New York's claims to rule over the Grants. Most of these "Yorkers" did not actually come from New York, but New England. Generally the preeminent inhabitants of their towns, they sought to ensure good order and respect for their local authority.

In 1765 these Grants Yorkers petitioned for the creation of a county. Their petitions complained that since becoming inhabitants of New York, "[we] have been ever since without Law, Notwithstanding we have made application to be protected." They only asked that New York open courts in the east, "that offenders may be Brought to Justice, and Creditors may Recover their Just Dues"; they could not understand why New York refused to act in favor of its own jurisdiction. By insisting that the Grants inhabitants remain part of Albany County, its courts a hundred miles away over the Green Mountains, the government placed them "under such a Disadvantage that Justice Cannot be had," caught in a legal limbo. One petition, signed by most of the leading men of the eastern towns, concluded with the dire warning "that unless there be a County made as prayed for, instead of good wholesome Inhabitants comeing and Settling amongst us, the Land will be filled with Nothing, but Villins and Murderers, as being an out Law'd place." [63]

Albany County's large landowners opposed the creation of a new county, fearing that autonomous courts and county officials would weaken their opportunities for future land grabs and lessen the settlers' dependence on their richer neighbors. In 1766 the legislature agreed to appoint justices of the peace, but it refused to organize a new county. The governor and council overrode the legislature and ordered the creation of Cumberland and Gloucester counties in the eastern Grants. The Privy Council vetoed this act when the legislature insisted on the right to appoint representatives for these counties. In 1768 the legislature capitulated and allowed the election of representatives, though it appointed most other officers, including a court of general sessions which could overrule the decision of any justice of the peace. The legislature sought to minimize local authority and maintain its control of the northeast, hoping, as its opponents appreciated, to divide the New Hampshire claimants by creating courts only in the east. New York gave preferment to the wealthiest eastern settlers while isolating those towns most hostile to its authority, bringing the west under the firm domination of Albany County's political and economic elite. The westside would be surrounded, separated from its base of support in New Hampshire. [64]

Having adopted a clever political strategy, New York's government could not make it work. From the point of view of the eastside settlers, the new county courts reflected a high level of inefficiency and insufficiency. The Gloucester County court finally opened in May 1770 in the county seat Kingsland, an uninhabited town whose chief virtue was its name. The first session of the court adjourned without transacting any business; the second session appointed four constables and then adjourned. The third session, in November, exemplified the major fault of the New York judiciary in the Grants: after two days of struggling through the snow, the court's officials could not find Kingsland and resolved to hold the court in the woods, continued all the cases on their agenda, and adjourned. Not until 1772—after a fit of rationality led them to move the shire to Newbury, which was inhabited—did the court resolve any cases. Even then, the record was dismal, with only eighteen court cases (15%) decided in four years. Only one of the resolved cases ended with the plaintiff receiving satisfaction. Not surprisingly, the county convention of 1774 complained bitterly of "the inconveniences to which the inhabitants were subjected in collecting" their debts.[65]

The Cumberland County court, a busier and marginally more successful bench, managed to resolve one-third of its cases. But then the officers of the Cumberland court demonstrated fewer scruples than their Gloucester peers. If the defendant failed to show, the court declared him guilty; and if the justices found the defendant's plea "not agreeable," they declared it void, ordering judgment for the plaintiff "for want of a plea." In all but two cases the court decided for the plaintiff.[66]

The history of New York's courts in Gloucester and Cumberland counties is a study of inaction and bias. The records are full of statements such as "Neither appearing, Nothing done" and "capi corpus" (the sheriff unable to locate the defendant), of bonds forfeited and summonses ignored. Judges appointed family and political allies to jury duty, even, or especially, when the judge himself was subject to a suit. In one curious instance Judge Samuel Sleeper appeared as defendant in a case and, though present at the beginning of the session, was declared "not appearing," and the case was continued. One cannot be certain if he stepped outside for a few minutes, ducked under the table, or simply created a legal fiction on paper. In any event, it served as a poor example, though a valuable lesson, to other defendants waiting their turn to appear before the vanishing judge.[67]

Such corruption did the courts little good. Their sessions started playing to empty houses; not even the constables would attend. That so many of those ordered to appear did not reflects the attitude of the settlers along the Connecticut River toward the New York courts, one of denial and contempt. Unable to collect costs from the losing party, the courts had to bear some fairly hefty expenses with nothing to show for their money but ill will.[68]

Despite these difficulties, New York insisted on rigorous adherence to the rules. The courts' technically minded decisions disgusted most of those who bothered to appear. The majority of people on both sides of the Green Mountains desired a court system that would work, but they found New York's system worthless, its decisions unenforceable, and its proceedings dominated by a clique of New York attorneys and their patrons.[69]

At best New York's northeastern courts proved as corrupt and alienating as those in the rest of the province. People who associated with New York's courts in any capacity, whether as defendants, plaintiffs, officials, or jury members, found their time wasted and unproductive. For instance, in *Kingsley* v. *Bigelow* (1773), the Cumberland court spent an entire day hearing fourteen witnesses. The jury's deliberations ran into the evening, with the verdict delivered the next morning. But the jury forgot to sign and seal its verdict after the evening session. The judges ruled a mistrial and ordered a new hearing in the next session, four months later. No decision was ever reached in this case.[70]

New York's courts produced controversy almost from the start, intensifying and becoming entangled in local factionalism, appointing unpopular officers, and failing to resolve the vast majority of their cases. The Cumberland County court responded to the interests of a small faction that circulated around the only lawyers in the region, John Grout and Charles Phelps. These two men saw the Grants as a land of litigious opportunity, a perception they did their best to enhance by creating work for themselves. Increased land speculation by New Yorkers added to their power: the greater the trade in real estate, the greater the level of litigation. Grout alone bore responsibility for the majority of the cases heard before the Cumberland court.[71]

Such a corrupted and confused atmosphere undermined New York's legitimacy. In 1770 the very structure of New York's northeastern courts unraveled and the support of the local elite began evaporating. Trouble began with Judge Samuel Wells's refusal to prosecute William and Willard Dean for violating the mast timber laws. The judge reasoned that such fine citizens and close friends would not intentionally cut down trees marked for His Majesty's Navy. Sheriff Benjamin Wait arrested the Deans anyway, finding it necessary to pummel John Grout in the process. In return Justice Thomas Chandler issued a warrant for the arrest of Benjamin and Joseph Wait and Nathan and Simon Stone for assaulting Grout.[72]

At the heart of this web two factions, both supporters of New York's authority, competed for land grants and political office. But allegiances became confused in the battle between these local factions. Though steadfast supporters of New York, Wells and his allies violated the spirit of the law by refusing to prosecute the Deans. Acting in New York's name, the court succeeded not only in alienating four of the most ambitious and respected men in the region but also in arousing a large portion of the population, as became clear when a crowd rescued the Stones and Waits from Sheriff Whipple. A few months later—New York officials moved slowly—Whipple organized a posse to retake his prisoners. A crowd three times larger than the posse confronted and seized Whipple, informing him that there would be no criminal prosecutions of any kind at the next meeting of the Westminster court. The mob would allow debt cases but not felony hearings.[73]

A few days later a crowd led by Nathan Stone disrupted the court, declaring—"with their Hatts on," as Judge Wells complained—New York's government a "sham," its courts ineffective and unjust, and its officers corrupt, and demanded the immediate disbarment of John Grout as a "bad man." The court adjourned hastily, leaving the crowd to its own justice. The crowd seized Grout, lectured him on his maleficence, and let him go, proclaiming that "we have now broke up the Court." Authority had been turned upside-down and lines clearly drawn, to the detriment of New York.[74]

New York issued warrants but failed to arrest anyone. The earl of Dunmore, briefly governor of New York, reported that the situation in Cumberland and Gloucester counties "is truly lamentable; a number of disorderly people are continually committing Riots." Dunmore felt that "the authority of the Civil Magistrate will avail little, when even the Courts of Justice are obstructed and their proceedings stopped." Many people believed that the king intended to turn the region over to New

Hampshire. Dunmore issued a proclamation denying the rumor but doubted its efficacy while local officials remained unable "to enforce their own authority, against those daring violators of the peace supported as they are, by their whole province." [75]

Dunmore read the situation accurately, though he expressed his class bias in thinking that a few more "men of quality" would succeed in holding a "whole province" in awe. New York's authority meant nothing in the routine operation of local government, being opposed by almost every inhabitant in the region—as a single example from the Cumberland County court records reveals. In 1771 Jonas Moore of Putney finally won a £40 judgment against Leonard Spaulding for an unpaid debt. Spaulding, an active New Hampshire adherent, refused to pay, leading the sheriff to seize some of Spaulding's cattle. Spaulding gathered together eighty of his neighbors, equal to the number of adults in Putney—minus Jonas Moore—and broke into Moore's barn, reclaiming the cattle. Judge Joseph Lord could do nothing but make excuses and resigned his office out of "a desire to retire from Publick business . . . & concern myself in nothing else, but doing good to my numerous family & Neighbours." A decision of the New York courts had been overridden, its authority nullified, and one of its judges driven into retirement. [76]

Other frontiers experienced similar lawlessness as a consequence of external efforts at economic and political control. For instance, in North Carolina the coastal elite dominated the legal and political structures of the western counties, attaining significant control of the economic life of these communities in the mid-1760s. Organizing themselves into extralegal militia companies, thousands of "Regulators" fought back against what they saw as a corrupt legal system which failed to protect their property, only to be crushed brutally at the Battle of Alamance in May 1771 by Governor Tryon and the coastal militia. In upstate New York a few elite families dominated every aspect of the region's economy and courts. In 1766 New England squatters living in the east part of Dutchess County resisted efforts by the landlords to collect rent. The uprising spread to tenants in Westchester and Albany counties, and within a year hostile groups of farmers, militia, and the landlords' private armies roamed destructively through upstate New York. Governor Henry Moore finally sent in four regiments of British regulars to put down this rebellion by what Robert Livingston, Jr., called "vile wicked animals." Similar conflicts occurred on the Maine and Pennsylvania frontiers as settlers saw their interests denied while the state fostered those of an external class of wealthy landlords.[77]

It seemed possible that the would-be landlords of northeast New York would be spared these troubles. Resistance to their authority languished in the absence of a collective identity, and an internal pro–New York faction worked to undermine such efforts. New York's opponents along the Connecticut River found it difficult to unite with those in other towns, and several local leaders, including Nathan Stone, gave in and accepted preferments from New York. In return, New York stopped issuing land titles in the settled parts of Cumberland County but insisted on its own form of local government. Real power lay outside the town, in the appointed county board of supervisors, the provincial assembly, and the Executive Council—all dominated by the wealthy landed elite. The struggle against New York authority on the east side of the Green Mountains flared in 1770 and 1771 and then dimmed, though it was not extinguished.[78]

To the west, the settlers' many failures drew the gentle pity of Anne Grant. But by 1771 Grant's sympathy shifted to hatred. The New Englanders "carried their insolence so far" as to attack a "particular friend of my father's, a worthy, upright man, named Munro." Lacking manners, these people seemed "let loose by the daemon of discord, for the destruction of public peace and private confidence." The region had become "a refuge for the vagabonds and banditti of the continent," and Grant applauded the efforts of Justice John Munro to evict the New Englanders and replace them with good, obedient Scot and German settlers. The worst of the outlaws was this new man brought in to lead the battle against the authorities. As one of Grant's respectable neighbors wrote, a certain Ethan Allen had arrived recently with "twelve or fifteen of the most blackguard fellows he can get," by which he meant Allen's family.[79]

The Allens were considered savages. Their unusual respect for Indian ways confirmed this estimation. In fact, Ethan and Levi Allen did learn a great deal from the region's natives. Trading pelts and furs, the Indians shared their knowledge of the best routes through the woods, familiarizing the Allens with the extensive network of Indian trails crisscrossing the Green Mountains, and told them where beavers dammed the waters and the best places to wait for deer to pass. The Allens found much to admire and even emulate in native ways. Indian notions of economic and political equity and honesty seemed superior to many European practices. Levi Allen wrote that the "Christians have not so much to boast over the American Indians as they Vainly attribute to themselves." Ethan Allen shared these sentiments but admired especially the natives' understanding of war.[80]

CHAPTER FOUR

"Riotous Persons & Parties"

P OLITICAL authorities in colonial America generally found coercion ineffective for maintaining social control. Lacking a standing army or regular police force, governors, legislators, and selectmen had to rely on the militia to preserve order. But far too often the government discovered that it could not call out the militia to suppress crowd actions because the majority of the militia had joined the crowd. Even conservative patriot leaders such as John Adams insisted that "more dangerous than crowd action was the power of a magistrate to crush it with force." Far better, then, that the militia give way before the crowd.[1]

In 1770 the "Bennington Mob," as the New York government labeled those resisting its rule in the northeast corner of Albany County, reversed the equation. In the New Hampshire Grants the crowd formed itself into a militia. The instigator of this revolutionary act, Ethan Allen, promised to "submit to every legal process" except those which "are manifestly illegal."[2]

Allen faced three challenges as a leader. First, the need to forge something approximating a collective identity and common political program on the west side of the Green Mountains. Second, to make life difficult for New York. And third and most difficult, to win over accommodationists, most of whom lived on the east side, and thus consolidate the resistance by unifying the entire region in opposition to New York. Allen did not act in a jurisdictional vacuum; he and his Green Mountain Boys created the vacuum which they then moved to fill. Ethan Allen brought more than just organizational skill to these tasks, treating the northern frontier to one of the greatest demonstrations of political sleight of hand seen in the eighteenth century.

I

I was amazed and sore troubled, and said, L—d how is it that thou sufferest thy chosen ones to be trodden down by the heathen? . . . And he said unto me, "Son of man, fear not, for in the fullness of time I will appear for my people, and confound the Yorkites." And the L—d stirred up the spirit of the valiant Green Mountain Boys.—Junus, the Benningtonite

In late 1769 Major John Small and the Reverend Michael Slaughter found squatters living on their land in northeastern New York. These families claimed that they held legitimate title to the land and resided in the town of Shaftsbury, New Hampshire. Small and Slaughter, whose titles came from the royal province of New York, scoffed at this folly and brought ejectment suits against the squatters. New Hampshire proprietors, both settled and absentee, recognized the ejectments as test cases of the validity of all their holdings. Meeting in Canaan, Connecticut, the nonresident proprietors formed a defense fund for the defendants and appointed Ethan Allen its manager.[3]

Allen rode immediately to Portsmouth, New Hampshire, where he met with Governor John Wentworth. The governor, like most people, saw the Grants as a lost cause but suggested that Allen speak with the New Haven lawyer Jared Ingersoll. One of Connecticut's most prominent and conservative attorneys, Ingersoll agreed to represent the Shaftsbury squatters and rode with Allen to Albany, arriving the day of the trial, 28 June 1770.[4]

A certain conflict of interest marked the court. The presiding judges, Robert Livingston and George Ludlow, both held New York deeds in the contested area, as did Attorney General John Tabor Kempe and the plaintiffs' attorney, James Duane. In the first case, *John Small* v. *Josiah Carpenter,* Ingersoll produced Carpenter's grant, issued under the king's seal. Duane objected that New Hampshire's governor had no authority to grant land in the area, rendering the deed immaterial. Though Carpenter's grant bore an earlier date than Small's charter, the justices upheld Duane's objection, destroying instantly any case the Grants' inhabitants could put forth.[5]

Within an hour of entering the New York court system, Allen gained a direct experience of what he saw as its corruption and hypocrisy. The plaintiffs enjoyed every advantage, arriving "in great state and magnificance which . . . made a brilliant appearance." In contrast, the defendants, "appearing but in ordinary fashion having been greatly fatigued by hard labor wrought on the disputed premises, . . . made a very disproportionate figure at court." The poor farmers lost before the trial began, for "interest, conviction and grandeur being all on one side, easily turned the scale against the honest defendants," and the court rendered "judgements without mercy," serving the specific economic interests of a small "junto of land thieves."[6]

Having lost, Allen held the cases meaningless. New York's courts could make their biased decisions but had no power to enforce their authority. Duane also recognized that New York's effective jurisdiction was limited, and the day after the trial he and Attorney General Kempe visited Allen. Duane and Kempe offered Allen cash and land, under New York title of course, if he would work for their side in the dispute. Allen took the money but rejected the land, telling Duane and Kempe that he would not aid their efforts at expropriation. Kempe countered that the settlers did not stand a chance because might usually triumphed no matter what the righteousness of a cause. Allen replied with a statement that became famous in the Grants, and which he delighted in repeating: "The gods of the hills are not the gods of the valley." When Kempe asked what this meant, Allen extended an invitation, "If you will accompany me to the hill of Bennington, the sense will be made clear." Kempe chose to stay in Albany.[7]

New York's courts brought Allen immediate prominence in the Grants. Returning to Bennington, Allen called a general meeting at Stephen Fay's tavern, describing the trial and his exploits in resisting bribery but keeping their money—a subtle distinction on Allen's part. Resolving to defend their New Hampshire titles, with violence if necessary, those attending the meeting formed an extralegal militia company with this new and forceful neighbor, Ethan Allen, as "Colonel Commandant." Though he had just moved to the Grants, Allen was well known to many of the settlers, and his lieutenants included cousins Remember Baker and Seth Warner, who had lived in the area for several years. On Allen's initiative the settlers undertook their first real act of resistance to New York's authority, creating a militia without provincial authorization. Allen's persuasiveness, confidence, and commanding presence made him a logical choice to head the group of outlaw farmers calling themselves the Green Mountain Boys.[8]

Colonel Allen turned to the New England militia for his model, except that the Green Mountain Boys remained entirely voluntary. Officially there were five companies of Green Mountain Boys, organized by vicinity. In practice, anyone could account himself a member by sticking a fir twig in his hat and opposing the authority of New York. Again and again during their long struggle with New York, officers of the Green Mountain Boys would ride into a town and call forth the inhabitants for action, whether a company of this militia existed in the area or not. This very looseness of structure formed the premier strength of the Green Mountain Boys, serving to draw ever more of the community into the resistance through this inclusive regional militia.[9]

Most Green Mountain Boys replicated Allen's experiences. With few exceptions, the Green Mountain Boys were born in New England, emigrated to the frontier in family groups, cleared a few acres and held title to many more, and enjoyed only rudimentary educations. Though their ages ranged from fourteen to seventy, those who took most active part tended to be in their twenties or early thirties; Allen himself was thirty-two when he took command. The only significant differences between Allen and most other Green Mountain Boys were his religious skepticism, verbal skills, and driving desire to attain notoriety.[10]

More importantly, Allen shared the core commitment of most Green Mountain Boys to secure their land titles. Allen's few land sales in the first years of the 1770s fulfilled his family's basic needs while tying his interests to the future of the New Hampshire Grants. He acquired sufficient land for those Allens who wished to move north, selling the remainder for notes payable in cattle or wheat. In these transactions, and this identity of political and economic goals, Allen was no different from the vast majority of Grants settlers. But brother Ira envisioned a far grander scheme.

After walking over most of the west side of the Grants, Ira Allen became convinced that the best land lay in the area where the Onion River ran into Lake Champlain. This land, far north of all current settlements and already granted by New York to a few wealthy and influential land speculators, could be acquired cheaply under New Hampshire title. Pooling all the family's capital plus that of cousin Remember Baker, the Allens formed "Ethan Allen & Company," also known as the Onion

River Company. Traveling about New York and New England, Ethan and Ira Allen bought dozens of New Hampshire grants in the Onion River region, most of them for only a few shillings per hundred acres.

Ethan Allen sought to increase the value of this land by erecting a fort at Colchester near Lake Champlain while negotiating a treaty with the northern natives. Meanwhile Ira Allen and Remember Baker cleared a road through the forests north from Castleton to the company's fort, a formidable achievement. But their hard work could not attract settlers to the region so long as New York threatened to pull the rug out from under them. Though the Allens offered Onion River land "at a moderate price," they found few takers. They made only one major sale, to their Salisbury friend Thomas Chittenden, who moved north to Arlington. Otherwise, despite the purple prose of Ethan Allen's advertisements, few people seemed interested in taking such an enormous risk. After all, even without the threat from New York, it appeared that the majority of Grants settlements faced collapse from internal pressure. By 1772 it seemed certain that the New Hampshire Grants would become a historical footnote.[11]

Despite inevitable failure, the Allens poured their entire meager resources into the Onion River Company. Of course, their youth would cushion the impact of this audacious gamble if, as seemed likely, New York voided all their claims; the Allens could return to Connecticut and eke out the modest living appropriate to their social status. One problem blocked the fulfillment of this common sequence of events that would put the overly ambitious in their place: Ethan Allen had failed too often. From being twice an outcast with few possessions, little property, and four children, he managed within a space of three years to build an estate of thousands of acres, all of it uncleared and all represented by worthless pieces of paper. He intended to fight for those scraps of paper, finding his first allies within his family, most particularly in his clever and manipulative younger brother, Ira, and in their fiery cousin, Remember Baker. From this personal base Ethan Allen expanded outward, linking his cause with that of one family after another.

The Green Mountain Boys elected Allen their leader before the formation of the Onion River Company. Allen's few hundred acres tied his interests to those of the other Grants settlers. But the Onion River Company linked the future of the Grants with the security of all the Allens and led Ethan Allen irrevocably into politics. He hesitated initially to take the plunge, as brother Heman seemed more qualified—smoother and more polished. But once he dove in, Ethan found politics bracing and himself a master of the game.[12]

Allen's political ideas emerged from his actions, or at least from his perception of necessity. Allen tried whatever he thought would work and then found words to make those actions consistent with his neighbors' beliefs. As a consequence, and primarily in response to the government of New York, his justifications for the resistance of the Grants settlers shifted among conservative, legalist, and radical positions from 1769 to 1774. By the end of 1774 Allen's arguments crystallized into a consistent, and democratic, political doctrine.

In his more conciliatory moments, Allen argued that New York held jurisdiction over the Grants, but no more. The Privy Council's 1764 decision brought the region within New York's borders but did not affect property relations. Allen maintained that New York annexed the Grants from New Hampshire and must respect preexisting land titles and local political structures. Instead, New York made illegal and immoral grants to settled areas, violating the crown's intention and threatening the livelihood of settlers who purchased the land in good faith. If New York acknowledged the settlers' rights and property, all the better; but if not, the settlers must organize. The king had changed his mind once, and he could do so again. "He may cede the said disputed lands, back again to the province of New-Hampshire or erect it into a new province." But no action of the king, no jurisdictional alteration could affect property rights. As Allen correctly pointed out, under common law only the owner could alienate property. The dispute centered on who owned the land.[13]

Generally, Allen's early arguments stuck to a strict legalism, premised on the notion that the Privy Council had erred. The Privy Council's decree did not state that the region had always been part of New York, a position reinforced by London officials who kept referring to the "transfer" to New York. Allen ridiculed New York's "endeavour to draw the curtain of the Duke of York over their Knavery." By appealing to the duke's charter, the New Yorkers were arguing that no one held title except the "papist" duke of York. As the theoretical justification for land grants remained the settlement of the king's lands, and since the governor of New Hampshire served as a crown officer, Tryon should be thankful that Wentworth saved him the trouble.[14]

Occasionally, and with increasing frequency after 1773, Allen advanced a more radical argument dismissing the decision of the Privy Council as irrelevant. By "the handle of jurisdiction" New York aimed "at the property of the inhabitants." But why, Allen asked, should New York have jurisdiction? He found no reason. The government usurped property rights and destroyed "faith in communities." How, then could it "expect obedience?" Allen put forth criteria for legitimate rule and upheld the right of "citizens" to disobey any authority which exceeded these parameters. Because New York abused the law to serve the economic ends of an elite, making war upon the "the numerous families settled upon the land," it had abandoned the right to rule in the Green Mountains. This "parcel of mean-spirited servile wretches" deserved a halter, not the lands of hardworking people.[15]

Within each argument distinctive themes stand out. First, Allen insisted that the Grants settlers respected the law and resisted only the illegal actions of the government of New York. But New York committed many such violations, seizing land "by force and without color or pretence of law." Tryon and his council claimed to be "great advocates for law, order, and good govt," Allen wrote; "these are their horns of iron, and with them do they push the poor and needy, when they get them into their net." New York's government used "what they call law" to steal the property of poor farmers, labeling all who opposed it outlaws. In contrast the Grants settlers waited for the king to make up his royal mind, obeying his command to issue no new land grants and to disturb no one in his property. Allen manipulated the history of recent events to make New York appear the aggressor.[16]

New England political tradition allowed the people to employ collective action if the state violated the welfare or norms of the community.[17] These values retained their force in the New Hampshire Grants. The settlers, Allen wrote, respected all laws, except those "subversive of property, and inconsistent with the first principles of common sense." Such were the laws of New York, which served solely to enrich the wealthy further. New York drove the people of the Grants to resistance: the settlers "are no further turbulent than what is necessary to defend their persons and properties, from the cruelty and monopoly of their rulers."[18]

Besides invoking traditional justifications of collective protest, Allen defended resistance to New York by appealing to natural law. At the root of Allen's ideas lay "the law of self-preservation." By this rubric Allen meant more than individual survival, stating that he thought it unnecessary to explain that the self could not be separated from the family. As Allen wrote in 1772, "Self preservation makes it necessary that the said Inhabitants hold together, and defend themselves against this execrable Cunning of New York," or find themselves reduced to poverty and "be by terms inslav'd." New York violated common and natural law by falsely indicting those "bound by the law of self and family preservation to maintain their liberties and properties." For Allen, the preservation of the family formed a core justification of political resistance to superior authority.[19] And he of course included his own family in this equation, for between them they held title to thousands of acres in the Grants, and Ethan now had a son and three daughters whose future depended on the validity of those deeds.[20]

In the New England context, preservation of the family depended upon the security of land. As late as 1774 Allen offered to respect the jurisdiction of New York so long as that state recognized the land titles of the Grants settlers. "But," he added, "be it known to that despotic fraternity of law-makers and law-breakers, that we will not be fooled or frightened out of our property." The Grants settlers would obey New York, Allen stated, when New York obeyed the law.[21]

But Allen's political philosophy rested on more than the sanctity of property rights. Declaring that the family's labor gave property its worth, Allen insisted that the settlers had a right to the land of the Green Mountains because they worked it. On the pretense of possessing the correct legal documents, the New York speculators "fancied themselves the owners of towns, fields and houses, that they builded not." New York's "pretended zeal for good order and government, is fallacious," a cover for its true desire, "the lands and labours of the . . . settlers." As a consequence, "we mean no more by that which is called the Mob, but to defend our just Rights and Properties."[22]

New York's response to complaints from the Grants had the advantage of simplicity: follow orders. Grievances must be filed with the proper authorities, and their decisions obeyed. New York's stance backfired as Allen identified this call to order with disorder. In 1772 Allen dashed off a lengthy and eloquent—and occasionally factual—defense of the Grants claimants' actions that repudiated New York's right to rule. "There seems to be a generation arisen" in New York, Allen wrote, "extravagent in their loyalty to the king, and talk much of implicit obedience to government. This seems to be the first and greatest article of their creed, mighty sticklers for loyalty and submissiveness to government." New York offered "[our] wonderful settlement of peasants" the chance to give up the property "made valuable by extream labor and fatigue to these loyalists" and either become tenants or try their luck in another wilderness. Allen acknowledged the value of political order. But when a demand for order cuts at the roots of a stable community, it "terminates in the destruction of that very society which it was designed to protect." [23]

James Lemon has argued that the legal concept of "property in fee simple" is central to the development of American democracy. Ethan Allen asserted that property rights are irrelevant if the government chooses to ignore one's deed. The only way to protect those rights is to control the government. Two years later, in 1774, he would develop these ideas most fully in an influential pamphlet, *A Brief Narrative of the Proceedings of the Government of New York.* But as early as 1772 the law of self-preservation led Allen irrevocably to radical political action and the expression of a democratic theory of government four years before Thomas Paine's *Common Sense.* [24]

Allen addressed the qualms many New Yorkers had about the actions and sincerity of their government. Reminding the government that it played with fire, Allen warned his neighbors to the west that they might be next. If New York's lawyers could throw the small farmers in the Grants off their land, they could do the same along the Hudson River, no matter what one's deed said. Allen hit hard at the existing weaknesses and divisions within New York society, immobilizing the government for several years. Many in New York found troubling evidence of resistance to the large proprietors spreading west to the Hudson River. John Munro complained to James Duane that "the very tenants which I have settled upon my land bid me defiance." [25]

The frontier's centrifugal qualities presented the Grants settlers with their gravest challenge. Allen's peculiar genius consisted of making this weakness, the absence of established collective institutions, into the frontier's greatest strength. Where the eastside settlers accepted outside authority to attain some sort of order, Allen persuaded his neighbors to create their own authority—to make the world anew according to their own vision. Only the people, Allen argued, could establish governments and borders. In this way, Allen offered both a conservative and radical critique, appealing to the past while raising hopes for the future.[26]

Allen's writings, especially *A Brief Narrative,* though criticized by the Yorkers as gross distortions, proved effective propaganda. Allen did not initiate the resistance in the New Hampshire Grants, but he strengthened and consolidated what had been a sporadic and uncoordinated collective protest. He brought to the Grants intelligent and energetic leadership, impressive organizational and oratorical skills, and a precise critique of New York's rule. The Green Mountain settlers began as unwilling outlaws, but Ethan Allen—and the government of New York—transformed them into rebels against tyranny.

II

Those bloody law-givers know we {must} oppose their execution of law, where it points directly at our property, . . . but there is one . . . consolation to us, viz. that printed sentences of death will not kill us when we are at a distance; and if the executioners approach us, they will be as likely to fall victims to death as we.—Ethan Allen

Allen not only voiced shared opinions, he gave form to traditional modes of political dissent, building on a heritage of nonviolent communal action to sustain a broad-based political movement. More than just the skillful manipulation of rhetoric accounts for Allen's leadership; his method of resistance relied on political theater and psychological warfare to win battles without the loss of life. At a personal level, Allen had turned self-dramatization into a psychological defense for coping with his fear of premature death and his inadequacy in supporting his family. The other Allens must have appreciated this tack, for they remained Ethan's prime promoters. By the time he had reached the Grants, Ethan Allen had elaborated this strategy of frontier swagger into an art form and a highly effective political tactic. Allen's techniques of threat, bluff, and outrageous self-exaggeration propelled him into the leadership of the Green Mountain rebellion and kept an essentially nonviolent conflict alive far longer than anyone could have reasonably expected—certainly longer than New York's government desired.

Allen did not operate in a historical vacuum. New Englanders had long exercised the community's right to voice its opposition to unpopular acts by the authorities. Colonial America's formula of resistance included standards of acceptable opposition which justified communal disobedience and popular uprisings in the face of the state's use of force. This pattern played itself out in the widespread opposition of Americans to acts of the British government in the 1760s and 1770s.[27]

A colonial community's first recourse remained the right of petition. As colonists petitioned Parliament in 1765 in opposition to the Stamp Act, so the Grants settlers sent a steady stream of petitions to New York, New Hampshire, and the Privy Council between 1764 and 1770. When their petitions went unanswered or received a rude rebuff, the colonists formed themselves into associations for peaceful noncompliance with the Stamp Act, held public meetings, erected symbols of their liberty, and burned effigies of British officials. In a similar fashion, the Green Mountain settlers refused to acknowledge the authority of New York's courts, held public meetings to solidify their dissent, and hanged effigies of Governor Tryon. If a British official attempted to enforce the Stamp Act or other odious measure, he faced the ultimate indication of the community's displeasure: public humiliation. While a few officials were tarred and feathered or whipped, most got away with a public confession of error. The Grants inhabitants followed this pattern—Ethan Allen becoming a master of the theater of humiliation—and in response to New York's continued efforts at dispossessing them of their property, carried the logic of resistance to its radical conclusion, as did other American patriots.

The fluidity of authority in colonial America helped to localize power and feed this revolutionary logic. A town meeting simply adjourned in order to reconstitute itself as some other organization, such as a committee of correspondence or a crowd. The crowd—or, in the appellation preferred by opponents, the "mob"—could just as easily become a "posse comitatus." Communities learned to look inward for political solutions, rather than to the more abstract authority of the state.[28]

Allen personalized traditional forms, making himself the symbolic center of Grants opposition. By 1771 just the threat of Allen's presence proved an effective deterrent to the exercise of New York's authority. Allen appeared everywhere in the Green Mountains in the 1770s, often in person, boisterously proclaiming his presence, and more often as a shadow, a hint of the terrors of the savage wilderness which awaited any

New York official foolish enough to attempt the fulfillment of his duties. In 1771 William Cockburn, surveying James Duane's Socialborough grants, confronted three Grants settlers. They informed Cockburn that he was violating the king's order of 1767 and that great harm would befall him if he persisted in this disloyalty, for "Nathan Allen was in the woods with another party blacked and dressed like Indians" and would kill any New York surveyors. The threat proved sufficient. Before fleeing to the fort at Crown Point, Cockburn promised never to survey in the Grants again.[29]

Victorious in court, New York needed only to enforce the law. Yet from 1771 on, every attempt by New York's officials to evict the New Hampshire landowners confronted the organized opposition of the Green Mountain Boys. Most of these efforts ended in failure with terrified New Yorkers running before a swirl of rumors announcing the "savage" Ethan Allen's intentions.[30]

New York responded to Allen's challenges with angry proclamations and frustrated appeals for British assistance. The government did little to support its authority, largely because it saw no need to do so. In a fine example of projection, New York's council argued that absentee speculators, not settlers, held most New Hampshire grants. The government thus imagined a conflict between competing elites rather than an effort to transfer landownership from hundreds of settled farmers to a few wealthy landowners. And since the law stood on the speculators' side, they required nothing more, assuming that the decisions of the Privy Council and New York's courts defeated the Grants claimants. Given English respect for property, the speculators felt they could do as they wished with their land, and they desired most to be rid of the "New-Hampshire Intruders." They therefore planned to settle the region with Scots and Germans, removing anyone currently living on these sites.[31]

But evicting the squatters proved more difficult than acquiring legal title to the land. From the beginning, such efforts collapsed before Allen's adroit use of time-honored methods of symbolic forms of resistance. In July 1771 Sheriff Henry Ten Eyck gathered a two hundred-man posse and rode for the Walloomsac intent on evicting James Breakenridge. Albany's mayor, Abraham Cuyler, thought this eviction of sufficient importance to join the posse. Ten Eyck hoped to surprise Breakenridge, but, as usual, word of the Yorker advance flew before them. Ten Eyck discovered a large force of Green Mountain Boys already on

Breakenridge's farm in a strong defensive position—with twenty men in the house, forty in the field to its right, and another hundred on the ridge above. The group on the ridge most unnerved the Albany posse. Not only did the men command the field, but placing their hats on their muskets and clubs, they kept moving about, expanding the group's size in the eyes of the larger New York force.[32]

Attempting to uphold the aura of New York authority, Mayor Cuyler ordered the crowd to leave immediately. When Breakenridge asked to see his writ, Cuyler angrily dismissed such formalism as irrelevant. The real question was why a force of armed men dared defy the decision of the courts? Here Breakenridge played his trump: he did not own the farm; the town of Bennington had taken possession and intended to protect its property. Cuyler proclaimed this ploy a clear evasion, as Breakenridge farmed the land. The Green Mountain Boys aggravated the New Yorkers' confusion and nervousness by taking half an hour to consider Cuyler's command to leave. They decided to stay.

Sheriff Ten Eyck ordered an advance. Shockingly, most of his force refused to move. "Not without reason," one member of the posse wrote, "for we had by that Time discovered that the Yankies had made all the necessary preparations to give us the warmest reception." With only twenty men, Ten Eyck advanced, confronting an argument rather than a fight. The settlers complained of their ill-use by New York's courts and insisted that the king would soon proclaim his support for their titles. A New York attorney answered that all loyal subjects must acquiesce in the decisions of His Majesty's courts. But, the settlers persisted, their titles bore the king's seal, and only he could decide the issue.

Right there, on the front step of a small backwoods farmhouse, the entire Grants/New York debate was argued out, the irreconcilable differences made abundantly clear, and the ultimate result anticipated. When the sheriff threatened to break down the door, Breakenridge's neighbors raised their guns and aimed at Ten Eyck. "Whereupon," a New York observer wrote, "considering the little probability of succeeding and the eminent Danger attending it, he by the advice of his friends, Desisted." Ten Eyck demonstrated discernment, for during this debate the majority of his posse had evaporated.[33]

The showdown at Breakenridge's farm proved decisive. New York's authorities discovered that they could not rely on the posse to stand before riotous squatters. Ethan Allen held that the Green Mountain

Boys owed their success to the support of New York's poor farmers, who made up the ranks of whatever posse entered the Grants. Much of the population along the Hudson River sympathized with the Grants farmers in their struggle with the large landed proprietors. They, too, suffered the legal harassment of a judiciary which represented solely the interests of the rich and well-connected. They, too, had resisted, only to be squashed by the armed power of the state which the proprietors had at their disposal. And they appeared unwilling to serve in posses which sought to dispossess other small farmers.[34]

Ethan Allen enthusiastically played on the weaknesses of his opposition. The victory at Breakenridge's farm validated his tactics and gave the Grants claimants confidence in their ability to plan, bluff, and out-maneuver New York's officials. Armed mostly with clubs, they had stood up to a superior force; with the authority of the governor of New York and the king of England arrayed against them, they had driven the invaders to open retreat without shedding a drop of blood.

With heightened self-assurance, the Green Mountain Boys acceler-ated their acts of open resistance. Allen never resorted to bloodshed to drive Yorker officials from the Grants; not a single person died in the conflict on the west side during the eight years before the Revolution. Humiliation and terror proved more effective, as when one company paraded at night around Justice Munro's house "laugh[ing] its scorn" and making sufficient noise to disturb his sleep. Allen did not seek to hurt or kill his opponents but to neutralize them. Dr. Samuel Adams of Arlington received several warnings after he urged his neighbors to abandon their New Hampshire deeds as worthless and purchase New York titles—preferably from him. Adams armed himself with a brace of pistols and announced that he would defend himself against all comers, a challenge Allen could not resist. Confronting Adams, Allen knocked the threatening pistols to the ground and took the Yorker to Stephen Fay's Bennington tavern. The Green Mountain Boys tried Adams, found him guilty, and sentenced the defendant to be tied to a chair and hoisted atop Fay's famous catamount sign. There the poor doctor sat for some hours above a crowd of jeering men and women, with Fay's stuffed cata-mount staring remorselessly at him. Adams returned home a chastened and apolitical man, avoiding public affairs for the next several years.[35]

Allen targeted New York surveyors, for without surveys there could be no land divisions. The Green Mountain Boys established extralegal

"Judgment seats" and tried surveyors for trespass. These courts always found the defendants guilty, occasionally ordering them tied to a tree and "chastised with the twigs of the wilderness," in other words, whipped. After breaking their instruments, Allen sent the surveyors scurrying back to New York, where they made immediate and bitter complaint to the governor. Allen enjoyed his courts immensely and in his enthusiasm often acted as both judge and prosecutor. Neither legal forms nor separation of powers concerned Allen.[36]

What did concern Allen was the mobilization and support of his neighbors. Public rituals of humiliation drew ever more of the community into political action while reminding the hesitant which side held power. Allen aimed not just to scare off Yorkers but to intimidate the undecided into joining the insurgents.[37]

The struggle for the town of Clarendon, or Durham, illustrates Allen's ability to persuade the wavering, as well as the formidable obstacles New York faced in responding to events in its northeast counties. In 1760 the Albany adventurer John Henry Lydius joined Allen's friend Thomas Young in purchasing land rights from the Mohawks. A group of Rhode Island settlers purchased Lydius's town of Durham and by 1770 had built houses, barns, and a mill. But lacking title from either New York or New Hampshire, Durham's settlers were caught in the middle of the conflict. Feeling the wind blowing toward New York, they offered James Duane one-third of the unsettled land if he gained them a New York title. In a three-cornered council hearing in 1771, Duane opposed two former allies: Crean Brush, representing the New York grantees, and Robert Livingston, Jr., acting for Joseph Willard and the New Hampshire investors. Ironically, Duane made the very argument often used against him, that actual settlement outweighed the equity of absentee speculators. The decision for the Durham settlers reflected Duane's greater influence with the council rather than the persuasiveness of his abstract arguments.[38]

Ethan Allen did not mind if Durham existed without either New York and New Hampshire grants, but to take a New York patent affronted his tolerance. In a "Friendly Appistle" to the people of Clarendon, Allen promised "to assist you in purchasing" the land under New Hampshire title at a "reasonable" price. Should land speculators such as Willard "Demand an Exhorbitant price for your Land we scorn it and will Assist you in Mobbing such Avaricious persons." The Green Mountain Boys "mean to use force against Oppression" whether from New York or New Hampshire speculators.[39]

Several Durham settlers took Allen's letter to heart and bought New Hampshire titles. As a consequence, the settlers, who had been united in resisting all outside pressure, now found themselves divided into three camps and turned to the courts and the local political apparatus to resolve their disputes. Those who appealed to the New York courts wasted their time, the courts of the Green Mountain Boys proving far more effective.[40]

Allen paid Durham a visit in fall 1773. Failure to recognize the Grants' legitimacy, Allen warned with typical extravagance, would incite the Green Mountain Boys to "Lay all Durham in Ashes and leave every person in it a Corpse." Durham's justice of the peace, Benjamin Spencer, told his neighbors to ignore these ravings.[41] Spencer learned his error on the night of November 20, when Allen and a company of Green Mountain Boys came calling. Breaking Spencer's door down with an axe, Allen rushed in and seized the sleeping justice. Mixing liberal theology with threats, Allen informed Spencer that "the day of Judgment was come when every man should be Judged according to his works."[42]

Allen set up a judgment seat and acted—in both meanings of the word—as prosecutor and judge. Allen the prosecutor accused Spencer of owning a New York grant and applying for more, of "cudling with the Land Jobbers," of holding a New York commission as justice of the peace, and of working to ensure that his neighbors obeyed the laws of New York. Judge Allen found Spencer guilty of all charges—and indeed he was, cuddling aside. The jury favored whipping the hapless justice, but Allen suggested a more "lenient and just" punishment: as Spencer's house stood on land lacking a New Hampshire title, it constituted a public nuisance and should be burned. The excited jury set the roof ablaze; but Spencer's pleading touched Allen, and he ordered the burning roof knocked off. Though exposed to the elements, the house still stood.[43]

After Allen's nocturnal visit, most of Clarendon's inhabitants purchased New Hampshire titles, with Allen intervening personally to keep prices down. Spencer reported that only 4 of the town's 228 citizens remained loyal to New York, the rest having turned to the outlaw Allen for protection. "You may ask," an embarrassed Spencer wrote James Duane, "why I do not proceed against them in a due course of law." The answer was simple: the Green Mountain Boys threatened to destroy the crops of Yorkers. And since everyone knew that New York would not act, Allen freely "bid defiance to any authority." Unless the government captured Allen, Spencer thought the whole region lost to New York.[44]

With Allen and his portable court roaming the woods, owners of New York patents found it impossible to hold their lands or to make their ejectments stick. By 1772 opposing the will of Ethan Allen and his Green Mountain Boys proved dangerous. Clarendon was the only westside town which required Allen's firm attention. Generally Allen employed friendly persuasion and regular visits to keep levels of commitment high. Most of the region's settlers agreed with Allen's goals and belonged to the Green Mountain Boys, local companies dealing with isolated cases of recalcitrance. Allen was called in only when New York entered the picture, which was surprisingly seldom.[45]

Allen recognized that resistance required unity. In large part, New York's actions fostered that unity. But a collective identity required more than just responding to New York's actions. In an effort to build political structures and formulate a public expression of the region's shared grievances, Allen led eleven western townships in forming committees of safety for their mutual defense at a pair of conventions in 1771. The second of these conventions passed a "decree" forbidding New York patents and the holding of New York offices within their communities. A competing authority had been established in the Grants.[46]

Allen gave shape to the Grants resistance in a series of documents approved by these conventions and published in New England's newspapers. In moralistic terms Allen ennobled the Grants settlers while exaggerating their trials, painting a lurid portrait of their struggle: "The Writs of Ejectment coming thick and faster. Women sobbing and lamenting, children crying and men pierc'd to the Heart with Sorrow and Indignation at the approaching Tyranny of New York." New York's elite "used all manner of deceit and fraud to accomplish their designs: their tenants groan under their usury and oppression; . . . and the innocent blood they have already shed, calls for heaven's vengeance on their guilty heads." Allen transformed New York's legislative acts into symbols of repression, "emblems of their insatiable, avaricious, overbearing, inhuman, barbarous" desires. Like an Old Testament prophet, Allen demanded that this "execreble race" be blasted "from the face of the earth!"[47]

While recasting New York's government as a ruthless tyranny, Allen made himself the symbol of necessary violence and frontier lawlessness. Allen played on popular images of wilderness disorder for all they were worth, encouraging the suspicion among his enemies that he was a borderline savage, a known associate of Indians, an infidel lacking Christian moral constraints. He terrorized New Yorkers with little more than words and the occasional shaken fist, forestalling the need for direct action. On one occasion, Allen seized two Albany County sheriffs and locked them in rooms on opposite sides of a building. While they slept he hung an effigy from a tree outside each of their windows. In the morning he informed each that the other had been hanged. Allowed to escape, each fled to Albany, where they spread tales of barbarism in the Green Mountains before discovering the trick.[48]

Unopposed by New York, Allen moved from defending to evicting. In October 1771 a group of former soldiers settled as tenants on a military grant in the Rupert area which overlapped the farm of Robert Cochran, who liked to call himself "a Son of Robin Hood." Cochran, some neighbors, and Ethan Allen descended on the tenants, driving them off with wild threats and much waving of muskets. Setting a house on fire, Allen told Charles Hutcheson that "they had resolved to offer a burnt Sacrifice to the Gods of the world" and advised him to "Go your way now & complain to that Damned Scoundrel your Governor. God Damn your Governor, Laws, King, Council & Assembly." Hutcheson warned New York that Allen boasted of being able on short notice to "raise many 100s New Hampshire men . . . & curse the regular troops. . . . Despondent is also credibly Inform'd that said Allen Denys the Being of a God & Denys that there is any Infernal Spirit existing." Many New Yorkers believed that Allen's heretical religious views made him particularly dangerous and placed him in league with the "Infernal Spirit."[49]

Prompted by the defiance of the Grants settlers, the ponderous authority of New York plodded into action. The governor's council ordered the arrest of Allen, Cochran, Remember Baker, and several others, offering a £20 reward for their capture. Governor Tryon issued a proclamation reasserting New York's jurisdiction and warning that his will would be enforced, though he did not specify by whom. Justice of the Peace Alexander McNaughton issued a warrant for the arrest of Allen and company and raised a posse for that purpose.[50]

It all appeared most impressive and august. But McNaughton revealed the reality of this shadow play when he reported to the council that he had issued the warrants for the "rioters & traitors . . . but their number & Situation in the mountains is such that I am of Opinion no sheriff or constable will apprehend them." Only a large reward for "these abominable wretches" would work, for then maybe "some person of their own sort will artfully betray them." [51]

But McNaughton's prediction that a large reward would do the job proved incorrect. No one captured Allen or any member of his gang, even when New York increased the reward to the tempting sum of £100 in 1772. Nor did the search for a Judas succeed. Rather, the Green Mountain Boys went beyond merely eluding the authorities; they established their own law. In a joke reflective of the changed political situation, Allen printed a poster offering £15 reward for the arrest and delivery to the Catamount Tavern of James Duane and £10 for John Tabor Kempe. Had anyone tried to collect the reward, Allen would have been hard put to come up with the cash. But the warrant—posted throughout the Grants and in Albany—went beyond mockery, denying the validity and efficacy of New York's authority and placing the legitimacy of the Grants claimants on an equal footing with the royal province. If New York could issue unenforceable warrants and offers for uncollectible rewards, so could the Green Mountain Boys. At least they could enforce their will in the area they claimed. As James Duane wrote, the Grants had "assumed the Importance of an independent State." [52]

One individual, Justice of the Peace John Munro, tried to halt the activities of these "ungovernable people (to say no worse of them)." Munro, a major landowner and agent for other New York speculators, continued to hold court and issue ejectments despite repeated warnings. The Green Mountain Boys contented themselves with disrupting his court until Munro counterattacked. [53] In the predawn hours of 21 March 1772, Munro led a posse to the Arlington farmhouse of Remember Baker, catching him in bed. In the ensuing struggle, Baker's thumb received a serious cut while his wife and son suffered injuries. The posse threw the bound and bleeding Baker into a sled and set off for Albany.

Her arm broken, Baker's wife slogged through the snow to the nearest farm. Aroused, a group of Baker's neighbors rushed to the rescue and overtook the posse. As Munro reported pathetically to Tryon, his posse "all run into the Woods when they ought to have resisted," and the justice himself was taken prisoner. Though released a few hours later,

Munro felt infuriated and humiliated, angry that his fellow Yorkers fled before a disorganized mob, embarrassed to find his authority so easily slighted and overturned. Munro wrote Tryon that as a consequence of the Yorkers' fear and the audacity of the "Rioters," New York could not maintain its jurisdiction and land titles. No other New York official, Munro stated, dared oppose the Green Mountain Boys.[54]

Allen played this one incident of violence for maximum drama. Writing a long and wonderfully excessive article for the New England papers, Allen maintained that the effort to kidnap Baker proved the "wicked, inhuman, most barbarous, infamous, cruel, villainous and thievish" nature of New York. The crime, "perpetrated, committed and carried into execution by one John Munro, a reputed Justice of the Peace . . . with a number of Ruffians . . . [on] the Lord's Day," demonstrated New York's malevolence. Munro, his "wicked noodle" overbalanced by desire for "Gain and Plunder" and a "Thirst for Blood," set about "cutting with Swords and bruising with Fire Arms and Clubs, Men, Women and Children." Carried away, Allen declared such conduct by "a pretended civil Magistrate" a disgrace to the "Regulations, Peace, Manners, good Order and Oeconomy both of the Laws of God and Man." Amidst this lavish rhetoric, Allen turned the tables on New York by accusing its officials of violating the law, thus calling into question its legitimacy. Allen extracted deep political meaning from Remember Baker's wounded thumb, leaving New York looking both cruel and clumsy, the most politically harmful combination.[55]

Allen exaggerated the threat from New York to argue the need for internal unity. He regularly reminded the Grants settlers of the use of British regulars against New York tenants and Tryon's bloody repression of the Regulator movement. Allen described Tryon's proclamations as dripping with "the crimson of N. Carolina," drew attention to Tryon's ordering the death of a Regulator who approached under a white flag, and rejected "the cursed doctrine of passive obedience and nonresistance." Adhering to the law carried an objective air of propriety, but such a tactic served the interests of those who already held power and wealth. The doctrine of obedience to properly constituted authority was invented by tyrants; "it is the very quintescence of tyranny." Allen referred often to earlier, losing struggles of poor farmers against formal law and swore not to repeat their mistakes.[56]

Allen threw down the gauntlet, challenging New York to battle.

In April 1772 rumors reported Tryon's advance up the Hudson with British troops to attack Bennington. Allen mobilized the Green Mountain Boys, making elaborate plans to ambush Tryon's forces and fight a guerilla war from bases in the Green Mountains. After much mustering, marching, and planning, Allen learned that the British troops were relief units bound for the garrisons in western New York. But the Green Mountain Boys gained confidence from their own resolve and unity, while Tryon and the New York council, which heard of these preparations, felt sobered by the willingness of the "Bennington Mob" to fight even British regulars. As Ira Allen stated, "This alarm answered every purpose that a victory possibly could have done, without shedding blood."[57]

Ten days later the New York council heard that the mob had acquired two cannon and a mortar from abandoned Fort Massachusetts. Unaware of the artillery's antiquity, the council and governor offered to negotiate with the Grants as long as it did not send the vile Ethan Allen. Tryon warned that "a perseverance in your disobedience . . . must soon draw forth against you the exertions of the Powers of Government," but he diluted his threats with cajoling, promising "to give such relief as the nature of your situation and circumstances will justify." The king, Tryon concluded, had "finally fixed Connecticut River" as the border between New York and New Hampshire. "Finally" the king had acted, and the governor of His Royal Province "flattered" himself that the Grants would accept "this final offer of reconciling yourselves to this Government."[58]

A committee drawn from several Grants towns met at Bennington and agreed to parley with New York. Though Allen wanted to confront Tryon personally, the convention respected the governor's wishes and selected Jonas and Stephen Fay as representatives. But Allen still got his say, sending a letter informing Tryon that the governor, not the Green Mountain Boys, was breaking the law. By continuing to issue patents, Tryon violated the Privy Council's order of 1767. Until the king made up his mind, any New York court which acted on the dispute was "impertinent." Allen turned the language of the king's men back on them, invalidating the New York courts and putting Tryon in the position of having to claim authority superior to the Privy Council and monarch. As good subjects, the Grants settlers resisted the unconstitutional incursions of New York's special interests, respecting Tryon's authority "except in Instances where such perverse Use has been made thereof, as would dispossess us of our Property and Country." The convention voted its approval of Allen's letter, finding it a damning indictment of misgovernment.[59]

Of course the New Yorkers failed to see it this way, though Tryon did write Lord Dartmouth for instructions. The colonial secretary told Tryon that New York's courts should decide the validity of land grants. Dartmouth thus contradicted orders Tryon had received from Lord Hillsborough, the secretary of state, not to deviate from his initial instructions. Amidst this confusion Allen scored a significant propaganda victory and forced Tryon to waste a year seeking guidance.[60]

Tryon did his best to resolve the Grants dispute in a fashion other than that which he had employed so effectively against North Carolina's Regulators. Tryon and his council treated the Fays respectfully, but the two sides talked past one another. The Fays did not seek a settlement but a truce. The council played inadvertently into their hands, admitting that it appeared "unreasonable" for the settlers to be dispossessed of their property even if they did not hold legal title, and promised to work out a compromise with New York's speculators. Given the great number of squatters, the council felt generosity a wise policy and urged the suspension of all criminal and civil suits until Tryon found out what the king thought. The council predicated these recommendations on the good behavior of the Grants settlers; they must conform with New York's laws and allow all those the Green Mountain Boys had scared off to return. Failure to meet these last stipulations would lead to the swift exercise of New York justice, an old and hollow threat.[61]

To the Green Mountain Boys it appeared that their actions, especially the acquisition of the decrepit cannon, had forced Tryon to proffer this olive branch. Upon the Fays' return to Bennington, representatives from several towns met and accepted unanimously New York's offer. Firing the dreadful cannon, they drank numerous toasts to the king, Governor Tryon, and "Peace, Liberty, and Plenty."[62]

The reign of peace and goodwill initiated by Tryon proved short-lived. While the Fays negotiated in New York, a company of Green Mountain Boys drove off a party of New Yorkers who had settled on Otter Creek and seized William Cockburn, who had broken his fear-induced promise and returned to survey land. Once news of the New York truce arrived, Allen set Cockburn free. Meanwhile Remember

Baker and Ira Allen, who had not heard of these events, also chased away a party of surveyors in the north, but not before confiscating five gallons of rum.[63]

Though the product of slow communications and completely non-violent, these actions impressed Governor Tryon as a "breach of faith and honor." Tryon demanded that New York's settlers and officials remain unmolested and offered a £100 reward for Baker and the Allens. Allen called a convention at Manchester to consider these events; despite the nervous fears of some representatives who suggested that Tryon could only be pushed so far, the meeting dismissed the governor's latest blast as just so much hot air. Allen wrote a smarmy letter in the convention's name assuring Tryon that the Green Mountain Boys had no desire to "insult governmental authority" and would prefer to continue the truce.[64]

But the two sides just did not understand one another. The New York council stated angrily that despite its generous offer to settle the dispute, the "riotous and disorderly people" of the Grants "rendered themselves still more obnoxious and inexcusable." Having started out by claiming only the land they lived on, the squatters now denied New York's rule and prevented the settlement of anyone under a New York patent. The council prophesied that "so pernicious an Example if not speedily check'd and punished, must be attended with the worst Consequences, by bringing the Authority of Government into Contempt." Then, contradicting itself, the council concluded with the equally accurate observation "that it is beyond the power of the Civil Magistrate to put a Stop to this Growing evil" and called on London to supply troops.[65]

Tryon endorsed this proposal and sent Hillsborough a copy of Allen's letter so the colonial secretary could appreciate what New York faced. Tryon expressed a certain testiness with the king, writing that "His Majesty's late order forbidding me to proceed in giving them titles" had "sowered and disgusted" New York's supporters in the Green Mountains. He proposed that New York annex all townships in the region at half fee and issue patents to the rest of the area immediately. It was vital to act quickly, as "the Bennington people and the adjacent Country daily increase in strength." If "uninterrupted by Governt," even conservative settlers would "combine in opposition to the jurisdiction of this Province." While Tryon and his council discerned the tide of affairs, they seemed incapable of reversing it.[66]

New York's problem remained a simple one: no speculator wanted to bear the expense of subduing the rebellion, and neither did the government. The case of Colonel John Reid illuminates New York's difficulty. In 1773 Reid settled a group of Scot tenants on his Otter Creek land. When Allen learned of this latest affront to the Grants cause, he marched on Reid's settlement with one hundred men, executing a stealthy encirclement of the unsuspecting settlers. The Green Mountain Boys confronted a company of angry Scottish women whose dialect Allen could not ken. After locating the men, Allen ordered the forlorn Scots to gather their belongings and depart. But Allen felt sorry for the now homeless immigrants and offered them freehold parcels of his Otter Creek land if they stayed. Many of Reid's tenants took Allen up on his offer and became active supporters of the Grants cause; the rest made the usual sad trek to the safety of Crown Point.[67]

For the next few days Allen held the field, awaiting a reaction to this latest provocation. But New York responded with the usual proclamation noting the inadequacies of the civil authority and called on General Frederick Haldimand, commanding British forces at St. Jean, to occupy Fort Ticonderoga with a strong body of troops. It seemed to the council that "nothing less than a Military Force" could stop "these daring outrages, and . . . enforce obedience to the Laws." Colonel Reid thought New York's a government of cowards. Both may have been correct.[68]

Either way, the Grants region developed the requisite military force to back up its law and enforce its authority, the Green Mountain Boys. The elite of New York relied on the British military to enforce order, seemingly incapable of conceiving or implementing alternative policies. General Haldimand demonstrated a keener grasp of colonial conditions, writing that given "the present circumstances of affairs in America," it would be dangerous to employ regulars, especially with militia available. The government of New York suffered from serious problems if "a few lawless vagabonds" could force it to "have recourse to the Regular Troops to suppress them." Haldimand reminded Tryon that seeking help elsewhere was a "reflection of weakness" and rendered New York "contemptible to the Inhabitants."[69]

Goaded by Haldimand, Tryon finally acted, using the Green Mountain Boys' mistreatment of Benjamin Hough as pretext. In early 1774 Allen tried and sentenced Hough, the last remaining New York official on the west side, to a public whipping and exile for betraying his neighbors. On the motion of Cumberland County's representative, Crean Brush, the General Assembly of New York declared Allen and several others outlaws. Allen, the legislature declared, had "put a period to the Administration of Justice, and spread Terror and Destruction throughout" New York's northeastern counties. The assembly therefore placed yet another reward on Allen's head and provided for his trial in absentia. In addition the assembly passed a Riot Act forbidding assemblies in Albany and Charlotte counties for two years and mandating the death penalty for resistance to New York's authority, unofficial assumption of judicial authority, or the destruction of buildings and crops.[70]

New York did not enforce the Riot Act, but its passage gave the government a bloodthirsty image. And just as the colonies united in opposition to Britain's Intolerable Acts, so did the disparate communities of the Grants move toward unification. In short, the New York assembly played directly into Allen's hands, validating all his accusations of tyranny without ever exercising tyrannical power.[71]

In Bennington the Riot Act initially inspired a sense of crisis and hopelessness. Now that New York had at last moved, many thought the Grants lost and feared Tryon's coming fury. Allen scoffed at these fears and circulated copies of "the Bloody Law" along with his response, both of which he printed in New England's newspapers. New York sought to contain the resistance, but the opposite ensued. At a series of conventions in spring 1774 Allen drew every town on the west side of the Green Mountains into his open conspiracy against New York. Allen now wanted more than just to drive the New Yorkers out of the region, hoping to unify both sides of the Green Mountains. But Allen had no family, no connections on the east side and could not have attained his desired end except for New York's surprising ability to alienate even its own supporters.[72]

III

We value not New York with all their powers,
For here we'll stay and work, the land is ours.

Thomas Rowley

By 1774 Ethan Allen had attained leadership of the west side of the Green Mountains, invalidating New York's government in the region.

Yet a greater challenge lay ahead, for the western Grants remained isolated between New York's hostility and the Connecticut River valley's indifference. Somehow Allen had to win over the eastern Grants, to forge a collective identity which would transcend the geographic barrier of the Green Mountains and overcome the attractions of a self-interested acquiescence in New York's authority.

From 1763 until 1773 the people of the east side demonstrated a willingness to accept New York's authority, and many attempted to re-purchase their lands under New York title. Yet the government often rebuffed this moderation. For instance, a 1765 petition from Windsor seeking New York deeds was twice rejected for failing to meet the correct technical forms and then got lost in a bureaucratic shuffle until 1772. The petition was finally granted when Nathan Stone hired twenty-three New Yorkers to put their names on the petition. Even when accommodating the eastside communities, New York's elite saw the area as a theater for their own aggrandizement, with agents like Crean Brush preserving their interests and serving as representatives in the assembly. The general ineptness of New York's agents provided Ethan Allen with an exploitable opening on the east side.[73]

Allen's timing proved fortuitous. His attacks on New York coincided with both a weakening of New York's will to impose its laws and the deepening imperial crisis which disrupted and distracted all the colonial governments. Using the resultant internal divisions to his advantage, Allen played New York's numerous political factions against one another. As early as 1772 New York officials noted that the Green Mountain Boys had many allies in Albany, including merchants and other officials. Excluded from their own government's land grants, these secret allies turned to the cheaper New Hampshire grants. And, as Munro observed, Allen relied steadily on the sympathy of New York's poor farmers.[74]

But Allen's greatest political accomplishment proved his carefully wrought linkage of the American cause and republican ideology with the Grants settlers' claims to their own land and institutions. Allen clothed the Grants cause in the language of American resistance to Parliament and king, equating the struggle of the Sons of Liberty with that of the Green Mountain Boys. America battled for control of its property and future; so did the New Hampshire Grants.

If the Grants equaled America, then New York was its Britain. Allen hit often on this theme, calling New York Britain's "favorite government." If Parliament had no right to pass taxes or to regulate trade, neither did the General Assembly of New York. The admiralty courts violated the English constitution and common law, and so did New York's courts. British officials, marked by luxury and avarice, corrupted traditional liberties; New York's officials seemed no different. England and New York both passed laws specifically affecting unrepresented citizens; as with America, "the first knowledge we had of said laws, was the completion of them." The American patriot fought to preserve his way of life, and so did the frontier farmers of the Green Mountains. From 1772 on Allen declared it the same struggle: what New York's Whigs objected to in British rule, the Grants objected to in New York's rule. Equal partners in the struggle against Britain's "ministerial tyranny," the Grants settlers faced a second tyranny closer to home.[75]

Allen was not alone in equating the Grants rebellion with a larger, continentwide resistance to British imperial authority. Feeling part of this larger American movement emboldened many eastside settlers. At the formation of the Chester Committee of Correspondence in October 1774, the town meeting linked its struggles against the tyrannies of New York and Britain, resolving "that Every Mans Estate Honestly Acquired is his own and no person on Earth has A Right to take it Away without the Proprietor Consent." Every good patriot condemned England's attack on the property rights of Americans. Patriots in the Green Mountains asked if any difference existed between that conspiracy and New York's efforts to take away their land.[76]

In November 1774 the Cumberland County court imprisoned Leonard Spaulding of Dummerston for high treason after he said that "if the King had signed the Quebec bill, in his opinion he had broke his coronation oath." After Spaulding's trial, a majority of Dummerston's population met on the town green and organized a committee of correspondence. The crowd proclaimed its intent "to joyne with other towns or respectable bodies of peopel . . . to secure and protect the rights and privileges of trusted and fellow creatures from the ravages and imbarassments of the British tyrant & his New York and other immesaries." Ten days later a crowd gathered from several towns marched on the Brattleboro jail and demanded Spaulding's release. Overwhelmed, the sheriff freed his prisoner. Solomon Harvey wrote in the Dummerston town records that the patience of "the brave sons of freedom . . . was worn out with the inhuman insults of the imps of power." The time had come for the people to act.[77]

Harvey looked around him in at the end of 1774 and saw a disordered world. New York's courts and officials served as the local agents of "the British tyrant George the third," supporting the encroachment of British imperial tyranny upon the peaceful communities of the Green Mountains in a common assault on property. Sick of "diving after redress in a Legal way, & finding that the Law was only made use of for the Emolument of its Creatures & the immesaries of the British tyrant," the people discovered an easier method of combating "the New York, Cut throatly, Jacobitish, High Church, Toretical minions of George the third, the pope of Canada & tyrant of Britain." Instead of floundering in the courts, they seized them.[78]

New York's legitimacy, already weakened by a perceived connection with English oppression, suffered further diminution as a consequence of its officials' loyalism. Attempts at unity between New Hampshire and New York claimants, such as the first Cumberland County Convention in October 1774, collapsed as the Yorkers themselves equated the Grants cause with support for resistance to Britain.[79] When the Loyalists Crean Brush and Noah Sabin ordered the arrest of Leonard Spaulding for treason, they were acting against the local leader of the Grants adherents. New York officials stated regularly that the Green Mountain Boys betrayed His Majesty when they denied Governor Tryon's authority. Those "evil minded persons" who attacked New York's courts sought to "break up and Destroy the courts of our Sovereign Lord the king."[80]

In 1774 Cumberland County's board of supervisors secreted a letter from the New York City Committee of Correspondence asking for the people's views on the patriot cause. The Reverend Reuben Jones and Azariah Wright of Westminster learned of the letter, calling town meetings which erupted in anger and resulted in a county convention of twelve eastside towns that discussed not only the letter but also Acts of Parliament and the legitimacy of the king. While declaring loyalty to the monarch, the delegates asserted their right to defend their liberties and condemned the supervisors. In November, John Hazeltine of Townshend received the First Continental Congress's resolutions and, on his own initiative, called another convention which endorsed the congressional resolutions. A third convention in February 1775 created a committee of correspondence with representatives from twenty-one towns that acted as a provisional county government for the next three years. These three conventions met without the approval of New York or of the county's officials, establishing a precedent for extralegal action on the east side.[81]

All these currents of opposition came to a head in March 1775. That month a number of eastsiders called on Cumberland County's chief justice, Thomas Chandler, and requested that no court be held until after harvest, so that debts might be more easily paid. Judge Chandler agreed to hear only a murder case, satisfying the petitioners. But discord had spread to the Yorker judges, and several hard-line New York officials intended to hear the complete docket. When word of these plans leaked out, anti–New York forces rushed to Westminster, seizing the courthouse on 13 March. Sheriff William Patterson, backed by fifty Yorkers, ordered the mob out, or "by God he would blow a lane through them." The occupying forces stated that they intended to stay as long as they pleased but suggested a discussion. The court's clerk, Samuel Gale, held his pistol aloft, declaring that he would "hold no parley with such damned rascals but by this." The sheriff and his posse retreated boldly to John Norton's tavern while Judge Chandler tried to smooth matters, assuring the anti-Yorkers that the posse lacked authority and that he would keep his promise to hear but one case. Trusting Chandler, many of those occupying the courthouse went home.[82]

At midnight, the well-fortified posse, which had spent several hours drinking rum at landlord Norton's, approached the courthouse and demanded entrance. Twice thrown to the ground by a burly anti-Yorker, Sheriff Patterson ordered his men to fire. Killing two men and wounding ten others, the posse rushed the courthouse, taking dozens of unarmed prisoners. In such circumstances, it proved difficult to determine who constituted the mob, who the guardians of law.[83]

The court assembled the next day and prepared a justification of the night's events. The Yorkers insisted that the rioters called the violence down on themselves and that all "reasonable Inhabitants" should rally to defend the New York court system—the only security for their life, liberty, and property. But the Cumberland County court never met again and many of its officers, including Judge Chandler, soon joined the anti–New York faction.[84]

By noon of 14 March, four hundred men crowded into Westminster and demanded the prisoners' release. Heavily outnumbered, the Yorkers agreed and by nightfall found themselves imprisoned. The next day a company of Green Mountain Boys under Robert Cochran arrived from the west, seeking revenge. An inquest returned a verdict of murder and ordered the prisoners transported to Massachusetts, most never to return.[85]

On the west side, Ethan Allen arrested and banished several new justices of the peace commissioned by New York.[86] Charged with usurping the courts' authority, Allen asserted that he and the Green Mountain Boys formed extralegal organizations because New York *"obliged us to it."* The Grants settlers denied New York's right to pass laws without their approval and created committees of safety to legitimate their actions and their expulsion of New York's officials.[87]

The scattered and diverse Grants communities acted independently, not looking to their representatives for guidance. When the Loyalist-dominated Cumberland Convention of November 1774 refused to enforce the congressional resolutions, most of the county's towns simply bypassed the convention and created their own committees. Dummerston, for example, appointed a seven-member committee of inspection, chaired by the radical Solomon Harvey, to observe the political conduct of the inhabitants. The committee of inspection, made up entirely of anti-Yorkers, removed Yorkers as well as Loyalists from public office, disarming them in the process.[88]

By the beginning of 1775 the Green Mountain Boys held a firm grip on every resistance organization in the Grants, even in Cumberland County, which had the greatest concentration of Yorkers. Settlers in the east appreciated the quick and effective reaction of the Green Mountain Boys to what Allen labeled "the Westminster Massacre," especially in contrast to New York's usual proclamations and threats.[89]

Building on this momentum, Allen called for representatives from both sides of the Green Mountains to meet in Westminster, deliberately keeping the tragedy fresh and emotions high. The convention resolved that closing New York's courts arose from necessity "as predicated on the eternal and immutable law of self-preservation." Allen then heard the words he had worked toward for the previous three years, an expression of unified opposition. The convention declared its duty to "wholly renounce and resist the administration of the government of New-York" and petitioned the king "to be taken out of so oppresive a jurisdiction, and, either annexed to some other government, or erected and incorporated into a new one." The Westminster manifesto voiced for only the second time the need for a new province, the first coming just a month before from Allen.[90]

The Green Mountain settlers wanted to respect the rule of law. Their petitions to New York calling for the establishment of counties, as well as their willingness to go first to New York's courts with their grievances, demonstrate such a desire. But their chief commitment remained the moral values they discovered at the law's root. With Allen they returned to the "original design" of law in preserving the people in their lives, liberties, and land. The "Good of Society" required that citizens respect the law. But government often degenerates from its original purposes, "terminating in the Ruin and Destruction of the Society it should secure & protect." At such times self-preservation requires the people "to resist and depose" their government.[91]

Underneath this vision of the proper ordering of society lay a more fundamental understanding of power. Back in 1773 Allen told Benjamin Spencer "that if he disliked their proceedings he might . . . take their Methods if he saw fit, or apply to Government if he tho't fit: That they damned the Government, said they valued not the Government nor even the Kingdom; That force was force in whatever Hands, & that they had force and power sufficient to protect themselves against either."[92] Government supplied order by protecting property and community, which in turn secured freedom. When New York could not deliver on the first and threatened the latter, the people of the Grants felt justified in using their collective power to seek independence.

In the Revolution lawlessness did not battle law; Whig law contested Loyalist law. The Whigs saw themselves upholding constitutional liberties, protecting traditional legal rights and structures against perceived threats of British tyranny. Whigs found destructive violence clearly illegal. But, as demonstrated in the Stamp Act riots of 1765, they thought the violence of intimidation acceptable. Allen's tactics, his use of humiliation as political theater, drew from this heritage. Whigs distinguished between bad laws and good; opposing the former did not negate the legitimacy of the latter. The same logic held in the Grants and found expression in Allen's rhetoric.[93]

In 1774 the Grants settlers became convinced that New York's leaders felt no commitment to American liberty, too often pursuing their own interests to the detriment of the common good. Reuben Jones condemned New York's officials for believing that the king might make whatever laws he chose "and he that said otherwise was guilty of high treason." To Jones, and many others in 1775, New York's assembly evidenced its illegitimacy by failing to approve the resolutions of the Continental Congress. "The people," Jones wrote, determined "that such men were not suitable to rule over them," and any who abided with such a government betrayed America. The people of the Grants knew it was "time to look to themselves."[94]

The British Empire pushed the people of the Green Mountains to autonomy, creating a crisis it could not resolve. Allen provided the settlers with the language, logic, and methodology of resistance and state building. After 1773 the Grants settlers looked to themselves for political solutions, erecting legal institutions which could maintain order, as they understood it.

Convinced that they must take responsibility for their governance, the Grants settlers turned to the competing structures of the Green Mountain Boys and the leadership of Ethan Allen. Allen brought two key qualities to the struggle with New York. He expressed the feelings and opinions of the majority of settlers in common language, verbally and in writing. More important, Allen translated words into action, finding the methods by which these settlers could combat the power of an established government. Allen combined aggressive language with peaceful tactics, creating a surprising unity which transcended other differences—political, economic, and religious. Ethan Allen molded a collective identity in the Grants out of mutual opposition to New York's authority.

Turning to "mob" action did not indicate social disintegration, but disorganization. The existence of extralegal action on the frontier indicates that official agencies failed to supply essential social services, such as police and reliable courts.[95] When they could not respect New York's law, finding only what Ethan Allen called "the empty Appearance of Law," the Grants settlers created their own and obeyed it.[96] Their judiciary generally operated on and adhered to legal principles, as they understood them, whereas New York's legal system appeared unreliable and hypocritical in operation. The Yorker Charles Phelps noted this tendency in the early 1770s, finding the settlers' dissatisfaction based on an "idolatrous reverence" for the laws and traditions of New England.[97] These "disruptive frontiersmen" respected the law, once it was theirs.

CHAPTER FIVE

"On Wings of Glory"

SURVEYING his world in June 1775, Ethan Allen saw limitless horizons stretching before the American people. America had reached the "critical juncture" when it must finally exert itself against "a tyrannical ministry." If only the colonies seized the opportunity, they "might rise on eagles wings and mount up to glory, freedom and immortal honour." And some portion of that glory should, Allen thought, alight upon his own heroic brow. Like so many members of the revolutionary generation, Allen saw himself facing one of those rare moments in history which offered the opportunity of eternal fame, of building new nations and attaining immortality. "A vast continent must now sink to slavery and poverty, bondage and horror, or rise to unconquerable freedom, immense wealth, inexpressible felicity, and immortal fame." In a few extraordinary weeks, Allen's military exploits brought him within reach of immortality.[1]

But Allen understood that to attain the stature he desired and to win acceptance for his separatist cause required more than a few quick battlefield victories. Somehow he must gain the confidence of the patriot leaders, military and civilian. Necessity decreed that Allen transform himself from an outlaw into a hero, from the leader of a local guerrilla insurgency into the embodiment of the national conflict.

The fluidity of American institutions in this crucial second half of the 1770s offered Allen and the Grants separatists their most certain route to acceptance. That same fluidity posed significant threats to the good order the patriot leaders struggled to establish in Philadelphia. As the newly formed American political and military command structure discovered, the rebellion against British tyranny raised a number of disruptive people to positions of authority, creating serious problems. Backed by the aura of military success and a loyal army, a revolutionary hero could rise above a virtuous glory, could exchange the plow of Cincinnatus for the crown of Caesar.

The more astute observers among Allen's peers, such as John Adams, recognized that the desire for fame could become devastatingly self-destructive. Adams thought it appropriate to seek fame, rating ambition and emulation among the premier motive forces of human history. Yet to seek it exclusively, without a solid sense of guilt for the selfishness represented by such a personal greed for glory, courted disaster, and Adams admitted that he was often himself "enslaved" by this desire. Allen would experience this truth to his detriment. In summer 1775 he saw the laurel crown resting before him.[2]

I

I was called by the Yorkers an outlaw, and afterwards, by the British, was called a rebel; and I humbly conceive, that there was as much propriety in the one name as the other.

—Ethan Allen, 1779

Ethan Allen grasped the political value of the Westminster Massacre immediately. New York handed him unity on a bloody platter, and Allen did not intend to let the moment slip from his control. A convention drawn from the eastside towns appointed Allen, a westsider, to join his old Salisbury partner John Hazeltine and Charles Phelps in writing a public protest against the tyranny of New York. The committee never finished its work, for on 21 April information arrived in Westminster which galvanized the Grants and redirected its energy toward a new enemy.[3]

Exhausted messengers told a stunned convention that on 19 April British regulars fired on American farmers at Lexington, Massachusetts. Advancing farther west, the British troops encountered stiff resistance at Concord. American militia units repulsed the British, forcing them into a disastrous retreat back to Boston, the regulars committing numerous atrocities along the way. Allen realized that resistance to ministerial authority had become war.

Rushing back over the mountains, Allen joined with the Green Mountain Boys at a convention in Bennington "and attempted to explore futurity, but it was found to be unfathomable." The Grants settlers felt "truly perplexed" by their situation. As Allen wrote four years later, the people of the Green Mountains had placed their hopes for "deliverance from the incroachments and oppressions of the government of New-York" in George III. On the other hand, "the ties of Consanguinity, personal acquaintance and friendship" with the rest of New England "weighed very heavy in their deliberations." Most of the Grants settlers believed that "the cause of the country" was just and that "resistance to Great-Britain had become the indispensible duty of a free people." With one dissent (Justus Sherwood) the Green Mountain Boys voted to stand with the rest of America "and thereby annihilate the old quarrel with the government of New-York by swallowing it up in the general conflict for liberty." Once the Grants settlers demonstrated their patriotism, Allen reasoned, the Continental Congress would not "countenance their being deprived of their liberty by subjecting them . . . [to] a government which they detest more than that of the British."[4]

Other frontier settlers with grievances against seaboard elites did not turn as quickly to the patriot cause. Upstate New York and the western Carolinas, rife with Loyalist sentiment, remained plagued by civil war throughout the Revolution. Many settlers in these regions found little to respect in their provincial governments and looked to the crown for political solutions until 1781. The inhabitants of the Green Mountains had also turned to the British monarch for resolution of their conflicts with the colonial government of New York. But unlike their tenant neighbors and the Carolina Regulators, the Green Mountain Boys had not yet tasted defeat at the hands of the Whig elite. Allen and his compatriots had appealed to George III as the only one who could legitimately override the authority of New York. But the farmers of Concord revealed British power as little more than a hostile facade. Strength, as Allen noted, lay not with the crown but with the people themselves.[5]

The "people" of the Green Mountains made the choice to join the patriot cause. Allen's skill as a leader came primarily in his ability to sense his followers' intended direction and place himself boisterously at the head of that column. The deference Allen received came not as a result of his age or social position. In 1775 Allen was thirty-seven and had been commander of the Green Mountain Boys for five years. His status in the community did not arise from church position, for he had none; from town office, for he held none; or from economic holdings, for his were problematic. Faced with the need to make a definitive choice, the Green Mountain Boys relied on Allen to give substance to what may have been a fairly obvious decision: to side with family and neighbors back in Connecticut and Massachusetts.

Deciding its cause would be best served by joining the struggle against Britain, the Bennington convention appointed Ethan Allen to lead the Green Mountain Boys into battle. By this act, the convention transformed Allen from the leader of a local insurgency into a military commander. Seeking to emphasize this new status, Allen turned his attention to the towering fortress of Ticonderoga on Lake Champlain.

Lake Champlain long served as an avenue for trade and war from Canada south to the Hudson River. The garrison at St. Jean, just twenty-five miles from Montreal, commanded the northern end of the lake. Seventy-five miles south, Lake George—which pointed like a dagger toward Albany, its southern tip only ten miles from the Hudson—emptied into Lake Champlain. Here the French built the formidable fortress of Carillon in 1755, where Montcalm won his stunning victory over Abercrombie's superior force of 15,000 men in 1758. With the Peace of Paris, the fortress, renamed Ticonderoga, came into British hands. During the war it acquired a reputation as a fearsome modern fortress which could be successfully held by a small force, making it the key to control of the northern colonies.

On a steep bluff, surrounded by water on three sides, Ticonderoga's star-shaped outer walls rose one hundred feet above a narrow portion of Lake Champlain. Ships and troop movements were visible at a great distance, and attackers came under the fire of over one hundred cannon before facing an uphill charge to the base of its high walls or a slow advance through the swamps to the south. In the popular imagination, Fort Ticonderoga loomed large and invincible.[6]

But a closer look told a different story. Many Grants settlers traded goods there and knew the British had allowed the fortress to decay in the fourteen years of peace. Captain William Delaplace's fifty-man garrison enjoyed a relaxed duty, responsible for guarding the shipment of goods between Canada and Albany while providing a symbolic restraint on the region's Indians, the Abenakis and Caughnawagas.

Familiar with the vulnerability of this apparently awesome fortress, Allen suggested seizing Ticonderoga as early as January 1775. While traveling around New England circulating *A Brief Narrative,* Allen stayed with the Pittsfield lawyer John Brown. The Boston Committee of

Correspondence had instructed Brown to open lines of communication with Canada, and Allen volunteered the assistance of some Green Mountain Boys. Brown asked Allen which side they would join if war started. Allen responded carefully that their conflict with New York complicated the question of Grants loyalty. But Allen felt that the Green Mountain Boys must capture Ticonderoga or lose control of the region to whoever held that fortress. Brown wrote a confidential communiqué to the Boston committee, announcing that he had established a dependable route to Canada. More importantly, Fort Ticonderoga "must be seized as soon as possible should hostilities be committed by the Kings Troops. The people on N. Hampshire Grants have ingaged to do this Business, and in my opinion they are the most proper Persons for this Jobb."[7]

It seems as though everyone but the British saw the strategic importance of Fort Ticonderoga. Heman Allen and Benedict Arnold independently advised the Hartford Committee of Correspondence that it should be prepared to gain control of Lake Champlain if the conflict intensified. The committee agreed, commissioning Heman and Levi Allen to raise the Green Mountain Boys. Heman found Ethan already making preparations, having mobilized the Green Mountain Boys and stationed guards on all roads. Levi arrived a few days later with Edward Mott from the Hartford committee, £300 borrowed from the Connecticut treasury, and fifty men from Pittsfield and Williamstown under the command of James Easton. Somehow all these actions remained secret from the British.[8]

The Grants proved better prepared for the Revolution than much of America, with an experienced and organized military force in the five companies of Green Mountain Boys. They took pride in the label "rebels" and had a commander anxious to establish his credibility as a military leader. Only three days after making the decision, in the early hours of 10 May 1775, the Green Mountain Boys moved to the attack.[9]

But theirs would be a democratic war, one demanding wide popular participation. The Grants patriots created a Council of War which operated like their towns' selectmen, reaching collective decisions and sharing responsibility. The council elected Mott chair, linking the Green Mountain Boys with the legitimacy of the Hartford committee, and ordered Samuel Herrick's company to steal Philip Skene's boats for a rendezvous with Allen at Hand's Cove in Shoreham. The council sent

Asa Douglas to rent boats for the assault from Crown Point's garrison, a misuse of government property which amused Allen.[10]

Hand's Cove is just a mile north of Fort Ticonderoga, its small harbor obscured by trees. Green Mountain Boys arrived throughout the night of the ninth, until Allen had three hundred men under his command. Earlier that day Noah Phelps entered the fort in search of a shave and discovered meager defenses and continued British ignorance of the outbreak of war. For some reason the governor of Canada, Guy Carleton, did not bother to inform Captain Delaplace of the emerging crisis. But, Phelps warned Allen, if the captain learned of the impending attack he could put up an effective resistance.[11]

As Allen waited for his transports, trouble arrived in the form of Colonel Benedict Arnold. Arnold carried a commission from the Cambridge Committee of Safety to seize Ticonderoga, and he demanded the command. Though Arnold's ego matched Allen's, his acute sensitivity and aloof sense of superiority won few admirers, and he, unlike Allen, was not a local. The Council of War informed Arnold that the soldiers elected their officers and that their choices would stand. Arnold hoped to bluff and intimidate his way to the command of the expedition. He picked the wrong men to overawe. The troops stated that they would sooner go home than follow Arnold, insisting that their neighbor Ethan Allen remained their choice. To soothe Arnold's fragile sense of honor, Allen offered the colonel a place at the head of the column. Arnold, who, after all, added only himself to the company's strength, accepted.[12]

While Allen had a large company of men and an officially commissioned militia captain in a bright red coat, he had only two boats that would hold eighty-five men between them. With dawn approaching and the moon down, Allen set out across Lake Champlain with a third of his force. Standing on the opposite shore beneath the cannon of Fort Ticonderoga at three in the morning, Allen inspired his troops with a quick speech on their virtue, or so he later remembered. Others recalled a whispered, "Let's go."[13]

The Green Mountain Boys started a fast march up toward the fortress. At their head, quick stepping side by side, strode Ethan Allen and Benedict Arnold. As they neared the fort and came in sight of the narrow covered entrance and the gate blocking it, the two men broke into an undignified trot, each determined to press the attack first. Allen won.[14]

The startled guard raised his musket at the enraged giant with the immense sword charging out of the fog. But the gun misfired as Allen knocked it aside with his sword. Allen crashed through the wicket gate and charged after the screaming sentry, while Green Mountain Boys filled the courtyard and climbed onto the walls. Shouting "No quarter!" they ran for the barracks. A British soldier lunged at one of the invaders, but Allen hit him over the head. Holding his sword aloft, Allen demanded that the dazed regular point out the commander's room.[15]

"Come out of there, you damned British rat!" Allen shouted as he ran up the stairs to the commandant's office, Arnold a constant shadow. Lieutenant Jocelyn Feltham appeared at the door wearing his coat and carrying his pants. As Allen described the scene, he called on Feltham to surrender the fort. The British officer demanded to know by what authority Allen had entered the king's fort. Allen responded in the Old Testament fashion he favored: "In the name of the great Jehovah and the Continental Congress." Aroused from his sleep, Delaplace came to the door, having taken the time to dress fully. Allen threatened to kill everyone if Delaplace did not surrender.[16]

Delaplace had no idea who these people might be. But seeing little alternative, he handed Allen his sword and ordered his soldiers, most of whom had already been captured in their bunks, to lay down their arms. Allen later described that perfect dawn of bloodless victory, as the "sun seemed to rise that morning with a superior lustre; and Ticonderoga and its dependencies smiled on its conquerers, who tossed about the flowing bowl, and wished success to Congress, and the liberty and freedom of America." It was the most glorious moment in Allen's life.[17]

Not forgetting his duty, Allen ordered Seth Warner and Levi Allen with one hundred men to capture Crown Point and then set about informing America of his surprising victory. Allen sent John Brown to Philadelphia with the captured flag and a message for the Second Continental Congress; its first meeting had begun a few hours after the taking of Ticonderoga. "Gentlemen," Allen wrote Congress, "I have to inform you with pleasure unfelt before, that on break of day of the tenth of May 1775 by the order of the General Assembly of the Colony of Connecticut [we] took the fortress of Ticonderoga by storm." Allen shared his glory with the Green Mountain Boys and the Massachusetts militiamen "under the command of Colonel James Easton, who behaved with great zeal and fortitude. . . . The Soldiery behaved with such resistless fury, that they so Terrified the King's Troops that they durst not fire on their assailants, and our soldiery was agreeably disappointed." A wondrous and bloodless victory, the fall of Ticonderoga proved the virtue of the Grants' cause, the Green Mountain Boys, and Ethan Allen.[18]

Brown also delivered a message to the Albany Committee of Correspondence, which included some of the Green Mountain Boys' most bitter opponents. Allen hoped their brilliant victory would win over these foes. He certainly enjoyed telling them that he acted "pursuant to my directions from sundry leading gentlemen of Massachusetts Bay and Connecticut." Pouring legitimacy over his dispatches like syrup, Allen informed New York's leaders that they must do their share: "I expect immediate assistance from you both in men and provisions. You cannot exert yourselves too much in so glorious a cause. . . . Pray be quick to our relief, and send us five hundred men immediately—fail not." Allen may have smiled as he signed himself "Your friend and humble servant."[19]

A small crisis ensued when Arnold again claimed the command, attempting ineffectually to maintain proper military discipline as the Green Mountain Boys expropriated Delaplace's stock of ninety gallons of rum. The soldiers "paraded, and declared they would go right home, for they would not be commanded by Arnold." The Council of War calmed the men with assurances that they would elect their officers. But Arnold insisted that without a commission, Allen could not direct operations. While Allen might be the "proper man to head his own wild people," he was "entirely unacquainted with military service" and commanded only because of his "ascendancy over his people." Arnold found no greater proof of the dangers of unrestrained democracy. The Council of War issued Allen a commission, meeting Arnold's first objection.[20]

While Arnold sulked, Allen turned his attention to more pressing matters. He sent his prisoners south as "a present" for Governor Jonathan Trumbull of Connecticut, hoping they might serve as ransom "for some of our friends at Boston" captured by the British. Soon thereafter, Allen learned that Warner had captured Crown Point without violence. Allen finally realized what he had gotten into. These two forts, while easy to capture, would be difficult to hold once British regulars in Canada launched a counterattack. With a trace of panic, Allen warned the Albany Committee of Safety that despite the great quantity of military supplies seized, his troops lacked "almost Every Necessary (Courage Excepted)," and he requested immediate reinforcement. New York should join Allen's Green Mountain Boys in defending the northern frontier and foot the bill.[21]

But help from New York or elsewhere remained a few weeks off, so Allen turned to the offensive, hoping for another easy victory. At the northern end of the lake loomed the St. Jean garrison and a heavily armed sloop, the largest ship on the lake. Allen had the second largest ship, Skene's schooner. Few of the Green Mountain Boys had any idea how to handle a ship, but Benedict Arnold did. The Council of War, having no choice, gave command of the newly named *Liberty* to Arnold, instructing him to seize the British sloop while Allen's troops followed up in four bateaux. Arnold did not wait, surprising St. Jean and its thirteen-man garrison. In retrospect, the inadequacy of British communications and defenses is amazing. All of Lake Champlain fell in four days to a roughly organized, crudely armed band of farmers.[22]

Galled by Arnold's success, Allen proclaimed that he would hold St. Jean. Arnold thought this a senseless idea as the Americans controlled the lake and the regulars marching from Montreal outnumbered Allen's small force. But Allen persisted and with "100 mad fellows," as Arnold put it, moved on St. Jean. The exhausted Green Mountain Boys had slept and eaten little in the previous three days, though they had drunk a great deal, and threw their blankets down next to the Sorel River for a rest. Their poor choice of campsite became apparent at dawn when the fire of British fieldpieces awakened the Americans. Running for their boats, the Green Mountain Boys fled before the British fusillade and sailed south. Allen reported that "the Musick" of the cannon "was both Terrible and Delightfull."[23]

Back at Ticonderoga, Allen sought to reclaim credibility with a bold initiative. He invited the Caughnawagas to join in fighting the British, whom "you know . . . stumble along close together rank and file," while the Green Mountain Boys "fight as Indians do. . . . Your Warriors [can] join with me and my Warriors, like brothers, and ambush the Regulars." In addition to entreating the natives, Allen started a stream of letters to the Continental Congress and various committees of safety calling for a full-scale invasion of Canada.[24]

It was a foolhardy plan. The colonies had no army, no chain of command, no quartermaster corps, no stockpiles of munitions, no unified government. But the capture of Ticonderoga electrified America and tempted many to overconfidence. The *Worcester Spy* reported one week after the "battle" that "the possession of this place affords us a key to all Canada. . . . *What think ye of the Yankees now?*" When Joseph Warren heard of the taking of Ticonderoga, he wrote, "Thus a War has begun." [25]

On the other hand, Allen's actions presented Congress with a series of headaches. It faced the jurisdictional difficulty of acknowledging a force in rebellion against New York, acting in America's name, as the successful captors of a British garrison within New York's boundaries. Further, the capture of Ticonderoga contradicted Congress's policy of only defensive reactions to direct British attack, as at Lexington and Concord. Seizing Ticonderoga could not be construed as a defensive response, as Joseph Warren noted. The Green Mountain Boys committed the first blatantly offensive act of the war, confronting Congress with the need to declare itself. Congress refused—setting a definitive precedent—and made a clumsy attempt at a middle course. The assembled luminaries thus resolved "that no expedition or incursion be undertaken . . . against or into Canada" and apologized to the Canadian people for the unfortunate attack on Ticonderoga. Congress ordered Allen to move the cannon and other goods at Ticonderoga south to the far end of Lake George and await a peace settlement with England. [26]

Allen thought Congress insane to believe reconciliation possible. Firing off an angry letter rejecting its orders, Allen warned Congress that "it is bad policy to fear the resentment of an enemy." For once, even Benedict Arnold agreed, though in endorsing an invasion of Canada he insisted that the American army should include "No Green Mountain Boys." [27]

Meanwhile the American command at Fort Ticonderoga faced its usual problem: Benedict Arnold. On 10 June Arnold ordered the Council of War to disperse as "I was at present the only legal Commanding Officer and should not suffer my command to be disputed." All the officers at Crown Point and Ticonderoga signed a letter supporting Allen's command. Confronting massive jurisdictional confusion—Congress had given responsibility to New York, which had asked Connecticut to deal with it—the council held it essential that the commander on the spot make the decisions. And the officers' choice for that position remained Ethan Allen. [28]

Arnold retaliated, declaring a "mutiny" and arresting several officers. Venting his frustrations on Major Samuel Elmore, Arnold "tooke the liberty of breaking his head. . . . I kicked him very heartily and ordered him from the Point immediately." Evident in this peculiar clash is a startling absence of discipline among the northern forces. The spectacle of Colonel Arnold assaulting a fellow officer did not set a good example of military order. As General Philip Schuyler, the new commander of the northern department, wrote to Congress, this "unhappy controversy" had "thrown everything into vast confusion. Troops have been dismissed, others refuse to serve if this or that man commands." And the man most insistent on military discipline proved the source of the problem.[29]

To address this chaos, Allen and Warner appealed directly to Congress. The two made a favorable impression in Philadelphia. Congress organized the Green Mountain Boys into a regiment in the new Continental army, commanded by officers of their choice; and President John Hancock wrote New York's Provincial Congress urging cooperation with the Green Mountain Boys. More startling, Congress reversed itself and instructed Schuyler to invade Canada if he found it "practicable, and that it will not be disagreeable to the Canadians." Allen infused Congress with a sense of confidence, persuading the Continental leadership to leave a decision of some magnitude in the hands of the local commanders.[30]

From Philadelphia, Allen and Warner rode to New York, requesting admission to the Provincial Congress. On 4 July 1775 Allen found himself speaking before the leadership of New York, trying to persuade his longtime opponents to support the Green Mountain Boys. Amazingly, he won them over. They, too, appeared willing to put aside previous animosities in support of the common cause, voting their aid for a Green Mountain Regiment. The crisis of empire transformed these frontier outlaws into patriotic allies of New York.[31]

Through June and July 1775 Congress exerted its authority over the scattered components of the American rebellion. Returning to Ticonderoga, Allen handed over his command to Colonel Timothy Hinman, the congressionally sanctioned commander. In contrast, Arnold first refused to defer to Hinman and then resigned his commission, declaring that he "would not be second in command to any person whomsoever." Arnold also threatened to deliver his vessels to the British and, as a final gesture of self-centered pique, discharged his few recruits.[32]

The summer of 1775 seemed a particularly bright and propitious one to Allen. The problems of the Grants settlers appeared resolved: Lake

Champlain was safely in their hands, Congress recognized the legitimacy of the Green Mountain Boys, New York and the Grants found friendship and unity in the common struggle against ministerial tyranny, an invasion of Canada was planned, Benedict Arnold was out of the way, and over it all, relishing his visions of glory, fluttered the banner of Ethan Allen, American hero. As Allen later noted, he fortunately had no idea of the reversal of fate which awaited him as he pursued his dangerous hunger for heroism to its logical and self-destructive conclusion.[33]

II

Ever since I . . . acquainted myself with the general history of mankind, I have felt a sincere passion for liberty. . . . so that the first systematical and bloody attempt at Lexington, to enslave America, thoroughly electrified my mind, and fully determined me to take part with my country.—Ethan Allen

Ethan Allen used the British imperial crisis to attain legitimacy for himself and his cause. When 1775 opened, the Green Mountain Boys appeared just another gang of outlaws disrupting the fringes of British civilization and Ethan Allen but head brigand. The capture of Fort Ticonderoga transformed the Green Mountain Boys into a regiment of regular troops in a national effort and Allen into a military hero.[34]

To some degree these changes came as an accident of events. Yet Allen learned early the advantages to be garnered by decisive and quick action and self-consciously played the crisis for all it was worth. But such certainty and success made many people nervous—and in Arnold's case, envious. The revolutionary generation, while lusting for fame and glory, feared the excesses of military heroes. What Don Higginbotham has called the "anti-Caesar complex" activated Congress in its efforts to retain strict control of the Continental army. Patriots and Loyalists feared a Caesar or Cromwell, a dictatorship created amidst the passions of a military crisis. Congress enjoyed good fortune in selecting George Washington as the army's commanding general, for Washington deferred to civilian authority throughout the war, no matter how much it galled him to do so. Ethan Allen was no Washington, and many of his Grants neighbors had reason to distrust his reliability as a leader and his willingness to acknowledge civilian control. Allen tended to reinforce these doubts, as when he wrote Governor Trumbull on 12 July that he was seriously considering invading Canada with the Green Mountain Boys, "exclusive of any help from the Colonies."[35]

Two weeks later the leadership of the westside committees of safety met at Dorset and ignored Congress's orders that the Green Mountain Boys elect their own officers. Suspicious of Allen's glory seeking and radical methods and certain that they could not control such a commander, the older community leaders of the Grants decided to take Allen down a notch. While the convention appointed Heman, Ira, and Ebenezer Allen and Gideon Brownson officers, command went to Allen's cousin Seth Warner, known for his conservative and cautious manner. The convention ignored Ethan Allen and four other fire-eating captains of the Green Mountain Boys—Remember Baker, Robert Cochran, Peleg Sunderland, and Gideon Warren—all of whom Allen had proposed as officers.[36]

Furious with this violation of congressional orders, Allen felt that his cousin should not accept the command. "Notwithstanding my zeal and success in my Countrys Cause," Allen wrote Governor Trumbull, "the old farmers on the New Hampshire Grants who do not incline to go to war . . . have wholly omited me." Allen knew that the young Green Mountain Boys would have elected him their commander. "How the old men came to reject me I cannot conceive inasmuch as I saved them from the incroachments of New York." But then "the old men" feared Allen's heroic stature and willingness to violate rules. Seth Warner matched the style of the older Grants settlers; careful, deliberate, unemotional, he was a man of few words. The Dorset Convention bypassed Allen out with a justifiable concern of where he might lead troops given into his hands; after all, attacking Ticonderoga so soon after the opening of hostilities had been a rather outlandish risk. They could not trust Allen in the routine activities of war, an assessment most historians have seconded.[37]

Some did not overcome their anger at being bypassed. Remember Baker headed north with a company of Green Mountain Boys, where he tragically met his death in a skirmish with a troop of Indians. Cochran joined Elmore's Connecticut regiment, and Peleg Sunderland returned home. Many Green Mountain Boys threatened to follow Sunderland's example, inducing General Schuyler to offer Allen a place at his headquarters. Allen accepted happily, considering it "an honorable offer," and agreed to do whatever Schuyler required, including keeping his

Green Mountain Boys in the army. Unlike Arnold, Allen could accept an affront to his honor and serve even without a command.[38]

Allen became a premier recruiter among the myriad cultures of the northern frontier. In September 1775, with the American army of the north advancing toward St. Jean, Schuyler sent Allen into the hinterland of Quebec in search of allies, or at least neutrals. Allen brought his years of experience rousing the inhabitants of the Green Mountains to the service of the new American army. In a strange land, among people who often spoke little if any English, Allen demonstrated a remarkable ability for inspiring fervor and a desire to join in the struggle for "liberty." Traveling north along the Sorel River, Allen spoke to hundreds of Quebecois and Caughnawaga Indians, also meeting with several Montreal merchants. The Americans, Allen assured his audiences, respected private property and religious freedom; their only target remained the British army.[39]

The Caughnawagas seemed particularly well-disposed. Presenting Allen "in a solemn manner" with jewelry and a wampum belt "as a lasting testimony of their friendship," they observed that the American army seemed "too weak to protect them against the severity of the English." Allen admired the Indians' reasoning: they would not risk taking up sides until they determined the likely victor. The Caughnawagas acted on sound "political principles," he wrote, respecting strength and, like the French, "watching the scale of power." The victories at Lake Champlain gave the Americans the appearance of power. Now they needed to match image with reality.[40]

After two weeks of "preaching politics," as he put it, Allen returned to find the Americans besieging St. Jean and Schuyler replaced by General Richard Montgomery. The new commander needed all the help he could get: his fluctuating and untrained collection of two thousand Americans did not get along well with one another. The Yorkers, whom Montgomery described as "the sweeping of the York streets," despised the Yankees, who returned their disdain. The New Englanders' "levelling spirit" disturbed Montgomery; he complained of the difficulty of commanding men "who carry the spirit of freedom into the field, and think for themselves." Curiously, Montgomery called on Ethan Allen, one of the most spirited of these men, to undertake a reconnaissance mission, promising his personal intervention should Allen be captured.[41]

Allen welcomed the action. With a small party of Canadians and

Connecticut militiamen, Allen roamed the countryside, recruiting and seizing wagons and supply boats bound for the British troops at St. Jean. Within three days Allen recruited 250 Canadians. Pleased with his "good success as an itinerant," Allen felt he had tapped into a local vein of resentment against the British. "As I march, they gather fast," he told Montgomery. Allen proceeded farther north, toward Montreal, in search of "the glory of a victory."

Reaching Longueuil across the St. Lawrence from Montreal, Allen contacted Warner at Laprairie, ten miles away. Warner suggested a concerted attack on Montreal, but Montgomery dismissed the suggestion, noting that although he had heard that Montreal stood undefended, Allen and Warner's troops lacked the experience for such an undertaking.[42]

In fact, British forces throughout Canada were in disarray. Governor Carleton had just two regiments of seven hundred regulars, a company of seventy volunteer Scottish veterans, a Canadian militia company of one hundred, and the frigate *Gaspé*. His resources stretched thin, his officials attacked by pro-American mobs, and rebel infiltrators having "succeeded in making Peace with the Savages," Carleton wrote the lord chancellor that "I cannot but fear that before this reaches your Lordship Canada will be as fully in the Posession of the Rebels as any other Province upon the Continent." Constant rumors of American armies around Montreal and Quebec created an air of panic; Quebec, as one Loyalist wrote, appeared "on the brink of falling into the hands of the most despicable wretches," like Ethan Allen.[43]

Allen, steadily feeding these rumors, set out to join Warner. Instead, he encountered Major John Brown and his force of two hundred men. Brown reported that only thirty regulars defended Montreal, Carleton having moved the rest of his troops to reinforce St. Jean. Deducing a golden opportunity to capture Montreal and disrupt British lines of communication, Brown and Allen hatched a scheme to take the city by storm. Allen would cross the St. Lawrence the next morning to the north side of Montreal, while Brown would cross and attack from the south, the assault synchronized by "three huzzas." Their plan was deeply flawed.[44]

"I will lay my life on it," Allen had told the New York Provincial Congress, "that with fifteen hundred men, and a proper artillery, I will take Montreal." Allen's problems arose from a failure to follow through on his own boast. His force consisted of eighty-five Canadians, mostly French, twenty-five New Englanders, and no artillery. It took three trips by canoe to cross the river to the north end of the island on the stormy morning of 24 September. Allen then waited two hours for some sound from Brown, having put himself in an impossible position, able neither to advance nor retreat. While Montreal's inhabitants panicked at the sight of a military force outside their walls and Carleton considered abandoning the city, Allen hurriedly sent messengers to find Brown. In the city General Robert Prescott prepared his paltry forces for a last-ditch defense, until his scouts detected Allen's weakness. Shifting to the offensive, Prescott's twenty officers, thirty-four regulars, six Indians, and two hundred citizens moved on Allen's position.[45]

Allen saw that "it would be a day of trouble, if not of rebuke." Taking a defensive position among some farm buildings, Allen tried to flank the English with a group of Canadians, who immediately ran away, as did a second detachment. With forty-five men left, Allen retreated toward the river, hoping to reach the canoes, but "the enemy kept closing round me." Exchanging shots with Peter Johnson, son of Sir William Johnson, Allen offered to surrender, "provided I could be . . . assured of good quarter." Johnson agreed, and Allen ordered his men to lay down their arms. There followed a peculiar dance, as an Indian took aim at Allen, who picked up Johnson and used him as a shield. An Irish soldier finally drove the Indians back, "swearing by Jasus he would kill them." Thus ended the military career of the victor of Ticonderoga.[46]

When news of Allen's capture reached the American army, his superiors rushed to discredit their recent hero. Schuyler wrote angrily to John Hancock: "I am very apprehensive of disagreeable consequences arising from Mr. Allen's imprudence. I always dreaded his impatience of subordination." Washington hoped that other ambitious officers would be taught a lesson of "prudence and subordination" to their superiors. To Allen's credit, he never blamed anyone else, not even John Brown, who had changed his mind when he saw the rough St. Lawrence and turned back south, leaving Allen to press the attack alone and suffer the consequences.[47]

The short confrontation outside of Montreal proved Allen's only pitched battle, the only one in which participants on both sides died, though it seems that Allen managed to avoid killing anyone. It was also the only battle in which Allen forgot his own basic rules of warfare:

to bring superior numbers quickly to bear, while leaving open lines of retreat and relying on threatening gestures rather than violence. More than a soldier, Allen was an actor. Unfortunately for Allen, speeches hardly sufficed in the middle of a battle.

His captors knew and hated Allen, not just because of his seizure of Ticonderoga but also for his efforts to arouse the Caughnawagas and the merchants of Montreal. General Prescott flew into a rage when he learned his prisoner's identity and "shook his cane over my head." Prescott wanted to shoot Allen on the spot, but some junior officers dissuaded him. If he could not execute him, Prescott could sentence Allen to maximum discomfort. British troops transferred Allen to the *Gaspé,* fastening irons on his feet and hands, and kept him and his fellow prisoners in a small room in the hold of the ship for six weeks. Unable even to lie down, Allen wrote Prescott the first in a long series of ineffectual letters. Reminding the British commander of his own generous treatment of the prisoners taken at Fort Ticonderoga, Allen demanded to be treated "as an officer of my rank and merit should." [48]

Having captured Allen, the British were stuck with him. The ministry feared American retaliation, especially as the rebels held so many British prisoners, and faced hostile questioning in Parliament on its handling of Allen. It resolved to keep all prisoners of war in America, thrusting the dilemma upon the field officers, who also had no idea how to treat their captives. Were they truly rebels, to be tried and hanged, or prisoners of war to be held for exchange? In typical imperial fashion, the British decided on neither and just muddled along for the war's duration. In Allen's case this indecision translated into a sequence of new prisons and inconsistent treatment, one of the longest and harshest confinements of an officer on either side during the Revolution. [49]

Confronted with a writ of habeas corpus for Allen, the government finally removed his irons and the problem, sending Allen to New York by way of Ireland, Madeira, North Carolina, and Halifax. While he languished in British ships, the tide of war turned against the Americans. Washington suffered defeat after defeat at Long Island, Manhattan, and White Plains. The final debacle occurred on 16 November, when General Sir William Howe's forces overwhelmed Fort Washington on the Hudson and captured nearly three thousand American troops. Allen arrived in New York just in time to witness this nadir of American fortunes. The British occupied New York City and crowded their prisoners into churches which quickly became filthy death holes. Allen tried to help the wounded but acknowledged he could do little. "Hollow groans saluted my ears, and despair seemed to be imprinted" on every face. The British fed the prisoners less than subsistence, giving them, Allen charged, bread thrown away as unfit for their own troops. And then came the carts, carrying away the dead Americans to a hasty burial. "I have seen whole gangs of tories making derision, and exulting over the dead, saying there goes another load of damned rebels."[50]

After fourteen months of harsh treatment, Allen and his fellow officers finally received a parole to Long Island on condition that they not attempt an escape. Seriously ill and without money, Allen settled in New Lots, roaming restlessly and uneventfully around his open prison for the next year. Denied his chance for immortality in battle, missing the main action, separated from his family, Allen found comfort in drinking, fighting in local taverns, and reliving his glory days. "Col. Allyn came in," one prisoner wrote, "& Repeated to us again, the Story of his Taking Ticonderogue."[51] The British concluded that Allen was mad, though not dangerously so. "My constitution was almost worn out by such a long and barbarous captivity," leading the British to believe "that I was crazy, and wholly unmanned."[52]

The final blow to Allen's precarious balance came in a letter from his brother Heman, informing Ethan that his son Joseph had died of small-pox. "I had promised myself great delight in clasping the charming boy in my arms, and in recounting to him my adventures. But mortality has frustrated my fond hopes, and with him my name expires—My only son, the darling of my soul—who should have inherited my fortune, and maintained the honour of the family." Later that year, Ethan wrote Levi Allen that "the death of my little boy closely affects the tender passions of my soul. . . . Do not fail to have an eye on the condition of my family; see that the girls be well schooled. I perceive that Ticonderoga, like other tenements and possessions of this changeable world, is snatched from hand to hand."

Ethan's cynosure and primary justification for all his actions, the struggles and manipulations, remained the well-being of his family. As the source of his greatest satisfaction and glory, Ticonderoga, had fallen again to the enemy in 1777, so the source of his greatest love and expectations for the future, his son Joseph, passed from "an impermanent world." Ethan's one definite hold on immortality was gone. Not only would there be no eternal fame from the Revolution, there would be no defeat of death through his son.[53]

Allen's experience replicated that of thousands of Americans who suffered devastating personal losses in the Revolution. Allen had the added pain of seeing himself as having fallen from a great height. In his abortive attack on Montreal, he had squandered his credibility as a military leader, and then suffered the ultimate humiliation of imprisonment. Allen saw his own irrelevance to the revolutions he had helped to make, on the Grants and in British North America. His culture thought the selfless pursuit of heroism noble, the ideal of the Roman republic exemplified. But that culture, and Allen, failed to note the self-destructive blade buried in the desire for glory.

Shortly after his letter to Levi, on 25 August 1777, Ethan simply wandered off. The British arrested him for parole violation, placing him in solitary confinement in New York's provost jail. Another prisoner wrote in his journal that he thought Allen, numb from the loss of his son, welcomed arrest. Allen wrote his brothers that he felt death nearby and begged them to care for and educate his daughters. After visiting Allen, the Connecticut commissary of prisoners reported to Governor Trumbull that the colonel "says he's forgot—He's spending his Life, his very prime" as a prisoner and had quite abandoned hope. For the first time in his life, Ethan Allen gave way to despair.[54]

CHAPTER SIX

"Our Injured Little Republic"

WHILE Ethan Allen languished in humiliating captivity for more than two years, events in the Grants moved swiftly. At the same time that the region took its first steps toward unification and independence, its inhabitants became militarized and mobilized by the arrival of war at their doorstep. Through 1776 and 1777 the Grants settlers followed a course of action which could not have conformed more exactly to Allen's wishes if he had been there to chart and steer them himself. During these years the Grants underwent a dramatic political transformation. The Green Mountains came to exemplify as few other places the highest ideals of republicanism, becoming a literal refuge for self-perceived republican heroes. Yet what unfolded in these crucial years compounded the difficulty of Allen's adjustment once he returned home.

Many scholars argue that the Revolution created a power vacuum in the Green Mountains, with the Green Mountain Boys stepping into this void to create the independent state of Vermont.[1] While essentially accurate, such a view is inherently passive: a vacuum existed. But the Green Mountain Boys created that vacuum by discrediting and then eliminating the authority of New York before the Revolution. Vermont filled a gap which its adherents had produced; which is to say, they made a revolution.

I

They were a people between the heavens and the earth, as free as is possible to conceive any people to be; and in this condition they formed government upon the true principles of liberty and natural right.—Ethan Allen, 1779

In the first confused days of the War for Independence, supporters of New York and the Grants each attempted to gain advantage from the sudden collapse of British authority. Neither side had an edge because, unlike every other province in America, the Grants citizenry had negated all colonial structures before Lexington. No preexisting offices beyond the local level remained for anyone to move into with claims of legitimacy. The route to political jurisdiction in the Grants shifted to popular approval or, at the very least, acquiescence. Such a political atmosphere benefited the group with a committed leadership and the widest popular following. For five years Ethan Allen had worked at fashioning just such a movement in his extralegal militia, the Green Mountain Boys. After Lexington, the Allens and their adherents seized the initiative, aided at every turn by the ineptness of New York's government and the intervention of the British army.[2]

Before his capture, Allen set the Grants on a course toward a distinct political identity, discerning opportunity in the weakening of New York's government in the first year of the Revolution. While insisting on the primacy of America's struggle with England, Allen saw no reason why that effort should exclude his separatist movement. On the contrary, Allen persuaded New York and the Continental Congress that their advantage lay in accepting the Green Mountain Boys on an equal footing with troops from other states. As a consequence of his efforts, the Green Mountain Regiment served under orders from Congress, a direct connection between the Grants and the new United States.

Initially, Allen hoped his zealous promotion of "the common cause" offered a peaceful solution to the controversy with New York, subsuming their dispute within the general revolutionary conflict. In a letter thanking New York's Congress for its "respectful treatment . . . [of] the Green Mountain Boys," Allen expressed confidence that "the friendship and union that hath lately taken place between the government and those its former discontented subjects" would lead to reconciliation.[3]

Rapprochement served practical purposes, for the Green Mountain Boys had few munitions and needed a source of supplies in the face of repeated British invasions. The old enemies thus enjoyed a brief period of détente. Albany's leaders sat across the table from representatives of the Green Mountain Boys, while the Grants towns provisioned the American army in the north. The Albany committee acquiesced in the harassment of Loyalists—most of them Yorkers as well—encouraged trade with the Grants, and even supported the validation of some New Hampshire land grants.[4]

Yet, despite protestations of friendship and mutual loyalty to America, neither side gave ground on basic positions, and the dialogue remained one between two distinct parties. The first demand in most rural uprisings is that the state simply listen to the rebels. By accepting the Allens as representatives of the Grants, New York validated their leadership and their cause. Considering that from New York's point of view the Green Mountains lay within four of its counties, the government committed a grave tactical error in treating the region as a single entity. At least one Yorker official in the Grants pointed out that it would be far wiser to manipulate the extensive factionalism of the region, especially divisions between the more conservative and economically established settlers along the Connecticut River and their poorer neighbors to the west. "The people are much divided—some for a new State, some for joining Hampshire, others Massachusetts, many for remaining under New-York."[5]

Most of the committees of safety along the Connecticut River contained a delicate balance of Yorkers and anti-Yorkers, sending representatives to both New York and Grants conventions. New York's government fed these divisions through its lukewarm support of the revolutionary cause. Many prominent officials doubted the wisdom of arousing the lower orders to political action, and the state made no effort to halt those New York City merchants who supplied the British warships throughout 1775. In the Grants, New York suffered particularly from the enthusiasm of its adherents, most of whom supported the British monarch. New York could not resolve the differences among its own supporters in Cumberland and Gloucester counties at the very time that it struggled to re-organize and legitimate its government, deciding to address the lesser issue of its unruly northeastern counties after eliminating ministerial tyranny.[6]

Military events in 1776 indicated that ministerial tyranny would be difficult to eradicate. The Americans barely kept the field against the British onslaught. But for the reckless heroism of Benedict Arnold in October, the northern frontier would have fallen to the British. The naval battle at Valcour Island in Lake Champlain proved the most brilliant defeat of the Revolution, gaining the Americans several months in which to prepare for the invasion they knew would come. It also gave the Grants inhabitants the opportunity to found a new state.[7]

In a series of six conventions between April 1775 and January 1777, the Grants moved slowly toward unification and independence. The circumstances of war delayed a declaration of independence, and each convention met in an atmosphere of heightened uncertainty, subject to sudden postponement due to the approach of British troops. No one could predict in the spring of 1775, or 1777, where the Revolution might lead.

Initially it seemed that the war would prevent unification. With so many Grants adherents busy invading Canada and then defending the northern frontier, the earliest conventions concentrated on military matters. Attempting to work within the system, these conventions petitioned Congress for protection of their land titles from New York's land jobbers. Congress offered a uniform response: it referred the matter to committee.[8]

In May 1776 Heman Allen wormed a resolution out of one of these congressional committees. The committee recommended that the Grants "for the present . . . submit to the government of New York," but it added a significant qualifier: submission to New York "ought not to prejudice the right of them or others to the lands in controversy, . . . nor be construed to affirm or admit the jurisdiction of New York in and over that country." Congress would address the subject again "when tranquility shall be restored." New York's representatives protested furiously and tabled the issue. But they acted too late. Allen had the ammunition he needed to persuade the hesitant. He also received sound advice from some members of Congress, who told him to ignore Congress and unite quickly.[9]

Unity required the participation of the eastside towns, only one of which, Townshend, sent a representative to any of the first four conventions. Attempting to overcome this coolness, the July 1776 Dorset Convention produced an "Association" for submission to the people. The association claimed to act for Congress, which had requested "that every honest Friend to the Liberties of America . . . should subscribe an Association, binding themselves as Members of some Body or Community." Signers of the association swore "at the Risque of our Lives and fortunes to Defend, by arms, the United American States," but not as New Yorkers. Swearing allegiance to the revolutionary struggle under an authority other than New York's marked the association as a significant political statement. Emphasizing its jurisdiction, the convention appointed a committee of war responsible for military procurement and overseeing the operations of the local committees of safety. The convention clarified the duties of these local committees by declaring those who refused to sign the association or signed any document supportive of New York to be enemies of the people.[10]

In August 1776 Heman Allen appeared boldly before a meeting of the eastside Yorker committees of safety. He asked those attending to sign the association and declare their support for an independent state. Hesitating to sign, the chairman, James Clay, sent a message to all eastside towns inquiring "wheather they Intend to Revolt from the State of New York or not?" It was an odd question to ask, especially as many towns had not considered it before. Marlborough called a town meeting "to consider the contents of a letter from the Chairman of the Comitte of this County . . . Requesting to know the mind of this town on acct of Revolting from New York." Marlborough's town meeting, uncertain what to make of the suggestion, tabled the matter for future discussion. Four other town meetings replied quickly in the affirmative.[11]

The Westminster Convention of January 1777 attempted to determine "the full sentiments of the People." Its methods are unknown, but a committee reported that three-fourths of those expressing an opinion favored independence. Receiving this report at face value, the convention voted unanimously that the New Hampshire Grants "be a new and separate state; and for the future conduct themselves as such."[12]

The convention's Declaration of Independence resembled Jefferson's in being a long list of grievances. The sixteen complaints against New York boiled down to four main points: New York attempted to extend its jurisdiction to the Connecticut River against the wishes of the people living in the region; its legal system was unjust; New York, like Britain, ignored the people's petitions and failed to operate as a proper government; and, most importantly, New York attempted to dispossess the people of their land. Finding their property and very lives threatened by the "monopolizing land traders" who controlled New York's government, which had withdrawn its protection, the people had a right to form themselves into a political community.

The Grants' separatists drew legitimacy from the congressional resolution of 10 May 1776. In this resolution John Adams recommended that "where no government sufficient to the exigencies of their affairs has been hitherto established," it was proper for the inhabitants "to adopt such government as shall in the opinion of the Representatives of the people best conduce to the happiness and safety of their constituents." It seemed an almost exact description of the Grants, now the independent state of New Connecticut. The declaration stated that all who resided within its borders—which extended north to Canada and "West as far as the New Hampshire Grants extends"—became citizens with the same rights as other Americans. The convention closed its business by applying for admission to Congress and voting to raise more troops for Warner's regiment, which it claimed as its own.[13]

New Connecticut's delegates returned from Congress without the recognition they desired. Instead, they brought an open letter addressed "To the Inhabitants of Vermont," from Ethan Allen's old friend Thomas Young. Young praised them for their continuing struggle against "the New York Monopolizers" and for taking matters into their own hands, playing the role of true revolutionaries. Now the people of "Vermont" must organize a government, for "you have as good a right to choose how you will be governed" as the other states. The ideals of the Revolution demanded that they maintain their independence, as "the people at large [are] the true proprietors of governmental power." Young found a name not only for Vermont but for what its conventions represented: "the supreme constituent power" of the people. But until the settlers of Vermont "incorporate" and become "a body politic," they could not expect to be treated as free men. The Allens published Young's letter and circulated it widely.[14]

The constitutional convention met in Windsor at the very moment when America's northern defenses crumbled before Burgoyne's army. The convention opened on 2 July 1777 with fifty delegates from thirty-one towns. They listened to the Reverend Aaron Hutchinson's sermon linking the "oppression and tyranny" of Britain with that of New York and then spent several days responding to the military crisis and debating their new constitution. On 8 July, during the last reading of the document, news arrived of Ticonderoga's fall and Warner's defeat at Hubbardton. The enemy had overrun the homes of many of the delegates and threatened the security of the entire region. The worth of their proceedings appeared suspect.[15]

In a time of such uncertainty, the authors of the Vermont Constitution placed their faith in a democracy. While the Vermont Constitution is often considered little more than a copy of Pennsylvania's, there are several significant and revealing differences.[16]

The preamble, written by Ira Allen and Thomas Chittenden, asserts the people's right to establish their own form of government. In consequence of New York's failure to maintain "the security and protection of the community, . . . it is absolutely necessary" that the region's inhabitants "by common consent, and without violence," create a government as the instrument for best promoting the happiness of the people "and their posterity . . . without partiality for, or prejudice against, any particular class, sect, or denomination." Allen and Chittenden found their only legitimation in the "authority of the people."[17]

The rhetoric of the preamble offers little innovation. Its language of the consent and will of the people formed part of the political vocabulary of the day. But Vermont's constitution demands attention for the way it lived up to its theoretical assertions, creating the most democratic structure of its time.[18] It clearly established and protected certain basic rights: freedom of speech, print, and public assembly, a modified freedom of religion,[19] the right to a fair and open trial before a jury, and the people's right to form new governments as they see fit. But liberty carried a price, and every citizen bore a responsibility to serve in the militia, unless individual conscience prevented such service.[20]

The state's voters controlled every branch of government, electing the state's executive officers and judges, as well as representatives to the unicameral legislature. Vermont failed to institute a separation of the branches of government: an individual could hold office simultaneously in the legislature, executive, and judiciary, with every member of the Executive Council automatically a justice of the peace.[21] But political power resided in the General Assembly. The governor and council of Vermont could not veto legislation, though they could recommend amendments to bills. In other states an upper house served as the embodiment of property, its members representing status and hierarchy. Critics of Vermont's constitution, like Timothy Dwight, fumed that "a Legislature by a single house is of course no other than an organized mob. Its deliberations are necessarily tumultuous, violent & indecent." The radicals of Pennsylvania and Vermont rejected this logic as aristocratic, insisting instead on the existence of a "homogeneous community of interest" which superseded class distinctions. This vision of a unified society was an image cast by their desires rather than by reality, though in Vermont the actual came closer to approximating the ideal.[22]

Vermont's radicals crafted mechanisms for the maintenance of their democratic vision. To attain maximum civic participation, the constitution required public legislative sessions and forbade the passage of any bill into law the same year it was proposed, mandating its printing for the public's information. Such a procedure intended to make the representatives dependent upon their constituents, who habitually issued instructions. A septennial Council of Censors was to review all legislative and executive acts to ensure that the constitution was being fulfilled, laws justly executed, and taxes fairly assessed. The Council of Censors could amend the constitution by calling a popularly elected convention, allowing "posterity the same privileges of choosing how they would be governed" without resort to "revolution or bloodshed."

Vermonters feared the power of the state to imprison those who fell onto the wrong side of the credit system. The constitution therefore spelled out several key limitations on the economic power of the courts, allowing no writ against the property or person of a debtor except in extreme circumstances, while guaranteeing a jury trial even in civil cases and allowing local control of fee schedules. Any officer of the court who accepted payment beyond that specified by law was disqualified for life from public office.[23]

The democratic orientation of Vermont's constitution is easily understood. The Windsor Convention did not consist of delegates appointed by the legislature, contrary to most other constitutional conventions. Vermont lacked a legislature, requiring the Grants settlers to produce all their own institutions. Representatives at this convention and the structures they created spoke for the desires and felt needs of the majority of Vermont's male citizens. Their government thus indicates popular political sentiment better than that of any other state in the Union.

But Vermont's leadership did not seek the approval of the people as an undifferentiated mass. Sovereignty lay in the distinct townships, which held the "unalienable and indefeasible right to reform, alter, or abolish government, in such manner as shall be, by that community, judged most conducive to the public weal." Pennsylvania established proportional representation, an exceedingly progressive concept, while New York apportioned representation by county. Vermont ignored these examples and returned to its New England roots, which nourished each town as an autonomous unit deserving its own voice in the legislature. Under New York's constitution, all of Cumberland County's towns would have joined together to elect three representatives, Gloucester would have shared two, and both counties would have united with Charlotte, on the other side of the Green Mountains, into a single senate district. Under Vermont's constitution, each community with more than eighty freemen received two representatives, all others one. In 1777, when the largest town numbered eight hundred inhabitants, or about two hundred freemen, this system was roughly equitable. The people of Vermont interacted with their state government through their community, not as isolated individuals.[24]

The state council in turn looked to the towns to conduct the state's business and deferred to their local understandings of the appropriateness of acts. The new government determined to enforce a basic consensus, adherence to the revolutionary cause of both America and Vermont, but the towns decided the fate of those who violated consensus. The Windsor Committee of Safety, for instance, adjudged its deposed leader, Nathan Stone, a "dangerous person" and placed him in the state jail as a proper lesson in the power and authority of Vermont. The towns made the decisions and the state carried out their will.[25]

The needs of the community took precedence over the Lockean standards of individualism expressed in the Pennsylvania Constitution. Vermont's Declaration of Rights proclaimed "that private Property ought to be subservient to public uses." In a harbinger of later notions of eminent domain, the state gained the right to seize private property for public use, the owner receiving fair compensation.[26] And to make certain that the state never got out of hand, the Declaration of Rights stipulated that the people reserved the right of review over every action of the state and its police. Even Pennsylvania found such a firm limitation on executive power too radical.

Vermont's radicalism is reflected in two key differences from every other American constitution of the 1770s and 1780s: Vermont was the first state to institute universal manhood suffrage and the first to outlaw slavery.

The constitution granted every male over the age of twenty-one "all the privileges of a freeman of this State." Vermont put forth an entirely new definition of citizenship in fundamental conflict with the British notion of perpetual allegiance, of the individual carrying the nationality of birth through his or her days. In place of "subjectship," Vermont proffered citizenship and the rule of "expatriation," the free choice to abandon former allegiances and adopt new ones.[27] And while as few as 10 percent of the adult males could vote just over the border in Dutchess and Albany counties, Vermont placed no property restrictions on the franchise. No state in the Union made such an effort to include so many of its inhabitants in its decision making. No other state succeeded in divorcing property from liberty.[28]

But it was the opening words of the Declaration of Rights which most shocked the world of the 1770s. In two sentences the founders of Vermont carried the logic of the Declaration of Independence to its obvious conclusion, stating: "That all men are born equally free and independent. . . . Therefore, no male person, born in this country, or brought from over sea, ought to be holden by law, to serve any person, as a servant, slave or apprentice, after he arrives at the age of twenty-one, nor female, in like manner, after she arrives at the age of eighteen." Pennsylvania's constitution stopped at the first sentence. As Ethan Allen stated two years earlier, a people claiming to fight for their liberty demonstrated a callous inconsistency in enslaving others. In contrast to New York, which allowed slavery, Vermont supported freedom with law: the legislature declared free any slaves brought into Vermont, for they became citizens upon entering and thus enjoyed the constitution's protection.[29]

Though distinctive in several particulars, the Vermont and Pennsylvania constitutions shared an essentially democratic orientation, especially when compared with the constitutions of the other states. And that similarity is what remains so curious. Pennsylvania and Vermont stood at the extremes of early American society. Pennsylvania had the largest urban center in North America, a remarkably diverse ethnic population, marked class divisions, and an economy based on trade and commercial farming. Vermont had nothing even remotely resembling a city, a nearly homogeneous population of New Englanders with few if any class distinctions, and a frontier subsistence agricultural economy. Yet these two states emerged from the Revolution with similar political structures. Perhaps two paths to a democratic ethos existed in colonial America: the more expected route of pluralism growing from the pressures of diversity, as represented by Pennsylvania; and the needs of localism, of communities seeking to preserve their primacy, as in the case of Vermont.[30]

But all such considerations appeared academic with a British army invading their new state. As Warner had at Hubbardton, the representatives at Vermont's constitutional convention endeavored to hold their ground, to complete their public duty. They finished their deliberations, approved unanimously the constitution of the new state of Vermont, and rushed to join their militia units. As a sign of their confidence, they ordered a statewide election for December 1777 and appointed a Council of Safety to act as an executive body until then. The crises of war postponed the election until March, and Ira Allen could not print the constitution until February 1778. But the people of the Grants finally had their own government and, as its first task, turned to confront the might of the British Empire.[31]

II

Burgoyne's army . . . had been victorious in every place. . . . The Green Mountain Boys were deeply interested in the fate of the day; for the very existence of the infant State of Vermont, their families, and property, were all pending on the event.—Ira Allen

On 13 June 1777 General John Burgoyne launched the long-awaited British invasion from the north. The British commander threatened all those who stood in his way with extermination, warning the rebels that he would unleash his Indian allies if he met opposition. Yet those Americans who stood first in his path, the citizens of the new state of Vermont, equated resistance to Burgoyne with the very survival of their communities. Though part of a national struggle for independence, the Vermont rebels acted out of local concerns. Burgoyne's invasion thus militarized the Vermonters, providing the nascent state government its first opportunity to demonstrate its loyalty to the United States and its effectiveness as a political unit.[32]

Conversely, the northern campaigns of 1777 had more than local significance. These battles represented a pivotal confrontation between classic and innovative methods of warfare. An aristocratic command structure encountered mobile revolutionary tactics and decentralized leadership. The outcome of this conflict should have taught British commanders a valuable lesson, but they ignored this instruction to their detriment. Ethan Allen at least understood that his followers had no real need for him or any other leaders in order to triumph over the old order.[33]

Vermonters made the American evolution their own struggle. Nearly fifteen hundred of them served in the Continental army, while almost all adult males served in the militia. The elected officers understood that their positions and success depended on the loyalty of their men, for nothing held them in line except their feelings for one another. Colonel John Chandler informed his troops that "the honor and interest of the Regiment will ever be the object of his attention, Sensible that his is inseperably connected with theirs." They could rely on his "constant aim that unanimity and harmony prevale."[34]

What appears repeatedly in the records is the personal nature of the Revolution for the people of the Vermont frontier. When the militia needed supplies, they were donated, usually with the hope of receiving eventual reimbursement but with no real expectation of quick recompense. During the crisis of 1777 settlers with money donated it for the raising of troops. Samuel Stevens, for instance, managed to acquire £13 in hard currency for the use of the militia. Some tried to make a profit from the war, usually by organizing town proprietorships with fellow soldiers and keeping an eye open for favorable land to settle. But very few Vermonters profited handsomely from the Revolution, except insofar as their land titles eventually were recognized and honored.[35]

The war brought the Vermont townships together in battle, intensifying each participant's identification with the state. Town militia acted as coherent units, and battles were often family affairs with sons and fathers, brothers and cousins standing side by side. The loss of a family member or neighbor further personalized the conflict. Constant militia mobilizations and the continued presence of Continental units at Fort Rutland and Fort Warren kept the Revolution and the threat of warfare before the Vermonters.

Militia companies served as what John Shy called "the infrastructure of revolutionary government" and as sources of political education. Risking one's life for a cause made political goals all the more intimate. Serving in the militia was a persistent reminder of the danger all Vermonters faced, of enemies within and without. The survival of the state became the preeminent political concern of the majority of the area's inhabitants, and anyone who threatened Vermont became a traitor, whether a loyalist to Britain or New York. Allen's efforts to connect the struggle for American independence with Vermont independence paid off.[36]

General Burgoyne demonstrated the deepest contempt for these units, and all other Americans, including his own Loyalist troops. He accused the latter of timidity in battle and of seeking personal profit through service to the king. Burgoyne placed his faith in his 4,000 British and 3,000 German troops as he aimed for Albany. General Arthur St. Clair's 2,500 poorly supplied troops at Ticonderoga alone stood in his path. Burgoyne foresaw few problems, for the Americans lacked "men of military science."[37]

Burgoyne moved down Lake Champlain at a stately pace of twenty miles a day, issuing several inspiring general orders along the way. He assured his troops that they fought "to vindicate law and relieve the oppressed; a cause in which his Majesties Troops . . . will feel equal excitement."[38] While less thrilled than their general with the prospect of saving the British constitution in America, the British and German troops enjoyed high morale as they moved south, convinced of their invincibility. On 1 July they landed three miles above Ticonderoga. The Americans abandoned the fortress.[39]

Burgoyne, disappointed that the Americans had slipped away, ordered a quick pursuit. On 7 July, General Simon Fraser's British troops fell on the American rear guard at Hubbardton. St. Clair hoped to block the British advance with his most reliable troops, Seth Warner's Green Mountain Regiment. As New York had long demanded, British regulars finally entered battle against the Green Mountain Boys. The Americans repulsed the initial attack and held their ground for the next half hour. Warner might have carried the day if two militia companies had not defied St. Clair's orders and refused to enter the fray. Instead, General Baron Frederick von Riedesel's Germans appeared suddenly and drove in Warner's right. In desperation, Warner shouted for his men to "Scatter and meet me at Manchester." The Green Mountain Boys melted into the woods, working their way to Manchester in small groups.[40] A fierce and bloody engagement, the Battle of Hubbardton claimed two hundred casualties from each side. But Warner's regiment stopped the British dead in their tracks, giving St. Clair the time he needed to escape south.[41]

Burgoyne had not eliminated any part of the American army. General

Schuyler, taking over from St. Clair, held Fort Edward on the Hudson, and Warner and the Green Mountain Boys hung on Burgoyne's flanks, sniping at him at every opportunity. Yet Burgoyne commanded the field and had his choice of directions: proceeding directly south through the swamps from Skenesboro to Fort Edward, or sailing down Lake George to its southern end, a mere ten miles from the Hudson River. In Burgoyne's own estimation the latter was "the most expeditious and commodious route to Albany," while the former was essentially "impassable." Yet for reasons Burgoyne could not explain to a later parliamentary inquiry, he headed for the swamps.[42]

The Americans could not believe their luck. The track Burgoyne followed forded Wood Creek forty times, passing through a morass of bogs and woods. Schuyler's experienced woodsmen made the way even more difficult—destroying every bridge, felling trees, digging ditches to extend the swamps, and using boulders to back up the creek—while local militia fired on the British from ambush. The area's residents abandoned their farms, removed all food and livestock, and burned unharvested crops.[43] For three weeks Burgoyne's troops hacked their way through this sixteen-mile-long obstacle course. Finally, on 29 July, the British advance companies arrived at Fort Edward, only to discover that Schuyler had abandoned the site, taking up position thirty miles south, at the mouth of the Mohawk.[44]

Though strategically sound, these retreats devastated American morale. The abandonment of Ticonderoga sent shock waves through New England; many thought that Schuyler had willingly sacrificed the northern frontier in order to avoid a fight. Near panic swept the towns of the new state of Vermont and their militia rushed west to join Seth Warner. Congress, angry over the fall of Ticonderoga, recalled Schuyler and St. Clair and gave command to General Horatio Gates.[45]

In contrast to the discouraged and anxious Americans, the British, at last free of the wilderness and moving through the cultivated lands of the Hudson Valley, felt confident of success. Baron von Riedesel, weary of having his dragoons acting as infantry, suggested a raid on the American military depot at Bennington to acquire horses. Burgoyne approved, hoping to end the Green Mountain Boys' constant attention to the British flank. Riedesel chose Lieutenant Colonel Frederick Baum "to try the affections of the people" of Bennington with a mixed force of Germans and Tories. Neither Baum nor Burgoyne realized that following the Battle of Hubbardton the newly constituted Vermont Council of Safety not only called out the Green Mountain Boys but also appealed to New Hampshire and Massachusetts for assistance, a step which had not occurred to any of the American generals.[46]

New Hampshire issued a call for volunteers, with impressive results. Within a week, New Hampshire filled a brigade of 1,500 men, 10 percent of those on the state's voting rolls. The General Court gave command to John Stark, accepting his condition that he not have to answer to the Continental Congress.[47] The New Hampshire troops moved quickly, crossing the White and Green Mountains inside a week. At Manchester, Stark joined forces with Warner, rebuffing General Benjamin Lincoln of the Continental army, who claimed command and tried to order these troops to the Hudson.[48]

As Baum approached Bennington, militia rushed to join Stark and Warner, not waiting for orders from their governments. Word reached the captain of the New Marlboro, Massachusetts, company in church. Rising from his pew, the captain interrupted service. "Mr. Turner," he shouted to the minister, "the British are at Bennington, and I forbid Sabby-day! Minute men, turn out and follow me!"[49] Thus reinforced, Stark moved forth to meet the Germans. His troops—militia from New Hampshire, Vermont, and Berkshire County, Massachusetts, and a company of Stockbridge Indians—had no uniforms and carried their own or borrowed guns, often in the worst condition. Facing them across the Walloomsac stood eight hundred trained, experienced, and well-armed Germans and Loyalists.[50]

On 16 August, Warner arrived in advance of his regiment and joined Stark in planning a complicated attack involving the simultaneous encirclement of Baum's entire force. The Tories and Indians, whom Baum put in the front line, fled before the first onslaught, their commanders leading the rout. The Germans, stationed on a steep hill above the river, drew themselves into a circle and fought the Americans off for two hours; it was "the hottest [battle] I ever saw in my life," Stark recalled. When the Germans' munitions wagon exploded in their midst, Baum desperately ordered his men to draw their swords and cut their way out. The Americans, who had no bayonets, used their muskets as clubs, withdrawing slowly before the Germans. Baum fell, mortally wounded. Without leadership or hope, his remaining troops surrendered.[51]

The victory his, Stark dispersed his forces to search the woods for

Loyalists, unaware that German reinforcements had just arrived on the scene. Lieutenant Colonel Henrick von Breymann's relief column of 650 men came into contact with the Americans at the very moment that Baum's units surrendered just five miles away. Four times the American militiamen formed and fired on the advancing Germans but could not stop them. The Americans, as one participant recalled, "retreated from tree to tree, firing as they left the trees, until they came to a ravine where there was a log fence, then made a halt, and held the ground." Stark frantically organized his scattered forces. Just before sunset Colonel Samuel Safford appeared with Warner's regiment.

Joining Stark's retreating companies, Warner's tired troops met Breymann's assault, "and the battle then became desperate." The Americans overran the German cannon, turned them on the fleeing enemy, "and mowed down a large number of them." The German retreat turned into a second rout. Breymann attempted to surrender, but the inexperienced Americans did not understand the message of his beating drums. Only Stark's calling off the attack because of darkness saved Breymann and the battered remnants of his force.[52]

Thirty Americans and two hundred Germans died at the Battle of Bennington. Stark took seven hundred prisoners, including thirty officers, four brass cannon, hundreds of high-quality muskets and swords, and a great deal of pride. These frontier farmers destroyed two units of professional soldiers in the same day. The first victory is surprising for its coordinated encirclement of a disciplined and well-led enemy; the second is phenomenal, given the equal size of the two forces and the Americans' unorganized and exhausted state. Several British officers expressed shock that "the peasants of the country" had "fought with great courage and obstinacy."[53] Neither Congress, which unanimously voted Stark's forces its thanks, nor Burgoyne missed the significance of this victory. The people of the northern frontier shared an obvious commitment to the cause of American independence and identified this struggle with an effective willingness to defend their homes. As Burgoyne wrote Lord George Germain, "Wherever the King's forces point, militia . . . assemble in twenty-four hours." Their inexperience proved irrelevant, for "the panic of the rebel troops is confined, and of short duration; the enthusiasm is extensive and permanent." The biggest mystery, and threat, lay in Vermont, "a country unpeopled, and most unknown [in] the last war." It "now abounds in the most active and most rebellious race of the continent, and hangs like a gathering storm upon my left."[54]

The news from Bennington stunned Burgoyne. Frozen by indecision—except in speedily fixing blame elsewhere—Burgoyne watched placidly as his Indian allies deserted. With American morale and numbers soaring, Burgoyne's wisest course, as his officers urged, would have been a retreat to Fort Ticonderoga. Instead, Burgoyne crossed the Hudson to the west bank and headed for the entrenched American positions at Bemis Heights.[55]

After their brilliant victory at Bennington, the New Hampshire and Vermont militias accelerated their campaign of harassment into full-scale attacks. They broke Burgoyne's lines of communication and retreat, driving the British into their defenses at Ticonderoga and Mount Independence, seizing Skenesboro and Mount Defiance, capturing hundreds of prisoners and most of the supplies bound for the dispirited British army. But the Vermonters hesitated to cross into New York, and Stark and his militia went home when their enlistments expired at the end of September. The New Englanders had defeated the Germans without any help from New York and saw no reason why they should come to that state's aid.[56] Gates overcame this parochialism, persuading the Vermonters to move. As the British and Americans maneuvered toward the climactic second Battle of Freeman's Farm, two thousand Vermont militia settled on the heights above Fort Edward. When Burgoyne finally attempted his retreat, he found his way blocked and his army completely encircled. On 16 October he surrendered.[57]

Few victories carried greater importance for the Americans, and the Vermonters expected to find equal value in the event. As the British hastily withdrew their garrisons from Lake Champlain, Vermont secured control of its borders. Burgoyne's invasion distracted New York from responding to the audacity of its northeast counties forming an independent state and gave Vermont an immediate national legitimacy through the active role it played in defeating the British—"a striking proof of the good policy of assuming government," as Ethan Allen put it.[58]

The end of 1777 should have been a time of triumph. Yet despite the startling courage of Warner's troops at Hubbardton, the brilliant victory at Bennington, and the successful guerrilla war against Burgoyne's lines of supply, Vermont received little credit and no gratitude. The ultimate blow came on 30 June 1777 when Congress ordered that Vermont cease to exist. Congress disclaimed any authority to "recommend or countenance anything injurious to the rights and jurisdictions of the several communities which it represents." Vermont could find no justification in America's independence or in the congressional resolution of May 1776—despite the fact that many states, including New York, used this resolution to legitimate their constitutions. Congress rejected all petitions from Vermont and denied that Warner's regiment validated a separate jurisdiction.

This 1777 congressional resolution denied many elements of the Revolution. In short, Congress stated that the United States consisted of the thirteen original states within their colonial borders, no matter how those borders contradicted one another, and that neither the people nor their communities had a right to determine which state to join. The jurisdictional rights of the thirteen congressional states subsumed the freedoms of every community.[59]

Vermont stood separate and alone. Its military service had not won it political legitimacy. Congress, it appeared, had betrayed Vermont's people in the face of their heroism. At this moment of doubt and confusion within Vermont, Ethan Allen finally returned home, two years and ten months after leaving Crown Point to conquer Canada. Burdened with grief over his son's death and worn from his long and brutal confinement, Colonel Allen rode into Bennington to find the Grants no longer existing and his brother Heman one week dead. Colonel Herrick ordered fourteen cannon fired in Allen's honor, "thirteen for the United States, and one for young Vermont." That last cannon shot was the sole hopeful sound Allen heard.[60]

III

{Allen's} fortitude and firmness seem to have placed him out of the reach of misfortune. There is an original something in him that commands admiration; and his long captivity and sufferings have only served to increase if possible, his enthusiastic zeal.— Washington to the President of Congress, 12 May 1778

Ethan Allen had returned to the Green Mountains, but not to the Grants. Surrounded by the marks of a quickly changing world, Allen sensed his own insignificance. He had thought himself the necessary leader of his community, but his followers had acted without him in forming a new state, writing a constitution, battling to defend their towns, crafting a political identity.

The Vermonters did not need Ethan Allen. The would-be hero found himself amidst proven military heroes and expected to be received as an embarrassment, held at arm's length for his foolish attack on Montreal. The laurel had fallen on other brows. Being a prisoner of war had left its wounds. Coming home, a captive of his own unfulfilled expectations, cut deeper. "I thought to have enrolled my name in the list of illustrious American heroes," Allen wrote, "but was nipped in the bud." He determined to alter that situation.[61]

Allen appreciated his significance as the most famous of the early prisoners of war. Washington himself had employed Allen as a symbol of America's suffering, repeatedly calling forth the image of "the brave Colonel Allen, sent to England in irons." Appropriating this symbolic value, Allen found meaning and even glory in his failure, writing a narrative linking the trials of those in captivity with the larger struggle for freedom. Allen would not allow a single defeat to diminish his hero's aura; he would confront America with the daily heroism of those left to rot in British prisons.[62]

Within a few months of his return, Allen wrote a small book, *A Narrative of Colonel Ethan Allen's Captivity*. The *Narrative* enjoyed great popularity, going through eight editions in two years. Its readers discovered their soldiers holding true to the cause of American liberty while suffering the privations and cruelty of British prisons. On its surface, the *Narrative* is a classic piece of war propaganda, a public tirade calculated to put the worst possible face on the British, the most heroic face on the rebels, and the rosiest cast on prospects for victory. Throughout, it stands with Tom Paine's *Crisis Papers* as one of the great eulogies to superior American virtue and endurance and an effective call for continued struggle at the very moment when rebel military fortunes nearly hit bottom.[63]

At a deeper level, however, Allen's *Narrative* is an intensely personal document. Allen used his book as a sort of therapy to banish his depression and restore his ruptured self-esteem. He did so in typically Allenesque fashion: self-dramatization. As in his earlier life, Allen responded to disappointment and defeat by boasting and strutting. Faced with his own insignificance, he convinced first himself and then others of his power and centrality. While a prisoner, Allen had sustained himself by telling stories about his heroism in battle; in the *Narrative* he revived his heroism by telling stories about his captivity. By asserting himself in the most vivid and dramatic ways, Allen not only became a legend in his own times (and his own mind) but also secured his sense of identity.

If the *Narrative* represents Allen's idiosyncratic effort to regain his sense of self-worth, its form replicated a traditional New England literary form, the captivity narrative. Allen made no effort in his *Narrative* to disguise the dismal failure of his capture at Montreal. But this disaster was personal, of no strategic consequence to America. In this, as in many other particulars, Allen drew on the heritage of captivity narratives. In the older narratives the Christian survivor of some native outrage endured initial brutalities only to confront the powerful temptations of Indian culture. Allen's tale of captivity borrowed that plot but replaced the Indians with the British. Allen told of refusing the offer of a colonelcy in a Tory regiment with all the concomitant status and salary, as well as title to a large tract of land in the Green Mountains. Allen's rendition of the captivity narrative also added a new twist to the old story. Instead of a conflict between Christian civilization and infidel barbarity, Allen's *Narrative* pitted a decadent, overcivilized culture against a natural, uncorrupted America—represented, of course, by Ethan Allen.[64]

Allen found himself "in the power of a haughty and cruel nation" which offered few examples of compassion. "The word rebel applied to any vanquished persons," Allen wrote, "was thought (by the enemy) sufficient to sanctify whatever cruelties they were pleased to inflict death itself not excepted." Everyone who came into contact with the British lost their humanity, as Allen demonstrated in relating the atrocities which followed the fall of Fort Washington to the British in November 1776. The "merciless Britons" killed many prisoners on the spot, bringing the rest to New York under "slavish Hessian guards, . . . who were sent to America for no other design but cruelty and desolation." Hundreds of prisoners, including one of Allen's cousins, died as a consequence of their mistreatment, to "the hellish delight and triumph of the tories." It was "too much for me to bear as . . . I saw the tories exulting over the dead bodies of their murdered countrymen." One British officer said that he "wished them all dead" and treated them accordingly.

Allen protested the excessive cruelty of such violent British officers as Captain William Cunningham, removed from his post largely in response to Allen's persistence. By turning the British and their Tory allies into monsters, Allen sought to reinforce American commitment in a dark time.[65]

As in the captivity narratives of an earlier age, Allen's years in the clutches of the British savages intensified his commitments and loyalties. From his fellow captives he learned the meaning of being an American. The experience of the prisoners of war replicated in microcosm the suffering of all America: in the grip of a hateful tyranny seeking to starve them into submission, willing to see them die if they would not obey, Americans learned to rely on one another. While "the malignant hand of Britain . . . greatly reduced my constitution with stroke upon stroke," Allen and his fellow prisoners almost sank beneath the weight of British oppression. They used "every argument and entreaty that could be well conceived of, in order to obtain gentleman-like usage, to no purpose." As with the colonies, the tyrant ignored all their petitions. Allen found the preservation of "[our] injured little republic" in the camaraderie and unity of the prisoners. At his own worst moments, Allen found himself lifted from his depression by fellow prisoners who persuaded him that he did not face the hardships alone. The American prisoners boosted one another's courage and united when necessary to free one of their number from a particular peril.[66]

Where previous captivity narratives taught the traditional message of total dependence on God, Allen's narrative evoked a dependence on fellow democrats. At each moment of crisis in the *Narrative,* the prisoners save one another or receive a sudden unexpected assistance from secret democrats within the British army itself. Allen thus found in his captivity the essence of a transatlantic democratic movement. When the prison ship *Soleby* arrived in Cork and Madeira, delegations of local sympathizers brought supplies for the relief of the American prisoners. The people of Cork even requested that Allen be allowed to come ashore and attend a dinner in his honor. All this attention directed at a rebel seemed strange and discouraging to the commander of the ship, but then English officials have rarely understood the ingratitude of subject peoples. Further, Allen insisted, the British military itself was undermined by a secret egalitarianism which aided the prisoners in their darkest moments.[67]

Allen's updated, republican rendition of the captivity narrative not only gave the rebel cause a needed boost, it also served two crucial functions in his personal recovery from depression. First, the *Narrative* allowed Allen to cast himself back in the center of the action, as he had been at Ticonderoga, even if he was in prison. Allen could not think of himself as standing anywhere but at the center of his known universe, with all action revolving around him. That is why he felt so threatened coming home to a fundamentally transformed Grants. The *Narrative* permitted Allen to regain a sense of himself. If captivity withdrew him from the center of that revolution, he would make captivity central to the revolution.

Second, in his *Narrative* Allen reassured himself and everyone else that even in captivity he remained courageous, defiant, and democratic. To show resolution in such adversity would "eclipse the other actions of my life." In the process, Allen fashioned a theory of revolutionary warfare, one which de-emphasized violent conflict. A revolution, Allen argued, is not a series of battles but an extended political movement. Military action should remain the last resort of a rebel, for the preexisting state is always better able to fight battles. But politics, which Allen found primarily the art of theater, determines a revolution's outcome.[68]

The commander at Pendennis Castle in Falmouth, England, held all power in his hands. But he erred in welcoming visitors to observe and talk with the rebel prisoners, as with other primitive curiosities at a sideshow. Allen thus obtained the opportunity to educate the British "on the impracticality of Great Britain's conquering the (then) colonies of America" and on democracy. When one gentleman visitor ordered his servant to bring Allen a bowl of punch, Allen rejected it as a token of inequality. The gentleman then offered the bowl himself but refused "to drink with me in consequence of my being a state criminal: However I took the punch and drank it all down at one draught, and handed the gentleman the bowl: This made the spectators as well as myself merry." Two clergymen with whom Allen discussed "moral philosophy and christianity" expressed astonishment "that I should be acquainted with such topics." Allen attributed their surprise to judging the quality of a person by appearance alone.

Allen's behavior shocked his genteel tormentors, while his descriptions in the *Narrative* delighted his American readers. Instead of hanging his head in shame, Allen fought back as best he could, hurling invective and insult, arguing on equal terms with the most exalted of those who visited him. On one occasion, "in a fit of anger," Allen used his teeth to rip a small nail which held his handcuffs together out of the mortise (leaving, incidentally, a permanent chip in a front tooth, which he enjoyed showing off in later years). The story spread that Colonel Allen ate iron, and a padlock was put on his cuffs for the continued safety of the British.[69]

Allen identified himself to his captors as a "conjurer." Through the alchemy of his rhetoric he transformed defeat and hopelessness into triumph and salvation. The *Narrative* created a mythology for Ethan Allen and restored to its author a sense of his own power. Allen never ceased playing the hero, remaining larger than life as he stood with bared chest before the onslaught of a terrible enemy. By such reported conduct did Allen stand forth as the equal of the heroes of the Battle of Bennington. In fact, he set a new standard for heroism, even in captivity.[70]

The majority of Allen's readers had little trouble accepting the explicit message on the *Narrative*. But Allen played a more subtle game, one closely attuned to his political interests, through his conjunction of Yorker and Tory. Allen recorded that Governor Tryon "and several other perfidious and over-grown tories and land jobbers," old enemies of the Green Mountain Boys, came aboard the *Mercury* in New York. In consequence of their visit, the prisoners suffered increasingly severe treatment. Allen attributed the British refusal to exchange him to the New York land speculators. Even while Allen's *Narrative* sought the legitimation of the American Revolution through its stories of British atrocities, it also legitimated the cause of the Grants' settlers as the logical extension of revolutionary principles.[71]

The two sets of heroes—prisoners of war and Green Mountain Boys— shared not just their enemies but also a deep democratic conviction which persisted in the face of the harshest adversity. The prisoners, confined in a room with nothing but "excrement tubs" and without "regard to rank, education, or any other accomplishment," learned democracy whether they wanted to or not. They shared in their sufferings and "divided our scanty allowance as exact as possible," casting aside all previous distinctions, even those of military rank. The soldiers offered Allen, as a colonel, a larger portion, but "I refused to accept it, as . . . in my opinion I ought to partake equally with the rest, and set an example of virtue and fortitude to our little commonwealth."[72]

As Allen endeavored in his *Narrative* to make the Vermont separatist movement into the embodiment of the national struggle, so he tried to transform himself from an archetypical republican frontiersman into a national folk hero. Allen sought to reflect and elaborate a distinctive form of character with its roots in the frontier experience which encompassed the emerging American national character. To secure the success of Vermont and his leadership of that movement, Allen projected himself and the frontier on a wider cultural screen, calling forth an American national identity even as he reasserted and affirmed his own.

The *Narrative* is full of heroes, of common men filled with exceptional courage and fortitude. Allen admitted he could offer no better advice to his fellow prisoners than to enlist with the British, build up their strength, and desert at the first opportunity. But they consistently rejected his suggestion: "The integrity of these suffering prisoners is hardly credible. Many hundreds, I am confident, submitted to death, rather than enlist in the British service." The stamina and bravery of these Americans, Allen wrote, should inspire pride and gratitude in his readers. If the British served as the perfect enemy—stupid and petty, cruel and cowardly, snobbish and vacillating—then the Americans appeared in Allen's *Narrative* as bright, egalitarian, physically courageous, and graceful under pressure. Allen did more than run down an opponent, he offered an American identity formed in a community of rebels. And Ethan Allen was, as Guy Johnson called him, the rebels' "most daring Partizan."[73]

Americans, Allen wrote, must stop thinking of themselves as English. Too many Americans regarded the British as cousins and the Revolution as a family dispute. Allen sought to persuade them that the British could not be trusted and that the war would have but one victor. He cautioned his readers to take the darkest experiences of war as a vision of the dire alternative to victory. "I was persuaded," Allen wrote in 1779, "that it was a premeditated and systematical plan of the British council, to destroy the youths of our land . . . and make it submit to their despotism." They should look to the fortitude of their prisoners of war as worthy examples and learn what Allen had, "the intrinsic worth of perseverance." More than just a military struggle, the Revolution hinged on psychological battles. Harbingers of eventual victory could be found in the internal divisions of the British, the support of democrats around the Atlantic world, the desperation and cruelty of the Tories, and the undying dedication of the American prisoners of war.[74]

Allen valued the lessons of his captivity. In the prisoners' "little commonwealth," a facade of strength evidenced its utility, as it had in Allen's earlier struggle with New York. But the power of unity, the necessity of holding together in the face of a superior foe, came to Allen as a revelation, and as a new weapon. Neither the image nor the reality of strength proved sufficient against an aroused people. "Your power," Allen told the English at the end of his *Narrative,* "is by no means sufficient to support your vanity." Power undirected "by virtue [and] wisdom . . . never fails finally to destroy itself." [75]

The errors of British policy stayed with Allen. He would take his bitterly learned lessons back with him to govern and protect a new state. Allen found the ultimate moral of his captivity in the heavy price of defeat. Ethan Allen would do everything in his power to save himself, and Vermont, from that fate. He would never lose another battle.

CHAPTER SEVEN

Law and Political Power

INSIDE the small wooden jailhouse in Bennington, Vermont, David Redding waited for frontier justice to exact its price. A Vermont court had found Redding, a New York Loyalist, guilty of fighting with the British against his fellow Americans and of stealing horses for Burgoyne's recently defeated army. But that morning, 4 June 1778, John Burnham, the only person in that part of Vermont who could make any claim to knowledge of the law, pointed out to the governor and his council that a jury of only six men had passed judgment on Redding, whereas English common law required twelve. The embarrassed council ordered a stay of execution. An angry crowd gathered outside the jail, denied the spectacle of a public execution, called for vengeance; it had come to hang Redding, not to protect his inalienable rights as a freeborn Englishman.

Just as the nervous sheriff sent for reinforcements, a long absent voice shouted clearly above the crowd's din, "Attention the whole!" After two years as a British prisoner, Ethan Allen made his dramatic reentry to Vermont politics, leaping onto a tree stump and obtaining the attention of the crowd in his usual flamboyant fashion. Witnesses reported that Allen made a colorful and amusing speech, quieting the crowd's disappointment and calling on it not to besmirch the fair name of Vermont with any hint of injustice. He closed with the peculiar assurance that the next day someone would be hanged—if not Redding, then Allen himself. The crowd roared its approval and dispersed to toast Ethan Allen.

To keep his promise, Allen had his old friend Governor Thomas Chittenden appoint him state prosecutor. Chittenden circumvented the fact that Redding's crimes occurred in New York, which requested his extradition, by appointing Allen, in effect, a United States attorney. The governor proclaimed Allen prosecutor "to act in the Capacity & to do the duty of State Attorney in the cause depending Between this & the United States of America & David Redding." Chittenden dismissed as irrelevant the facts that Redding had committed no crime in Vermont other than escaping from its officers and that Vermont, which was not part of the United States, had no authority to appoint attorneys to act in the nation's interests. But then, such technicalities had never mattered to the Grants' inhabitants, now self-proclaimed Vermonters. As Allen persuaded Chittenden and his council, the appearance of legality and legitimacy remained all-important. Vermont gained an aura of power and comradeship with the United States, while thumbing its nose at the authority of New York.[1]

Redding's new trial on 6 June proved brief and effective. Defense counsel John Burnham's knowledge of correct legal procedures proved no match for Allen's rhetoric, and the properly constituted twelve-man jury duly found Redding guilty. He was hanged to great public approval the same afternoon. The presence of the entire General Assembly at Redding's hanging just two days after Burnham won his stay suggests the importance attached to this execution by the state of Vermont.[2]

Redding's trial represented a crucial moment in Vermont's thirty-year struggle with New York. With the courtroom the main battlefield of that conflict, the efficacy of the legal system sponsored by the states contending for legitimacy proved essential to the process of revolution and state formation in Vermont. Inability to triumph in the courthouse translated into a failure to win the consent of the governed. Thus, the Vermont government's prosecution of Redding, despite New York's request for his transportation to its jurisdiction, served to emphasize the independence of the new state. Allen's quick actions demonstrated that the power of Vermont and its courts was at least equal to that of New York and obviously superior within the contested jurisdiction of the former New Hampshire Grants. In the process Allen prevented a lynching, an act of lawlessness that would have been a black mark against the state—though in the end Allen's intervention made no difference to David Redding.[3]

Redding's trial also represented a crucial moment in the political career of Ethan Allen. With his *Narrative*, Allen resolved his first great crisis, restoring his credibility on the national scale and overcoming the stigma of personal defeat. Likewise, Allen used the Redding case and his appointment as prosecutor to reassert his leadership on the local scene after the hiatus of captivity. Two powerful weapons supported his efforts: a functioning court system and a democratic constitution. Allen manipulated each with his own style of confrontational politics, winning internal unity for Vermont while depriving New York of its legitimacy to rule. In the years from 1778 through 1783, Ethan Allen and his adherents would employ the courts, as well as the militia and the constitution, to punish their nearest enemies: Vermont's resident Loyalists, conservatives, and Yorkers. In the same years the Allen faction would use these same institutions in a populist strategy to capture the hearts and minds of the majority of Vermonters and, of course, to gain certain personal advantages.

I

The government of New-York . . . received its life and spirit by a mistical communication . . . from the sovereign will of the royal adjudicator; . . . and the declaration of independence cutting the vital union, occasioned this line like a lamp to go out which is exhausted of oil, and leave no traces of its existence.
—Ethan Allen, 1779

The American Revolution should have ended the dispute with New York, or so Ethan Allen thought. The order extending New York's border to the Connecticut River "may be well accounted one of the cruel acts of the Crown" negated by the Declaration of Independence. The Revolution placed all Americans in a state of nature, free to rewrite their social contract.[4]

The new government of the state of New York and the Continental Congress disagreed. In their view the old colonial borders held, despite their many contradictions. In order to protect its component states, Congress employed what amounted to Loyalist reasoning: only existing governments enjoy legitimacy. In contrast, Vermont used revolutionary logic, what Thomas Jefferson called the "Vermont doctrine": the people can create their own states. Congressional resistance eventually forced Vermont to establish that its independence did not depend on the independence of the United States, effectively proving its point that the citizens actuated government.[5]

New York's reasoning in favor of its right to the Green Mountains did not change much in twenty years. In fact, the most cogent presentations of its case, both before and after the Revolution, were made by the same man, James Duane. Duane's opinion remained unchanged: the king of England had granted the region to New York. To his original evidence, royal charters and decisions of the Privy Council, Duane added only the opinion of Congress that New York retained its colonial borders. Duane rejected Vermont's argument that it had an equal right to declare independence as striking at the "very foundation of all social liberty, Government and security." Duane desperately wanted to have it both ways. On the one hand he argued that the royal province of New York no longer existed, so that the inhabitants of the Grants had no cause for complaint "under our present free and happy Constitution." On the other hand, as a former member of the provincial government, Duane assured everyone that the crown government had never oppressed anyone.[6]

Supporters of New York within the Grants appreciated the limited appeal of Duane's views and argued instead from expediency against the existence of Vermont. The Cumberland County Yorkers issued a proclamation in 1777 declaring it "impolitic and dangerous" to form a new state, offering four objections to "this offspring of anarchy": the "confusion" of acting without congressional approval; the "inability of the people to support a separate government, however frugally the public moneys are managed"; "the very great scarcity of men properly qualified to make and put into execution a wise system of laws"; and the need to unite in the common struggle with the British. Supporters of Vermont were all people with "little, or not any property which they can claim under any grant whatever." Creating a propertyless lower class in their imaginations, the eastside Yorkers proceeded to feel threatened by that class and begged for outside intervention. They closed by calling the Vermonters back to the "tranquillity and submission to the just and necessary authority of those who . . . are regularly appointed to rule over us." Strange words in the midst of a revolution.[7]

But the Yorkers expected little tranquillity from their neighbors and warned their government that the Vermonters "will never submit to the authority of the State of New York until compelled to do so by the sword." New York turned to Congress for that aid, insisting that it had not itself crushed these "wicked disaffected and turbulent Persons" only "from an apprehension that it might . . . weaken our Exertions in the common Cause." Despite the common cause, New York wanted to sack the "outlaw" Seth Warner from his command and dissolve his regiment. As the disputed counties "are of great Extent and Fertility" and constituted a "very valuable Part of this State," New York's Provincial Congress threatened to abandon the war if Congress did not "take speedy and vigorous measures for reducing them [Vermont] to an obedience" to New York. Responsibility had been passed from Cumberland County to New York to the Continental Congress.[8]

Congress passed more resolutions. Seeking to avoid an open conflict in the midst of war, Congress hoped that the Vermonters would listen to reason and abandon their government for that of New York.[9] In late July 1777 James Clay, chair of New York's Committee of Safety in Cumberland County, ordered town meetings to read the congressional resolutions. The Vermont Council of Safety arrested Clay and outlawed his committee. The congressional resolutions remained just that, intentions rather than deeds.[10]

Vermont's quick action damaged the authority and prestige of New York, but New York itself provided the most persuasive arguments for Vermont's existence. New York continued to base its claim to the Green Mountains on crown decisions, validating for many Allen's assertion that the Revolution had not diminished the power of the same old land jobbers who sought to steal "the lands from under our feet." New York's legislature reinforced this close identification between the colony and state of New York by voting to retain quitrents, now due to the state government rather than the king. It followed this act with the constitution of 1777, which shoved the majority of Grants inhabitants off the fence.[11]

A conservative document, New York's constitution seemed to many in Vermont a step backwards. Primogeniture and entail and the appointment of local officials, violations of New England ways, aroused especial condemnation; but far more threatening, the constitution affirmed all land grants by the colony of New York, invalidating the deeds held by nearly every settler in Vermont. To enforce these provisions, the constitution retained the colonial judiciary largely unchanged, even to the hated court of chancery.

A political disaster to most Vermonters, the New York Constitution lacked a bill of rights, created a strong central government with a powerful executive who had the right to prorogue the legislature and a Council of Revision with veto power over all legislation, and maintained a strict property qualification for the franchise which excluded the vast majority of those living in the Green Mountains. Compared to Vermont's constitution, New York's appeared little different from prerevolutionary structures. As one New York historian put it, "the Constitution of 1777 was conspicuous for the absence of pronounced democratic innovations." [12]

To ensure that the northeast counties learned of its constitution, New York's Provincial Congress sent copies with orders to hold an election. Most town meetings which considered the matter rejected New York's authority. Ebenezer Hoisington, Windsor's county committee representative, left no doubt as to the feelings of his town: "[I] Do now in behalf of sd town Enter my protest against any proceeding under the State of New York either directly or indirectly." Refusing to conduct New York's elections, Jacob Bayley of Newbury informed the New York council that "the people before they saw the constitution, were not willing to trouble themselves about a separation from the state of New York, but now almost to a man they are violent for it." Bayley decided that the new constitution posed a greater threat to his way of life than the "heads of the Green [Mountain] men." The Allens could not have asked for a better inducement to support their independent state. By June 1777 only nine Cumberland County towns remained undecided or loyal to New York. [13]

Ira Allen spent much of 1777 traveling through Vermont, inviting each town to compare the constitutions of Vermont and New York. The town meetings must decide the merits of each constitution, since neither carried any other legitimation. Allen thought the distinction simple: Vermont offered a democratic constitution while New York did not. [14]

Establishing mechanisms by which the people's will might be known formed the key problem for republicanism. Vermont asked its towns. Forty towns validated this approach by approving the constitution and participating in the first state election. The towns' representatives renewed their social contract four times over the next fifteen years. [15]

The Vermonters established a government actuated by "the consent, approbation and authority of the people, which is the fountain of all temporal power." Doing so, Ethan Allen wrote, put them on "an equal footing with their New-York adversaries, and will finally enable them to baffle all [New York's] machinations and devices." New Hampshire's government recognized this equality by treating Vermont as an independent state in their joint resistance to the British invasion. The interim Vermont government responded by acting quickly and effectively to meet Burgoyne, provisioning Stark's troops and raising a regiment of rangers to be paid for, on Ira Allen's suggestion, by confiscating the estates of their enemies.[16]

In the context of minimal orthodoxy—every state's constitution was an experiment on some level—Vermont's system of government bore the same legitimacy as the rest. It grew from the Vermonters' experience with committees of safety, which acted like unicameral assemblies complete with executive councils. The Vermont Constitution re-created this experiential structure on the state level just as had the province-wide committees of safety in New York and New Hampshire. Most states abandoned political experimentation with their constitutions and returned to traditional political hierarchies.[17] Vermont, as Ethan and Ira Allen wrote, institutionalized the American Revolution in its constitution, which stood as the foundation of all laws.[18]

Political power in Vermont operated on four levels. Town meetings had the greatest impact on the daily lives of most people, deciding local issues from the control and marking of livestock to the construction of roads. The representatives of these town meetings met for a few weeks every year in the General Assembly to pass legislation necessary for the state's security and the maintenance of the courts. The legislature claimed sovereignty but met too seldom to exercise control in a consistent and rigorous fashion. To manage the regular operation of and gain credibility for the state of Vermont, the people elected the governor and his twelve-member council, who acted in concert with the assembly during its sessions, attending its meetings and participating in its committees. Commanding extensive powers, the council operated only so far as the towns allowed their own authority to be circumvented. Generally the council addressed matters requiring immediate action which no single town could handle, from intratown disputes to paying the militia.[19]

Such were the three official rankings of political authority. But a fourth locus of power served as a unifying symbol and carried the weight of enforcement—Ethan Allen and the Green Mountain Boys. What made Vermont unique was its crowd transmuted into a military force, its frontier outlaws reincarnated as revolutionary heroes. No other state boasted such a militia, which, ignoring official forms, created and activated itself. At the center of the Green Mountain Boys' effectiveness stood the even more original Ethan Allen and his popular theater of Old Testament invective and vengeance.[20]

The Green Mountain Boys became the symbol of Vermont's legitimacy as the Continental army did for the United States, with the key difference that the Green Mountain Boys never came into significant conflict with the supporting population, as they were one and the same. The Green Mountain Boys bridged the gap between militia ineffectiveness and the threat of a standing army by their political orientation. The group was created and existed for a precise political purpose, to maintain local autonomy. Hundreds of Grants settlers participated in the invasion of Canada and the later defense of the northern frontier. Operating in their own units, the Green Mountain Boys became soldiers in a just cause rather than outlaws. And along the way they acquired experience which New York and the Continental Congress came to fear, learning the trade of war in defeat and victory. By 1780 few adult males in the Grants had not served under arms. These soldiers felt a right to an equal share of the Revolution and its promises of liberty and independence.[21]

The Green Mountain Boys also formed the activist core of the pro-Vermont and pro-Allen political faction. Ethan Allen worked hard to equate his faction's leadership with the very existence of Vermont. Hardly a political party, the Allen faction, as it is usually identified by historians, was a network of personal connections moving outward from the Allen family and dedicated to the maintenance of Vermont and its democratic constitution. In the first decade of Vermont statehood this faction filled nearly every state office, including Governor Thomas Chittenden, Treasurer Ira Allen, state's attorney Stephen Bradley, and almost every member of the governor's council and Superior Court.

Allen's leadership rested on the personalization of political authority. His power did not emerge from elected office, and his sole official position was commander of the state militia. But this rank proved sufficient, especially as he freely sat in on any governmental body he chose, from the council to the courts. Command of the Green Mountain Boys made Allen the defender of the frontiers and the stability of Vermont while supplying him with the requisite force for coercing Yorkers and other hesitant citizens. The assembly showed its support by passing resolutions giving Allen the right "to transact the political businesses of this state

as often as it may be found Necessary"—wonderfully inclusive word-
ing. After his much-appreciated handling of the Redding trial, Allen
became the state's spokesman, responding in Vermont's name to issues
as diverse as requests for official appointments to informing Congress of
Vermont's intention to sequester the estates of Tories. As a professional
troubleshooter, Allen regularly received notes against the state from the
governor for settling "some discontent among the People" and attending
to "important Public Business." Allen used these notes to purchase state
lands, closing the circle from desire to action.[22]

The lost children of Eldad Taylor exemplify Allen's ability to draw
others to him. In the last days of May 1780, Taylor's two daughters,
aged four and seven, wandered into the woods. With night falling, the
parents called on their neighbors to help search for the girls. Through
the night and all the next day the worried adults combed the thick
Sunderland woods without success. On the second day volunteers from
adjacent towns arrived, dozens of people walking through the woods
with torches, shouting for the lost girls. At mid-afternoon of the third
day the exhausted searchers gathered together with the despairing parents, indicating their intention to give up.

But one of the Taylors' neighbors was Ethan Allen. Allen pointed to
the mother and father, insisting that everyone present make the Taylors' case their own, feel their grief and fear, and then ask themselves if
they could return home without making one more effort to find the lost
girls, who even now spent their last energy in crying for their father and
mother to save them. Tears rolling down his cheeks, Allen swayed the
crowd with his passion as he swore that he would not quit. Witnesses
reported that the volunteers joined him in tears and renewed their resolve to find the lost girls. Just before nightfall the searchers discovered
the children, weak with hunger and hiding in terror in a shattered tree
trunk, but still alive. Until the end of his life, Eldad Taylor would allow
no one to speak ill of Allen in his company. Family and community
aroused such emotions in frontier Vermont; Ethan Allen called forth
such loyalty. Through appeals to personal allegiance, Allen convinced
the people of Vermont that they could stand alone against the world.[23]

And it did seem as though the world opposed them. While the British
army and a hostile Congress confronted Vermont, Allen deemed these
less immediate obstacles than his three internal opponents: loyalists,
Yorkers, and conservative Vermonters.

A few Loyalists supported the Grants cause but opposed Allen's patriot stance. Distinguishing one issue as local and the other as imperial, these Loyalists found no contradiction between Grants autonomy and British sovereignty. Most Loyalists, though, remained pro–New York, allowing the Allens to lump both groups together as "Tories," labeling even patriot Yorkers British supporters. Using this conjunction of Loyalists with Yorkers as justification, Vermont's constitutional convention required every male over sixteen to pledge loyalty to its "Covenant" and to the new United States. Neither Yorkers nor Loyalists could take this oath in good conscience, further isolating them from their communities and opening them to the charge of treason.[24]

Opposition to the Allens among pro-Vermonters grew slowly. Initially this fragmented, internal opposition relied on Jacob Bayley to combat Allen's leadership. But Bayley originally supported New York and changed sides grudgingly, limiting his influence to the Coos country of northeastern Vermont. In the same way, other potential competitors for leadership, such as Nathan Stone, discredited themselves by their indecisiveness and history of shifting loyalties.[25]

Conservatives who supported both Vermont and American independence but worked to undermine the radical political changes instituted by the Allens found their leadership in the newcomers Nathaniel Chipman and Isaac Tichenor—"Jersey Slick" as Ira Allen labeled him. In the late 1770s and early 1780s Chipman and Tichenor worked with the Allens to maintain Vermont's independence, while doing their best to alter the nature and future character of that autonomy by battling the Allens for control of the legislature. They found most of their supporters among the larger landowners along the Connecticut River, other ambitious newcomers, and former Loyalists and Yorkers. The conservative patriots distrusted the committees of safety and democratic enthusiasm. In place of the committees, the conservatives favored a forceful legislature and an independent judiciary, heaping contempt on elected judges and the Green Mountain Boys.[26]

It is not easy to pin down either faction as personal networks superseded political opinions. Several leading conservatives and Loyalists supported the Allens. For instance, the Knowlton family of Newfane remained staunch Allen adherents after Ethan Allen saved the Loyalist Luke Knowlton from an angry mob. The conservatives, while few in number, enjoyed great influence in the state because of their higher level of education, with nearly every lawyer supporting Tichenor and Chipman in their efforts to displace the Allens. Yet only once in Vermont's first twenty years did the conservatives gain control of the state government, and then by subterfuge. A broad-based coalition, the Allen faction consistently commanded large majorities in statewide elections, especially dominating the west side of the Green Mountains. Nonetheless, the Chipman-Tichenor faction remained a major annoyance to the Allens.[27]

Ira Allen found the perfect weapon to combat all three opponents in the courts. In July 1777 Allen suggested that the Vermont Council of Safety create a commission of confiscation to seize the property of Loyalists, finding precedent in New York's commissioners of sequestration. Allen went beyond previous conceptions in calling on the commissioners to act in a judicial capacity to expropriate the property of those "enemical" to the state's interests. This careful choice of words included anyone who opposed the continued independence of Vermont, whether through support of England or New York. Allen appreciated fully the political usefulness of an activist judiciary.[28]

Ethan Allen, who often served as a judge on the courts of sequestration, argued that all Yorkers were Tories, and the only good Tory was a propertyless one. Shortly after the Redding trial, Allen transported "seventeen wicked Tories" to the Albany jail. These men insisted they were guilty only of "acknowledging themselves to be subjects of the State of New York, and not recognizing the validity and existence of the State of Vermont." Allen remained unmoved, for the Albany seventeen had become New York's problem, leaving their land for Vermont to expropriate. Vermont got in the habit early on of trying Yorkers as Loyalists and banishing them.[29]

The funds raised from the rent or sale of confiscated lands paid for military defenses against the British, further enhancing Vermont's legitimacy by linking its cause ever closer to that of revolutionary America. As Ira Allen honestly acknowledged, "In consequence of internal divisions, and to make government popular, it was thought good policy not to lay any taxes on the people but to raise a sufficient revenue out of the property confiscated." The courts of sequestration attained Allen's goals, winning the enthusiastic support and loyalty of most Vermonters while undercutting the political opposition. This policy proved a boon to Vermonters who did not have to pay for their revolution.[30]

The commissions of sequestration served primarily as a tool of the Allen faction, as is evidenced by the greater number of confiscations in the west. Between October 1778 and February 1779 the state sold thirty-three parcels in Bennington County but none in Cumberland County. In the single month of April 1778 the westside commissioners brought writs against 158 people in twenty-four towns, declaring that they had abandoned their property rights through treasonable activities. Sequestration thus touched the life of almost every community on the west side of the mountains. The east sought compromise and accommodation with the Yorkers, while the west—in more immediate danger from New York—followed the Allens in seeing no reason to pull its punches.

This policy division ended in 1779, when the assembly passed the Banishment Act forbidding enemies of the state from returning to Vermont and confiscating their property. To enforce this law, Governor Chittenden created a new court of sequestration under Ethan Allen's personal control which quickly sold a hundred parcels of land on both sides of the Green Mountains. The assembly followed up by authorizing itself to dispose of all unappropriated lands in the north of Vermont, tens of thousands of acres with which to meet government expenses while attracting new settlers.[31]

The gears of this self-legitimating machine remained the Green Mountain Boys and their commanding general, Ethan Allen. Allen petitioned the assembly to meet government expenses by confiscating Loyalist estates, saw that act through the assembly and into law, served on the first court of sequestration, and led the court through the western townships on its journey of retribution. While the commission let most Loyalists off with a small fine, the largest landowners lost everything: William Smith listed his losses at £26,000; Crean Brush, nearly 30,000 acres; Samuel Peters, 56,000 acres; Justus Sherwood, 13,000 acres; James Rogers, 47,000 acres.[32]

The government wanted to leave no doubt that only its approval could end exile and return an individual to his community. The Vermont council recommended leniency to those with small holdings and allowed Loyalists to return so long as they saw "their Eror confess their fault & are willing to defend their Country's Cause." On several occasions the council ordered that the families of expropriated Loyalists, even of old enemies like John Munro and Dr. Samuel Adams, be left sufficient property and livestock to assure that they did not suffer for the folly of one of their number. But a banished person who returned to Vermont before a family member procured absolution from the assembly faced forty lashes a week until he left the state. In brief, the Allens had discovered a legal method of overcoming all their internal opponents. The courts served either to win over or to dispossess those who refused to accept Ethan Allen's vision of Vermont.[33]

Allen came up with one more imaginative use for confiscated land; he gave it to powerful rebel leaders outside Vermont. Stealing the trick from Benning Wentworth, Allen often included prominent members of Congress or the Continental army in grants for northern lands, took blank deeds with him when visiting some dispenser of influence, and circulated land grant petitions among Continental soldiers. Thus did John and Abigail Adams, John Witherspoon, General James Sullivan, and John Paul Jones, among others, find themselves the surprised owners of Vermont lands. Pierce Butler angrily condemned this "shameful and scandalous affair," but to no effect.[34]

As a final advantage, the commissions of sequestration linked the towns closer to the state government. The council required that representatives from three towns review all cases. Consultation established a common bond while in no way threatening local power; and because all fines and proceeds from sales went to the state, a local committee could not attempt to gain someone's property for its own use. Neither did the commissioners for sequestration become an entrenched officialdom, a prime complaint against the British. The commissions remained ad hoc, appointed by the council to treat a precise caseload and then dissolved. The council hoped to promote unity through the amelioration of local animosities; the courts of sequestration served this intent well.[35]

With the legislature's approval, commissioners sold the land of those they thought Vermont better rid of and confiscated movable goods— primarily crops and livestock—to intimidate those reluctant to acknowledge Vermont's government. The former method was more profitable; the latter more effective in controlling the populace without losing population and support. As a compromise between local demands and the needs of the state, and mindful of the dangers of disrupting family connections needlessly, the Council of Safety often confined non-Loyalist "enemical persons" to their property "for the time being." Thus the state ordered Samuel Wells, a patriot Yorker judge, to stay on his farm for the war's duration. Confinement did not prevent Wells from protecting the interests of son-in-law Samuel Gale who had joined the British army. Moved by the threat of economic loss, Yorkers generally kept their views private. And silence was good enough for the Allens.[36]

Most important for Vermont's residents, the commissioners heard cases of conflicting title. Not surprisingly, disputes between New York and New Hampshire grants ended with the latter being upheld. In 1780 Chittenden simplified the process by declaring all New York titles null and void.[37]

Vermont went further than other American states in its use of the courts of sequestration as a tool for determining social policy. The Allens had long encouraged settlement and saw sequestration as a means toward that end. At the 1779 and 1780 land auctions, the council gave preference to new settlers, especially veterans—or active members—of the Continental army. As Ira Allen said, former soldiers tended to be "staunch friends of the new government," for Vermont fulfilled Congress's long-deferred promise of cheap land. The commissioners also expropriated the lands of absentee owners, though they first had to label the owners Tories—a simple matter. On the other hand, Ethan Allen persuaded the assembly that its land grants should allow all those already settled to retain their property, with the right to become proprietors. The state thus encouraged those who owned land in Vermont to live there.[38]

Some corruption and outright theft marked this system. The Vermont Superior Court heard a dozen cases in its first three years against local officials who stole confiscated property. As one complaint stated, "Coll. Williams can Enform Where a Number of horses is Gone that are cared by Certain Persons who think tis No Harm to Stele from a State because a Tory once owned them." The court tended to deal severely with such miscreants.[39]

Despite the government's best efforts, some people used the courts to settle old scores. Leonard Spaulding got back at the Lovells, who had hauled him into New York's courts several times, by preventing them from taking over the land titles of a Loyalist family member. Jacob Bayley hounded his Loyalist opponent John Peters out of the state and saw to the confiscation of his property. Bayley thought that being on the winning side should bring some recompense.[40]

Perhaps the greatest abuse of the system came from the council itself. Ethan Allen and his family and friends invested heavily in sequestered properties, acquiring thousands of acres in addition to their Onion River lands. At the first auction Allen paid £200 for 150 acres from the estate of William Marsh. As one Loyalist wrote, "Claimants title being under a New York Patent was reckoned bad. . . . Col. Allen has got the land." [41]

II

As the people seemed inclined for a popular government, the Constitution was so made. —Ira Allen

Vermonters need not have put up with such corruption. In the years immediately following the establishment of Vermont, New York still held the superior legal claim to the region, the support of the majority of the Continental Congress, and the allegiance of a great number of Vermont's wealthiest settlers. On the other hand, Vermont's courts operated the one translocal institution which truly mattered to the average citizen, regulating the economy through the quick and efficient settlement of debt cases and enforcing their decisions with a vigor unknown to New York's courts. Just as the courts undermined the enemies of Vermont's independence and the Allen faction, so they operated constructively to foster collective loyalty to the new state of Vermont and its leadership.

Before 1777 the Grants had to rely on the town structure or turn to New York's courts for the resolution of conflicts. Most Grants settlers, wedded to New England's heritage of distrust for the fine points of law and a perception of the legal system as necessarily responsive to local needs, thought New York's legal structure heavy with technicalities and extracommunal powers. For Yorkers, the judiciary operated to protect the interest and property of the hierarchy as the best means of maintaining order. For Vermonters, the courts reinforced community standards while protecting property. As Allen wrote in 1774, the law should be servant to the "labouring Men that support the World." While centralizing tendencies emerged in the settled regions of New England during the eighteenth century, frontier institutions, including courts, remained based in the individual community and represented local concerns. [42]

The seedbed of Vermont's ad hoc legal structure lay in this background of practical, localized law. Most Grants settlers shared the sentiments expressed in the Connecticut law of 1686 which stated that judgments should not be reversed due to technical errors. In contrast, New

York granted appeals only on technical grounds. These writs of error could not consider the merits of the case or mitigating circumstances. Lieutenant Governor Cadwallader Colden held that the great proprietors preserved this structure for their own advantage, fearing appeal past the judges they owned. These few great families ruled the assembly and courts "in all Matters of Importance." Independence changed little. The legislature proclaimed the statutes and common law of the colony of New York the law of the new state, except insofar as the legislature decided otherwise. In essence it said nothing but that the elite intended to retain their power.[43]

In contrast, the new state of Vermont rejected a strict adherence to common law.[44] With all legal decisions open to appeal to the legislature, statute law reigned supreme. Making the legislature the final authority in all legal matters also removed the one alternative standard to which dissidents might appeal. But Allen, like other radical republicans, insisted that the people needed no protection from their own representatives. The only real threat to liberty could come from a corrupt executive or judiciary.

In Ethan Allen's view, the state served only two functions beyond his personal aggrandizement: protecting the frontiers and maintaining economic order and social stability through the courts. And not even Allen could twist Vermont's courts to his personal service; he often lost cases, and his Loyalist brother Levi lost his lands.[45] Vermonters knew exactly what their courts were about: upholding their land titles, maintaining the equilibrium of a delicately balanced debt-based economy, enforcing the newly established political and social structures, and eliminating any enemies of that system. That such a judiciary often served the interests of the Allens is correct; that those interests tended to coincide with those of almost all holders of titles from New Hampshire is equally true.[46]

Vermonters sought and attained an informal and flexible legal structure. Points of law had their place, but justice came first. Lawyers, every one of whom had supported New York, evoked such popular metaphors as vultures, creeping parasites, and agents of oppression. Several times in the 1780s the assembly considered limiting the number of attorneys and their fees. In one memorable proclamation Governor Chittenden rejected the suggestion that lawyers and deputy sheriffs be put to death, suggesting instead that lawsuits be taxed. As Stephen Jacob wrote Ezra Stiles, "Ethan Allen swore *by himself* that the man who should presume

to make use of Law Logick should be cut off from among his People."
Given the popular election of judges, it is not surprising that only one
lawyer held that office in Vermont's first fifteen years. Lawyers remained
rarer than Yale divinity school graduates in the Green Mountains, and
even less popular.[47]

The judges shared their constituents' dislike of lawyers and preference
for informality. When an attorney protested a deed as invalid for lack of a
proper seal, the judge sealed it on the spot, declaring that "the objection
is removed." The courtroom environment encouraged a relaxed attitude toward the law. The Bennington County court met at Jonas Fay's
Catamount Tavern, where Ethan Allen spent his free time drinking.
Rutland's county court convened at Solomon Bingham's tavern, holding
its sessions in the bar, the jury retiring to the barn to deliberate, with
the outhouse serving as jail. Formality in such a courthouse would have
proved difficult.[48]

Vermont's judges reinforced the popular conception of a natural sense
of justice understandable by anyone. In a landmark decision, a run-
away slave appeared in court demanding recognition of his right to
stay in Vermont. His "master" responded by producing the bill of sale
from the previous owner. The judge demanded a bill of sale from "God
Almighty" as original proprietor before he would recognize title. The
former slave stayed in Vermont, a free man. Such creative interpretation
of the law allowed Vermont to maintain its jurisdiction in the face of
hostile superior authority, including the Continental Congress. Just as
in the Redding case, Vermont's judges did not hesitate to extend their
jurisdiction into whatever areas they deemed necessary for the security of
the state. And as Ethan Allen had so often argued, communal security
on the frontier required the preservation of economic order, which in
turn necessitated the recognition of the settlers' land titles.[49]

Economic uncertainty propelled Vermont's early courts to widespread
acceptance. The poverty of the northern frontier required some regulating mechanism, a system which would compensate for the lack of
capital. The structuring of debts formed the cornerstone of this frontier
economy. Vermont's courts ensured the trust such a system necessitated.[50]

Not part of a market economy, the northern frontier operated on a
careful accounting of localized exchanges. The Green Mountain settlers
recorded every transaction, no matter how small, in their account books,

reckoning relative indebtedness every few years. The state of Vermont functioned under this same structure: balancing book accounts, exchanging pieces of paper, working entirely on credit, and postponing its own payments as long as possible.[51]

Vermonters institutionalized their economic weakness. Lacking a currency, they made everything serve the function of exchange; not being part of an extended market system which could support specialized business enterprises, they got along without specialization and relied on each other; devoid of capital, they transformed mutual obligation into a viable economic structure. They glorified independence but understood it as based on interdependence. As the French visitor Jacques-Pierre Brissot concluded, "Their mutual wants produce mutual dependence."[52]

But their trust-based economy required some means of enforcement, and thus arose the need for an effective court system. New York's courts had failed to fill that simple criterion. Vermont's competing system earned the confidence of local creditors and debtors, executing most debt cases to the satisfaction of the plaintiffs within a few months of the court's decision. New York's courts had demanded payment in specie, which almost no family on the frontier could acquire. Vermont's judiciary allowed and expected that damages and court costs would be paid in kind and accepted. As with all other debts, people paid with whatever they had, from rum to labor to corn. Debtors even produced currency, though plaintiffs avoided such payment as it carried little functional value.[53] Occasionally defendants executed debts by enacting new debts, agreeing to pay as soon as they got in the harvest, or some other forestalling tactic. But rarely did a losing defendant avoid payment for as long as a year without finding his property seized, as Ethan Allen—who made a political virtue of waiting out one's opponents—discovered on several occasions. When Benjamin Bird sued Allen for payment of an old debt, Allen asked for a continuance. Instead, the court ordered him to pay Bird £33. Shortly thereafter, Bird found himself the proud owner of Onion River land. The court accepted delays but not unnecessary avoidance.[54]

Like Allen, most Green Mountain settlers relied on land as a source of debt payment, or capital transference, since it was the one commodity which most everyone owned in excess of immediate use. Debtors most often paid small debts or fines with crops and livestock. But for obligations above £25, land titles usually traded hands. In the absence of specie, land titles functioned as currency, as an agreed-upon medium of exchange. The courts guaranteed this system by protecting and regulating the land titles of the Vermonters, something New York's courts would not do.[55]

In securing the settlers in their lands, Vermont's courts also secured them in their communities. A highly litigious people, like all New Englanders, Vermonters averaged fifty court cases per one thousand inhabitants a year. Yet Vermonters hesitated to sue neighbors. Outsiders—social outcasts or members of a political minority—and newcomers served as regular targets and instigators of lawsuits. Dragging a neighbor into court more than once a year indicated a high degree of alienation from the community. People such as the much reviled lawyer Crean Brush, the Yorker Francis Prouty, and the Loyalist Luke Knowlton appear constantly in the court records on one side or another of a lawsuit. Newcomers, who needed to borrow most of the goods necessary to establish a farm, should have been an obvious target for lawsuits. But their creditors usually allowed the notes to lapse until the newcomer had a successful harvest and entered actively into the local trade networks. Only if the new arrival failed to integrate himself into the life of the town—proselytizing an unpopular religion, refusing to attend town meetings, or taking the wrong side politically—would he find himself called into court. Even in the most divided town in Vermont, Guilford, the number of intratown suits was only one-third that of intertown suits.[56]

Most particularly, Vermonters punished those who upheld the supremacy of New York. Anyone who dared to be as disastrously on the wrong side as Seth Smith of Brattleboro found Vermont's courts a hostile venue. The freemen hauled Smith into court for "attempting the alteration and subversion of . . . [our] frame of government" by betraying Vermont "into the hands of a foreign power," i.e., New York. A long series of lawsuits cost him his farm and gristmill and eventually drove him out of the state. Not surprisingly, it became increasingly difficult for New York to find anyone to accept its local appointments.[57]

But most plaintiffs just wanted to keep peace with their neighbors, to avoid threatening communal structures already weakened by political discord. In a great many Vermont court cases there are notations that the victorious party declined punitive damages and court costs, and plaintiffs regularly accepted new notes in acknowledgment of old debts.

On the surface of it, the plaintiffs gained little, but they reinforced the town's values and order. Creditors deferred debts for years, as long as delay upheld the economic harmony of the town and as long as the creditor did not need a few extra bushels of wheat. This procedure did not deny the loser his voice and opinions; it did moderate and even disguise differences.

The most common exceptions demonstrate the rule. Most suits between neighbors involved estates of the recently deceased and recently departed. Executors worked to clear the deceased's debts, usually by transferring them to heirs. Straightening out old debt patterns required time, but after the lapse of an appropriate period, usually two years, executors took the recalcitrant to court. More disruptive than death, at least to a region's economy, were those who left town. Though friendships might endure, economic trust could not, especially if great distances intervened. As the goodwill of the departed no longer mattered to the town's stability, a spate of lawsuits often followed the departure of a once-trusted neighbor. But such cases remained relatively rare, as Vermonters tended to stay put.[58]

So who could one sue, if not one's neighbors? Most often, defendants shared economic but not communal connections. The vast majority of court cases in frontier Vermont involved litigants from different towns, but within the same county, and usually within a ten-mile radius—the average maximum distance an individual could travel in a single day and still return before nightfall. Most of these suits contested small claims. The average court case heard in the Vermont courts in the 1780s was for £20, with the median even lower at £12. This median equaled about five acres of undeveloped land or one good cow—and that does not include the minor debt cases heard by justices of the peace.[59]

Vermont's informal lay courts, and their relatively low costs, proved congenial to a steady reliance on the judiciary for the settlement of minor debts. Further, Vermonters anticipated the future in their rejection of legal formalism. After the Revolution, courts in Massachusetts acted to eliminate pleading based on excessive technicality. Legal procedures became separated from the substance of a case, allowing judges to develop the law and gain independence from British formalism. Vermonters foreshadowed these developments in their reaction to the excessive formalism and Anglicization of New York's courts. Less technical tribunals, Vermont's courts sought the abstract goal of justice, even if the wrong writ had been filed. Their innovations grew from their New England heritage and, except for the absence of lawyers on the bench, prefigured the pattern followed elsewhere in the last two decades of the eighteenth century.[60]

Vermont's courts remained more flexible, more responsive to growth and change, and more democratic than any of their predecessors or competitors. Local conservatives and outside observers questioned the quality of Vermont justice, shocked by what they deemed an anarchic and archaic approach to the law, one unsuited to the complex economy and society of the new nation.[61] Yet it is doubtful that a state so isolated and economically undeveloped as Vermont truly required the predictability and regularity of a professional legal system. The local orientation of Vermont's lay courts served well the overwhelmingly rural state and its primitive trade networks.[62]

In sum, the Green Mountain settlers created a court system that ensured the state's survival by actively involving citizens in its legal proceedings. New York would not enforce its will: its leaders refused to expend the funds necessary to send their own forces into the Grants, preferring to rely at first on the British, their troops and their authority, and later on the American Congress and its army. New York's government did not look to its own strength to assert and maintain its legitimacy but to the power of higher governmental levels, a reflection of its leaders' hierarchical worldview.[63]

In contrast, Vermont looked entirely to itself and its people for validation. Vermont's military, the Green Mountain Boys, enforced the decisions of its executive, legislature, and judiciary. Allen did not scruple sending a company of troops to enforce a court decision. Allen did not turn to the superior legitimacy of the American nation to justify such actions but to the will of the Vermonters as a self-realized and self-reliant people. In the most liberal definition of citizenship then existing, Vermont required only that an individual acknowledge the right of Vermont to exist and state his willingness to be part of it. Vermont's Declaration of Rights made clear who claimed the state's protection. The fourth article declared the "the sole, exclusive, and inherent right of governing and regulating" Vermont vested in all those who acknowledged its jurisdiction.[64]

In the same fashion, those who used its courts recognized the legitimacy of Vermont and had a stake in preserving its structures. As yet no creditor or debtor class polarized Vermont's economy and legal system; almost everyone fell on both sides of the ledger. A defendant might begrudge a state that ordered payment on a note of hand, but most defendants understood that the next day might bring a reversal of roles— the defendant would become a plaintiff. They needed courts to keep the economy functioning and to protect land titles and transfers. In establishing courts, the people of the Green Mountains employed what they saw as legitimate methods, creating a potentially inclusive and democratic legal system that recognized the rights of any who in turn would acknowledge the legitimacy of Vermont.

The enormous number of people who flooded Vermont's courts attests to the level of popular support commanded by the Allen faction and the success of its strategy. The Bennington and Windham county courts alone heard 176 cases in 1781 and 250 the next year; approximately one-tenth of the adult males living in these counties appeared before a Vermont county court in the single year of 1782. Again, such a figure does not include the justice courts. John Strong, justice of the peace for Dorset, heard thirty cases in 1781 and fifty-nine in 1782, in a town with a population of 400. By 1780 the people of Vermont had come to rely on its structures; they went to its courts to resolve conflicts, respected its decisions, and paid as ordered.[65]

Why did the inhabitants of these scattered frontier communities turn enthusiastically to Vermont's courts? What did Vermont offer in place of New York's discredited structures? First, the court system worked; it could reach and enforce decisions. Vermont's court records are not crowded with the endless stream of continuations that filled New York's dockets, nor did a long line of frustrated constables report that they lacked power to collect the ordered fines. Vermont's courts decided most cases in the years from 1777 to 1790 within two hearings, executing the majority within a few months of the decision. New York's courts resolved quickly only those cases involving the lands of wealthy New York speculators. In Vermont's courts even the smallest debt received prompt attention.

Second, Vermont's court system addressed the needs of its clientele, meeting public requirements for flexibility and the regulation of the economy. Debt litigation made up more than 90 percent of all cases heard by Vermont's courts before 1790. While a large number of the disputes involved debts as much as ten years overdue, the majority came to trial within six months of the date payment fell due, demonstrating the substantial confidence of creditors in the efficacy of the courts. Creditors did not turn to the courts as the last and usually useless resort, as they had under New York authority. As intended, the courts replaced violence with law. Rather than seize the debtor's goods by brute force to reclaim unpaid debts, a creditor turned to the courts with the expectation of some peaceful resolution. Seizure was now the last resort, used only when a debtor refused to pay court-ordered damages and undertaken by officials of the state rather than by the claimant and a few burly friends.[66]

Third, Vermont's courts fulfilled the expectations of the Grants settlers, performing only those functions they felt appropriate. New York used its courts as instruments of the central state government and the interests that ran it. While Vermonters also saw courts as a means of social control, that conception emphasized the well-being of the immediate community rather than the success of a distant elite. To New Englanders, with their heightened sensitivity to encroachments upon local autonomy and stability, the exercise of such unrestrained outside authority remained intolerable.

And fourth, Vermont's court system punished its enemies and rewarded its friends. Behind all other justifications, economic or intellectual, stood military power. The casual nature of the Green Mountain Boys, allowing companies to form and disband on short notice, constituted their greatest strength. Along with the courts, they comprised the one agency encountered by the average settler that surpassed local authority. As such this posse comitatus functioned as a vital theoretical and practical prop of Vermont's stability. Serving with Ethan Allen for even a short time made a frontier farmer into a Vermonter.

The timing of Vermont's effort to create its own judiciary seemed perfect. In 1777 and 1778, with much of the state occupied by the British, New York's legal system sank beneath its own confusion. The court records demonstrate the uncertainty of the period: transcripts break off, old forms bear new names, and new forms are printed in old styles. Court clerks wrote the busy Provincial Congress for instructions on a steady stream of cases, most of which it postponed indefinitely. In contrast, the assurance and briskness of Vermont's judiciary anchored the new state. Ironically, the frontier attained quick stability while established communities remained unformed. But then Vermont did not carry the burden of an imperial heritage.[67]

Historians have seen law and order as generated principally from above. Some have written of the direct transportation of common law to the American frontier as though the settlers carried copies of Blackstone in their luggage.[68] But the case of the Green Mountain frontier indicates that legal structures can be generated from below and represent a broadly felt desire for consistent standards and comprehensible notions of justice. New York's efforts to impose law from above ended an abysmal failure. As a consequence, the inhabitants of the Green Mountains acted in concert to create and operate a court system that would protect their land titles and serve the needs of their fragile frontier economy. These settlers, though called outlaws by New York, did not feel lawless in resisting the government of New York, finding its use of the law to impede the region's development illegitimate. In rejecting New York's courts as inadequate, as the empty shell Allen labeled them, they rejected all aspects of that province's rule. When the settlers created their own state, the courts occupied the core of its legitimation. The perception and operation of legal institutions thus proved vital in shaping the society of revolutionary Vermont.[69]

III

Those . . . who have suffered so much from Yorkish and British tyranny, will yet take the field against the government of New-York (if need be) and at the muzzle of their firelocks convince them of the independency of the state of Vermont.—Ethan Allen

Having taken care of the Loyalists and conservatives, Ethan Allen used the courts with great effectiveness to finish off the Yorkers. The contest with New York became a shadowboxing match, with Allen throwing all the punches.

In 1778 New York governor George Clinton tried to woo the Vermonters with a new proposal. Every title would receive a fair hearing in court, Clinton promised, with priority given to those who actually worked the land. Allen acted unconcerned, assured that his fellow settlers knew what to expect from New York's courts. Their charters had always been ignored in the past and would be again. "This proposal is really whimsical," Allen concluded.[70]

New York's supporters within the Green Mountains felt otherwise and thought to put the issue to a vote. The New York Committee of Safety for Cumberland County asked its voters which state they favored. Supporters of Vermont boycotted the election, and several communities refused to hold the election. Newfane reported that "ye Inhabitants being about equally divided, have come to some agreement of neutrality" and decided that no one would vote. The results were devastating for New York, which received 480 votes to 320 for Vermont and 185 neutrals. New York failed to acquire a majority even in its stronghold.[71]

Lest there be any doubt on this point, Ethan Allen made the power of Vermont conclusively evident in his brilliant coup d'état of 24 May 1779. On that day, in a masterfully organized and executed power play, Allen and the Green Mountain Boys terminated whatever pretense to a functioning jurisdiction New York might still have within the Green Mountains.

Governor Clinton's failure to understand local politics assisted Allen at every step. In 1778 Clinton instructed his officials to resist the "usurpation [of] the ideal Vermont state." To head his militia in Cumberland County, the main force in his battle against Vermont, Clinton, a patriot, appointed Eleazer Patterson, an infamous Loyalist. It was an odd choice for New York's premier representative, but Patterson told Clinton what he wanted to hear, assuring New York's governor that a regiment of five hundred stood ready to oppose the Green Mountain Boys. Clinton, returning one lie for another, promised that if Vermont harmed a New York official, he would instantly raise New York's militia and march to the Connecticut River. Having stoked each other's courage, Clinton turned to other business while Patterson looked for an opportunity to defy Vermont.[72]

Ethan Allen was also ready for action. "To establish Government in the minds of the people," Allen prevailed upon the legislature to pass a law empowering the Superior Court to inflict corporal punishment on any who opposed the laws of Vermont—a vague and therefore useful law.[73]

Patterson accommodated Allen by making himself a nuisance. The commander of the New York militia publicly proclaimed his intention to disrupt Vermont's militia, called forth in response to the Continental army's plea for help in defending the northern frontier. Under Vermont's militia law of February 1779, the state authorized the commander of each militia unit to meet his complement by drafting whomever he chose. This arrangement often led to those most odious to the local militia leaders, namely Yorkers, being the first drafted. But those called up could buy their way out with £18 worth of goods or property, notes accepted. So a Yorker could contribute one good cow to the American cause if he did not desire to serve with Vermonters. Nonetheless, the militia law put those who disavowed the existence of "the pretended state of Vermont" in a difficult position. Putney's Vermont militia captain, Daniel Jewet, targeted two such men, New York militia officers James Clay and Benjamin Willson. When Clay and Willson refused to serve, Sergeant William McWain seized one cow from each to be sold at public auction on 28 April. On that date Colonel Patterson and a hundred Yorkers showed up, not wanting to bid for the cows but to seize them. Allen found his opportunity.

Governor Chittenden proclaimed Patterson and the other New York officers rioters and secretly ordered Allen to move against them. Allen quietly collected his troops together for the coup that he hoped would put an end to his New York competition. On 24 May, Allen sprang his trap. His Green Mountain Boys captured all but one of New York's officials in the region, plus 100 pounds of gunpowder sent by Clinton for Patterson's use. Though it was hardly news, Samuel Minott, chair of New York's Cumberland County committee, warned Clinton that Allen "bids defiance to the State of New-York, declares that they will establish their State by the Sword, and fight all who shall attempt to oppose them." Minott closed with the usual Yorker appeal for outside assistance: "Nothing but the reluctance the people here have to shedding human Blood could hinder them from attempting to rescue the Prisoners. . . . we therefore beseech your Excellency to take the most speedy & effectual Measures for our Relief; otherwise our Persons and Property must be at the disposal of Ethan Allin which is more to be dreaded than Death with all its Terrors." [74]

It is difficult to understand why the Yorkers offered no resistance, other than a likely fear of shedding their own blood. Perhaps the answer can be found in Allen's amazing ability to make everything seem larger than life, such as convincing the Yorkers that he had five hundred men when his official report listed only one hundred. Or perhaps the speed

and efficient organization of the Green Mountain Boys cowed the Yorkers. Either way, Allen played on their fears, thoroughly intimidating
the Yorkers. Carting his forty-one prisoners, many of them "Gentlemen
of property and great respectability," off to the Westminster jail, Allen
humiliated them and New York.[75]

Allen did not keep quiet about his coup. In fact, he allowed the prisoners to draw up a petition to Governor Clinton begging for immediate
relief, preferably military, and released one of the prisoners to deliver
it to Clinton with proper passion. Allen then sat back and waited, letting his prisoners swelter in their cramped confinement. In frustration,
the prisoners' families appealed to New Hampshire for help, asking
that state to send its militia to rescue New York's officials. The Yorkers
waited for Clinton to respond, while Vermont's courts tried them for
impersonating officials under a bogus authority.[76]

The court appointed Stephen Bradley, Allen's friend and the Superior
Court's clerk, to represent the accused. Bradley managed to gain the
dismissal of the first six defendants, three for lack of evidence and three
as minors. Allen rebelled at such impartial justice. Resplendent in his
gold-laced uniform, Allen pressed through the crowd from the back of
the courtroom, bowed to Chief Justice Moses Robinson and began to
harangue the court for paying so much attention to legal deceptions.
Robinson told Allen that while a private citizen could address the court,
a soldier could not. With a dramatic flourish, Allen threw his hat on
the table, laid his sword beside it, and voiced some undemocratic but
pragmatic sentiments:

> For forms of government, let fools contest;
> Whate'er is best administer'd, is best.

Pausing for effect—and to let everyone appreciate his ability to quote
Alexander Pope—Allen turned and surveyed the court. "Fifty miles, I
have come through the woods with my brave men, to support the civil
with the military arm . . . and to aid . . . in prosecuting these Yorkers—
the enemies of our noble state. I see, however, that some of them, by
the quirks of this artful lawyer, Bradley, are escaping from the punishment they so richly deserve." Allen turned to Justice Robinson, "Let me
warn your Honor to be on your guard, lest these delinquents should slip
through your fingers, and thus escape the rewards so justly due their

crimes." Gathering up his sword and hat with the utmost dignity, Allen strode from the courtroom. In this case, as so many others, his dramatic flair—and implied threat of force—swayed the audience Allen knew so well. The jury found thirty of the remaining defendants guilty, and Robinson issued stiff fines.[77]

Meanwhile Clinton answered with an expression of his horror and concern. His loyal supporters in Vermont assured him that if New York did not send help soon, "we shall be under the disagreeable Necessity of submitting tho' reluctantly, to be governed by the Enemies of the State." But Clinton would not send his own unreliable militia into the mountains to become embroiled in another war, a war which, Washington had told him, New York would fight on its own and would probably lose. So Clinton settled for confirming, yet again, his authority and demanded the immediate release of his officials.[78]

Vermont, on the other hand, demonstrated that it meant business. Shortly after the Westminster show trials, the assembly passed an act threatening much worse punishment if the Yorkers who lived in Vermont did not toe the line—a somber reminder that Vermont's laws, unlike New York's, had force. And to show its approval of Allen's actions, the assembly made him a general. Then, in the first major expression of legislative sovereignty, the assembly ordered the selectmen of every town to seize all Yorker ammunition, without exception. The leadership of Vermont capitalized quickly on its victory.[79]

Allen exulted. He had humbled New York before everyone on both sides of the alleged border; and the government of Vermont, in all its audacity and temerity, had demonstrated its complete control over its jurisdiction. After the requisite boasting, Allen intelligently offered the guilty Yorkers a way out. Instead of releasing them in complete humiliation, to nurture their grudges and plot, Allen presented them with the chance to serve the obviously sovereign state of Vermont. On 3 June 1779 Chittenden issued a general pardon while the council forgave the Yorkers their fines.[80]

Thanks to the ineptness of its enemies, Vermont's government could ease up on those who opposed its authority. Acting on Allen's orders, Colonel Samuel Fletcher instructed his captains "to call upon those called Yorkers" in filling their enlistment quotas, "but not to proseade in Law against them in Case of Refusial." While many Yorkers left in bitterness, some never to return, others took Allen up on his offer to work for the winning side and rose quickly to positions of prominence within Vermont.[81]

Allen's policy of conciliation toward Yorkers was one of his most clever and controversial moves. By welcoming into the Vermont structure any former enemy, whether Loyalist or Yorker or both, who swore to respect the new state's authority, Allen succeeded in precluding future resistance. As Ira Allen explained his brother's actions years later, "The object was to shew power and lenity at once, as the most effectual mode of uniting the inhabitants of Vermont in the cause of their own Government."[82]

With this final sweeping assault on all vestiges of New York's rule, the Allens convincingly demonstrated the greater strength and viability of Vermont's legal system and government. Power and efficiency, not abstract theory or legal correctness, legitimated authority to the practical settlers of the Vermont frontier. The question of allegiance rarely came up again after Allen's coup convinced most settlers that Vermont's government could fulfill its functions while New York's could not.[83]

New York insisted upon its jurisdiction over all the land as far east as the Connecticut River for eleven more years and contested its border with Vermont until 1936, more than a century and a half. But after 1780 its assertions of authority contained not a shadow of reality, and most of the Green Mountain settlers knew that. The climactic event of this three-decade-long struggle came in 1779, when Ethan Allen directly and explicitly challenged the most basic instrument of New York's sovereignty, its right to appoint officials. Vermont's existence remained uncertain for the next six years, but when New York declined to react to Allen's attack, it effectively abdicated all claims to authority.

The core of Vermont's strength lay in its merging of state interest with local town structures. A violator of state decrees chanced alienating the rest of the community. Resisting the distant and impotent authority of New York seemed almost an abstract act. Contesting the legitimacy of Vermont risked calling down the wrath of Ethan Allen, who could raise up the dissident's neighbors against him—as Allen demonstrated to everyone's satisfaction in 1779. By 1780 most, though not all, Yorkers had been recruited to the Vermont cause or had withdrawn to the quiet contemplation of their grievances.[84]

The practical exercise of power constituted the crucial determinant in

Vermont's struggle for self-created statehood. New York had no individual or group that it could rely on in its efforts to enforce its legal will. The Grants, and later Vermont, had Ethan Allen and the Green Mountain Boys. They prevented a counterrevolution by ensuring that New York's authority never got beyond the assertion stage while the people obeyed Vermont's courts. New York had claims, threats, and legal correctness on its side; Vermont had weak arguments, a sloppy understanding of the law, and power. Allen and his few companies of ad hoc militia were more powerful than New York's hundred years of established authority.[85]

CHAPTER EIGHT

War, Diplomacy, and Independence

ETHAN Allen's coup of 1779 left no doubt; New York could not
rule in the Green Mountains. But Vermont still had a string of
sizable problems to address. First and foremost, a hostile British
army threatened from the north, its disposition toward Vermont unknown. At the same time, the Continental Congress resented Vermont's
continued insistence that the inhabitants of the Green Mountains should
decide their own fate. Equally resentful, New York persisted in demanding that Congress and the Continental army should terminate "the
pretended state of Vermont." In addition to these external enemies—
and from time to time Massachusetts and New Hampshire joined in the
contest—Vermont's government faced an array of internal opponents
who wanted power taken from the Allens and placed in worthier hands.

A fine irony lay at the core of Vermont's problems in the 1780s. Patriots demanded and fought for self-determination. But most Americans
lived within preexisting legal structures: colonies become states, bypass-
ing questions of the sources of sovereignty. Vermont shared the patriot
emphasis on independence and the right of local self-determination, and
every action taken by the Allen government from 1777 on held true
to these goals. Unfortunately for Vermont, most outsiders refused to
see it this way. Patriots, Loyalists, and British perceived an illegitimate
state seeking its own selfish ends and based their actions toward Vermont on this perception. A complex, multisided struggle emerged from
Vermont's anomalous position.

In response, Ethan Allen attempted to turn Scylla and Charybdis
against one another. Faced with an indignant Congress on one side and a
British army on the other, Vermont benefited from Allen's artful combination of promises, threats, and creative procrastination. By 1784 Ver-

mont was an accepted fact, and Allen proved again that revolutionary politics is often more illusion than violence.

Allen developed his political methodology from a close observation of the Native Americans. Historians often note the importance of the Indian style of fighting to America's revolutionary victory, and the American preference for shooting from cover certainly discomfited the British. But Indian methods of war included more than just firing from behind trees. As the weaker party in most military conflicts, several Indian peoples developed an appreciation for the political and diplomatic character of warfare. Allen learned much from the Iroquois practice of constant negotiation with equally powerful enemies. Through most of the eighteenth century the Iroquois manipulated the aggressive designs of France and England, keeping the two nations in suspense over which side they would join, using this tension to preserve their autonomy. The Iroquois began the American Revolution with the same policy but made the fatal error of eventually siding with the British. Ethan Allen avoided that mistake.[1]

Allen learned from the Indians that warfare has a strong psychological component, and that violence can be limited by manipulating an enemy's fears and desires. Allen used these methods to win and preserve Vermont's independence. Like the Iroquois, Allen did not seek conquest but survival in a hostile world. As the British spy Micah Townshend complained after another humiliating Yorker defeat, "Allin knows Indian ways too well."[2]

I

Come York or come Hampshire—come traitors and knaves,
If ye rule o'er our land, ye shall rule o'er our graves;
Our vow is recorded—our banner unfurled;
In the name of Vermont we defy all the world!
"The Song of the Vermonters"

Vermont's governor and council moved quickly to seize a commanding position in the economic life of the region, a power which grew steadily with every victory over their opponents. The council did not limit itself to prosecuting and persecuting Loyalists and Yorkers; it devoted most of its time to fiduciary matters such as collecting bills and allocating funds, juggling the hundreds of notes it received, and persuading towns to contribute more toward the support of Vermont's militia and Continental regiment. Governor Chittenden and his council also settled a host of details relative to the political and social life of the state: responding to individual requests for assistance, from locating American prisoners of war held in Canada to providing financial aid during the winter; acting as a tribunal of last resort while also enforcing decisions of the state's courts; considering cases of fraud and overcharging; granting divorces; suggesting legislation; and issuing certificates of "Fidelity to the United States" to suspected Loyalists. The council buttressed the region's informal exchange network—of which it was an integral part—with its courts, police, land deeds, notes, and efforts to regulate trade.[3]

By 1780 Vermont had attained a rough economic stability. For instance, Manchester, like many Vermont towns, did not hold a tax sale until 1813. Vermonters did not get wealthy, but their economy became routinized through the intermediary influence of the state, the one financial force connecting the isolated local markets of the Green Mountains.[4]

Vermont's constitution, as Thomas Chittenden said, "placed no embarrassing restrictions on the power of the legislature respecting the finances" of the state. The assembly and the state treasurer, Ira Allen, could do just about whatever they wanted to raise funds, with every citizen "bound to contribute his proportion towards the expense of that protection" of life, liberty, and property guaranteed in the constitution. For example, when Jonathan Fassett presented a bill against the state for £6, Ira Allen persuaded him to accept a note against Parish Coburn for the same amount, thus recycling the state's credit. Since the state was chronically short of hard currency, the redemption of these notes—payable in wheat, public lands, or Continental currency—aided the state and its economy.[5]

For the most part, the state remained honest in its dealings, which surprised many of its creditors. In 1780 Ethan Allen bought half a ton of powder from Jedediah Elderkin. Discovering the shipment fourteen pounds over the purchased weight, Allen made out a note to Elderkin for the extra powder. Such actions encouraged confidence in Vermont.[6]

Vermont's towns, unlike New York's, retained a free hand in raising local taxes. In 1780 the legislature clarified this authority, declaring that town meetings might impose whatever taxes they chose for whatever "purposes which they might find necessary, not inconsistent with the Constitution of this State." At the first tax rating in 1778 the state authorized each town's lister to determine value and exceptions as he saw fit, subject to appeal. It should be added that such a tax system, while conducive to local autonomy, proved highly inefficient. In 1786 the first Council of Censors estimated that this collection procedure had defrauded the state of thousands of dollars. But given the uncertain survival of Vermont in its first fifteen years, inefficiency in tax collection seemed a small price to pay for the support of its component towns.[7]

The state's leaders demonstrated an acute comprehension of their political limitations in carefully balancing executive power, the needs of the state, and the continued authority of the towns. That the Allens found a successful formula for maintaining their own status without alienating Vermont's town meetings is evidenced by the acceptance of their actions by the legislature. The assembly negated only one act of the council, which Allen packed with his adherents, in the state's first three years. And only one issue in the first decade brought a noticeable minority of the assembly into conflict with Vermont's executive branch: the eastern union.[8]

From 1774 on, town meetings on the east side of the Green Mountains clamored for union with western New Hampshire. Towns on either side of the Connecticut River maintained close ties of kinship, trade, politics, and religion. Militia companies often consisted of men from towns facing each other across the river, while the area's congregations did not respect the Connecticut as a jurisdictional boundary. To many, the White Mountains, just twenty miles east of the Connecticut River, offered a more logical border than a river which served as their principal avenue of communication.

Until 1777 the majority of Grants settlers supported union with New Hampshire. But just as New York's constitution alienated most Vermonters, so did New Hampshire's conservative constitution remove the only probable alternative to independence. In early 1777 a convention of western towns met at Lebanon and declared New Hampshire's constitution in violation of basic human liberties. Borrowing words from an article written by Ethan Allen which had just appeared in the *Connecticut Courant*, the convention contended "that the only legal Bonds" between its towns and New Hampshire's government were the royal commissions. With these commissions now "extinct," the people of all the Grants—meaning both sides of the Connecticut—were "unconnected with the former Government of New Hampshire . . . and are so far reverted to a State of nature." A state of nature did not mean, as Jeremy Belknap put it, "that each individual was reduced to such a state; but that each town returned to its corporate unity, unconnected with any superior jurisdiction." [9]

New Hampshire's system of representation, which ensured the continued underrepresentation of the western towns, became the focus of opposition. A small coastal clique had dominated colonial New Hampshire; and its new constitution, as the Chesterfield town meeting said, promised to perpetuate this control by "the dregs of Monarchical and Aristocratical tyranny in imitation of their late British oppressors." But while independence had advantages, the leadership of the Connecticut Valley towns indicated a willingness to be part of New Hampshire should the Allens prove intractable and New Hampshire flexible. [10]

The opposite proved the case. The government of New Hampshire refused to compromise with the western towns while the Allens welcomed them, hoping not only to co-opt the leadership of the Connecticut River towns but to convince Congress to take Vermont seriously. In March 1778 the Vermont assembly voted to submit the question of unification to the town meetings. Large majorities in most Vermont towns and all sixteen western New Hampshire towns favored annexation, a move immediately validated by the Vermont assembly. Vermont had expanded to the White Mountains. [11]

New Hampshire responded quickly to this infringement of its sovereignty. But it did so in the same fashion as New York, with threats but little action. President Meshech Weare rejected the protests of the western towns and warned Chittenden that Vermont faced "anarchy and confusion" if it did not abandon the union. Weare's true concern, as he admitted to Congress, was that "the affair will end in the shedding of blood." Ethan Allen played continually on this fear for his own purposes. [12]

The day after he read Weare's letter, Allen left for Philadelphia, audaciously passing through New York on the way. Allen had developed friendships during his captivity and shortly thereafter with several members of Congress, including President Henry Laurens. In discussions with Laurens, New Hampshire's Josiah Bartlett, and several others, Allen worked out a deal whereby Vermont would renounce its annexations in return for a concerted effort to convince New York to accept Vermont as the fourteenth state. Allen maintained that Laurens gave the plan his personal approval and assured Allen that statehood was within sight.[13]

Allen spent a week working the members of Congress. As a sign of goodwill, his friends nominated Allen for an active commission in the Continental army, but they could not overcome Gouverneur Morris's opposition to the man who had "debauched" the Green Mountains. Instead, Congress voted Allen a lieutenant colonel's pay of $75 a month, a handsome stipend for someone who regularly denied congressional authority. A major political coup for Allen, the ultimate success of these negotiations depended on the Vermont assembly expelling sixteen of its member towns and on New York's final acquiescence in Vermont's existence. The first lay within Allen's power, the second did not.[14]

After another ten days' hard riding, Allen arrived at Windsor in time for the assembly's opening. In his absence Arlington had elected him one of its representatives. Allen alienated many in the assembly by refusing to take the religious oath. Yet, contrary to any normal procedure, the assembly invited Allen to attend its sessions as a nonvoting delegate and elected him to several committees. Despite his public impiety, Allen remained well placed to work his deal. After five days of conversations and contrivances, Allen submitted his report to the assembly, warning that unless Vermont dropped its eastern union, "the whole power of the confederacy . . . will join to annihilate the state of Vermont."[15]

The annexed towns rejected Allen's arrangement with Congress. The assembly, attempting to reach a consensus, appointed a committee chaired by Allen to justify the union. Though outnumbered by those favoring the union, Allen twisted consensus into support for his agenda. The committee recommended organizing new counties; the assembly agreed but voted to retain the old boundaries. Since the Connecticut River was the old eastern border, the legislature effectively excluded the sixteen New Hampshire towns from Vermont.

Allen had counted his votes and waited. And since he did not vote, he remained free of blame—above the battle, merely the assembly's servant. The representatives of thirteen east-bank and eleven west-bank towns protested the union's dissolution as a violation of "the public faith." The assembly submitted the whole matter to the consideration of the state's town meetings, which voted their approval.[16]

Allen wrote President Weare announcing the end of their disagreement. Explaining the annexation as the work of "designing men," Allen hoped that Weare would "excuse the Imbecility of Vermont" and asked New Hampshire to fulfill its part of the bargain. Members of New Hampshire's assembly pointed out that Vermont failed to dissociate itself from any future connection with the western towns. But that was precisely Allen's intent, to leave this option available. Politics, Allen reasoned, consisted of a subtle play of threats and courtesies.[17]

The courtesy Allen had in mind could be called bribery by the less generous. Before leaving for Philadelphia to again press Vermont's case, Allen convinced the assembly to issue an immense land grant of more than 200,000 acres around Lake Memphrenagog in northernmost Vermont. The legislature had never given more than one grant to an individual, "to prevent undue influence, & to encourage population," as well as "for the greater preservation of equality." But the state's grants remained matters of policy, and Allen took this one out for six hundred unnamed proprietors, allowing him to take a stack of blank deeds to oil the wheels of Continental government.[18]

His first night in Philadelphia, Allen dined with Laurens, presenting the assembly minutes declaring the dissolution of the eastern union. Statehood seemed imminent, one New York representative informing Clinton that "two thirds of the Members of Congress favor the pretended State of Vermont."[19]

Unfortunately, John Wheelock arrived on Allen's heels as representative of the sixteen east-bank towns and announced that they continued in revolt against New Hampshire. Using Wheelock's statement as pretext, New York's delegates tabled consideration of Vermont statehood. Morris wrote Clinton that Congress resolved "to keep matters quiet untill the Enemy leave us, when the Forces of the whole Continent may be turned to reduce" Vermont. Allen furiously accused Congress of reneging on its bargain.[20]

The eastern union appeared a wasteful interlude and failure for Vermont. All parties ended where they started, only with an increase in the level of animosity. Responding to Clinton's complaints, Congress resolved that New Hampshire, Massachusetts, and New York should arrange a final arbitration of their contest for the Green Mountains. Congress ordered what "they call the State of Vermont . . . to abstain, in the meantime, from exercising any power." Since Congress called on the other states to do likewise, it in essence ordered a suspension of all law in the region.[21]

"The influence of Congress at the time was great," wrote Ira Allen, "being considered the pillar of liberty; and their advice was deemed a law." Many in the Vermont assembly thought it should cease confiscating property and selling land, as ordered. Again, Ethan Allen came to Vermont's rescue, listing to the council and assembly all the reasons for ignoring Congress as irrelevant to Vermont's legitimacy. A community created itself and had no need for outside authorization; Vermont's existence "as a body politic (upon revolutionary principles) is at least equally right with the existence of any other free State of America." Vermont, while a "faithful Ally," remained unrepresented in Congress. Given time and the people's natural democratic impulses, Congress would rectify that error. Until then, its own Articles of Confederation prohibited Congress from interfering in the internal affairs of any state. Persuaded, the assembly voted unanimously to proceed with the sale of all remaining confiscated estates and public lands. Perhaps coincidentally, the assembly's next land grant went to a group that included thirteen members of Congress and several Continental officers.[22]

The assembly sent Ira Allen to explain to that "pillar of liberty," Congress, Vermont's intention "to demonstrate the natural and divine right the people have to form a Government for themselves." Governor Chittenden stated plainly this political understanding in his proclamation of pardon for all those who previously opposed Vermont. He grieved that some citizens resisted the community's will "through their own mistaken notions of government" built "on a false hypothesis, that a public acknowledgment of the powers of the earth is essential to the existence of a distinct, separate state." These individuals had forgotten "that all power originated from the people, whose voice is the voice of God."[23]

A congressional committee met with Chittenden to determine whether the Vermonters would "return under the Jurisdiction of New-York" if their land titles "were perfectly secured to you." Chittenden responded with a ringing negative. "We are in the fullest sense as unwilling to be under the Jurisdiction of New-York as we can conceive America would [be] to revert back under the Power of Great Britain." The die was cast.[24]

Congress and Vermont entered upon a phase of benign neglect which lasted eleven years and served Vermont well. As Ira Allen stated, "Procrastination was essential to Vermont." While New York persisted in pressuring Congress and the Continental army to do something about its wayward northeastern counties, Vermont went its own way. Betrayed by Congress, Ethan Allen and the Vermont leadership felt free to do as they pleased, even to negotiate with the much-hated British.[25]

II

He said I might tell Capt. Sherwood he was tired of fighting and did not intend to fight the British nor no others any more. And that all the people wished for a settlement of the war.

—Crowfoot to Justus Sherwood, 1781

After Burgoyne's defeat, Vermont plagued Congress with plans for invading Canada. On several occasions Washington showed interest, sending Lafayette to organize such an effort in late 1777. But nothing came of these schemes, and Allen never realized his dream of leading the Green Mountain Boys and Warner's regiment back into Canada. Instead, Allen found that Congress dismissed Vermont as a bad seed, an unfortunate annoyance to be resolved after America finally defeated Britain. Until then, the rebel state would just be ignored, if possible.[26]

In 1779 Governor Chittenden requested ammunition for the state militia from Isaac Tichenor, commissary general of the Continental army's Bennington arsenal. Tichenor, with congressional support, refused this request. Seeing Vermont abandoned by the United States, Ethan Allen rushed to Connecticut and purchased munitions on his personal credit. Allen then formed an independent strategy for Vermont's defense while the assembly retaliated against the United States by prohibiting the export of all provisions, a blow to the northern army.[27]

The real threat to Vermont between 1780 and 1783 came not from Congress or New York but from the north. In the Royalton raid of October 1780, Indians and Loyalists killed two people, burned the town, and took thirty-two captives. Aside from the Royalton raid, there occurred only a few isolated attacks in this period. But the terror generated by these examples became a potent political reality, one richly exploited by Ethan Allen.[28]

The settlers noted, and Allen reminded them, that Congress did not come to their defense, but the Green Mountain Boys did. Allen established garrisons across the state from Barnet on the Connecticut River, to Pittsford in the Green Mountains, to Castleton in the west, making his headquarters in the house he shared with Ira. Vermont's Board of War proclaimed a defensive line and relocated women and children to homes in the safer southern districts, advising those staying behind to "work in collective bodies, with their arms." Convinced of the imminence of invasion, Allen kept the militia in constant readiness and called it out several times in early 1780 to respond to British probes. Allen knew but did not admit publicly that a British attack would be a losing proposition for Vermont. While making the requisite warlike noises, Allen quietly sought alternatives.[29]

To Allen's advantage, the British lacked a coherent policy. The colonial secretary, Lord George Germain, thought to end the Revolution through the direct purchase of several key officials, writing Henry Clinton that "gaining respectable members of Congress or officers of influence or reputation is, next to destroying Washington's army, the speediest way of ending the rebellion." Clinton targeted generals Israel Putnam, Benedict Arnold, and Ethan Allen. Allen looked particularly promising as he commanded an entire region and stood at odds with Congress. On the other hand, Allen had just written one of the war's most virulent denunciations of British character, a popular call for continued struggle against the British beast. But informed that Allen was "a man of no principles," Clinton sent a message that "I will give Allen everything he has asked of Congress."[30]

Up in Canada, an old Loyalist friend of Allen's, Justus Sherwood, made suggestions similar to Germain's. Sherwood advised the new British commander in Canada, Frederick Haldimand, that Allen and his supporters would "accept any proposal rather than give up their possessions to the N. York Claimers." Suspicious of his southern adversary, Haldimand questioned every informed source that came his way about Ethan Allen. "I am assured by all, that no dependence can be had in him—his character is well known, and his Followers, or dependents, are a collection of the most abandoned wretches that ever lived, to be bound by no Laws or Ties." But Haldimand promised Clinton further study.[31]

As word of these inquiries leaked out, Allen became the center of conspiracies and conspiracy theories. Washington received word that his errant Green Mountain commander had been in New York City speaking with Sir Henry Clinton on 2 July 1780. Aware of Vermont's dissatisfaction with Congress, Washington dispatched John Lansing and Peter Cuyler to investigate. Lansing and Cuyler put a negative slant on every aspect of Allen's whirlwind of activity in late June and early July. He went to Connecticut "under the pretext of procuring a supply of powder," supervised the transportation and distribution of munitions, reviewed troops in several towns, helped rescue Eldad Taylor's daughters, met with Colonel Samuel Herrick to discuss militia matters and drink to excess, and gave speeches. The two spies concluded that not even Allen could have rushed from Bennington, where he "harangued" the militia on 1 July, to New York City by 2 July. But that did not mean that they trusted him, and Washington suggested to General Schuyler that they might need to kidnap Allen. While Schuyler thought Allen guilty of treason, he advised against seizing him—just yet.[32]

In June 1780 Congress again ordered Vermont to cease operation, promising to determine the fate of the Green Mountains within three months; and this time it meant business. On his way to a council meeting called to respond to Congress, Allen was handed a letter from Colonel Beverly Robinson of the Royal Americans. Allen read the council the letter, in which Robinson assured Allen that if Vermont came over to the British side "you may obtain a separate government under the king and constitution of England." Robinson offered more than Congress ever had.

The council's response was quick, decisive, and threatening. Allen wrote Congress that if it would not acknowledge Vermont, Vermont would not acknowledge Congress. He sent another message to Governor Clinton by way of a known New York spy. Showing John Williams the letter to Congress, Allen swore "that he will fight, nay even run on the mountains & live on mouse meat before he will subject himself to New York, or Congress." Williams relayed this message in all seriousness to Clinton. Chittenden followed with a startling proclamation offering passports to "all Tories who choose to join the Enemies of this & the United States." Nine Loyalists accepted the offer and left for Canada.[33]

This public act in favor of Loyalists presented a positive response to the British overture without making a definite commitment. At the same time it sent a hostile message to Congress, which had tried bullying Vermont into surrendering without a fight. But Allen did not want to give the impression that Vermont had quit the American cause. Playing with both sides at once while holding his own cards, Allen wrote Washington promises of continued support for "a thorough retaliation" against the barbaric British. Given the fervor and anger of Allen's language, Washington found it difficult to believe that such a man would betray America. But then Benedict Arnold's treachery was not discovered until September 1780.[34]

Allen sought Washington's help in arranging an exchange with the British for some of Warner's regiment, including his wife's brother. Washington responded that he was doing all he could, but the British continued obdurate. Allen sought an alternative route, contacting Justus Sherwood. During their discussion about a prisoner exchange, Allen complained that with Congress manifesting its willingness to sacrifice the northern frontier to New York's elite, there seemed little reason for Vermont to remain loyal to the Philadelphia government. Sherwood came away convinced that Vermont could be won over by the British.[35]

In fall 1780 Haldimand sent Major Charles Carleton with one thousand men down Lake Champlain. They met no opposition. The Continental army maintained only token garrisons at its northern outposts while New York's militia would protect Albany but not Lake Champlain. Frantically, Governor Clinton called on Chittenden for help, in effect recognizing Vermont's existence—though he later denied it. Chittenden promised his cooperation and called out the state's militia.[36]

Vermont's militia prepared for the attack, while New York's militia refused to march. But General Allen preferred to avoid battle. With three hundred men he shadowed the British as they moved south, trying to determine their objective. Carleton accommodated the Vermonters: his army swept down Lake Champlain to Skenesboro and then over to the Hudson, destroying Fort Edward. The New York command was in panic, beseeching Washington for aid. Hoping to avoid the harassment which so damaged Burgoyne's army, Carleton sent Justus Sherwood into the Green Mountains to make a few suggestions.[37]

Sherwood proposed a truce and negotiations for a prisoner exchange. Allen found this a workable idea. Sherwood then asked if Allen would be open to hearing a further suggestion from Haldimand. Allen had no objection so long as it was "no damned Arnold plan to sell his country and his honor by betraying the trust reposed in him." In fact, the British commander had exactly that in mind. Aware of Congress's recent unfriendliness, Haldimand thought Vermont might be interested in returning to the protection of the British monarch as a separate province.

Allen's reply, a study in contradictions and evasively noncommittal, set the tone for three years of negotiations. He insisted "that he was not to be purchased at any rate"; the British had already tried that approach with him. But since the proposals seemed "to concern the whole people of Vermont whose liberties and properties" had been his premier concern for many years, he would give them serious consideration. Still, Allen promised nothing but "neutrality, nor even that to take place except Congress force them to it by their Tyranny." Having made clear the ambiguity of his position, Allen stated that Vermont could go it alone as "a neutral power free and independent of any other power on earth." Should Congress foolishly attempt an attack, Allen would "take possession of Albany and invite all friends to the liberties of America to join him." Only if this effort failed would he consider uniting an autonomous Vermont with Britain.[38]

Despite his verbiage and convoluted qualification, Allen actually stated his position. Allen's top priority remained Vermont's independence and security. The very nature of both Vermont's government, which included opponents of the Allens, and the Vermonters, who continued loyal to the American cause despite Congress, precluded a switch to the British. Nothing short of a series of unmitigated disasters culminating in an invasion by the Continental army would make union with England attractive, and even then the whole affair would have to be conducted slyly. Though the most powerful man in Vermont, Allen could not order its direction without popular approval. And congressional acceptance of Vermont would terminate all discussions with Haldimand. But Sherwood and the British command missed these points and hoped for the best. Henry Clinton boasted to the duke of Gloucester that "it appears that Ethan Allen has joined the King's troops. I have been for these two years tempting that chief, and I have offered him what Congress have refused him." Like most others, Clinton misunderstood the situation.[39]

Calling together his officers, Allen explained that Haldimand offered a complete cessation of hostilities with Vermont. The officers saw no fault in the plan, except that it would leave Haldimand free to attack New York with his lines of communication secured. Sherwood, knowing Carleton's force too small for such an endeavor, promised that not even raids would be conducted by the British. Delighted, Vermont's military command saw an opportunity to remain loyal to America, protect the northern frontier, and return to their harvests. They approved the plan unanimously.[40]

Allen demobilized the Vermont militia and informed New York's Colonel Alexander Webster, commander of the Albany County militia, that he had arranged a truce which included New York, ordering him to conduct only defensive operations. Orders from an outlaw led Webster to expect treachery. Admitting dependence on Vermont for protection of New York's northern flank, Webster wrote Schuyler that it appeared "that the Grants have left us to ourselves, either to stand or fall." Schuyler thought defeat imminent, as he could not pry any Continental forces out of Washington.[41]

Allen did his old enemies a good turn, though they never admitted it. It galled Governor Clinton even to imply in a letter to Washington that Ethan Allen had saved New York. When Carleton demonstrated some hesitance to include New York in the cartel, Allen held firm until Carleton agreed. Allen had done very well in his opening discussions with Sherwood. Having promised nothing more than a willingness to talk, and that only through others, Allen gained a much-needed truce, an exchange of prisoners, and peace for the entire northern frontier a year before Yorktown. A combination of circumstance, the wishes of others, and the clever manipulation of both by Allen won Vermont a breathing space.[42]

The threat of invasion removed, Vermont's assembly convened, examined Allen's dealings with Sherwood, and voted its approval and appreciation. A few people rejected this turn of events, feeling that Vermont had a duty to continue the battle against the English no matter what the odds or costs. Two men submitted remonstrances to the assembly questioning Allen's motives. Allen jumped to his feet shouting that "it was beneath his character to sit there and hear such false and igniminious" charges and then walked out. The assembly considered, rejected, and destroyed the remonstrances. The next day Allen tendered his resignation as commander of Vermont's militia because the assembly had even listened to attacks on his character. It is unlikely that Allen resigned unless he saw some advantage in doing so, and he promised to return if the state needed him. To show that there were no hard feelings, the assembly approved Allen's petition for a grant to the town of

Easthaven, expressing its gratitude for all his "good services." It hardly mattered to Allen if he held public office; his power did not depend on position but connections. And being out of public office freed Allen from official responsibility for his double-dealing with the British.[43]

Allen mastered the art of mixed messages to keep Vermont afloat. Major Joseph McCracken of the New York militia called on Allen and asked what Vermont would do if the British invaded again. Allen replied that he would "neither give nor take any assistance" from New York. McCracken reported the conversation to Schuyler, as Allen knew he would. Two weeks later Allen warned Schuyler that while in Canada, Ira Allen had learned of a plot to kidnap Schuyler. "I must Confess that such Conversation before my flag, seems rather flummery than real premeditated design," but he thought Schuyler should know. Schuyler told Washington that Allen's letter aroused more suspicions than it quelled. Yet a group of Loyalists did attempt to kidnap Schuyler, being driven off by the guard he had placed around his house after receiving Allen's letter.[44]

Schuyler did not know what to make of his uncertain ally. Like most patriot leaders, he saw the Vermonters as "artful and cunning full of thrift and design." The Vermonters were equally baffled. When Allen heard that he had upset Congress with his independent actions, he wrote General Stark promising a full explanation. But, he concluded, "I am at a loss to form an idea what the United States would have Vermont to do."[45]

Vermont's leadership never disguised its intentions. Chittenden told all the northern governors, Congress, and General Washington that Vermont could not resist the British alone, yet Congress left it to that fate. If attacked, Vermont faced "the disagreeable necessity of making the best terms with the British that may be in their power." Any governor in the same position betrayed his people if he did not seek peace over annihilation. Chittenden insisted that Vermont could be of no assistance to the American cause if not admitted to it. Abandoned and isolated, the Vermonters declared openly that they would treat with the enemy unless Congress presented an alternative.[46]

Far from secret, Allen's negotiations formed the core of a program aimed at persuading Congress to let Vermont into the Union. Attempting to convince Massachusetts to give up its claim to Vermont's territory, Chittenden wrote Governor John Hancock that Vermont required "better assurances . . . whether, at the conclusion of the present war, she may without molestation enjoy her independence, or whether she is only struggling in a bloody war to establish neighboring states" in theirs so that they might "swallow up" Vermont. The Massachusetts legislature found Chittenden's request fair and abandoned its claims.[47]

New York proved less understanding. In 1780 Chittenden suggested to Governor Clinton that they settle their differences and "join in a solid union . . . for mutual defense against the British forces." The bearer of this message, Ira Allen, received a chill welcome in Albany. After Clinton twice refused to see him, Allen swore that "he might be damned if ever he would court [Clinton's] favor again." Frustrated that New York and Congress rejected Vermont's petitions without a reading, Allen relayed a warning to the New York government. "There was a North pole and a South pole, and should a Thunder gust come from the South they would close the door opposite that point and open the door facing the north." Allen knew, and Clinton suspected, that the Vermonters were already testing the northern winds.[48]

Yet distrust shrouded Ethan Allen's actions. Proclaiming his disdain for both Britain and Congress, Allen stated publicly that he would have nothing to do with either. Rumors circulated of his storing grain for a coming confrontation with Britain and of his raising a Loyalist regiment, of trips to Quebec and to Albany to discuss plans with and against the British. Allen himself put out many of these rumors. In the circumstances neither Clinton—Governor George Clinton in Albany nor Sir Henry Clinton in New York City—knew how to proceed, and both attempted to acquire more information. Neither accepted the obvious, that Allen really did disdain both sides.[49]

Hearing these rumors, Seth Warner decided to confront his cousin. Allen told Warner all about the letters the British had been sending him and even volunteered to send them to Congress. Warner thought he had forced Allen's hand. It seems more likely that Allen did not want the rumors against him to build to a damaging indictment when he could so easily demonstrate his own patriotism and the importance of Vermont to the American cause.[50]

In sending the evidence of Britain's courtship of Vermont, Allen assured Congress that Vermont's government would "take no further notice of the matter." Vermont would stand fast against the British, securing the northern frontier, including New York, although that "government could have but little claim on my protection." Yet, Allen could not help noting, Congress still denied Vermont its due, allowing self-interested parties to pursue their "avaricious designs." No wonder the British thought Vermont might be available for a change of partners. Allen stated bluntly the consequences should Congress persist in slighting Vermont: a separate peace with Britain. Allen thought it ridiculous that the Vermonters should be "obliged to defend the independence of the United claiming States, and they, at the same time, at full liberty to overturn and ruin the independence of Vermont." Allen threatened to retreat into the Green Mountains "and wage war with human nature at large."[51]

The assembly issued a ringing endorsement of Allen's actions and words, reappointing him general of the militia. Allen declined, preferring to be free of any official responsibilities and oaths, to do what needed to be done. Allen seemed to think Vermont's preservation hinged on the sowing of confusion. He sent a letter to Governor Clinton offering the services of the Green Mountain Boys to New York. "We would Esteam it the greatest happiness of our lives lastly to defend the State of New-York against their Cruel Invaders." Seemingly satire, the letter was a political document intended to confound and to hint at a possible resolution. Allen often stated and demonstrated that Vermont anxiously wished to fight alongside New York, but only as an equal.[52]

Adding a threat to his offer, Allen produced his master stroke: he annexed part of New York. Between Bennington and the Hudson lay more than a dozen towns settled primarily by Scots, New Englanders, and Quakers. They shared a history of abuse and neglect from New York's government, hated the land system they lived under, suspected the government of ignoring their defense, and feared a new British invasion. One town, Granville, voted to flee south should the British again move down Lake Champlain, while others sent petitions to the governor and legislature begging relief. In contrast, Vermont's government acted to defend all of its towns and had just concluded a successful truce with the British. So when officials in the town of Cambridge called out the militia to defend New York's borders, the townspeople refused and instead petitioned the Vermont assembly for protection.[53] Allen seized the tide at its crest and rode immediately to Cambridge, persuading the town meeting of the wisdom of uniting with Vermont. As Ira Allen later wrote, "The people of this district had great confidence in General

Allen." Cambridge and thirteen other New York towns petitioned for admission to Vermont, and the assembly granted their request.[54]

The assembly received another interesting petition. Across the Connecticut River in Cornish, a convention of forty-three New Hampshire towns suggested that Vermont again annex western New Hampshire, only this time more of it. The Vermont assembly accepted this proposal, annexing New Hampshire as far east as the Mason line, most of the state. But as council member Moses Robinson put it, they intended "to take the East side of the River only to get Rid of them [at] the first opportunity." This union, like the last, would be a bargaining chip in a larger political game.[55]

Similar motivations held on the other side of the Connecticut. Just as Vermont cajoled Congress to accept its independence, so New Hampshire's western towns had attempted for years to win democratic concessions from their coastal government. By uniting with Vermont, the western towns left themselves open to a deal with New Hampshire's government while avoiding taxes and the control of their courts by a distant oligarchy. At worst they would be forced to rejoin New Hampshire; at best they would be within a state without taxes and with a maximum of local autonomy.[56]

The Allens did not really care what logic the New Hampshire towns followed. A larger and more threatening presence on the northern frontier, Vermont became a more attractive prize to whoever cared to win its alliance. Vermont's leaders confidently expected Congress to understand these points. General Haldimand certainly did, writing Lord Germain that the Vermonters "are in every respect better provided than the continental troops and in their principles more determined."[57]

Once more the council assigned Ethan Allen to justify Vermont's actions. His pamphlet *The Present State of the Controversy* demonstrates a brusque regard for consequence over ideals, with expediency the main justification. Vermont's unions had nothing to do with "whether it accords with old homespun honesty, as whether it is politically so." Since the British were the aggressors, any reasonable person would see a truce as a positive step. Taken together, the truce and annexations preserved the government. To their enemies "it is a mystery that Vermont yet lives; they think that having prevented its union with the United States it must have terminated in their destruction: and inasmuch as they are at a loss about these and those things, it may be best that they remain so." Allen's book "is by no means meant to open their eyes, but leaves them to grope in the dark, conjecturing what to their depraved ideas of politics appears most eligible." Allen thought he held all the cards but bluffed anyway.[58]

The western union almost produced the desired effect. Pushed by Schuyler, the New York senate voted with only a single dissent to abandon its claims to Vermont as "inexpedient." Only Governor Clinton's threat to prorogue the assembly prevented the house from also approving this resolution. Clinton, who seems to have internalized his dispute with Allen, castigated the assembly for listening to Schuyler's argument that an armed and friendly Vermont better served New York. Clinton guessed accurately that many of New York's legislators speculated in Vermont titles. But Schuyler was also correct; an alienated Vermont could not be relied on to defend New York's borders.[59]

The second union met Allen's other goal of lessening Vermont's internal factionalism. Those who left the assembly over the dissolution of the first union returned with enthusiasm, and the former Yorker towns of Brattleboro and Hinsdale elected their first delegates. Loyalists and Yorkers such as Luke Knowlton and Micah Townshend served alongside radical democrats like Matthew Lyon and Leonard Spaulding in the state government. Easing its former religious intolerance, the legislature allowed Quakers "to wear their hats in this House." As a sign of reconciliation and unity, the state elected Elisha Payne, from an eastbank town, lieutenant governor and established its printing press at Dartmouth College.[60]

Few Yorkers and Loyalists failed to recognize the defeat of their causes. Instead of allowing them to form a bitter opposition, Allen drew them into the government of the state, tying their interests to Vermont's survival. Evidencing its new goodwill toward former enemies, the government let its committee of sequestration lapse and did not interfere when banished persons slipped quietly back into their old communities. The paucity of petitions complaining of the return of one-time Loyalists and Yorkers indicates that most towns welcomed their old neighbors back, hopeful that the war was finally over. Frontier communities prized unity, and many towns elected former outcasts to public office as a sign of restored amity.[61]

Allen and the Vermont leadership perceived little alternative to the eastern union or to their policy of playing for time. If the Vermonters could maintain their balancing act between the British and Congress for just another year, America might realize Vermont's value to the cause. The longer the war lasted, the better for Vermont, so long as the English did not decide to invade again. In spring 1781 Ira Allen persuaded the British of the wisdom of not fighting on Vermont's territory, agreeing to another truce and prisoner exchange with Haldimand.[62]

On the surface, Ethan Allen took advantage of the peaceful summer of 1781 to spend time with his family. Ira Allen told Haldimand that "General Allen has resigned and taken to his old studies, philosophy." But in fact he busily pursued several projects at once: traveling through New England to encourage settlement in Vermont, meeting with the council and various militia companies, receiving British spies at his house in Sunderland, and writing a book. The British could not have been more obliging, keeping Allen informed of their own plans, which remained happily unaggressive.[63]

But by fall 1781 the British became suspicious that Allen was using them for his own purposes. Haldimand, who thought Vermont a formidable enemy, was "at a loss to see into the real intention of that designing people," thinking that they sought only to make Congress jealous so that Vermont could enter the Union. Sherwood thought the Allens "wish to have two strings in their bow, that they may choose the strongest." The Vermonters sought protection from invasions by either the United States or Britain "by spinning out the summer and autumn with truces, cartels and negotiations." Sherwood concluded sadly that the Vermonters "are as ready as they ever were to assist their rebel neighbors."

Haldimand agreed that "nothing is to be expected from Vermont but cursed hypocrisy and deceit." Nonetheless, he decided to try again, presenting Ira Allen with a plan. In October, British troops would sail up Lake Champlain and issue a proclamation offering Vermont the status of an autonomous colony within the empire. Haldimand intended moving south anyway, so Allen lost nothing by agreeing to the proposal.[64]

One of the more farcical episodes of the Revolution ensued. Haldimand's force, commanded by Lieutenant Colonel Barry St. Leger, sailed calmly up Lake Champlain to Ticonderoga. In attempting to capture a Vermont soldier to act as messenger for Haldimand's proclamation, Sherwood accidentally killed one Sergeant Tupper. Sherwood took the rest of the company prisoner, releasing them with a letter of apology from St. Leger to Governor Chittenden.

An enemy of the Allens intercepted this letter and took it straight to the assembly. Ira Allen and Chittenden spent the next several days explaining why a British commander apologized for killing an American soldier. Then came news that though not yet attacked, St. Leger had retreated. A few days later word arrived that Cornwallis had surrendered at Yorktown, and St. Leger returned to St. Jean. In an uproar, the assembly demanded to know what was going on. Though they could discover no evidence of conspiracy, they suspected such.[65]

As a fitting end to this bizarre little invasion, Governor Clinton finally decided to move against his rebellious subjects. With the victory at Yorktown, the time had come to settle old scores. Showing both contempt for and ignorance of the forces he faced, Clinton sent only two hundred militia under General Peter Gansevoort east toward Bennington. Chittenden sent an equal number, and the two miniature armies met at the Walloomsac on 20 December. After exchanging insults and threats, the two sides settled in, each claiming to be laying siege to the other.[66]

Ann Bleecker joined the New Yorkers while the two armies glared at each other. Bringing her husband food, she wanted to see the "illegitimate Vermonters" for herself. Just in time to witness Ethan Allen's arrival on the opposite bank with reinforcements, Bleecker wrote a friend that "General Allen was bound up in gold-lace, and felt himself grand as the Great Mogul." He brought along "an old spiked up field piece, which, however, looked martial." With Allen's arrival the New York militia broke up, stating that they would not fight their neighbors. Allen won the field without firing a shot. Vermont maintained its acquisitions in New York, drove the Yorkers into ignominious retreat, and sent Clinton into another rage. By the end of 1781 Ethan Allen had succeeded in repelling a British fleet by spinning out treaties and words and a New York army with a grand show. A brilliant, if occasionally embarrassing, sequence of victories.[67]

III

Ethan Allen said that he could go to Albany and be head monarch if he had but orders in three weeks, and he had a good mind to do it; and further Allen God damned Clinton over and over from time to time.—A Yorker prisoner, 1782

With another military victory under his belt, Ethan Allen turned to deal with Congress. But this time none other than General George Washington entered the fray. Washington offered the Vermonters a deal. Taking "it for granted that their right was good," Washington stated that "you have nothing to do but withdraw your jurisdiction to your old limits" in order to "obtain an acknowledgement of independence and sovereignty." Washington found the northern crisis "of the utmost political importance to the future union and peace and justice of this great country." Vermont's admission as the first new state would be a positive precedent for those who hoped to see American sectionalism subsumed into a national identity. Washington added that he had shown his letter to several members of Congress, and all supported his sentiments. And then, in August 1781, Congress voted to admit Vermont to statehood if it dropped its annexations.[68]

A promise from General Washington could not be doubted or refused. Vermont's assembly hastily annulled both the eastern and western unions, leaving those towns to work out their problems on their own. The assembly thought this breach of honor a small price to pay for finally joining the Union. Washington's letter seemed the culmination of the Allens' strategy. The time had come to cash in the annexationist chips and claim statehood. But Vermont's leadership made a common error in assuming George Washington synonymous with America. In fact, he did not even have a seat in the Congress which now ignored its commanding general's promise and its own previous resolutions. Having defeated Cornwallis, Washington effectively ended the war and thus terminated Vermont's usefulness to the struggle.[69]

More than New York now blocked Vermont's admission. As James Madison noted, "The two great objects, which predominate in the politics of Congress at this juncture, are Vermont and the Western Territory." Madison feared that the resolution of the former could decisively influence the latter, with Vermont not only casting another vote in Congress against Virginia's western claims but also serving as an example for the creation of new states in the West. The French observer Achard deBonvouloir wrote in 1778 that Vermont represented a "principle that the various States found a great deal more alarming" than its constitution. The Vermonters held all colonial charters void. In their place Ethan Allen put the will of the people—a truly revolutionary doctrine.[70]

Vermont's government felt swindled by Congress. Convinced, correctly, that Congress planned to partition Vermont among its neighbors, Allen returned to his negotiations with Haldimand. Honestly informing Haldimand of his reasons—Washington's trickery, Vermont's error of annulling the unions, Congress's actions—Allen indicated that the time had come to consider rejoining the empire. "Jealousy rages high about us in the United States," with all parties seeking profit in the division of Vermont. "The turning point" had arrived where, if the Continental Congress would not have it, then the British might.[71]

But the sentiments of most Vermonters limited Allen's action. They could conceive of independence from the United States but not of returning to the British crown. Throughout 1782 stories of Allen's negotiations with the English sparked several ugly confrontations. In April a company of Green Mountain Boys captured the British scout Crowfoot and seventeen New York Loyalists he was guiding to Canada. Chittenden and Allen headed a special court that found Crowfoot and the Tories guilty of treason. Promising that justice would be done, Allen dispelled a crowd gathered at Chittenden's house to demand a hanging. Fortunately for the government, Ira Allen negotiated the exchange of forty Continental soldiers, mostly Vermonters, for Crowfoot's party. Despite this favorable conclusion, many Vermonters remained suspicious of the state's leadership.[72]

Allen's amicable correspondence with Haldimand justified such skepticism. But Allen only wrote, taking no substantive actions to meet Haldimand's demands. Allen filled his letters with encouragement, but when Haldimand pressed for a meeting, Allen managed to agree while refusing. Stating his desire for such a personal encounter with the British commander, Allen thought the time not yet propitious. Just a few more months, he assured Haldimand time and again.[73]

Allen's obfuscation no longer fooled Haldimand, who found his own needs served by their negotiations. After Yorktown the British command feared Washington would invade Canada. In addition to strengthening defenses and expanding intelligence operations, Haldimand followed Germain's order "to make the recovery of Vermont to the king's obedience the primary object of my attention." Haldimand hoped that the Vermont sideshow would keep the Americans off balance, and the chance existed that Congress would finally succeed in driving the Vermonters into Britain's arms, giving Haldimand a valuable buffer.[74]

So the negotiations dragged purposely on for another two years. With the Treaty of Paris in 1783 Vermont found itself within the United States but not of it. The borders conceded to the United States included Vermont, yet that region considered itself an independent republic. With the war over, Allen's policy focused on a "specious show of union with Congress" while promoting conflicts between and within the states to prevent concerted action against Vermont. The eventual goal remained statehood in the confederacy, but Allen discovered obtaining this end the trickiest task of his life, with timing essential.[75]

Allen found certain advantages in delaying union. Vermont emerged from the Revolution without debt, having relied for its defense in the previous five years on the confiscation of estates and on Allen's negotiations. By staying independent for a while longer, Vermont might avoid contributing toward the debts of the other states. Even those Vermonters who had been "most zealous" for admission to the Union on any terms, Allen wrote, now "dread taking on them the burden of the Continental debt."[76]

Keeping his options open, Allen continued corresponding with Haldimand beyond the war's conclusion. Allen even went so far as to assure Haldimand that if Congress did not accept Vermont by February 1784, he would attack New York. Haldimand did not take this promise seriously, coming as part of a request for munitions. Haldimand continued writing in case the peace treaty fell through. Until the future became clearer, Haldimand was content to "amuse the messenger."[77]

Allen could not be so sanguine. Certain the Continental army planned to invade Vermont in the spring of 1783, Allen went to Poughkeepsie to discover Clinton's plans. He could not understand why the Yorkers did not launch an attack and suspected subterfuge where there was merely indecision. In February 1783 Allen received word that New York had moved at last, sending an army of invasion against Vermont. Within hours he mobilized the militia. The panic passed as the invaders shrank to phantoms. But months of dwelling on the possibility of an American invasion convinced Allen that, as he wrote Sherwood, Vermont might be forced to reach an accommodation with Congress for its own protection. Sherwood promised to do all he could to aid the Vermonters, but the time had passed when Vermont might return to the empire. The two conspirators finally admitted the truth.

Ira Allen's comments on this last exchange are revealing. Complimenting Haldimand on his "generous conduct," Allen emphasized the

fortuitousness of the negotiations and the intelligence of the participants. "The facts are," Allen wrote in his *History of Vermont,* "that these
negotiations . . . were from necessity." Though moved by different
motives, they found common ground and ended their discussion with
"impressions of friendship." A model for effecting peace between Vermont and New York, the negotiations addressed "mutual interests" of
security and trade.[78]

Trade held particular interest for Ira Allen. He established business
connections in Canada with Sherwood, Luke Knowlton, and Levi Allen.
The Haldimand negotiations had also served to bring Levi back into the
Allen fold. For the next fifteen years, Levi Allen served as Vermont's unofficial ambassador to Britain, crossing the border and the Atlantic often
to arrange numerous deals, political and business. Ethan welcomed Levi
back into the family with great warmth but did not always agree with
him that trade was above morality. When Haldimand proposed a little
scheme to make some money by trading salt and other items to New
York by way of Vermont, Ethan applauded the idea but asked that the
British avoid Vermont's territory.[79]

Allen refused to take part in war profiteering. On the contrary, he
financed, without interest, more than half of Vermont's £13,600 debt
between 1777 and 1786. Allen did not know much about business and
resignedly expected his brothers to get the family hopelessly enmeshed
in speculative enterprises. He did know that land always pulled them
through and held them together. So he took land in payment for his services. And the protection of that land led him into negotiations with the
British. At their most pro-British, the Haldimand negotiations aimed
at an alliance and trade treaty on strict terms of political equality. By
keeping the British and Congress uncertain, the negotiations maintained
Vermont's security, bringing the region a period of relative peace while
the rest of the United States bore the burden of the Revolution.[80]

The experience of other frontiers convinced many Vermonters of the
wisdom of Allen's policies. British raids devastated militia on several
frontiers. After the Cherry Valley massacre in 1778, Governor Clinton
proclaimed the militia insufficient to defend his state's borders. In contrast, the Green Mountain Boys could and did protect their borders
with the least possible loss of life. Ethan Allen's treatment of warfare
as primarily a political contest minimized cruelty and destruction while
preserving the state of Vermont. General Ethan Allen, perceiving his

duty in avoiding the loss of life and maintaining peace, thought his frontier war a successful enterprise. After all, Allen pointed out, the goal of
the Revolution was not to kill the aggressor but to attain independence.[81]

The Haldimand negotiations did have one more unexpected result
which proved highly favorable for the independent state of Vermont:
an uprising by its few remaining Yorker citizens, also known as the
case of the Yorker cow. In Vermont's southeast corner—in the towns of
Guilford, Halifax, and Brattleboro—the Yorkers made their last stand.
Though numbering only a few score, the Yorkers, by their concentration in this area, contested every election. Town meetings in all three
towns swung back and forth between bare majorities. With Cornwallis's surrender, the Yorkers imagined that Congress would move against
the treasonous Ethan Allen and his illegitimate state. The Haldimand
negotiations justified the Yorkers in calling for immediate intervention.[82]

In early 1782 Guilford narrowly returned a pro-Vermont slate of officials. The new militia board drafted a number of Yorkers who had
avoided service. Sheriff Barzilla Rice seized a cow from one reluctant
draftee, only to be confronted by a crowd of fifty Yorkers who drove
him, and the cow, off. In response, the Vermont assembly passed an act
making any gathering of six or more persons to hinder the execution of
the law a felony punishable by banishment. Like most states during the
Revolution, Vermont saw no contradiction between denying rights to
dissidents while fighting for liberty. The security of the Revolution took
precedence over abstract consistency, a sentiment not limited to radicals
like the Allens. Isaac Tichenor, Allen's bitter opponent, went to Guilford to explain the new legislation and the consequences of disobeying
its laws. As a conservative and official of the Continental army, Tichenor seemed qualified to persuade recalcitrant Yorkers to give in with a
minimum of conflict.[83]

But the Guilford Yorkers ignored Tichenor. Instead, they petitioned
Washington for cannon and requested Clinton's permission to march
on the Vermonters, convinced that as long as "Old Ethan" did not de-
scend on them "with weapons of terror to scare or frighten us" that they
could easily regain control of Cumberland County. They erred in seeking permission. Ira Allen arrived in Guilford while the Yorkers awaited
an answer and started a campaign to undermine their morale and support. And when Clinton did send his approval to act, he did so in the
oddest fashion, telling his subjects that Congress would never approve

New York's claims. Clinton promised defeat for his followers even while urging them to go forth into battle.[84]

Clinton's unencouraging letter convinced Ira Allen that the time had come to end New York's pretensions permanently. On 22 August 1782 Allen sent Sheriff Jonathan Hunt to arrest Timothy Church, commander of the Yorker militia. Church's Yorker neighbors joined in resisting Hunt, and the sheriff retreated to Arlington to tell Governor Chittenden of this latest outrage. Demonstrating the differences between New York's and Vermont's exercise of power, Chittenden ordered General Ethan Allen to call out the militia and march over the Green Mountains to enforce Vermont's authority.[85]

Allen mobilized the Green Mountain Boys around Bennington and marched over the mountains to rendezvous with General Samuel Fletcher and the eastside militia. Dividing his force to march on Brattleboro, Halifax, and Guilford simultaneously, Allen moved on the latter town with one hundred men. Classic Ethan Allen military theater followed. About forty Yorkers ambushed Allen's advance unit just outside of Guilford. The Green Mountain Boys fled at the first shots, suffering no casualties. Getting his men back in line, Allen rode at their head toward Guilford. Within sight of the Yorkers' barricade, he halted the column and approached alone. He then gave one of his short yet grandiose Old Testament speeches. Declaring he would "give no quarter to Man, Woman, or child who should oppose him," Allen warned that unless Guilford peaceably submitted, "he would lay it as desolate as Sodom and Gomorrah." The Yorkers ran away, and Allen rode unopposed into Guilford, taking twenty prisoners.[86]

Allen sent his prisoners to Westminster, where a grand jury determined that, "seduced at the instigation of the devil," the Yorkers "did with force of arms treacherously and perfidiously conspire . . . [to] destroy the constitution of this state and subvert [its] freedom and independence." As he had three years before, Allen attempted to persuade his prisoners to join Vermont. He advised them that "Congress had no right to pass any resolution respecting Vermont" and could not enforce its resolutions anyway. But if the people of the Green Mountains "would be united, they might make independent fortunes, while the thirteen united States were quarrelling among themselves and becoming bankrupts." State prosecutor Stephen Bradley added in court that Vermont had no need for Congress, "for they had strength enough to defend their

State and policy enough to regulate their laws." On September 19, ten days after Allen passed over the mountains, all but four Yorkers pleaded guilty to "enemical conduct" and were fined. The court banished the four who pleaded not guilty and confiscated their property. New York made the usual response to these outrages: a protest to Congress, an assertion of jurisdiction, and nothing more.[87]

Most Yorkers made peace with Vermont, especially after the assembly offered full pardons. A few diehards retreated to Guilford and organized a competing town meeting. When Governor Clinton recommended kidnapping some leading Vermonters, the Yorkers, after a few bungled efforts, grabbed Benjamin Carpenter—a former Yorker and onetime lieutenant governor of Vermont. In retaliation, Brattleboro's constable arrested some Yorkers. The Yorkers released Carpenter on condition that he petition the Vermont government to free its prisoners—which he did and it did not.[88]

The *Vermont Gazette* cried out for retribution. "Since the most lenient means prove ineffectual in quieting the insurgents in that quarter, the most decided measures is to be carried into immediate execution." The assembly denied any who still favored New York's jurisdiction the right to commence a lawsuit, economic death in Vermont. Chittenden decreed that now "nothing short of an immediate and universal submission" would be accepted.[89]

In January 1784 after a brief battle at a Brattleboro inn, General Samuel Fletcher mobilized the Vermont militia. The last hundred Yorkers took a solemn oath to fight to the death. Vermont's troops marched through the snow toward Guilford, taking the Yorkers' advance scouts prisoner and surprising the rest at Stowell's tavern. The Yorkers fled and regrouped at Lucretia Houghton's tavern on the outskirts of town. Again vowing to stand and fight, the Yorkers fled before the Vermont militia. Outside of town, the remaining thirty Yorkers—pub-hopping had taken its toll—met at Packer's tavern. One of these Yorkers took a shot out the window at the advancing militia and mortally wounded Sergeant Silvanus Fisk. The sight of blood apparently unnerved the Yorkers, who again ran, the next tavern being well to the south, over the Massachusetts line.[90]

Two days later Ethan Allen arrived with several hundred reinforcements and placed Guilford under martial law. Vermont had had enough. Allen marched every Yorker he found off to jail and quartered a regiment in Guilford, ordering the arrest of any returning Yorkers. The Guilford Yorkers apologized to the Vermont assembly and petitioned for pardon, promising to behave in the future. But Vermont no longer needed their acknowledgment, and Allen arrested their messenger. At Benjamin Carpenter's urging, the assembly considered and granted individual petitions for amnesty over the next year. Guilford's Vermont town meeting offered reconciliation to all those who took an oath of allegiance to Vermont. Even Allen's old enemy Charles Phelps stood before the governor and council to apologize and take the oath—a fitting denouement, indicating that the struggle was over. Only Vermonters remained in the Green Mountains.[91]

New York again threatened to quit the Union, even while requesting Continental troops. The *Vermont Gazette* called the rival assembly's actions "a mere New York puff." Chittenden assured Congress of Vermont's willingness to fight New York should it attack, expecting that "Congress and the twelve States will observe a strict neutrality." Congress voted with only New York's dissent to reject its request for troops. In the words of Gouverneur Morris, Vermont was now "independent de facto."[92]

Not many in Vermont in 1784 expressed dissatisfaction with their government or opposed its continuation, and if they did, they kept quiet about it. As the numerous petitions to the legislature—more than a thousand in its first decade—indicate, even those who complained did not question Vermont's sovereignty as the final arbiter of all grievances. The creation of independent Vermont had solved the settlers' political and economic problems, soldering together the diverse ends of fragmented communities and a fragile economy. Intelligent enough to understand how best to attain their interests, the inhabitants of the Green Mountains appreciated the government they created and nurtured.[93]

In February 1783 Washington had rejected a congressional resolution that the Continental army invade Vermont, noting the internal agreement between otherwise hostile factions as the source of Vermont's strength. Such unity guaranteed that "it is not a trifling force that will subdue them, even supposing they derive no aid from the enemy in Canada." Congress wanted him to invade a well-defended fortress inhabited by "a hardy race, composed of that kind of people who are best calculated for soldiers; in truth who *are* soldiers." Hundreds had served in the Continental army, hundreds more had experience with the Green Mountain Boys. Washington did not think they would step aside for the Continental army.

Nor did Washington think his soldiers would fight. The officers expressed "the utmost horror at the idea of shedding blood in this dispute, comparing it . . . to the quarrel with Great Britain, who thought she was only to hold up the rod and all would be hushed." Neither would common soldiers have "the blood of their brethren" on their hands. Ethan Allen's latest pamphlet made all these points, and, Washington told Congress, Vermonters circulated it, and land grants, among his soldiers. "I shall only lament," he closed, "that Congress did not in the commencement of this dispute act decidedly." Vermont had acted decidedly and, as Washington perceived, had won. Congress and New York must now admit that fact.[94]

As Washington understood, Vermont prevented invasion by constantly planning to resist it. Removing supporters of external authority and involving the majority of the citizenry in its defense plans denied an invader of both internal support and hope of success. Any would-be conqueror faced the sort of guerrilla war which had plagued New York before and during the Revolution and would have necessitated the maintenance of an occupying army. These preparations convinced Vermont's opponents not to attack. Washington, Haldimand, and eventually Governor Clinton realized that they would have to fight not just the government of Vermont but its people as well.[95]

In the years from 1778 to 1784 Ethan Allen made it clear that no one else could govern New England's northern frontier. New York tried with proclamations and a few officials. Congress attempted to use its central position and revolutionary status to coerce the Vermonters. Britain turned to negotiation and hidden manipulations. None proved effective. The state of Vermont exercised power, established institutions, addressed local needs, and ignored claims to any legitimacy beyond the will of the people. Allen expressed these primary and determinative political ideas in his writings. The people formed the only constituent power and had governed themselves since 1774 with the organization of their committees of safety. The state they created fulfilled the function of government, protecting its citizens and their livelihoods. In defending the Haldimand negotiations, Allen thought Vermont's actions self-evidently wise, sparing the region the bloodshed of war; its "citizens have much the largest quantity of seed wheat now in the ground that has been in any one season since the first settlement." That was good enough.[96]

By 1784 Ethan Allen felt that he had resolved all crises. With external and internal political upheavals settled, a court system capable of regulating the economy in place, land titles secured, and even his family reunited, Allen could retire from politics and turn his attention to other concerns. It was only a matter of time and negotiation before Congress accepted the inevitable and admitted Vermont into the Union. On the surface, peace seemed attained. But the Revolution had distracted the people from what had once been a basic motivating force, one of the two primary reasons they had initially moved to the frontier. With the War for Independence at an end, religious factionalism again came to the fore, though with a fervor magnified by Vermont's democratic ethos.

CHAPTER NINE

Frontier Philosopher

POLITICAL independence opened the floodgates of diversity. Released from traditional political and social restraints, many common Americans reached the startling conclusion that they had the right and ability to make important political decisions. In the Green Mountains the Revolution produced a democratic effervescence from which emerged a new state.

This unique faith in individual determination did not end with politics. Exactly what revolutionary leaders like John Adams and Gouverneur Morris most feared happened on the northern frontier, an apparent end to dependence on inherited structures and doctrines. As Nathan Hatch has argued, Americans emerged from their Revolution convinced of their ability to think for themselves, even about the Bible. These democratic impulses did not undermine social stability, as Adams and Morris feared, but enhanced and justified the legitimacy of America's new states.[1]

The Revolution temporarily dampened and redirected religious disputes. The language of religion had fueled revolutionary fires, even when coming from the lips of a skeptic such as Ethan Allen. But congregations in the midst of bitter controversy with competing denominations or on the verge of splitting asunder put aside their differences for the duration of the war.[2] With the victory at Yorktown, détente vanished and sectarian conflict returned, the storms given added force by the thunderous new logic of individualism. A few people went so far as to cast aside all anchors, and set forth under the sails of their own religions. Ethan Allen was not alone in navigating uncharted theological seas, but few dared to proclaim so publicly their refusal to travel by the known sightings of Christianity.

I

His soul's ship foresaw the inevitable rocks, but resolved to sail on, and make a courageous wreck. Now he gave jeer for jeer, and taunted the apes that jibed him. With the soul of an Atheist, he wrote down the godliest things.—Herman Melville

In 1789 the Reverend Nathan Perkins left his home in Connecticut for a missionary journey on the Vermont frontier. He did not like what he found. Perkins complained about everything. The food was terrible, the company worse. His evenings "passed in dullness and insipidity" with people he described as "nasty, low-lived, indelicate, and miserable cooks." Worst of all, Perkins found himself among "deists & proper heathens." [3]

In every community people turned out in great numbers to hear Perkins and to argue with him. Conceiving "a high opinion of my abilities & address," his audiences bestowed "encomiums which it would be vain in me to repeat, such as ye very first-rate, philosophical, Deep, penetrating, a great Scholar, angelic, the angel Gabriel could not go before him," etc. Yet they rejected his theology. In Manchester he met Lucy Hitchcock, who charmed him with her education and good manners. His admiration turned to dismay when he learned that Hitchcock was Ethan Allen's daughter and a "rank deist." It infuriated Perkins that she listened to him so politely and displayed more civility than his compatriots, who wanted to argue points of theology. [4]

Though a "profane" lot, Vermonters appeared oddly "cheerful & much more contented than in Hartford, and the women more contented than ye men." How could they be happy in such adverse conditions? The settlers of this wilderness worked hard and suffered much, and yet the women were "serene, peaceable . . . loving their husbands, their home, wanting never to return. . . . I think how strange!" Strange indeed. Even the governor, Thomas Chittenden, was "a vulgar man, clownish," who lived "in a very indifferent house"—though Perkins admitted that Chittenden understood "extremely well ye mysteries of Vermont." Surely, Perkins thought, the "woods make people love one another," teaching them to trust and rely on their neighbors. But how then could they reject the true light of religion? There seemed no explanation for the many contradictions Perkins witnessed. [5]

Surely the paucity and poor quality of frontier ministers explained in part the settlers' lack of religion. But Perkins saw a deeper explanation of "ye mysteries of Vermont." The new state's problems originated in the people allowing all kinds of theologies free rein. Failing to enforce true religion, Vermont harbored the irreligious. The consequences appeared obvious: anarchy and eventual ruin. Perkins returned to Connecticut a frustrated man, writing Vermont off as a total loss. "The frowns of ye Almighty are on this State for its sins."[6]

In labeling the entire state irreligious, while noting the profusion of sects, Perkins missed the obvious. His audiences listened so attentively and yet rebuffed his theology not because they lacked religion but because they took it so seriously. Perkins, like most travelers, saw only infidelity in Vermont. But the Vermonters did not reject religion; the observers rejected the religious sentiments of the settlers.[7]

Perkins associated diversity and deism, finding them the unfortunate effect of the same environment. The frontier seemed to dissolve traditional cultural standards. Like so many of early America's leaders, Perkins lacked confidence that the frontier could be integrated into the new nation without dealing damaging, perhaps crippling, blows to social order. Yet that very diversity which Perkins feared guaranteed that religion played no significant role in the new order.[8]

Perkins had his reasons for portraying the frontier as irreligious. Using Vermont as a cautionary tale, he hoped to shore up Connecticut's sagging Congregationalist establishment and to raise money for missionary efforts, while obscuring the presence of religious diversity, and even a few deists, in his own state.[9] Allowing for these qualifications, Perkins did have a valid point that Vermont's religious culture lacked consistency and verged on chaos. Everywhere he rode, Perkins discovered not just the Separates and New Light Congregationalists he expected, but also Episcopalians, Presbyterians, Baptists, and sectarians of all types. During the Revolution, Vermont became a refuge for a number of unpopular denominations, including Quakers and other pacifists. Already more diverse than any New England colony before the Revolution, Vermont went wild in the 1780s. By 1790 a patchwork of theologies stretched across Vermont.[10]

While political and religious leaders in the rest of New England struggled to maintain the Congregational establishment, Vermonters rejected state support for religion. Many settlers—primarily Baptists, Separates, and Quakers—had moved north after having their beliefs rejected as heresy and their property seized for the benefit of a minister whose sermons they abhorred. Their experiences made them fervent supporters of Vermont's secular constitution. Whether persecuted previously or not, most Vermonters agreed with the Reverend Thomas Fessenden, who told his audiences in 1776 that no earthly ruler could make laws binding personal beliefs, as everyone had a "right of private Judgment in things both civil and religious." [11]

Some Vermonters did feel that the towns should be able to support churches. Whenever this issue arose in the assembly, the legislators agreed to leave the matter to those towns which could command a substantial majority for a single denomination. In 1780 the legislature empowered towns to levy taxes in support of a minister. But the minister's selection required a majority of the male inhabitants, and the act operated only "provided always that no person be compelled . . . [to] support a worship, or minister of the gospel, contrary to the dictates of conscience." [12] Three years later the assembly passed an act which required two-thirds of the town meeting to establish a minister or collect a church tax; a dissenter could avoid payments of any kind by producing a certificate of exemption from any other church, certificates easy to come by. [13] Even these acts proved highly controversial, violating, as opponents pointed out, the Vermont Declaration of Rights. Others turned to the Bible, "Fidelity" writing that "from the first of Genesis to the last of Revelations, it cannot be found that any house of worship was built by rate or tax." The assembly moved cautiously but surely toward voluntarism, reaching that point in the 1790s. [14]

Vermont's medley of sects seemed to many observers the source of its stability. Contemporary observer John Graham wrote that these frontier congregations had no choice but to leave each other alone since "they stand in need of each other's assistance in the common concerns of life." It was not "toleration, but equality in this respect, which the people of Vermont aim at." The state's peace and prosperity "are the result of this religious freedom." [15]

Traditional religious structures, never fully established in Vermont, crumbled in the years following the Revolution. As relations between church and state became ever more tenuous, religious competition in-

creased, leading to the further division of congregations and the proliferation of sects, several of which originated in Vermont. Some of
these new churches flashed briefly across America's theological firma-
ment; others persisted. Among the former were the Dorrellites, who,
guided by the Loyalist William Dorrell, enjoyed visions from "the light
of nature" and lived in a vegetarian commune in Guilford into the early
nineteenth century.[16] The Universalists proved more influential. The
argument that Christ gained pardon for the sins of all humanity in a
universal atonement made Universalism one of the leading sects in the
northern United States, particularly along the frontier. For many Vermonters, Universalism marked the final stop on their spiritual journey
from New Light Calvinism. Growing from Calvinist roots, Universalism
stood Puritanism on its head, positing a benevolent deity incapable of
creating men only to cast them into hell. The most inclusive of commu-
nions, Universalism sought to unite communities on a theological basis.
It ended dividing them, permanently.[17]

But before these champions of universal salvation organized, the Vermont frontier was rocked by a number of rationalist proponents of
natural religion and deism. Thomas Fessenden, a Harvard graduate
and creator of a "science of sanctity," could not keep a pulpit until he
found his way to the frontier town of Walpole in 1767. Over the next
forty years Fessenden shocked and delighted audiences with his sense
of "whimsey," which went so far as to encourage dancing and youthful
"frolics," and his outrageous theological views, which extended to questioning the divinity of Christ. Drawing his listeners' attention to the
world outside the meetinghouse, Fessenden declared that "the Gospel
had its Foundation laid in the Religion of Nature, and that we were not
required to believe anything that our Reason could not comprehend."
Like the Universalists and most frontier rationalists, Fessenden feared
that religion divided people from one another by feeding doubts of salvation. Everyone should find a good "companion, friend, and brother"
in religion, not dread of the afterlife. Churches should reflect this theological communalism by taking all in, "to shine in the midst" of each
town rather than "to live separate in a Corner."[18]

Fessenden bordered on deism but did not cross the line into a denial
of Christian revelation. While demanding a stronger evidential base for
belief in the Christian deity, he held fast, like most eighteenth-century

rationalists, to the sacred truths of the Bible. A very few went over the line, most notoriously the author of the first published defense of natural religion and deism in America: Ethan Allen.[19]

II

Behold him move ye staunch divines!
His tall head bustling through the pines;
All front he seems like wall of brass,
And brays tremendous as an ass;
One hand is clench'd to batter noses,
While t'other scrawls 'gainst Paul and Moses.

Lemuel Hopkins
on General Ethan Allen

Allen saw the book he entitled *Reason the Only Oracle of Man* as the most important work of his life. In the long lull between the Yorker trials of 1780 and the final battles around Guilford in 1784, Allen worked on his manuscript. As he wrote St. John Crèvecoeur, "My late publication had been expencive and has engrossed my attention" to the point where he had no time to attend the legislature or pursue any other activities. But, Allen told his friend Stephen Bradley, his sense of duty required that he attempt to save "the human Species, from this ghostly Tyranny, (as far as in me lay) . . . an Object worthy of Genl. Allen, whatever his success may be." Shortly after the Guilford battle, the publishers Haswell and Russell of Bennington agreed to print 1,500 copies of *Reason,* with the stipulation that Allen pay them as printing progressed. To raise this money, Allen sold off large tracts of land worth £1,022 in 1784 and 1785. *Reason* appeared in November 1785. Its publication marked Allen's withdrawal from Vermont's leadership.[20]

The depth of Allen's commitment to theology can be measured by trying to locate a contemporary political leader devoting several years to the publication of a work rejecting mainstream religious beliefs and offering a uniquely personal vision of humanity's place in the cosmos. Just as Francis Bacon changed his mind late in life about the founder of nations holding the pinnacle of fame and placed the great philosophers in that coveted position, so Ethan Allen turned from action to thought with grandiose hopes of serving all mankind with his theological relativism.[21]

Allen's book appears an anomaly in many ways. Most deists of America's revolutionary generation were either cosmopolitan, elite intellectuals or freethinking artisans in major seaports, not frontier farmers. While Vermont produced much in the way of religious diversity, it is difficult to discover many people there who rejected Christianity and advanced positive arguments for natural religion. Further, it seems rather odd that someone like Allen, who reveled in popular acclaim, would relinquish his political career by publishing ideas he knew to be anathema to the great majority of his neighbors. Allen longed for immortality and fame, not notoriety and opprobrium. It is appropriate, therefore, to ask what compelled Allen to commit himself in print? The answer may be found in what he wrote.

In most particulars Allen's book is similar to its British predecessors and American successors. Roughly a fourth of *Reason* is devoted to demonstrating the contradictions, inconsistencies, and logical absurdities of the Bible and the various Christian creeds. Most of these criticisms appear in other eighteenth-century rationalist works. Allen thought that in highlighting logical errors in the Bible, such as Moses describing his own funeral, he would undermine the acceptance of that book as divine text—as though accuracy is a necessary component of faith.[22]

Allen thought a holy text should be useful and credible. The word of the Bible's god remained so unreliable as to be worthy only of ridicule. In the Old Testament the Sabbath is Saturday, and that is the word of God. In the New Testament it is Sunday, and that is the word of God. Beyond this contradiction, Allen found reason to question making a passage of time holy. Why would God establish a holy period which would be an hour later for a region fifteen degrees farther west and already over for the other side of the globe? It may make sense for a small flat earth but is inane when the world is known to be of a rather different shape and the universe of a disturbingly different character. Allen pitied the poor Israelite put to death for gathering sticks on the Sabbath. If he had done so at that precise moment on a different part of the planet or in modern Vermont, "he might . . . receive his wages for it."[23]

Like Thomas Jefferson, Allen thought Jesus Christ an admirable moral philosopher whose message found little adherence among Christians. They took some "absurd" stories in the Bible literally, while dismissing as allegorical words of great importance. Anyone with a modicum of common sense could see that the Trinity lacked any logical foundation, while doctrines such as the Incarnation and the Virgin Birth struck Allen as so childish and primitive as to not warrant consideration.[24]

More importantly, Allen focused attention on widely shared doubts over the Christian doctrines of original sin and the imputation of Adam's guilt to later generations. The story of Adam's fall appeared sordid and "unnatural". If Adam and Eve gained the power to reason by eating some fruit, then they must not have been rational before the act and could hardly be held accountable for choosing to eat it. Like a frontier lawyer, Allen presented a metaphysical brief, insisting that if the defendants did not yet know the difference between good and evil, then they could not have transgressed any law. At the very least the jury, God, should recognize the inequity of pitting a wily and sophisticated opponent, Satan, against "a woman who just before had been taken out of Adam's broadside." The defendants had a "right to plead non-age," attorney Allen argued, especially against such a trivial charge. The devil, as "the efficient cause of the apostacy," should be punished, assuming God granted an appeal.[25]

Instead, the Christian god, not content with punishing those first innocents, extended guilt to all of their progeny. Allen placed the doctrine of original sin, which imputed guilt to the offspring of Adam and Eve for all time, at the core of everything wrong with Christianity. Moral worth and demerit, Allen held, could not be freely transferred like a bushel of wheat. One might as well assume that the wicked deserve to "share the joys and salvation of the righteous" and that the righteous should bear the punishments of the wicked. Extending the logic saves and damns everyone; all share the same contradictory fate. In short, imputation "confounds virtue and vice, and saps the very foundation of moral government, both divine and human."[26] Take away personal responsibility, and morality ceases.

But if one questioned original sin, then Christian salvation itself must be challenged. As a youth, Allen heard a Calvinist minister explain that without imputation, Christ did not need to save humanity and pass on the imputation of salvation to those already saved through predestination. After his head stopped spinning, Allen admitted the clergyman's argument irrefutable. After much "painful" reflection, Allen found "that I must concede to it entirely or not at all, or else believe inconsistently." In finding all humanity guilty with Adam and Eve and subject to salvation with Christ—though they had nothing to do with Adam and Eve's alleged sin or Christ's sacrifices—imputation hinges on the transference of virtue and vice from one person to another. If sin or salvation cannot be transferred to all succeeding generations, original sin vanishes, and there is no guilt which all humans must answer for from birth, no need for atonement, no need for Christ. All that remains are individuals accountable to the Creator for their own actions. Ridiculous, then, that anyone should feel guilty because of "a premised eating [of] a pleasant apple." [27]

Allen attributed the longevity of such unreasonable doctrines to clerical power. Once a minister convinces his people that God answers his prayers, there begins ministerial authority, wealth, and titles. Moses presented a deity at the beck and call of his minister—"God had the power, but Moses had the dictation of it." From this first pretension the "Creedmongers" spread their "pious fraud," making "all Christendom . . . dupes to the See of Rome" by shrouding God's revelations in mystery and disseminating superstition as the most effective means of gaining and retaining power. [28]

Allen rejected the elitism of deists like Voltaire and Franklin, who thought religion necessary for keeping the lower orders moral. As Allen pointed out, history offers little evidence that religion produces morality, as Christians go about killing in the name of Christ. The reason for this adulteration of Christ's peaceful message seemed obvious: the clergy's manipulation of religious myths and sentiments. Organized religion appeared to Allen a negative historical force. [29]

Given these failings, Allen argued that the best system of religion is one which replaces clergy and creeds with individual intelligence and conscience. The individual is best able, through the conscientious application of innate, though limited, reason, to discover the laws of a deity who is perfectly rational. This rationality indicates, for Allen, a just and benevolent god, desiring only the happiness of mankind, unlike the capricious and irrational Calvinist deity Allen found in his youth. [30]

Allen sought to individualize theology. All forms of human happiness grow from the "consciousness of liberty." Just as there is no real social good without political freedom, so does true morality require free will. Allen rejected predestination for allowing people to evade blame for their actions. God becomes the author of moral evil, and men are passive innocents. Free will makes people responsible, while "our own consciences," not faith, make people good. [31]

Free will, which is seated in the "intelligent nature" of humanity, allowed people to discover and act upon god's truths. From Lord Kames, Allen borrowed the notion that everyone could differentiate right from wrong. Though weak in some, this moral sense remained present in all and could be strengthened by education. Allen once asked an Indian to describe his soul. "It is my think," the Indian replied. Allen found this answer "both laconic and pertinent." The soul emerges from thought.[32]

Demanding equity of the universe, Allen defended human free agency as more moral and just. All would agree that a modern judge should not punish a person for a crime known to have been committed by another, so why hold the deity to a lesser standard of justice? Finding the Calvinist god vindictive and cruel, Allen stated that he would remove such a judge from the bench of a Vermont court, so why accept such as the final arbiter of a soul's fate?[33] God intended people to judge themselves, Allen insisted. Truth tends toward the greatest "order and harmony"; sin and evil are but deviations from that rational order. Truth punishes violations of morality with internal sufferings of guilt. Allen's theology required justice. Largely unavailable in this world, he found it in the next.

A perception of a benevolent deity fostered Allen's belief in human reason and universal salvation. Contemporary Methodists, Universalists, and Baptists shared with Allen a view of man's inherent goodness; all possessed free will and the capacity for "morality, compassion, and generosity," as Thomas Jefferson put it. Deists and Protestant liberals also agreed that one glorified God by serving humanity; dogma and creed held little importance compared with ethical behavior.[34]

But freedom is not enough. "The actions of mankind may be free, but . . . the omniscience of God" gives order to the universe. And it is possible to tap into that omniscience through the exercise of reason. The necessary first step is divesting ourselves of inherited biases. "As the Pagan, Jewish, Christian and Mahometan countries . . . have been overwhelmed with a multiplicity of revelations diverse from each other," Allen thought his readers absolved, "without a lengthy course of arguing," in dismissing the lot to pursue their own truths. Such personal searches, conducted by the light of reason, would transform theology into a science, the most essential science.[35]

Reason is superior to revelation for discerning the laws of nature and of God, which are, Allen thought, the same thing. Those who rely on "dreams and visions" to understand the universe are subject to their own "deceptions, blunders and inaccuracies." If God intends to relay information to humanity, the deity will, in "the spirit of truth and uniformity," tell everyone. History is full of messages straight from God, most of which contradict each other, so why accept the vision of one lunatic over another? Because the Bible originates in a claimed revelation, it too should be questioned. At some point reason and "the deistical Bible" of nature must be consulted, even to understand the Christian Bible. Remove reason, and only superstition remains—and Allen claimed he attacked superstition, not Christianity. As "all true religion originates from reason," its opposite, superstition, stands as the enemy of religion. Only the free use of individual intelligence can clarify the difference.[36]

People need only turn to nature to see "the immutable perfection of a God" displayed. "For all rational and accountable agents must stand or fall upon the principles of the laws of nature." Here lay the simple root of Allen's theology and of his intellectual self-confidence: since he saw order in the universe, an ordering force must exist.[37]

But Allen's deity lacks personality. Omniscient and omnipotent, it has none of the human faults, such as jealousy, anger, or a desire for vengeance. Nothing should be ascribed to the deity "which is inconsistent with reason," and we should be "wise enough not to charge God with injustice and contradictions, which we should scorn to be charged with ourselves." Those who behold a vengeful God are ignorant of or alienated from nature. An angry deity "is only the idol of their own imagination, which they truly ought to hate and be ashamed of." Allen insisted that God rise above human emotions and obsessions. Any deity unable to meet this minimum standard must be the creation of humans, not the creator of the universe.[38]

Allen noted that one person's revelation was another's superstition, and that people criticized others for what they suffered from themselves—what psychologists call projection. Every culture, "blind with respect" for its own traditions and superstitions, despises others for similar faiths. Christians of all kinds regularly accuse one another of heresy. "With equal facility do Christians and Mahometans spy out each others inconsistencies, and both have an admirable sagacity to descry the superstition of the heathen nations." That we so freely criticize the adherence of others to their traditions should make us question our own and not "rest satisfied until we have regulated our faith by reason." Allen calculated such tolerance and mutual exploration highly unlikely and believed most people would continue to cling to the religions of their parents.[39]

Allen's relativism extended further than that of perhaps any contemporary, including Paine and Jefferson.[40] Mankind's diversity, Allen argued, precluded a single revelation. Divine truth for one person could hardly be the same for an individual in another culture. Each person must independently determine truth and personal beliefs. The seeker needed only intellectual consistency, which meant questioning every received truth.[41]

While all religions shared an equal relative value, Allen found natural religion methodologically superior. Not dependent upon a culturally determined text, natural religion is open to all rational beings. Natural religion's reliance on human reasoning opens the door to natural laws, permitting people to determine correct moral conduct, and thus to merit their eternal salvation—or to deserve their eternal damnation.[42]

Natural religion's great strength is its constant and universal accessibility. Christianity and other religions premised on revelation "came too late into the world to be essential to the well being of mankind." The revelatory religions "began the same as human traditions have ever done, in very small circumstances . . . and made their progress as time, chance and opportunity presented. Does this look like the contrivance of heaven and the only way of salvation? Or is it not more like this world and the device of man?" To assume the systematic exclusion from salvation of all those who lived in times or nations without access to the one truth convicted God of a vicious favoritism. God intended better for humanity than guesswork. Nature is available for all to observe and reflect upon and is thus a more reliable source of the divine will. "The knowledge of nature is the revelation of God."[43]

Faith, Allen thought, requires less effort than education and thus holds an attraction for many people. The purposefully ignorant "are most fond of miracles" and seek easy explanations for what they do not understand and refuse to learn. The ignorant respond to the unknown as children to a "Jack-with-a-lanthorn," running away in the night rather than discovering the source of their fright. If people studied their environment, their superstitions and fears would vanish. Not "a supernatural whirligig" subject to chance or the inconsistent actions of angels and devils, the universe operates in a systematic and predictable fashion.

Nature offers a "regular standard . . . whereby to acertain the truth and reality of things." If humanity but tried to determine that standard, all notions of luck, fate, astrology, and portents would vanish.[44]

Allen's deistic perfectionism shone with optimism. The "glorious purpose" of creation is human "existence and happiness." The route toward that end is nature, the medium "through which God dispenses his benignity to mankind." God's providence is evidenced in "the air we breathe in, the light of the sun, and the waters of the murmuring rills, . . . and well it is that they are given in so great profusion that they cannot by the monopoly of the rich be engrossed from the poor." A selfish elite try to limit nature's blessings but will not succeed as the divine intention is human equality. Nature must ultimately lead to "this single point" of "infinite perfection . . . eternally displayed." Having established the existence of a deity, it is "our obligation to love and adore God, because he provides for, and is beneficent to us." Humanity is dependent on nature and on the creator of that bounty.[45]

Most of Allen's arguments can be found in one rationalist work or another in eighteenth-century France or England. But *Reason the Only Oracle* grew from native roots. Allen's book is an adumbration and extension of popular anticlericalism, lay assertiveness, ecclesiastical democracy, impatience with the theological hairsplitting and contradictions of Calvinism, and concerns for preserving the balance between individualism and the community. In many particulars, Allen was not that iconoclastic. Of course, most of Allen's Christian neighbors accepted the authority of revelation, the reality of a personal god, and, in some instances, predestinarianism—vital differences to be sure. Still, the similarities of outlook toward religious authority figures may explain why people like Nathan Perkins found Vermont's Christian culture and Allen's deism all of a piece. Allen represented only the rankest form of democratic, individualist infidelity and rejection of traditional, hierarchical social theory and practices. In these ways, Allen's work echoed three major theological trends which characterized Vermont's pluralist sectarianism and struck fear in the hearts of orthodox ministers such as Nathan Perkins.[46]

First, a widely held preference for lay control of churches marked religious development on the Vermont frontier. With the exception of some Anglicans and Presbyterians, most religious Vermonters moved during the Revolution toward a strong attachment to democratic forms of church government, marked by an intense suspicion of ministerial prerogatives and an educated clergy. The chronic shortage of trained ministers in Vermont fostered this preference. Congregations grew accustomed to running their own meetings and showed little enthusiasm for relinquishing control of their churches.[47]

Some Vermonters expressed concern with the paucity of ministers in their state. As early as 1770 several Grants townships petitioned the New Hampshire association of Congregational Ministers for help. Settlers could not afford a minister, opening them to the danger "of falling into a heathenish State and bringing up their Children without any knowledge of God & Religion, or of being drawn into gross Errors, Heresies & disorderly Practices." But the Association found it inexpedient and prohibitively expensive to become involved in what was, after all, a local issue. In religion as in politics, frontier settlers had to solve their problems themselves. Their solutions were not always to the liking of the orthodox leadership.[48]

When possible, towns shared available ministers. Throughout the 1760s the Reverend Peter Powers of Hollis served his own community as well as Newbury and Haverhill on the other side of the river. Like the few other settled ministers in the state, the Reverend Abner Reeve of Brattleboro conducted meetings in the 1770s and 1780s on alternate Sundays at barns in neighboring towns. Just as the frontierspeople relied on one another for essentials like plows, so they "rented" ministers and lay readers from each other, writing notes for these services. In the process they may have enjoyed a greater variety in their Sunday meetings than did their relatives to the south.[49]

This self-reliance in the face of a shortage of ordained ministers promoted the confidence of congregations in their ability to do without. Wallingford's church fragmented in 1783 when its minister insisted on greater authority. Seeking to attain theological peace, the town meeting selected Baptist Henry Green as the town's settled minister if he passed an examination before local Congregationalists and Presbyterians. Green passed, delivering his cautious sermons to a very mixed congregation which united on the primacy of lay authority.[50]

The shortage of educated clergy and insistence on lay authority partially fueled the second major pattern in this period: the proliferation of diverse theological opinions. Bereft of a clergy to define and defend orthodoxy—as understood throughout most of New England—Vermonters relied more on their own judgments and the persuasive power of itinerant ministers. Orthodox predestinarian Calvinism, whose logic mystified congregations, became the major casualty of this diversity of opinion, while Methodism and Universalism flourished on the northern frontier, their theologies welcomed as commonsensical.

In most frontier communities, so many different religious views competed that no one group could support a meetinghouse. All came together to listen to any traveling minister, no matter what his specific theological message. As late as 1801 William Babcock of Springfield addressed congregations in a dozen Vermont towns consisting of Anglicans, Methodists, Congregationalists, and his own Baptists. He admitted that this diverse audience came to hear him preach for lack of an alternative. Another itinerant, Thomas Robbins, wrote that "the people wish to have ministers and will listen to any who come by," even the occasional grump, like Nathan Perkins.[51]

Some ministers, such as the Baptist Aaron Leland, overcame initial doubts to embrace this diversity. When the people of Chester, none of them Baptist, wrote Leland to request that he settle among them, he rejected the proposal as "unpromising." But after a brief visit, Leland felt the call to Chester and stayed for fifty successful years, serving seven towns and ending his career as Vermont's lieutenant governor.[52]

Not all ministers were willing to compromise their theology in this way. Based on his own experiences, Isaac Lyman wrote that Calvinist missionaries met with hostility in these new communities. While still a theological force to be reckoned with in Vermont, Calvinism fell into disrepute after the Revolution, a decline assisted by the spiritual elitism of Samuel Hopkins's "New Divinity." An exacting theology which called for a return to the Puritan church of visible saints, its adherents— labeled "the professors of Fatelism" by Ethan Allen—saw little hope for the mass of humanity. Many Vermonters resented these demands for theological purity divorced from social reality and the constant reminders of their own damnation. Lyman wrote that frontier congregations did not wish to hear sermons "of Hell & Damnation" as they already "suffer all these torments . . . to a perfection." Another minister gave a brilliant example of this rejection when he attempted to quantify the chances of a dead child getting into heaven, placing the odds at ten to one against. The father gave "a heavy stampt with his foot and said, 'Hold your tongue, I will have no such talk in my house. I don't believe my child has gone to hell. I believe it has gone to heaven, and I just mean to go there too.' He turned to a friend and said, 'Brother Norton, won't you bring a Methodist preacher to see me?' " [53] And Methodists they got.

What did Vermonters expect from religion, if not to be told that the odds are that they would burn in hell for all eternity? In a world of accentuated uncertainty, they sought support for their families and communities. William Babcock found Calvinism's greatest fault in its "wicked & uncharitable, illiberally narrow Doctrine of Close Communion." When a member of his church objected to the admission of those baptized only at birth, Babcock responded that he "could not answer to God, [for] the crime of Shutting out one of his children from the table." The Wallingford Baptist Church covenant stated that "the laying on of hands is an ordinance of Christ, to be administered on all . . . that see it to be their duty when baptized, but not to be as a bar with those who do not." Vermonters took theology seriously but tried to prevent it from disrupting their churches. [54]

Congregations organized themselves. As Ezra Stiles wrote, "Wherever they find a Bunch of ten or a dozen baptist Families they form a Chh & ordain a Brother an Elder." [55] Occasionally trouble arose when someone demanded that the entire church practice in conformity to his or her private perception of truth. For instance, a "Sister M" withdrew from Shaftsbury's First Church with the complaint that the congregation neglected washing one another's feet. She did not find a church which did so but always had the option exercised by Benjamin Randall, who started as a Congregationalist, became a Baptist and then a self-proclaimed Arminian, and finally founded his own church, the Freewill Baptists. The wide choice of denominations actually lessened theological conflict. [56]

Calvinist exclusivity threatened the cohesion of their communities while an open communion brought people together and held them in a bond of hope. Babcock recorded "a Sorrowful day to all of our family— Brother Newton being obliged to flea his Country, being insolvent." After joining with him in prayer and "Giving the Right hand of fellowship & the kiss of Charity," Babcock observed that "it is not at all probable I shall ever see him again on the shores of time . . . hereafter may we meet; where Assemblies never break up; & where friendship shall be as lasting as Eternity." Religion could not hold together societies before such economic forces of dissolution, but it need not interfere.

Babcock's congregation, like others in Vermont, downplayed differences while emphasizing commonalties. The open communion matched this need while offering condolence, comfort, and the dream of assemblies which would "never break up." [57]

New England's learned ministers had difficulty dealing with these un-tutored yet powerful religious emotions. Many felt an elitist contempt for their congregations. Asa Burton, a noted trainer of ministers, wrote of his flock at Thetford in 1779 that they were "quarrelsome, intemperate, immoral, clownish and vulgar." Even the much-heralded "Apostle of Vermont," Job Swift, failed consistently to understand or exploit the sentiments of his congregations, expecting them to follow his lead while they broke new ground. Four congregations dismissed Swift on the same complaint of theological intolerance and excessive exercise of ministerial discipline. Telling frontier settlers that a Yale degree gave one special insight into the mind of God did not work well for Swift and his ministerial colleagues. [58]

But then Vermonters no more needed ministers than church buildings in order to seek religious truths. As Ethan Allen mockingly wrote, "The uncultivated part of mankind . . . do not distrust their conscious knowledge, this is a privilidge we derive from learned sophestry." The diversity and theological independence of Vermont daunted many of the organized religions. The would-be Episcopal bishop of Vermont, Samuel Peters, wrote that "the Deists and various kinds of Dissenters compose eight tenths of its inhabitants, its wealth, and power." As a consequence, many in his own church "believe me mad, if I should further think of trying to build up a prelatic Church in the howling wilderness" of Vermont. Where Perkins and Peters saw chaos and irreligion in the frontier proliferation of sects, Allen saw democracy and the doom of religious hierarchy. [59]

The third trend appears at first glance contradictory. In the 1780s some Vermont congregations retreated from their former exclusivity, becoming ever more inclusive and open, while some Separates and Baptists called for closer attention to the purity of membership and practices, generally splintering congregations as a consequence. Although the effects differ, they derived from the same source: the desire and perceived need to grant individual conscience primacy within a viable religious community. Some congregations met this need through greater inclusivity; others by subdividing.

Most of Vermont's early settlers followed the Separate path to the Green Mountains. These congregations sought to separate themselves from those lacking in sanctity and, like the original Puritans, went into exile in the wilderness. But as church after church in Vermont discovered, Separatist theology quickly reached a critical stage bordering on complete dissolution. Separate churches fell apart into first two or three and then a dozen religious societies. Every person became his and even her own minister. Congregations routinely reached a crisis where individual parishioners felt as qualified as the minister to interpret the Bible. And what they tended to conclude did not bode well for ministerial authority. If no one recognized the saved, how could the minister? Separatism reached a point of logical inversion. Ethan Allen was just one of hundreds of Vermonters who reasoned that by the logic of Calvinism either no one or everyone was saved—finding the latter proposition more intellectually comforting and socially useful. Confronted with the social realities of the frontier, Separatism became more relaxed in its discipline and more open theologically—and the church became a component of a secular community, rather than its defining institution.[60]

Vermont's first Separatist congregation reflects both sides of this paradoxical theological development. Within the Bennington church's first few years, those who favored a more restrictive membership separated themselves from their fellow Separates, attaining their goal of isolation on the side of Mount Anthony. The town's first minister, the Calvinist Jedediah Dewey, opened the congregation to the entire community. Dewey did not require public confessions of faith, and nonmembers, those who had not experienced saving grace, enjoyed equal rights within the church and often held church offices. Even "ye awful deist Ethan Allen" attended regularly, carrying on a lively, good-natured dispute with Dewey for a decade until Dewey's death in 1779.[61]

The career of Dewey's successor evidences the importance of an open communion to Bennington's unity. Before seeking a replacement for Dewey, the church rewrote its covenant, accepting the Cambridge Platform—the rock upon which the New Lights built their churches—except for its grant of authority to the minister. The new covenant held that "the decisive power in cases of discipline" and doctrinal disputes lay with the body of the church, and not the minister. With that qualification, a committee found a minister worthy of the leading town of an independent state, an outstanding representative of New Light Congregationalism named David Avery.

Born in Norwich, Connecticut, like many in his congregation, Avery had been converted by George Whitefield and later graduated from Yale. His first congregation dismissed him in 1777 for his extended absence as a chaplain in the Continental army, a recommendation in Bennington. But Avery arrived in town with a woman he called a slave, in one stroke violating Vermont law and the policy of his church not to commune with anyone who owned a slave. Avery polarized the town from his first day, and many followed the example of General Ebenezer Walbridge in refusing to attend any service presided over by a slave owner. In defending himself, Avery compounded his crime by informing this congregation which just signed a covenant with God affirming the supremacy of the laity that the minister commanded final authority on all matters of theology and discipline. He even attacked Dewey's "liberal principles," a terrible blunder in a community which idolized its former minister's memory. Within weeks of his arrival, Avery confronted opposition from both ends of the theological spectrum.[62]

Avery's spiritual superiority emptied his church. A follower of the New Divinity, Avery swore to limit church membership to the visibly saved, insisting that only he could judge this virtue. Discipline is to a church as regulations to an army, its absence reducing the church to "a wild ungovernable mob." The congregation, Avery said, found its sacred duty in silence and obedience to the minister, whose authority could not be questioned without affronting God. Like Jonathan Edwards, Avery insisted on individual salvation and group acquiescence.[63]

Had Avery aimed to keep the likes of Ethan Allen—busily convincing Avery's slave to sue for her freedom—out of church, his congregation might have supported him. But the new minister directed his fire at other believers, dividing his congregation and Bennington. Avery clung to a hierarchical view of society shared by few of his neighbors. Expecting deference from the whole town, Avery warned against a "levelling disposition" which is "not only dangerous to society, but is expressly forbidden in God's word." Democracy was the new devil, promoting the unchristian view that "I am not inferior to any one" and thus confounding "the distinctions nature had made, and which time immemorial has sanctified." Guided by that arch-demon Ethan Allen, "this daring leveling spirit of the times has pervaded all our land, and shakes even the pillars of church and state." The tyranny of democracy must be opposed. Like so many conservatives over the past two centuries, Avery accepted independence but rejected the Revolution.[64]

The effort to remove Avery from his pulpit became a public event. The *Vermont Gazette* carried articles calling for Avery's dismissal, asking if "a flock may . . . be more happy in the absence of a shepherd, than in the presence of one" so disruptive of "the flock's tranquility?" Opponents went door to door calling for a boycott of what they insisted was the town's church and circulated petitions during services. Avery challenged the dissenters to press charges in court—a surprisingly secular solution that alienated his remaining supporters. After two years of fighting, Avery finally acquiesced in the calling of an ecclesiastical council.[65]

The council of Avery's fellow Yale graduates, meeting in June 1783, upheld Avery's theology and stated that "we are of the opinion that those who make this complaint are blameable!" Having vindicated Avery, the council dismissed him. The moderator, Eliphalet Wright, condemned "our aggrieved brethren" for denying "the great truths on which the faith and hope of the people of God depend. . . . I earnestly beseech you to consider whether you are not really doing the devil's work."[66]

In a bitter farewell Avery faulted his congregation for failing to exclude dissenters from communion. But an insistence on exclusion asked too much of a frontier community, as Avery dimly understood. The church members "put up with evils" so that they might "get along" with their neighbors. Efforts to preserve harmony must be secondary to God's law, which Avery knew and offered Bennington. Avery attacked the "vile churls" who opposed him as not only wrong theologically and corrupt personally but responsible for "the growth of vice, the abounding of lust, the spread and prevalence of infidelity, of heresy and hardness of heart." Avery battled the "antichrist" and lost.[67]

In the very year the Revolution ended, New England's standing order entered battle against the dangerous new theologies of the frontier. Avery spoke for many colleagues in warning against democrats who believed that "the rights of man allow to him this licence of his tongue," creating new religions with "new gospels." To avoid the corrosive impact of democracy and diversity, congregations should draw inward and obey their minister. Avery tried sustaining deferential structures in a society where they served no visible function and had no economic equivalent. The absence of social hierarchy on the Vermont frontier subverted deference.[68]

Avery encountered opposition not from irreligious skeptics but from deeply religious people. Their dissent began with disapproval of his power and ended with a surprising transition to a belief in universal salvation. The discovery that the council of their choice did not share their radicalism shocked Avery's opponents. Assuming their Calvinist purity, the dissenters were stunned and offended when accused of serving the devil. On the other hand, they took pride in their identification with the democratic thrust of the American Revolution.[69]

In the years of Ethan Allen's carefully purchased peace, from 1778 to 1784, Vermont became a caldron of new religions. Many historians regard this "New Light Stir" as a revival, taking ministers such as Job Swift at their word in seeing the people they converted as previously irreligious because their towns did not have ministers and church buildings. This emphasis on formal institutions assumes a great deal about the nature of religious sentiment while missing the fact that most of these towns did not have church buildings and ministers for years after the "Stir" either. Not so much revival as reorganization occurred in these years; well-ordered New England churches did not emerge, but dozens of competing sects did. The foremost historian of the "New Light Stir" identified three leaders of the revival: Joseph Marshall, David Avery, and Ithmar Hibbard. Avery converted only one person at Bennington; Hibbard led one of the five small Baptist churches in Shaftsbury; and Marshall, a well-known eccentric, never had his own congregation, dividing churches instead into Separate gatherings. These ministers assumed every person added to a congregation a convert. Yet the overwhelming majority of the new members in any of Vermont's churches in the 1780s were youths, returning soldiers, or people who already belonged to another congregation. In Bennington forty-seven new members joined the church after Avery's departure and without benefit of a minister; they just waited for one to leave.[70]

Town after town in Vermont experienced religious strife akin to that which disrupted Bennington. No simple statistical relation properly relates the traumatic effect such theological discord exerted on the delicate structure of new communities or the diversity of communal strategies for dealing with these conflicts. Yet this diversity in no way threatened the social order of Vermont, for the northern frontier had never

premised communal harmony on religious unity.[71] Towns either followed
Bennington's example of an inclusive covenant or did not establish a
single community church, making no effort to discriminate among the
various denominations which held their meetings in homes, barns, and
taverns. As one disturbed settler stated, "Among this motley crew there
was no regular place of worship, not any likely prospect that there should
[be], for their religions had as many shades of difference as the leaves
in autumn. . . . To hear their people talk, one would think time had
run back to the days of the levellers." The separation of church and state
came without extended debate on the Vermont frontier, making it an
attractive haven for religious dissenters.[72]

While Vermont's congregations continued to admonish those who violated the rules, willing confessions of error became much rarer. The most
common concluding entry to an individual censorship for drunkenness,
fornication, fraudulent business practices, or heresy became excommu-
nication, as the offender "left the fellowship" for another church. Far
easier to join one of the burgeoning sects of Vermont than to be subjected to the humiliation of a public confession. Church records are
riddled with such excommunications in the later 1780s and 1790s, and
one can trace a single individual through two, three, and even four
churches as the excommunications pile up.[73] Competition devastated the
power of the congregation to maintain its version of good order, placing
the responsibility for stability increasingly on the secular structures of
the community.

III

*I offer it as my candid opinion, that a proffer of religion to man-
kind which tenders salvation to them, merely upon condition of
believing it . . . and which dooms all those who disbelieve it to
damnation, has too much the appearance of human craft, and
ought to be suspected as to its divinity.*—Ethan Allen

In many ways Allen's logic of "universal plenitude" anticipated America's emerging democratic religions. Allen's assault on the clergy drew
upon Enlightenment attitudes but also presaged the antielitism inherent in the later attacks on the ministry by the Disciples of Christ,
among others. Most nineteenth-century Christians would have recog-

nized Allen's benevolent deity and his confidence in man's inherent goodness. Protestant liberals agreed that man possessed free will and innate morality and best glorified God by serving humanity; dogma and creed had little importance compared with ethical behavior.[74]

As with much nineteenth-century American theology, Allen's cosmology centered on rationality, equity, and inclusion; everyone got back what they put in, a fair spiritual price. An individual worked toward understanding and received proper divine recompense. Allen's system included everyone, like those efforts at open communion so common in Vermont's churches. All would reach heaven, all had an equal chance for divine justice in a rational universe. Anyone, Allen thought, could comprehend the world, even those lacking a Yale education.[75]

While significant aspects of Allen's theology rested comfortably in the mainstream of religious development on the frontier, his rejection— and ridicule—of revelation separated him from his Christian neighbors. Many of Allen's contemporaries found such ideas deeply disturbing and intellectually radical, especially coming from a self-educated frontier farmer. A few Vermonters tried to win Allen from the devil; most simply disregarded *Reason the Only Oracle.* The unkindest cut of all came in winter 1786, when a fire at Haswell's printshop destroyed *Reason*'s remaining stock. While some deity or another may have started the blaze, many saw the more tangible hand of one of God's evangelical tools, the Reverend Joseph Marshall. There were a number of other possible arsonists, for *Reason* did not enjoy a popular reception.[76]

Allen gloried in being a "clodhopper philosopher." Appealing to the image of the rugged frontiersman, he apologized for his "untutored logic" while boasting of "a mind nursed principally in the Mountainous wilds of America."[77] Allen received mail from readers applauding his common touch and asking why so few copies circulated. He wrote Crèvecoeur that *Reason* had "pleased more individuals than I expected and caused considerable speculation & argumentation." In fact, Allen was roundly ignored, and his book deliberately forgotten.[78]

Not surprisingly, ministers were Allen's foremost critics. As Allen admitted to Crèvecoeur, "The Clergy of this Country reprobate the work and anathemize the writer of it." Those who wrote reviews refused to mention the book's contents, moving directly to insults. Lemuel Hopkins armed Allen with a "mob-collecting club / Black from the forge of Belzebub, / And grim with metaphysic scowl," appearing "in hyperborean skies, / To tell the world the bible lies." One reader, upset with both *Reason* and Rhode Island's continued existence, suggested that soon Rhode Islanders would begin "worshipping Ethan Allen for Mahomet, and Adopting the *Oracle of Reason* for an Alcoran." Timothy Dwight called Allen that "great Clodhopping oracle of man," imbued with the "reptility of a angle worm . . . in the contemptible plagerism of every rotten, worn-out dogma of the English deistical writers," full of the "deformity, the venom, and the ill nature of the toad . . . in the sputterings" against "Truth, virtue, providence, and the Creator." A shabby, awkward book, *Reason* evidenced the "rusticity of the expression, the jolting of the stile, the head-and-tail pomposity of the dogmaticism, and general naggishness" of the uneducated. No person "in his right senses" could suppose "that this thing was intended as an exhibition of reason." Dwight did not like the book. But he offered no specific criticism, gave no examples of its failings, no indication of what the book discussed. Instead, he called it "heathen" and dismissed it as the product of "the wilds of Vermont."[79]

Most reviews followed these lines. In 1810 John J. Henry, who had known Allen, wrote a long letter of warning to his children. Henry remembered Allen well as a man possessing "a most ferocious temper (fearing neither God nor man), of a most daring courage, . . . and very astonishing in all his undertakings." But his religion reeked of immorality. While he did not wish to censor their readings, Henry insisted that his children not read the "diabolical" *Reason*. Allen had limited his education to history and other "books of little account." A major "topic of discourse" in Philadelphia after the war, *Reason* had now thankfully vanished from circulation. Even those who admired Allen for his character and bravery, his political actions and opinions, despised him for writing *Reason*.[80]

Though often presented as such, *Reason* is not the railings of a village atheist alienated from Vermont's Christian majority. Usually Allen touched the deepest convictions of his fellow Vermonters, but not in *Reason*. While *Reason* does draw upon a number of shared values, it failed utterly as a persuasive work, swerving far off the main traveled roads of New England. As a writer and speaker, Allen's strength lay in his use of common idiom and a vernacular growl. Yet he aspired to be accepted as a man of learning, "the Philosopher." He failed utterly at that task, in part because of his inability or refusal to express himself in simple terms.

Wanting to sound like a philosopher, Allen came across as a heretic. As he knew it would, *Reason* put Allen beyond the pale, terminating his political career. Allen was as a man possessed—selling off land, calling in lawsuits and debts, turning to every expedient to get his book published. Why did he print his theological views at such great personal and financial sacrifice?

Perhaps the answer lies in the only significant difference between *Reason* and every other deist work of the time: Allen devoted the bulk of his book to a discussion of immortality and the afterlife. From the moment of his father's death, Ethan Allen entered on a lifelong obsession with immortality and justice in the afterlife. Every major psychological crisis of Allen's life involved coming to terms with death—his father's, his son's, his own. And in June 1783 Mary Brownson Allen, who for many years had carried the primary responsibility for the family farm and their five children, died at the age of fifty.[81]

Hardly a typical deist concern, the afterlife was of great importance to most of Allen's neighbors. In this age before unchecked individualism, the generation of children, especially sons and heirs, mitigated the fear of death as a reassuring extension of the lineal family across time. The majority of Vermonters turned to their religious faiths and ritual for comfort, or at least resignation. But at the time he wrote *Reason*, Allen had neither sons nor Christian faith. Allen followed Hume in seeing religion entirely as a human construct intended to quiet fears of uncertainty and death. As if to prove the point, Allen's own theology was born of that anxiety.

In this context the timing of *Reason* is significant. Allen started wrestling with this inner demon at a time when he felt particularly strong, after regaining his self-esteem in the sweeping victories over his longtime Yorker opponents. He certainly could not have opened this private Pandora's box at a better moment. Convinced that he had assured his own secular "immortality" as a founder of Vermont, he felt secure enough to tackle his one remaining enemy: death.

His need to affirm immortality compelled Allen to abandon his reliance on reason alone. By insisting on observation and thought as the basis for understanding the universe, Allen had reasoned himself into a difficult position from which the logical conclusion could have been atheism. To retain his "darling hope of immortality," he had to make at least one logical leap: that humans cannot understand the next world with their limited abilities.[82] But this assertion called into doubt the efficacy of human reason to understand God's will. Allen cleverly, though tautologically, anticipated this logistical trap by insisting that God formed the senses precisely so people could comprehend their world, but no more. Allen's God did humanity a favor by limiting their view of the afterlife, for if they saw beyond death, the vision might "imbitter all our present enjoyments, and make us discontented and miserable from the anticipation." It was all speculation, but necessary speculation, just like the Onion River Company.[83]

Seeking escape from mortality, Allen contorted his reasoning until, in keeping with his sense of democracy, he attained certainty not just of his immortality but of everyone's. Given a benevolent god, Allen reasoned, there must be a soul which lives beyond physical death, because this life is too short and painful. And the afterlife must be pleasant, because eternal punishment reflected cruelty and iniquity, the actions of a few years deciding the individual's fate.[84]

Allen limited physical manifestations, whether good or evil, to this world. God would not punish sin with "pain, sickness or mortality" or reward virtue with "sensual happiness"; "to reward moral actions with a glass of wine or a shoulder of mutton, would be as inadequate, as to measure a triangle with sound; for virtue and vice pertain to the mind." Human souls progress into the afterlife while human bodies return to the cycles of nature. Allen envisioned life as a "progressive state of being and action" in which God intended that all improve, evolving toward greater understanding and deeper wisdom. Infant death, a paradox for many contemporary theologians, convinced Allen that the soul must continue to grow beyond the limitations of this world, reducing death to "no more than a dissolution of the form and . . . particles" of our bodies. With death only a step forward in inevitable human progress, Allen thought he had refuted both "a particular day of judgment" and atheist finality.[85]

It was not sufficient, though, for Allen to reach this intellectual and psychological resolution in private. A satisfying—which, for Allen, by definition meant self-dramatizing—catharsis required an audience. Just as his *Narrative* reasserted his heroic identity, so *Reason* removed the one remaining inner doubt for this supremely self-confident individual. None of which is meant to imply that Allen wrote *Reason* solely as an exercise in self-therapy. He believed in the validity of his message and the necessity of presenting it to the public. But at the same time, it seems clear that an unusual compulsion drove him to publish his thoughts at all costs.

In *Reason* Allen exorcised the inner demons that had haunted him since the premature death of his father. Hence his need to believe that the afterlife functioned as a sort of college—a Yale without entrance requirements or degrees. This self-educated would-be philosopher could not imagine an end to learning and intellectual development. Human happiness demanded change, so Allen rejected as unacceptable the stultifying steady state of the Christian heaven. If a mind received no new ideas, it lost its purpose. As humans are "always capable of additional knowledge" and find happiness in education, it must be expected that they will continue to exercise their minds after death. Humans are imperfect and finite creatures, "probationers," but capable of improvement. In his heaven Allen finally would continue the education interrupted by his father's death and rise above the limitations of his class. Yet his afterlife would be like his present life: active, energetic, and unpredictable.[86]

As if to seal the resolution he reached with *Reason,* Allen remarried shortly before finishing his manuscript. Frances Montresor Buchanan, the daughter of a French officer and widow of a British officer, came to Vermont to claim land she inherited from her stepfather, the Yorker attorney Crean Brush. She and her mother, Margaret Wall, rented a room at Stephen Bradley's house in Westminster.[87] It was here that twenty-four-year-old Frances Buchanan met the widower Ethan Allen, still the most influential man in the state. The young widow enjoyed teasing the overbearing general who managed to find daily reasons for visiting. When a mutual friend noticed Allen's interest in Buchanan, he joked that she could easily become queen of Vermont. Unimpressed with the honor, Buchanan observed that if she married the devil she would become queen of hell.[88]

But Frances Buchanan felt differently about Ethan Allen than about the devil. The popular story of their marriage accords with Allen's impetuous nature. On the morning of 9 February 1784 Allen stopped at Bradley's house and called on Buchanan. "If we are to be married," Allen is reported to have said, "now is the time, for I am on my way to Arlington." "Very well," Buchanan is reported to have answered, "but give me time to put on my Joseph [a colorful coat]." Some versions add that Allen saw little reason to bother with marriage except that "as a decent respect for the customs of society require it of us, we are willing to have the ceremony performed." What is known for certain is that the chief justice of Vermont, Allen's friend Moses Robinson, married them that same day. Nine months later Fanny gave birth to Hannibal Montresor Allen.[89]

At the age of forty-six, Ethan Allen found happiness. Allen respected his wife for her learning and wit, and there is every evidence that they enjoyed their life together. He presented a copy of *Reason* to "Dear Fanny wise, the beautiful and young, / The partner of my joys, my dearest self, / My love, pride of my life."[90] Allen's retirement from politics had as much to do with his stated desire to stay home with his family as with a concern for the reaction to *Reason the Only Oracle.*

Allen noted the tendency of men to create "scarecrows" with which to frighten themselves. He knew from experience that "men will face destructive cannon and mortars, engage each other in the clashing of arms, and meet the horrors of war undaunted," yet flee in terror from some "supernatural whirligig." Though religion had long been the prime source of these devils, clever political leaders often manipulated this psychology of fear to their own purposes. Allen himself had made ample use of imagined horrors to avoid violence, successfully casting himself in the role of wilderness demon. By the middle of the 1780s Ethan Allen had become a scarecrow for the emerging conservative elite of the United States. In the last political acts of his life, Allen would play on this image finally to win acknowledgment for Vermont's independence.[91]

CHAPTER TEN

The Fate of Revolutionary Republicanism

I N AUGUST 1784 Ethan Allen wrote his brother Ira of his "positive determination" to retire to his farm, the care of his family, and the cultivation of his thoughts. He asked Ira's help in building a house and added, "Do not Think that I will change my scheme, for the Decree is gone forthwith." He signed himself, "the Philosopher." The week after his son Hannibal's birth, Allen published his farewell to the Vermont public, defending the Haldimand negotiations and supporting Ira Allen and Thomas Chittenden for reelection.[1]

When Allen left the center of power and moved north, he did not know that a final challenge awaited him. In the wake of Shays' Rebellion, Ethan Allen performed his last public role, this time paradoxically as protector of the oppressed *and* of established order. By supporting one group of agrarian insurgents while denying support to another, Allen finally won Vermont statehood.

I

Behold inspired from Vermont's dens,
The seer of Antichrist descends,
To feed new mobs with Hell-born manna
In Gentile lands of Susquehanna.
Lemuel Hopkins

In the years after the Revolution, Allen emerged as one of America's first national figures, an authentic frontier folk hero. Through his unique blend of republicanism, pragmatism, and self-promotion, Allen established himself at center stage of a dozen revolutionary dramas. Even after Allen's retirement from Vermont politics, the state government used him as a valuable symbol in exceptional cases. None proved more exceptional than the uprising to the south known as Shays's Rebellion.

Only one of several political disorders in the 1780s, the rebellion in Massachusetts came in response to a larger crisis of economic stagnation gripping the northern United States. Vermont also experienced these pressures. In the early 1780s the assembly passed a number of acts encouraging settlement and threatening the confiscation of lands not settled by fall 1786. These policies seemed to work too well as thousands of people poured into Vermont between 1783 and 1787.

Vermont changed, fast. In the decade after Yorktown the population more than tripled, most of the increase coming from migration. A Boston paper reported in 1787 that "more families have moved into [Vermont] . . . for six months past, than has done in the same space of time since the first settlement of that country." Added to this migration, Vermont enjoyed a remarkable persistence rate in its first decades: 95 percent of more than two thousand families identified as resident in the Green Mountains in 1775 can be found on the Vermont census of 1791, 70 percent in the same towns.[2]

Since newcomers ran up more debts and faced lawsuits sooner than long-settled residents, Vermont's courts filled with debt cases, attorneys joined the rush north, and the assembly received dozens of petitions complaining of lawyers and court costs.[3] Tensions rose in early 1786 as citizens petitioned for the expulsion of lawyers and the cancellation of all debts and angry crowds gathered outside courthouses.[4] Most people tried to get extensions from their creditors. Ethan Allen, for instance, offered an impatient creditor named Hudson partial restitution in cattle and a new note, the way things had always been done. But Hudson insisted on the full amount and rejected the request for an extension from Allen's attorney, Stephen Bradley. In court Bradley denied that the signature on the note was Allen's. Furiously, Allen disrupted the court, saying something to the effect that he did not hire Bradley to lie for him but to get an extension. "That is a true note," Allen told the court. "I signed it, I'll swear to it, and I'll pay it. I want no shuffling— I want time." The judges granted Allen an extension, and the story spread quickly through the state, becoming an allegory for common sentiments.[5]

In October a crowd tried to close the court in Windsor, but the sheriff persuaded them to go home. That same month nine towns petitioned the assembly for relief from taxes and lawyers and the lowering of court costs. After a series of crowd actions directed at those "pick-pockets" and "bandittie" known as attorneys, and fearing even more radical measures such as paper currency, the conservative leadership of the assembly reached a compromise with Governor Chittenden. The assembly passed a series of acts designed to meet the economic crisis, most notably the Specific Tender Act requiring creditors to accept payment in kind, even personal items. Ira Allen pushed through a popular act preventing creditors from states in which Vermonters could not press suits—in other words New York—from suing in Vermont's courts. These acts were temporary, as the constitution required. The conservatives bought more time by convincing the assembly to call on the town meetings to decide in January 1787 what measures should follow. Under the constitution any recommended acts would take another year to implement.[6]

Most of the state seemed satisfied with the assembly's efforts, the only other crowd action coming in Rutland in late November. A crowd of about one hundred, mostly veterans, surrounded the county court and demanded its closure. The judges asked the defendants if they desired postponements, which they did not, leading the court to deny the crowd's request. The crowd held the building for a few hours and then dispersed before the arrival of the militia. The state arrested and fined forty-seven people, ending the matter there. The *Vermont Gazette* reported that "the affair was conducted with . . . prudence and firmness on the part of the government." More to the point, the government enjoyed substantial support, with hundreds of local inhabitants turning out in their militia companies to defend the state's courts.[7]

The uprising in Rutland coincided with popular crowd activity in Massachusetts which closed the courts in the Berkshires and brought the entire state to a standstill. Vermont handled the affair quickly and effectively, but then its government also responded to citizens' petitions and passed laws to meet their needs. Since leadership shared these concerns, the responsiveness and popularity of Vermont's government are not surprising. In Massachusetts the leadership removed itself from the citizenry, physically and economically. In Vermont the crowds remained loyal to the state, and the government could depend on its militia to maintain order. In Massachusetts the militia was the crowd, and the government turned to a private army under General Benjamin Lincoln to put down the rebellion. Vermont's conservative minority compromised; in Massachusetts the conservatives ran the show.[8]

Amidst the political upheaval of 1786 Ethan Allen found one more arena in which to employ the rhetoric of the Revolution to the advantage of a group of frontier farmers. New Englanders began moving into the Wyoming Valley on the northern reaches of the Susquehannah River in Pennsylvania in the late 1760s. Their deeds came from the Susquehannah Company chartered by Connecticut, and they refused to repurchase their land from Pennsylvania speculators. This disagreement over the validity of land titles, so common on the eighteenth-century frontier, started a long dispute between the region's settlers and Pennsylvania's government. Officials in Philadelphia thought convincing Connecticut to drop its claims would end the settlers' pretensions. When Connecticut complied in 1783, Pennsylvania dealt with the Wyoming Valley as "a conquered Nation." Rather than trying to win over the settlers, Pennsylvania indicated that it would brook no compromise in the exercise of its jurisdiction. Pennsylvania based its authority in the region on an interstate agreement, not the consent of the governed.[9]

This policy showed signs of succeeding. As in the Green Mountains, the inhabitants of the Wyoming Valley willingly accepted any jurisdiction that respected their land titles. When Pennsylvania denied the validity of their deeds, most Wyoming settlers resisted. But by 1785, after fifteen years of struggle against the proprietary and revolutionary governments of Pennsylvania, and with Congress unable to resolve the dispute, many settlers lost their stomach for the fight and sought accommodation with the Philadelphia speculators.[10]

In desperation some of the settlers in the Wyoming Valley turned to a veteran defender of local autonomy, Ethan Allen. Convinced that Allen's military and organizational skills would render him "particularly serviceable" to their cause, the Wyoming settlers hoped that Allen's notoriety and charisma would rekindle their lagging enthusiasm while striking terror in the hearts of the Pennsylvania oligarchy. To the Wyoming claimants Allen embodied the success of Vermont, which "rose in such a storm" as they now faced to become "too strong to fear an attack." They thought that Allen's presence—in fact, just the act of inviting Allen—would force Pennsylvania to negotiate rather than fight.[11]

The Wyoming settlers lured Allen with that most common yet most desired of frontier commodities, land. Allen took the bait. "I am very sensible that our cause is just," he wrote, and their opponents evil men who conspired to aid the British during the Revolution. He promised to fight to the death these "avaricious men [who] make interest their God" and then offered a string of practical recommendations.[12]

Following Allen's advice, John Franklin acquired arms and ammunition for the settlers and worked to crowd the settlements with as many landholders under Connecticut title as possible. In late December, Franklin organized a small army of four hundred men, looking forward to the arrival of the "Head Doctor from the North . . . with his apparatus Glister Pipe and all," to lead these troops.[13]

But Allen did not rush into the fray. First he sent Levi Allen to reconnoiter and wrote William Samuel Johnson, Connecticut's congressional representative, seeking information and dropping several threats which might find their way into congressional deliberations. He told Johnson that he intended to "spedily repair to Wyoming with a small detachment of green Mountain Boys to Vindicate (if it appears to me practicable) the right of soil of those proprietors." Allen thought most American states captives of the rich and wondered if the "land Jobbers" controlled Pennsylvania's legislature and could raise troops at public expense. He trusted that Johnson would inform him what "the land scheming Fraternity would be able to do in the hostile way against me." The intelligence Allen gained from Johnson and Levi encouraged him to make the trip south.[14]

Allen's arrival on 27 April 1786 had a dramatic impact, reviving the spirit of the disheartened Wyoming settlers. Pennsylvania's agent in the region, William Shaw, wrote that until Allen showed up the settlers looked ready to capitulate. Now everything had changed. Allen boasted to the crowd "that he had formed one new State" and would now do the same "in defiance of Pennsya." Another Pennsylvania official wrote that Allen's presence ended their hopes for subduing the region: "since [his] arrival every idea of submission to the Laws of Pennsa. has vanished."[15]

Pleased with Allen's forcefulness, John Franklin placed him on the four-man ruling committee. Allen stated that "my policy will be to publish propositions of amity with the government" of Pennsylvania, provided its officials respected the land titles of the Wyoming settlers, "which I know they will not do." But the appearance of moderation and a willingness to compromise were "apt to make friends in Pensylvenia and divide them and give me a better plea in the eyes of the world." [16]

In August, Allen issued a broadside redolent with the rhetoric of his earlier assaults on New York. Scorning "the tribunal of land monopolizers" who ran Pennsylvania, Allen addressed himself to "the court of conscience, of the people at large," and proclaimed that the Wyoming Valley settlers "will not tamely surrender our farms, orchards, tenements, neighbours, and right to soil, to a junto of land thieves." The "pious legalists" who ran the government would "stand aloof in the day of battle, with lawbooks in their hands," looking on as the people "smoke it out at the muzzle of the firelock." Could it be, Allen asked, that they had fought the Revolution in vain? They thought they won their freedom, but Pennsylvania's government sought to "cram their laws down our throats." Allen and the Wyoming settlers would not abandon the heritage of the Revolution.

But devotion to the cause did not preclude striking deals, and Allen offered one. The Wyoming settlers would acknowledge Pennsylvania's jurisdiction if that state guaranteed their landholdings in return. Allen issued "a gentle admonition" that, should Pennsylvania hesitate, the settlers would turn next to Congress, as an independent state. And if the new American nation failed to respect their rights, foreign powers might. But that was a remote possibility, he added, for the people of Pennsylvania would not allow their government to trample the rights of their fellow yeomen. "Your land-jobbers will be confounded and curse their stars, since it amounts to a moral certainty, that you, Gentlemen of the Militia, will not come forth in arms against us." [17]

Ethan Allen made practical arguments. He offered reasons why Pennsylvania should leave the Wyoming alone and be content with productive citizens, no matter where their land titles originated. But Allen ended his broadside by switching from land rights to radical republicanism. When the rich subvert government and law and attempt "to dispossess and ruin a large settlement of industrious yeomanry (the supporters of the world of mankind)," then the people are in "a state of nature" and have the right to resist under "the greatest of all laws, to wit, that of self-preservation." Allen hurled the logic of the American Revolution back at the revolutionary government of Pennsylvania. [18]

Allen's adversaries reacted with alacrity to the threats of his "atheistical Highness." Attacking Allen as a heretic, the Pennsylvania land speculators attempted to discredit their new enemy as an anarchist, out to destroy government and religion in Pennsylvania. The atmosphere in Philadelphia neared panic; rumors flew of an approaching army of Green Mountain Boys. The legislature reported that "banditties [are] rising up against law and good order in all quarters of our country," declaring Daniel Shays and Ethan Allen part of the same lawless plot to destroy America.[19]

Allen's strategy succeeded. The Pennsylvania legislature responded to his threat with the Confirming Act of March 1787, securing the land titles of those settled in the Wyoming and forming it into an independent county, thus meeting the New Englanders' demands. Three years later conservative members of the assembly attempted to repeal the Confirming Act, complaining that they passed it under duress, the state being "at ye time much alarmed or scared with danger from Shays, Allen, &c." Timothy Pickering, battling the repeal, agreed, maintaining that only the Confirming Act had prevented Allen from turning the Wyoming Valley into "another Vermont." The Confirming Act held. In Allen's eyes, he had forced another officious and remote government to bend before the will and rights of the people.[20]

In his two brief but energetic visits to the Wyoming, Allen made a difference. The Wyoming settlers gave him credit for reversing the tide and eventually winning them the right to retain their lands. Twenty years later, the town of Luzerne, expressing dissatisfaction with Pennsylvania's government, reminded the assembly of the success of "the Allen's in forming the State of Vermont, saying the same thing may be done here with greater ease." For generations after his visit, people along the Susquehannah defined a brave man as one who "was not afraid of bears—he had heard Ethan Allen swear."[21]

II

And since it is almost the universal foible of Mankind to aspire to something or other beyond their natural or acquired abilities, I feel the infection.—Ethan Allen to St. John Crèvecoeur

Ethan Allen gained more from his Wyoming adventure than mythic stature on another frontier. His successful campaign in the Wyoming

Valley coincided with the crushing of Shays's Rebellion and a mounting concern that more agrarian insurrections would follow. Allen had shown that it took only energetic leadership to bring a government to its knees. What he had done in Pennsylvania could be repeated in western Massachusetts or the Hudson River valley, unless the danger was removed. George Washington wrote James Madison that "we are fast verging to anarchy and confusion" as the "levellers" sought agrarian laws which would reapportion wealth. The best way to eliminate that threat, concluded national leaders from Madison to Hamilton, was to grant Vermont statehood.[22]

While the Wyoming settlers were winning their demands without bloodshed, Lincoln's volunteer army routed the Shaysites in Massachusetts. Not satisfied with crushing the rebellion, Governor James Bowdoin of Massachusetts wanted to punish the rebels and called on the neighboring states to arrest the scattered "malcontents." The governors of Connecticut, New Hampshire, and New York promised assistance, Governor Clinton marching with three regiments of New York militia to join General Lincoln. As for Vermont, Lincoln twice sought Governor Chittenden's help. Chittenden said that he would see what he could do and then did the least he could.[23]

Most members of Vermont's legislature feared that they would be dragged into war with their neighboring states but disagreed on how to avoid conflict. Many agreed with Chittenden and Allen in believing that a few thinly veiled but unfulfilled threats to intervene in Massachusetts would make Vermont appear more valuable to the United States. But a bare majority of the assembly held that Vermont's security demanded a disavowal of any connection with Shays. At their insistence, Chittenden issued a proclamation at the end of February 1787, warning the citizens of Vermont that they should not "harbor, entertain or conceal" Daniel Shays and three other insurgent leaders. At that time Shays and several other rebels were staying at the farm next to Chittenden's.[24]

Vermont's inaction worried Massachusetts and New York. Both governments expressed anxiety that Vermont might annex the insurgent regions, or something even worse, that revolutionary activity would intensify. Ethan Allen had demonstrated his effectiveness in Pennsylvania, and reports reached Bowdoin that hundreds of Shaysites camped near Allen's home. And Allen made no secret of his sympathies: he declared that those who "held the reins of government in Massachusetts were a pack of Damned Rascals and there was no virtue among them."[25]

Alexander Hamilton determined to buy off Vermont with a straight bargain: statehood for acquiescence. In February 1787 Hamilton introduced a bill in the New York assembly directing the state's congressional delegates to support statehood for Vermont. "Vermont is in fact *independent,* but she is not *confederated,*" and Hamilton thought this situation threatened the United States because of "the means which they employ to secure that independence." Having no taxes, Vermont had long offered a bad example to bordering states and "make proselytes to their government." Hamilton appreciated the shrewdness of Vermont's government in availing itself "of the discontents of a neighbouring state," manipulating events in Massachusetts to secure its own borders. Such a policy was consistent with the Haldimand negotiations: "Is it not natural" for a free people, "irritated by neglect . . . [to] provide for their own safety, by seeking connections elsewhere?" It made sense that Vermont turned first to the British and now to Shays. Logic dictated that New York seek the best possible settlement with a powerful opponent. As Hamilton recognized, "They are useless to us now, and if they continue as they are, they will be formidable to us hereafter." The time had come to put an end to the "Vermont principle." The New York assembly agreed.[26]

Receiving a political message, Vermont returned one. When Daniel Shays sent two fellow rebels, Luke Day and Eli Parsons, to offer Ethan Allen command of the "revolutionary army," Allen "contemptuously refused" and ordered Day and Parsons out of Vermont. Publicizing this refusal, the Vermont government entered on a sustained effort to persuade Massachusetts that it would have nothing to do with that state's "malcontents."[27]

Vermont's repudiation of rebels who shared so many of its ideals appears hypocritical, and indeed it may have been so. But Vermont's priority remained its own autonomy and internal stability, and admission to the Union guaranteed both. Most Vermonters sympathized with the farmers of western Massachusetts but dreaded the "Consequences that may arise, if this State . . . shall intermeddle in that Quarrel." Intervention might lead to dissension "Amongst ourselves [and] . . . bring this State into Confusion and Destress." Localism circumscribed the sympathies and democratic sentiments of the Vermonters. Ethan Allen believed, erroneously, that economic dislocations were regional concerns, to be dealt with by the communities involved. If the people of western Massachusetts chose to revolt, that was their affair. Thus Vermont bombarded the government of Massachusetts with public statements condemning the Shaysites while giving them refuge, keeping all options open while baffling its neighbors, and even some of its own citizens.[28]

The culminating act of this public campaign of conciliation with Massachusetts came with Ethan Allen's last service to the state. Allen wrote Colonel Benjamin Simmons of the Massachusetts militia in July 1787 that though "the malcontents of your State appear to be forming unlawful Associations in this State," Vermont would take "the most effectual measures to prevent the mischievious consequences" which might follow. As in his correspondence with Haldimand, Allen relied on purposeful ambiguity. The only Shaysites Vermont turned over to Massachusetts were a pair of horse thieves arrested in fall 1787. Vermont did only what it must to maintain its autonomy.[29]

Allen gave Simmons permission to circulate and publish his letter. Simmons did so, sending a copy to Bowdoin, who in turn sent copies to Clinton and the Boston papers.[30] Allen's letter meant to demonstrate Vermont's reliability, a stabilizing force and no longer a threat, a state worthy of admission to the Union. It took three more years to settle the details, but the reality of Vermont's authority had been acknowledged, even by New York. Republicanism played an important rhetorical role in supporting the creation of an independent Vermont. But practical politics on a new national scale brought Vermont at last into the Union in 1791.

With the Revolution secured, Ethan Allen faded from public life. On 1 May 1787 he and Ira dissolved the Onion River Company. Ira gained possession of most of the land, supplying Ethan with a thousand-acre farm of excellent quality just north of Burlington, £100 worth of goods annually for seven years, and the lumber to build his new house. After seventeen years of struggle, Ethan Allen received his reward. His family, both lineal and extended, was well established, with prosperity promised, and attained, in the years ahead. In 1769 Ethan Allen left a rocky farm in Connecticut that he shared with six siblings and their mother. At the end of his life he owned one of the finest farms in the Green

Mountains and left hundreds of acres to each of his six surviving children, more than enough to promise a comfortable sufficiency for them and their children.[31]

Though he was only forty-nine years old in 1787, Ethan Allen's health declined quickly—the consequence, Ira felt, of his long and harsh captivity. Bringing his father's body with him, Ethan and his family moved north to Lake Champlain that spring, built their new home, and tended their garden, with the help of two free blacks Ethan had befriended. Ethan wrote Levi Allen, "I Embrace this opportunity to write you on the Subject of wheat." Tiring easily, Ethan welcomed his freedom from political responsibilities. "My farming business goes very brisk," he wrote Levi, but he "trembled" for his crops. With Ira down in "Quaker Danbe" trading hogs, "it is a pinch with us and will be so till Harvest, pray help us." The family was whole; Levi sent Ethan the wheat he needed.[32]

Allen loved his new farm. He wrote Stephen Bradley of its 350 acres of "choice river intervale" and rich upland meadows with "the finest of wheat land and pasture land well watered and . . . by nature equal to any tract of land of the same number of acres that I ever saw." He was pleased with how quickly settlement proceeded; "I wish that you was well settled in it, [for] little is said about Philosophy here." Instead, "our 'talk is of Bullocks and our glory is in the gad,' " he wrote, mocking the accent and concerns of his neighbors. "We mind earthly things."[33]

Bradley stayed in Westminster, but Ira settled directly across the Onion River from Ethan. Cousins Caleb and Ebenezer Allen moved to nearby South Hero Island and Thomas Chittenden to the neighboring town of Williston, giving Ethan a small group of intimates with whom he talked of matters not bovine. Ira Allen remained busy, keeping the family's fingers in a dozen plots, economic and political. He eventually would be known as "the founder of the University of Vermont," complete with a pious statue in front of its main building.[34] Ethan was content to farm, father children, and write an "Appendix" to *Reason the Only Oracle.* In this postscript to *Reason,* Allen explained the "universal plentitude of Being": the universe was full of life and goodness, and the spirituality of the soul flowed forth from a benevolent deity which abhorred vacuums. As a personal document, the "Appendix" reflects the happiness Allen found in retirement. In the last two years of his life he may have attained a philosophical detachment, a satisfaction with the limited audience of his own family. He had to settle for this constituency, his ideas denied any larger circulation.[35]

The autumn of 1788 fell hard on the settlers of the northern frontier. It rained incessantly, the frosts came early, and many people lost their crops. Ebenezer Allen offered Ethan hay for his cattle. With Lake Champlain frozen, Ethan took a sleigh across to Ebenezer's farm on South Hero on 16 February 1789. Ethan Allen died the next morning on his way home. He was fifty-one years old. The Allens held the funeral at Ira's house, burying General Allen with full military honors. Following Ethan's last wishes, Ira excluded ministers, sermons, and public prayers.[36]

In London, Levi Allen "gave no credit" to stories of his brother's death. But stunning confirmation came in a letter from Ira. It did not seem possible that Ethan could have died so soon. Reminded of his own precarious mortality, Levi wrote Ira that he longed to return home and live his last years quietly with his family.[37]

Ezra Stiles, that gentle Puritan whose nephew Benjamin was Allen's oldest friend, confidently stated that Allen was in hell getting his much-deserved punishment. John Graham, who also hated Allen for his impiety, admitted that he had "proved a valuable friend to the people, and a firm supporter of their rights." Joseph Fay wrote his son that "the old general was truly my friend and worthy my best rememberance." The *Vermont Gazette* reported "with much regret . . . the death of General ETHAN ALLEN." The public lamented the loss of this *"Great man"* who had "rendered them great services, both in council and in arms."[38]

Many contemporaries thought Allen a "Great man." A national hero from the taking of Ticonderoga through the publication of his *Narrative,* Allen chose to be a Vermont patriot rather than an American one, and for a decade the two were incompatible. By the mid-1780s Allen represented everything the American elite feared from the excesses of democracy. Looking to the example of the Roman republic, many American Whigs warned against agrarian laws and the redistribution of property, of using political means to attain economic ends.[39] New York's government accused Vermont of doing just that, of taking land from the wealthy and giving it to the unworthy poor. Vermonters saw matters differently, holding that they only turned property over to its proper owners, those who worked the soil. New York's elite saw the Green

Mountains inhabited by envious and greedy transients. Vermonters saw themselves as settlers. New York could have defeated the Vermonters; they probably never could have won them over.[40]

Fortunately for the national elite, Allen's radical republicanism was confined to local goals. At the fulcrum of American politics in these years stood George Washington, the new nation's surety against the dangers of democratic anarchy and military dictatorship. As Washington used his symbolic power in an effort to unify the new nation, so Ethan Allen used his to strike bargains for his followers in their struggle for independence. Allen's final compromise demonstrated the effectiveness of the new national government in containing the radical forces released by the Revolution. The Vermonters proved willing to draw back from further revolution in exchange for being part of the new national union. In the same fashion, other autonomy movements would sacrifice larger goals in exchange for a position in the American republic. As Garry Wills has pointed out, the meaning of George Washington emerged from his resignation, his refusal of power, assuaging fears of a military dictatorship and inspiring faith in the new government. Likewise, Ethan Allen's meaning derived from a final refusal to lead a revolution. The outlaw became a symbol of restraint.[41]

III

Arrived at Onion-river falls & passed by Ethan Allyn's grave. An awful Infidel, one of ye wickedest men that ever walked this guilty globe. I stopped & looked at his grave with a pious horror.—Nathan Perkins, 1789

A hero needs a community. Conversely, the hero serves to create a community, to give it an identity.[42] Such was surely the case with Ethan Allen. Dixon Ryan Fox found Ethan Allen the essential man in Vermont's separation from New York, yet "no one man could have done this without responsive sentiment behind him." Allen did not create Vermont, but he certainly played the leading role in giving it form. Or as Dorothy Canfield Fisher simply put it: "He was the voice of Vermont. He still is."[43]

Allen possessed that elusive quality, charisma. Max Weber found charisma inherent in those who transform society, who break down traditional authority and replace it with structures legitimated by some divine force. If we take popular sovereignty as a form of sacred legitimation, then Weber's analysis applies to the case of Vermont. In a Weberian sense, Allen willed Vermont into being and swept the public along with him in a passion of revolutionary state building.[44]

The popular imagination discovered in Allen some attachment to a transcendent good, to "order-determining powers."[45] In the minds of most Vermonters, Allen embodied not only their state but the forces which created it: popular action, nature and the frontier, the virtues of a freeholding yeomanry, and independence—political, economic, and intellectual. By coming into contact with Allen, a Vermonter touched these powers. In circular fashion, Vermonters imputed special qualities to Allen which they found in themselves by their association with this charismatic leader.

Allen's genius was to link the preservation of daily routines to revolutionary action. He even made social conventions the ultimate legitimation of his political movement. Perpetuating a system of family economy based on the freehold and autonomous communities justified two decades of radical political activity which irrevocably transformed the face of the New England frontier. Allen led the fight for a new world in the name of the old.[46]

Vermont is often left out of the American story because it subverts too many generalizations. Many historians prefer to leave the impression that popular sovereignty was not "the product of popular demand." "Yeomen did not declare their own independence. Their lordly neighbors declared it," and the commoners did their bidding. While such statements may be true for the rest of America, they do not hold for Vermont. The people of Vermont declared their independence without the legitimation of superior authority, and Vermont was the first state in which a popularly elected convention met for the exclusive purpose of producing a constitution to be submitted to the voters for their approval.[47]

The Revolution drew forth extensive individual political commitments and produced dramatic changes. Vermont emerged from the Revolution with an independent government based on New England models infused with new democratic elements. On one hand, the state of Vermont remained true to several older ideals. Life remained organized around the family, church, and community. But now every town housed several churches, and several levels of community operated within the state. Though Congregationalists might still suspect the Quakers of being in league with the devil, they now had no choice but to accept them, as Baptists, Methodists, Universalists, Unitarians, and even deists like Ethan Allen competed for theological loyalty. The town meeting stayed the center of political life; but statewide political factions emerged, factions premised initially on opposition to or support of Ethan Allen and his family and later on one's response to Thomas Jefferson. Land continued as the basis of the economic life of every family; but the new state of Vermont made available cheap land to the north, helping to make every farmer a speculator while securing the economic future of most families. The frontier functioned as a safety valve, absorbing thousands of settlers from overpopulated areas, and as a destabilizing force, exporting its disputes to the settled regions of New York and New England and even to the center of national government.

The American Revolution produced results often contrary to the initial expectations and hopes of its participants. While seeking the familiar, the Grants settlers created something new: striving for community, they established a new state; hoping for churches of the like-minded, they produced sects; fighting for security, they attained a measure of democracy; in attempting to re-create the New England they knew, they found themselves part of a new nation; pursuing unity, they ended with diversity; expecting traditional leadership, they made use of Ethan Allen.

Vermont was a very different place in 1789 from what it had been in 1780. The late 1780s saw the end of the New England frontier as structures and culture stabilized into routine forms. Settlers still came to Vermont in family groups but no longer journeyed to the frontier in entire communities. The newcomers lacked the political commitment to Vermont shared by those who had served as Green Mountain Boys. The new arrivals rejected communitarian values and looked to the federal government for legitimation. Finally stable in the eyes of the world, Vermont placed greater limits on popular political participation in each revision of its constitution.

Political values moved away from localism. Citizens identified with national issues and political parties, with most of Allen's old adherents lining up with the Jeffersonians. The new men sided with the Federalists, insisting that government should be left to those properly qualified by birth, wealth, and education, people suspiciously like themselves.[48] This change is reflected by the increased acceptance of imprisoning debtors in the 1790s—a direct violation of the Vermont Constitution. By 1800 imprisonment had become a common punishment for those who fell into debt, and Ethan Allen's own brother Levi died while being held for debt in the Burlington jail.[49]

What had been a major grievance against the government in the 1770s had become appropriate treatment for the poor, and ideas once considered Tory now found acceptance in political discourse. When Daniel Chipman wrote in 1824 on the evolution of Vermont law, he did not even mention Ethan Allen and the Green Mountain Boys. Instead, a few respectable families established Vermont's independence for purely religious reasons. And what they established should never be altered, Chipman wrote, as "it is unwise to change our course, merely because we have experienced evils in pursuing it." Foolish to leave traditional paths because human nature itself resists change, and "experiments are generally made by visionaries and wild projectors, and of course, usually fail." From this, Chipman concluded that "intelligible" legal codes cannot be established by legislatures but must follow the British style, "by an uniform and settled course of Judicial decisions only."[50] Chipman and his fellow conservatives had traveled a long way from the Revolution.

In other ways Vermont remained the same, producing some of the most interesting and eccentric individuals in nineteenth-century America, especially in religion: John Humphrey Noyes, founder of Oneida; the Mormons Joseph Smith, Heber C. Kimball, and Brigham Young; the Davidsonians, who believed that a Mrs. Thompson was Jesus Christ; William Miller, founder of the Adventists; Jedidiah Burchard, a former circus performer who did acrobatic stunts as evidence of energetic Christianity; George Perkins Marsh, who wrote books of racial theories with New Englanders the Gothic descendants of heroic Vikings; Fanny Allen, "the Beautiful American Nun" and daughter of Ethan Allen; and General Ethan Allen Hitchcock, Ethan Allen's grandson, a leading Swedenborgian and scholarly alchemist.[51] But these were the exceptions. On the whole, nineteenth-century Vermont would have little room for someone like Ethan Allen. As Vermont became ever more conservative, Ethan Allen retreated into legend—and not always a very acceptable one at that.[52]

Even while alive, Allen was a symbol to be exploited.[53] Vermont used

Allen as a talisman to frighten opponents, his very presence sufficient to quell rebellions and drive off invading armies. Allen fed this mythology from his youth, spreading rumors of his viciousness and circulating stories of his invincibility, proving so successful at self-promotion that rebels in other states called on him to give their causes that magic aura. His demand for the surrender of Ticonderoga carried divine and civil legitimation, both of which the Revolution lacked, and he succeeded in maintaining his mythology through captivity by turning his defeat into a triumph of the American will. Allen also muddied his class position, constantly labeling himself both peasant and gentleman while seeking to lift himself to the status of philosopher. Such pretensions matched those of his neighbors; visitors to the Green Mountains complained regularly that yeomen expected to be treated as gentlemen. On the other hand, Allen is always the frontiersman, in his own writings and in the works of others. Allen understood his audience, which saw virtue in rustic simplicity. As one scholar wrote, Allen left "a perplexingly inconsistent body of legendary material which could readily be shaped into varying kinds of representative men." [54]

More than anyone else, Daniel Thompson fixed the popular image of Allen and his revolutionary compatriots in his *Green Mountain Boys*. One of the best-selling historical novels of the antebellum period, Thompson's book appeared in fifty editions between 1839 and 1860. A Free-Soil secretary of state in Vermont, Thompson made his heroes simple farmers, close to the earth and proud of their labors, innocents who are good at tricking Yorkers and the British. Noble and generous and motivated solely by principle, Thompson's Allen is a Natty Bumpo frontiersman, devoid of intellectual pretensions or abilities, his love of liberty emerging from nature rather than thought. [55] This Allen was a trickster, constantly baffling his opponents. But to make him safe, Thompson, like James Fenimore Cooper with Natty Bumpo, makes Allen chivalrous. A short step from Thompson to Henry Hall's 1892 biography *Ethan Allen: The Robin Hood of Vermont,* with the Green Mountain Boys as the Merry Men.

Running through all studies of Allen, including the most recent, is a series of tall tales. A great many focus on Allen's very real strength, though they reached ridiculous proportions in this century. Thus Allen could "tear a pack of cards into eighths and when deep in thought was known to twist ten-penny nails in two with his teeth." He also used his teeth to flip hundred-pound sacks of salt over his shoulder. Such tales often contain a hint of veracity, usually as variations on material in Allen's *Narrative*. But most are unverifiable and have little connection to any known reality.[56]

Folklore rather than "fakelore," to borrow Richard Dorson's phrase, the Ethan Allen stories were not made up by New York City hacks for almanacs or dime novels. Nor were they created—as with Daniel Boone and Paul Bunyon stories—to promote the sale of land or lumber. Even in legend, Allen is not the pawn of "a moneyed elite." Unlike most frontier folklore, which is expansionist, violent, and racist, the Allen stories tend to aim inward, addressing religious and political affiliation and community identity. Though set on the frontier, these stories fail to portray Indians as savages or to kill them off in great numbers. Allen never abandons his culture in order to defeat his enemies; he never tries to be anything other than himself.[57]

Tall tales serve some function for the teller, validating or questioning norms or attempting to explain the unusual.[58] Allen's *Narrative,* for instance, provided a wealth of stories which demonstrated the superiority of simple frontier American gentlemen over the corrupted British. Abraham Lincoln enjoyed telling a story of Allen using a British toilet above which his hosts hung a portrait of Washington, intending to annoy their guest with the imputation that Washington belonged in that room. But Allen coarsely retorted to his hosts that the sight of Washington always had scared the crap out of the British. Lincoln just wished that he could find a general whose portrait would be worthy of hanging over a Confederate toilet.[59]

Lincoln found simple American virtues expressed in such stories; truth lay within Allen's crudeness. What truths did Ethan Allen represent? What then is American about Ethan Allen? Most dramatically, he demonstrated a lack of concern for legal technicalities, appealing to the popular emphasis on a commonsense interpretation of the law and a belief in what John William Ward called the "sagacity of the common man."

The American hero rises above the savages, representing civilization to the wilderness. Allen created an outpost of civilization, the state of Vermont. As a founder, he personified the greatest American myth, maintaining the facade of rugged individualism which covers the reality of essential family and communal networks. Admired as a man of action,

Allen refused to bend before any adversity and transferred his determination to others, living proof of the liberal creed of gaining one's own salvation through action. Yet the strong-willed must be democratic, respecting his fellow citizens and obeying the laws when absolutely necessary. Anarchistic individualism would not do; the man of will acts in the name of a higher law, not against the law. A society which came to insist on individualism and change while extolling family and tradition created ambiguities not resolved simply. A mythology of those caught between these worlds eased the tensions.[60]

An exemplar of republican values, Allen transformed defects in aristocratic cultures into democratic virtues. "He was but partially educated and obscurely brought up," one historian wrote, "yet no one was more at ease in the polished ranks than he." Allen did not conform to the "artificial rules of etiquette" but followed "the dictates of natural good sense and good humor."[61] The finest portrayal of this frontier balance came in 1854, with Herman Melville's serialized novel, *Israel Potter*.

Israel Potter did exist. Returning to America in the 1820s, Potter claimed a pension as a Revolutionary War soldier, asserting that the British had taken him prisoner during the war, but that he had escaped to London, where he lived in poverty for forty years.[62] Melville presented Potter as a revolutionary Everyman, making his painful progress through a series of republican alternatives. With the spirit of the early republic fading, Melville directed his cautionary tale at contemporaries torn between materialism and savagery. Potter wandered the "wilderness of the world's extremest hardships and ills," encountering the choices America faced.[63]

Drifting across Europe in search of passage home, Potter first meets Benjamin Franklin. A conjurer dressed in a dark robe covered with strange symbols, Franklin sits in a dark room with his strange foreign books, the walls hung with drawings of "surprising inventions." Old age and the Old World shroud the "antediluvian" Franklin. Appearing the sage, Franklin speaks in clichés drawn mostly from his writings. A crafty opportunist, Franklin depicts civilization in self-interested decay. He is no help to Potter.[64]

The exile next encounters John Paul Jones, covered with tattoos and wearing the "tokens of the primeval savageness which ever slumbers in human kind." Though courageous, Jones symbolizes a dark alternative: "unprincipled, reckless, predatory, with boundless ambition, civilized in externals but a savage at heart," given to orgiastic violence. Melville feared that "America is, or may yet be, the Paul Jones of nations."[65]

Finally, Potter discovers the symbol of Melville's preferred alternative, Ethan Allen in captivity. Like some "wild beast; but of a royal sort," the "Titanic Vermonter" is surrounded by "parlour-men, dancing masters" who shrug "their laced shoulders" at the very idea of Ethan Allen. Decadent and weakened by luxury, the English torment their captive lion, only to be trapped in their own terror by Allen. Drawing directly from Allen's *Narrative*, Melville's hero shouts: "Brag no more, Old England! Order back your broken battalions! home and repent in ashes!" Though crude, Allen remains the democratic gentleman: "Back, dogs! Respect a gentleman and a Christian, though he be in rags and smell of bilgewater." Women, purer in nature, realize the truth of these claims and sense the giant's virtue, requesting locks of their Samson's hair, which they find half gold and half straw.[66]

Glorious in his refusal to cower before British power, Allen resists all affronts. With a "wild, heroic sort of levity" Allen disdains adversity and orders up another bowl of punch. Though from New England, Allen is Melville's westerner, the symbol of what Melville hoped the West of the 1850s would yet be: honest, intelligent, and simple. Dressed like a frontiersman, "half-Indian, half-Canadian," Allen wears worsted stockings and moccasins, the perfect mix of civilization and wilderness.

The pilgrim stands "transfixed" by Allen but fails to see that Allen lights the way to his and America's salvation. Instead of bearing his burden like Allen, Israel Potter thrice disavows his nationality—a modern play on Paul's denial of Christ. Potter's deliverance lay in noble defiance and acknowledgment of his Americanness; instead, he flees from Allen to the loneliness of London. The city is the real wilderness, a desert devoid of life or "any green thing," the "flagging as flat an tombstones . . . worn heavily down, by sorrowful tramping." The city is home to death; the Thames flowed through London "polluted by continual vicinity to man." From the "entailed misery" of London, the "wanderer" and his son finally sail for "the Promised Land" of America, amidst whose forests civilization finds its natural home.[67]

There is delicious irony in Melville's fiction of three masters of artifice in a book based on the alleged adventures of yet another fraud. *Israel Potter* has the flavor of myth and reality, both aimed at warning his culture of the dangers they confront. Jones fights for himself, Franklin fights for no one, Allen fights for humanity against tyranny. Allen remains the frontiersman and leaves the corrupted Old World to Franklin and the untamed seas to Jones. By suffering, Allen instructs; his lesson: that determination and the acceptance of responsibilities constitute true heroism. In short, the individual has a duty to his community. Allen's American spirit would transform his nation and save it from selfish materialism and violent barbarism.[68]

Melville cut right to the heart of much of Ethan Allen's message. The American Revolution aggravated a preexisting tension between unrestrained individualism and communal unity. Allen's law of self-preservation did not excuse careless individualism or selfish personal aggrandizement. The self was not a person but a collective identification. If one member of a family faced starvation, the others had a duty to provide sustenance. If outsiders threatened the community, all shared responsibility for defending the group. Within this context of mutual dependence, settlers on the northern frontier beheld their greatest need as ensuring the economic independence of their families.[69]

The government of New York described Allen as a self-interested land thief, a view that has influenced historians for two centuries. Yet this mountain bandit unified the towns of the Green Mountains with a covenant. Allen did not leave Connecticut out of self-interest; self-interest dictated that he stay put. Likewise, self-interest demanded that he avoid conflict, take the bribes offered by first New York and then Britain, cut his losses and run, and certainly not risk his life by attacking Fort Ticonderoga and joining in the revolution against established government. Economic self-interest compelled him to abandon politics before he began, to sell his loyalty to the highest bidder, and to keep his mouth shut instead of expressing his unpopular religious ideas. As Allen said, self-interest rationalizes political and intellectual quiescence. The settlers of the Green Mountains linked "self" with the family and then the community so closely as to blur conventional distinctions. Unrestrained individualism had no place on this frontier.[70]

Historians of Vermont's early years have understood the Green Mountain insurgency in many different ways. For some, it amounted to a clash between rival groups of land speculators; others have discerned a controversy between two competing orders; another perspective emphasizes class conflict, casting the insurgents as frontier "peasants" battling New York's landlord class. Each of these interpretations illuminates some dimension of the struggle for independence on the northern frontier. Yet key questions remain unanswered, most especially: Why did these settlers risk so much in order to control the political organization of the Green Mountains? Supposing they acted for the private profit of a small group of New England speculators accords undue influence to the leaders of the insurgency while underestimating the independence of ordinary frontier settlers. Assuming they fought in the name of particular political ideals attributes enormous determinative power to abstractions. Arguing for class conflict on the northern frontier distorts the intentions of the Grants' freehold farmers, whose families were in no danger of being confused with landless "peasants."[71]

Land speculation and political idealism certainly influenced the development of the Green Mountain frontier, and class conflict characterized the insurgency which disrupted the region. But concerns centering on family and community, the twin poles of New England's social conceptions, politicized and mobilized the great mass of ordinary frontier families. The security of land ownership was essential to both, and New York's claims posed a basic threat to titles. At the same time the Grants' settlers perceived New York's pretended jurisdiction, which sought to bring local structures under its centralized control, as a threat to their communal order. Looking at their poorer New York neighbors, the Grants' settlers understood the choice before them: either give in and be reduced to the status of landless tenants dominated by a distant oligarchy or resist. Eventually the majority chose the latter course, nudged on, because of both interest and principle, by Ethan Allen.[72]

Allen's law of self-preservation linked life, liberty, and land. Remove one, Allen argued, and the others vanish. First New York, then Britain, and finally the Continental Congress threatened the self-preservation of the inhabitants of the Green Mountain frontier by denying the validity of their land titles, transforming these settlers into "outlaws" and leaving them no recourse but revolution. In that revolution these outlaws fashioned their own legal structures and, given the opportunity to choose, wrote the most democratic constitution of their time. Together they created the state of Vermont.

Appendixes

Notes

Bibliography

Index

Appendix A

Economic Distribution on the Northern Frontier: Probate Records

Jackson Turner Main has described a farm of less than 500 acres as "small." Yet in his study of a frontier town (Warren, New Hampshire), 73 percent of the decedents owned farms of less than 500 acres and 23 percent were propertyless. In the Green Mountains 500 acres was a very large tract, 100 acres being the median. It is also important to note that the figures include cleared and uncleared land. In the Green Mountains the latter dominated. Main found that in Suffolk County, Massachusetts, in 1764–71 and 1782–88 there were numerous estates worth more than £1,000 and even £2,000, with 46 percent of 315 inventories he studied valued at greater than £500. Drawing on over 5,000 probated estates, Main gave the following suspiciously symmetrical structure of personal property; to which I have added the figures for Vermont for the years 1774–88 based on 300 probate records.

PERSONAL PROPERTY IN PROBATE ESTATES

Values in £	% of total	% of farmers	% of Vermont
2000+	3	4	2
1,000–999	7	8	4
500–999	10	12	19
200–499	20	25	25
100–199	20	20	28
50–99	20	16	9
1–49	20	15	13

Source: Main, *Social Structure*, 11, 31–32, 113n; probate records for Bennington County, Manchester District, Rutland County, Windham County, and Windsor County.

It is important to note that Main apparently did not subtract debts from the total value of the estate. In this table, I have adhered to Main's structure. The statistics for Hampshire County, Massachusetts, listed in Jones, *American Colonial Wealth* 2:801–46, are roughly the same as those for Vermont.

As values varied widely and were inflated and confused by changing currency rates during the revolutionary period, percentages are more useful for comparison than gross figures. Main drew upon various sources for the following information about the holdings by the top decile of the total wealth of these towns:

Warren, N.H.(1781)	30%	Waltham, Mass.(1771)	43.5%
Groton, Conn.(1783)	29%	Milford, Conn.(n.d.)	36%
York, Maine(1775)	43%	Albany, N.Y.(n.d.)	44%
Kittery, Maine(n.d.)	45%	Boston, Mass.(n.d.)	57%

Warren was "a typical frontier community," while Groton was a "commercial farm society," and the rest were "urban centers" (Main, *Social Structure,* 11, 29–31, 35–36). Main drew his figures for Warren from Little, *History of Warren,* 551.

Main considered £20 worth of furniture in a probate a sign of poverty. By this standard, all but a very few Green Mountain settlers were poor (Main, *Social Structure,* 29, 131, 175–76).

Bidwell and Falconer found that the average holding of livestock in frontier Falmouth, Maine, in 1760 was one horse, a yoke of oxen, three to four cows, nine to ten sheep, and one to two swine. In comparison, more prosperous farms in eastern Massachusetts had one to two horses, a yoke or two of oxen, ten to twenty sheep, fifteen cattle and the same number of swine (Bidwell and Falconer, *History of Agriculture,* 105–6; Judd, *History of Hadley,* 385). Relying on 185 probate records for Rutland, Bennington, and Windham counties before 1789 and Jones's figures for Hampshire County, Mass., the average holdings were:

County	Cattle	Swine	Horses	Oxen	Sheep
Hampshire	2.25	1.5	1	1.3	8.5
Bennington	5.2	2.2	1.5	0.74	9.5
Windham	5.1	1.25	0.86	1	5.86
Rutland	3.2	2.2	1	0.75	3.9
Total	4.4	2	1.14	0.82	6.5

Probate records reveal that in both Vermont and Hampshire County, Massachusetts, the bulk of total wealth consisted of land titles.

PERCENTAGE OF TOTAL PROBATED WEALTH

	Vermont, 1773–89	Hampshire Co., Mass., 1773–75
Landholdings	65%	66%
Notes of credit	14.9	4.4
Livestock	8.5	10.2
Tools	3.1	3.6
Farm stocks*	1.5	4.1
Household goods	5.1	9.5
Luxuries	1.3	1.9
Cash	0.6	0.3

Sources: Probate records of Rutland, Windham, and Bennington counties; Jones, *American Colonial Wealth* 2:801–46.
*Seeds, stored hay, and surplus crops.

The vast majority of those probated owned land, with a large percentage owning land for investment, both within and outside of the home town. But the home farm constituted the largest component of property value, and land held outside of the home town was generally given a low value by the appraisers.

PROPERTY OWNERSHIP

	Hampshire Co.	Vermont
As percentage of total probated estates		
Owned property	81.5%	80.9%
Home farm	77.7	79.0
Other property		
Within town	44.4	27.8
Outside town	18.5	17.4
Commercial	11.0	8.7
As percentage of total property valuation		
Home farm	77.7	79.7
Other property		

PROPERTY OWNERSHIP (*continued*)

Hampshire Co.   *Vermont*

As percentage of
total probated estates

	Hampshire Co.	Vermont
Within town	44.4	12.4
Outside town	18.5	5.7
Commercial	11.0	2.2

A final component of probate records is the network of debt relations. Of the three hundred Vermont probate records available for the years 1773–89, 171 listed credits and debts. The range of credits ran from one shilling to £366 and of debts from one shilling to £390. The following are averages per probate account, based on those records.

DEBT NETWORKS IN VERMONT
PROBATE RECORDS, 1773–89

	Debtors	Creditors
Number	31	20
Size	£14.4	£4.6
Total	£134	£48.2
% of total valuation	35.5	12.8

In other words, based on those accounts which listed creditors and debtors, one-third of the total evaluation consisted of money owed to the estate by an average of thirty-one people. But one-eighth of the total value of an estate was owed to an average of twenty creditors.

Appendix B

Economic Distribution on the Northern Frontier: Tax Records

Charles Grant, in his study of Kent, Connecticut, established a tax assessment of £29 as the poverty level, finding that one-fourth of Kent's heads of household fell into this category. In Manchester 60 percent, in Clarendon 70 percent, and in Westminster 59 percent of the assessed households were in Grant's "poor class," small farmers who lacked a cash crop and produced just enough to survive. Grant's figures are for the period from 1740 to 1777 (Grant, *Democracy in Kent*, 96–98). Main agreed with these figures, finding one-third of the tax list for Goshen, Connecticut, in 1751 below the £29 assessment (Main, *Social Structure*, 29, 131, 175–76).

Grant found the following structure in both the 1751 and 1771 tax records for Kent, to which I have added the information for eleven Vermont towns from the early 1780s.

ECONOMIC DISTRIBUTION OF FRONTIER TOWNS

	£49+	£30 to £48	£29 *and below*
	"Upper middle class"	*"Lower middle class"*	*"Poor class"*
Kent, Conn.	46.0%	29.0%	25.0%
Barnard, Vt.	5.5	18.7	75.8
Cavendish	6.0	9.0	85.0
Clarendon	7.6	22	70.4
Fairlee	4.3	10.9	84.8
Lunenburg	4.6	31.8	63.6
Manchester	16.5	23.4	60.1
Newfane	3.8	19.2	77.0
Poultney	12.5	39.8	47.7
Randolph	0	10.3	89.7

ECONOMIC DISTRIBUTION OF FRONTIER TOWNS (*continued*)

	£49+	£30 to £48	£29 and below
	"Upper middle class"	"Lower middle class"	"Poor class"
Townshend	5.7	14.3	80.7
Westminster	25.9	15.3	58.8

Sources: Grant, *Kent*, 96; Manchester tax list in Hoyt, *General Petitions*, 240–44; Westminster tax list in Henry A. Willard Collection, box 2, LC; remainder in Tax files, Vermont State Archives.
Note: poll fixed at £6.

More than three-quarters of those assessed in four of these eleven towns fell in the narrow range between £10 and £59, and more than half in the remaining towns.

ASSESSMENTS

	£60+	£59–£10	£9–0
Barnard	2.2%	71.4%	26.4%
Cavendish	0	51.5	48.5
Clarendon	5.0	79.0	16.0
Fairlee	2.2	54.3	43.5
Lunenburg	0	90.9	9.1
Manchester	10.0	76.0	14.0
Newfane	3.8	57.7	38.5
Poultney	4.6	81.8	13.6
Randolph	0	64.1	35.9
Townshend	2.9	72.8	24.3
Westminster	16.5	55.3	28.2

The data for these towns are:

EVALUATIONS

Town	Heads of household	Total wealth	Median	Average	Highest evaluation
Barnard	91	£1,856	£17	£20.4	£ 76
Cavendish	33	553	12	16.8	52
Clarendon	145	3,668	22	25	152
Fairlee	46	787	12	17	82
Lunenburg	22	541	23	24.6	49

EVALUATIONS (*continued*)

Town	Heads of household	Total wealth	Median	Average	Highest evaluation
Manchester	188	5,539	23	29	130
Newfane	78	1,632	16	21	140
Poultney	88	2,365	17	27	90
Randolph	78	1,184	13	15.2	39
Townshend	70	1,420	18	20.3	98
Westminster	85	2,730	26	32	103

The distribution of wealth in these communities is also noticeably similar.

PERCENTAGE OF TOTAL WEALTH

	Standing on tax list		
	Top 10%	Middle 80%	Bottom 10%
Barnard	24.9%	72.6%	2.5%
Cavendish	26.8	70.5	2.7
Clarendon	26.5	71.2	2.3
Fairlee	33.7	64.4	1.9
Lunenburg	17.4	80.4	2.2
Manchester	26.4	71.2	2.4
Newfane	33.3	64.0	2.7
Poultney	23.9	73.6	2.5
Randolph	21.7	74.3	4.0
Townshend	28.0	69.4	2.6
Westminster	28.9	69.7	1.4

Looked at a different way:

PERCENTAGE OF TOTAL WEALTH

	Standing on tax list		
	Top 25%	Middle 50%	Bottom 25%
Barnard	51.3%	40.0%	8.7%
Cavendish	53.5	38.4	8.1

PERCENTAGE OF TOTAL WEALTH (*continued*)

	Standing on tax list		
	Top 25%	*Middle 50%*	*Bottom 25%*
Clarendon	49.0	44.5	6.5
Fairlee	55.2	38.4	6.4
Lunenburg	41.6	47.2	11.2
Manchester	50.9	41.2	7.9
Newfane	57.0	35.6	7.4
Poultney	48.3	43.4	8.3
Randolph	45.1	43.5	11.4
Townshend	51.7	38.6	9.7
Westminster	54.7	41	4.3

For statistics similar to those for Vermont on another early American frontier, see Harper, "The Class Structure of Western Pennsylvania."

There are four existing Vermont tax lists for the years 1782–85. These records break down property ownership more precisely in two recently settled towns, Cavendish and Lunenburg, and two towns settled before the Revolution. The entries under Land refer to cultivated land only.

VERMONT TAX LISTS, 1782–85

	No. (%) of evaluations	No. listed	Average holding
Cavendish, 1782			
Total ratings = 33			
Polls	31 (94%)	37	1.2
Oxen	10 (30)	16	1.6
Cows	23 (70)	53	2.3
Horses	13 (39)	13	1.0
Swine	5 (15)	7	1.4
Land	7 (21)	104 a.	14.9 a.
Money	2 (6)	£525	£262.5
Lunenburg, 1784			
Total ratings = 22			
Polls	20 (91%)	27	1.4
Oxen	9 (41)	20	2.2

VERMONT TAX LISTS, 1782–85 (*continued*)

	No. (%) of evaluations	No. listed	Average holding
Cows	17 (77)	29	1.7
Horses	15 (68)	25	1.6
Swine	9 (41)	16	1.7
Land	13 (59)	160 a.	20.0 a.
Money	1 (4.5)	£18	£18.0

Fairlee, 1784
Total ratings = 46

Polls	38 (83%)	53	1.4
Oxen	14 (30)	30	2.1
Cows	28 (61)	52	1.9
Horses	14 (30)	26	1.9
Swine	8 (17)	17	2.1
Land	20 (44)	342 a.	17.1 a.

Poultney, 1785
Total ratings = 135

Polls	127 (94%)	163	1.3
Oxen	43 (32)	86	2.0
Cows	125 (93)	281	2.3
Horses	75 (56)	100	1.3
Swine	37 (27)	55	1.5
Land	110 (82)	1,748 a.	15.9 a.
Money	1 (4.5)	£18	£18.0

These assessments were to be used only if a tax was passed, which happened twice in the state's first fifteen years, 1781 and 1783. All males between sixteen and sixty (except ministers, teachers, and students, who were not rated) were to be assessed at £6, lawyers at £50. Livestock was rated at from £1 to £4, money on hand in excess of debts at £6/£100, improved land at 10s./acre. Each town's lister was allowed complete latitude in determining the assessment. In 1781 the grand list for the entire state was £149,542, with the tax fixed at 1s. 3d. on the pound of assessed value (Slade, *State Papers*, 295, 424, 440, 511–16, 531–44; Williams, *Chittenden Papers*, 364–65).

Appendix C

Vermont Court Cases, 1777–88

This table is based on 1,014 cases heard before Vermont's county courts and Superior Court (also known as the Supreme Court) in the years from 1777 to 1788.

DISTRIBUTION OF COURT CASES

	Criminal cases		Debt cases		Other civil suits	
	No.	(% of total)	No.	(%)	No.	(%)
Total	94	(9.3)	796	(78.5)	124	(12.2)
Resolved	89	(94.5)	747	(93.8)	108	(87.1)
1st hearing	62	(66)	579	(72.7)	38	(30.6)
within a year	86	(91.5)	683	(85.8)	72	(58.1)
Of those resolved						
for plft.	79	(88.8)	653	(87.4)	71	(65.7)
for deft.	10	(11.2)	94	(12.6)	37	(34.3)
Average:						
debt			£12.5			
fine	£20		£6		£10	
Intratown	32	(34)	163	(20.5)	37	(29.8)
Intertown	58	(61.7)	549	(69)	71	(57.3)
Within day's travel*	33	(35.1)	327	(41.1)	38	(30.7)
Within two days' travel	19	(20.2)	157	(19.7)	26	(21)
Outside immediate region	6	(6.4)	65	(8.2)	7	(5.6)
Unknown	4	(4.3)	84	(10.5)	16	(12.9)

*Defined as ten miles one way, as a twenty-mile round-trip was considered a hard day's travel. The state legislature used this figure for reimbursement purposes, and most contemporary accounts concur (Williams, Laws of Vermont 14:188).

For a similar study—and similar statistics—in Plymouth County, Massachusetts, see Nelson, *Dispute and Conflict Resolution,* 52–53.

Appendix D

Population of Vermont and Its Persistence, 1775 and 1791

These town-by-town estimates for 1775 are based largely on freemen and militia lists. In a few instances, exact censuses exist and are noted. The province of New York conducted a census of the eastside towns in 1771. The returns are available in Holbrook, *Vermont 1771 Census*.

In the 1791 census the ratio of males over the age of sixteen to the total population was 1:3.8; while the ratio of heads of household to total population was 1:5.7. These ratios have been employed in estimating the population for 1775. Comparison of selected freemen lists to total population in 1791 produced a ratio of 1:5. In several instances the militia company lists available represent only one of two or three companies for a community. Wherever possible, the lists have been correlated with other sources, such as tax and church records. In a few instances, listed as "est." an estimate has been based on some other source, such as a church record.

POPULATION OF VERMONT

Town	Source	Number in record	Estimates 1775	1791	% increase
Andover	est.		30	275	816.7%
Arlington	town, 1775	61	320	992	210.0
Barnard	militia, 1776	28	107	673	529.0
Barnet	census, 1771	9	140	477	240.7
Bennington	militia, 1764	64	585	2,350	301.7
	militia, 1776	154			
Benson	est.		60	658	996.7
Bradford	freemen, 1775	71	355	654	84.2
	militia, 1777	25			
	census, 1771	28			
Brandon	court, 1776		80	637	696.3
Brattleboro	census, 1771	403	675	1,589	135.4
Bromley	est.		20	71	255.0
Castleton	town, 1775		175	809	362.3
Cavendish	town, 1776		120	491	309.2
Chester	freemen, 1778	47	235	981	317.4
	census, 1771	152			
Clarendon	militia, 1776	27	400	1,480	270.0
	census, 1770	160			
Corinth	freemen, 1777	9	45	578	1184.4
Danby	freemen, 1777	101	480	1,206	151.3
Dorset	town, 1775		250	957	282.8
Dumerston	census, 1771	189	340	1,490	338.2
Fair Haven	est.		40	545	1262.5
Fairlee	est.		100	463	363.0
Glastonbury	est.		15	34	126.7
Guildhall	petition, 1776	20	114	158	38.6
Guildford	militia, 1777	26	825	2,422	193.6
	census, 1772	586			
	census, 1771	436			
Halifax	census, 1771	329	480	1,209	151.9
Hartford	militia, 1771	88	308	988	220.8
	census, 1771	190			
	militia, 1775	40			
Hartland	census, 1771	144	380	1,652	334.7
Harwich	est.		30	165	450.0
Hinsdale	census, 1771	107	215	482	124.2

POPULATION OF VERMONT (*continued*)

Town	Source	Number in record	Estimates 1775	1791	% increase
Hubbardton	freemen, 1777	9	45	410	811.1
Ira	freemen, 1779	52	260	312	20.0
Jamaica	est.		50	263	426.0
Jericho	town, 1775	3	20	381	1805.0
Landgrove	town		18	31	72.2
Londonderry	census, 1771	28	50	362	624.0
Manchester	militia, 1776	37	340	1,278	275.9
Marlboro	freemen, 1777	22	190	629	231.1
	census, 1771	50			
Newbury	census, 1771	46	310	872	181.3
Newfane	census, 1771	52	200	660	230.0
Norwich	militia, 1776	33	350	1,158	230.9
	census, 1771	206			
Orwell	est.		50	778	1456.0
Pawlet	town, 1775		400	1,458	264.5
Pittsfield	est.		10	49	390.0
Pittsford	town, 1776		160	850	431.3
Pomfret	freemen, 1778	68	340	710	108.8
	census, 1771	39			
Poultney	freemen, 1775	46	230	1,120	387.0
Pownall	town, 1775		350	1,734	395.4
Putney	census, 1771	301	470	1,848	293.2
Reading	est.		100	747	647.0
Readsboro	est.		25	63	152.0
Rockingham	militia, 1775	82	410	1,235	201.2
	census, 1771	225			
Royalton	est.		20	748	3640.0
Rupert	town, 1776		230	1,034	349.6
Rutland	freemen, 1778	129	615	1,417	130.4
Ryegate	est.		100	187	87.0
Sandgate	est		150	773	415.3
Shaftsbury	town, 1775		500	1,990	298.0
Sharon	freemen, 1778	20	100	569	469.0
	census, 1771	68			
Shoreham	town, 1775	6	30	701	2236.7
Shrewsbury	est.		100	382	282.0
Somerset	town, 1774		50	111	122.0

POPULATION OF VERMONT (*continued*)

Town	Source	Number in record	Estimates 1775	1791	% increase
Springfield	census, 1771	141	340	1,097	222.6
Stamford	est.		100	272	172.0
Strafford	militia, 1776	27	125	844	575.2
	census, 1771	9			
Stratton	est.		20	95	375.0
Sudbury	est.		30	258	760.0
Sunderland	est.		150	414	176.0
Thetford	militia, 1776	34	130	862	563.1
	census, 1771	29			
Thomlinson	est.		200	561	180.5
Tinmouth	town, 1776		150	935	523.3
Townshend	census, 1771	136	250	678	171.2
Wallingford	freemen, 1778	16	80	538	572.5
Wardsboro	est.		30	753	2410.0
Weathersfield	tax, 1775	24	137	1,146	736.5
	freemen, 1775	22			
	census, 1771	20			
Wells	freemen, 1778	24	120	620	416.7
Westminster	census, 1771	478	650	1,599	146.0
Whitingham	est.		100	442	342.0
Wilmington	census, 1771	71	180	645	258.3
Winhall	est.		30	155	416.7
Windsor	census, 1771	203	500	1,542	208.4
Woodford	est.		15	60	300.0
Woodstock	census, 1771	42	350	1,597	356.3
Other towns			500	22,048	4309.6
TOTALS			17,384	86,507	397.6

A sample has been made for the following thirty towns, tracing family persistence within towns and the state of Vermont from 1775–76, with a few noted exceptions, to the 1791 census. The contrast with the southern frontier is striking. According to Richard Beeman 17.5 percent of the population of Lunenburg County, Virginia, left that county every year (*Evolution of the Southern Backcountry,* 29, 67).

PERSISTENCE IN VERMONT

Town	Source	Number in record	% of persistence In town	% of persistence In state
Barnard	militia, 1776	28	75	93
Barnet	census, 1771	9	44	89
Bennington	militia, 1776	154	59	95
Bradford	freemen, 1775	71	52	90
Chester	freemen, 1778	47	83	96
Clarendon	militia, 1776	27	55.5	96
Corinth	freemen, 1777	9	66	100
Danby	freemen, 1777	101	63	96
Guildhall	petition, 1776	20	30	80
Guilford	census, 1772	586	76	95
Hartford	militia, 1771	88	78	97
Hubbardton	freemen, 1777	9	89	100
Ira	freemen, 1779	52	75	100
Manchester	militia, 1776	37	65	97
Marlboro	freemen, 1777	22	82	100
Newbury	census, 1771	46	76	98
Norwich	census, 1771	206	87.5	97.5
Pomfret	freemen, 1778	68	87	97
Poultney	freemen, 1775	46	83	98
Rockingham	militia, 1775	82	67	97.5
Rutland	freemen, 1778	129	77	96
Sharon	freemen, 1778	20	85	100
Strafford	militia, 1776	27	93	100
Thetford	militia, 1776	34	82	94
Wallingford	freemen, 1778	16	69	94
Weathersfield	tax, 1775	24	83	96
Wells	freemen, 1778	24	75	96
Windsor	census, 1771	203	63	97
TOTALS		2,148	70.16	95.89

Appendix E

Biographical Profile of the Green Mountain Boys

PLACE OF ORIGIN

	No.	%		No.	%
Conn.	43	38.7	Ireland	2	1.8
Mass.	41	37.0	N.H.	2	1.8
R.I.	6	5.4	N.J.	1	0.9
N.Y.	6	5.4	England	1	0.9
Grants	5	4.5	At sea	1	0.9
Scotland	3	2.7	TOTAL	111	100

AGE AT FIRST PARTICIPATION

	No.	%
14–19	16	14.8
20–30	39	36.1
30–40	31	28.7
40–50	12	11.1
50+	10	9.3
Total	108	100

Robert Gross's figures indicate that Concord's ninety-one minutemen were much younger than the Green Mountain Boys. To use Gross's age distribution (*Minutemen and Their World*, 206):

	Concord	*Green Mountain Boys*
Under 21	29.7	21.3
21–24	27.5	12.0
25–29	14.3	17.6
30 & over	28.6	49.1

See also the figures of Mark E. Lender, "The Social Structure of the New Jersey Brigade: The Continental Line as an American Standing Army," in Karsted, *The Military in America,* 68.

PROPERTY OWNERSHIP OF THE
GREEN MOUNTAIN BOYS

	No.	*%*
At time of joining	73	69
At some point before 1790	106	100

Lender found that 63 percent of the Continental soldiers from New Jersey owned land (ibid., 69).

PERSISTENCE IN VERMONT, 1775–91

	No.	*%*
In same town	61	57.5
In state	104	98

Note: These 111 Green Mountain Boys represent less than 10 percent of the total number who belonged at one time or another to that group and therefore cannot form a very solid base for generalization. The very fact that this biographical information exists indicates that these men were to some degree prominent and thus more likely to stay in Vermont and enjoy some level of relative prosperity.

Appendix F

Patterns of Town Office Holding

This table is based on those of Gregory Nobles, *Divisions throughout the Whole*, 189, 197. The last three towns listed are from Nobles's study and are added for the sake of comparison.

DISTRIBUTION OF TOWN OFFICES

Town	Total no. of selectmen	Distribution by no. of terms			Average no. of terms per selectman
		1	*2–4*	*5+*	
Bennington	51	29	14	8	2.5
(1762–86)		(56.9%)	(27.5)	(15.6)	
Brattleboro*	31	16	11	4	2.2
(1768–85)		(51.6)	(35.5)	(12.9)	
Danby	33	11	21	1	2.1
(1769–88)		(33.3)	(63.7)	(3.0)	
Guilford*	41	27	13	1	1.7
(1772–86)		(65.9)	(31.7)	(2.4)	
Newbury	35	20	13	2	2.0
(1764–88)		(29)	(50.7)	(20.3)	
Newfane	18	9	5	4	2.7
(1774–89)		(50)	(27.8)	(22.2)	
Blandford, Mass.	39	11	16	12	4.3
(1742–75)		(28.2)	(41)	(30.8)	
Pelham, Mass.	54	11	33	10	3.0
(1743–75)		(20.4)	(61.1)	(18.5)	
Northampton, Mass.	92	32	24	36	5.0
(1655–1750)		(34.8)	(26.1)	(29.1)	

*Town officers went by a number of different names as these towns swung between New York and New England structures. I have combined the equivalents of selectmen into that category for these towns.

Edward Cook found that 40–50 percent of all taxpayers could expect to hold town office (Cook, *Fathers of the Towns*, 27–32). In the Vermont towns above, the figure is 78 percent.

Appendix G

Vermont Ministers to 1789

DISTRIBUTION OF MINISTERS

| Years in Vermont | | | | | College |
1–3	3–9	10+	Total	Dismissed	graduate
Congregationalist					
8	18	19	45	29 (64.4%)	37 (82.2%)
Presbyterian					
	2	3	5	2 (40)	5 (100)
Baptist					
3	5	1	9	3 (33.3)	2 (22.2)
Church of England					
		1	1		1 (100)
TOTALS					
11	25	24	60	34 (56.6)	45 (75)

These figures refer to the denomination when these ministers first arrived in the Grants or Vermont. At least five of the Congregationalists became Baptist and/or Universalist, one Presbyterian became Congregationalist, and most of the Baptists spent some time in some other denomination. These figures also do not include the great number of itinerants and lay readers active in the region.

Appendix H

Ethan Allen's Land Acquisitions and Sales

According to Lewis D. Stilwell, Ethan Allen owned 300,000 acres of Vermont land. James B. Wilbur put the figure at 75,000 acres. Based on the following information, Wilbur's seems the more accurate figure for the mid-1780s, the period of Allen's greatest land ownership. At the time of his death, Allen appears to have owned approximately 2,000 acres plus land rights in eight towns (Stilwell, *Migration from Vermont*, 84; Wilbur, *Ira Allen* 2: 520).

The papers of the Onion River Company are widely scattered, and most of the actual business records have long been lost. Kevin Graffagnino has done a fine job tracing many of the Onion River Company papers in " 'The Country My Soul Delighted In.' " According to one probate document in Wilbur, *Ira Allen* 2:520–25, the company purchased a total of 230 rights in eleven different townships. By 1775 the company had sold 16,793 acres in seven townships. Ethan Allen held a one-fifth share, or the equivalent of 46 rights. In 1775 these rights were worth £4 to £10 each.

LAND TRANSACTIONS BY ETHAN ALLEN

Date	Place	Acreage	From	Price	Partner
			Acquisitions		
1761	Cornwall	50	J. Squier	£50	Elihu Allen
1762	Salisbury	share in ironworks	S. & L. Forbes	54	J. Hazeltine
1762	Salisbury	water rights	L. E. & E. Owen	20	Hazeltine, S. & L. Forbes Heman Allen

LAND TRANSACTIONS BY ETHAN ALLEN (*continued*)

Date	Place	Acreage	From	Price	Partner

Acquisitions (continued)

Date	Place	Acreage	From	Price	Partner
1763	Salisbury	27.5	S. & L. Forbes	20	Hazeltine, H. Allen
	Salisbury	48	L. Owen	430	H. Allen
	Salisbury	95	E. Buell	500	H. Allen
	Cornwall	25	H. Allen	85	
1764	Woodbury	21	L. Baker	50	
1770	Poultney	1 right	D. Warner	4	
	Castleton	1 right	Z. Person	6	
1771	Poultney	house lot	S. Brown	?	
	Hubbardton	1 right	I. Searles		
1772	Castleton	1 right	S. Robinson	17	
1773	Onion R.	1 right	E. Burling	?	ORC
	Charlotte	1 right	B. Farris	9	ORC
	Charlotte	½ right	J. Akin	3	ORC
	Charlotte	1 right	J. Brownson	11	ORC
	Onion R.	1 right	J. Hart	4	ORC
	Onion R.	1 right	I. Newel	4	ORC
1778	Onion R.	150	CCP	300	
1779	Sunderland	?	S. Folsom	250	I. Allen
1781	Sunderland	10	S. Folsom	0.05	I. Allen
1783	N. Hero	1 right	W. Williams	1.5	
	N. Hero	1 right	R. Cochran	6	
1783	Two Heroes	1 right	L. Filmore	6	
	Two Heroes	2 rights	B. Purdy	14	
	N. Hero	2 rights	J. Underwood	12	
1784	Two Heroes	2 rights	W. Gallup	40	
1785	Susquehanna	12 rights	J. Hamilton	gift	
1787	Charlotte	200	A. White	50	

Date	Place	Acreage	To	Price	Partner

Sales

Date	Place	Acreage	To	Price	Partner
1763	Cornwall	25	E. Allen	£60	
1764	Salisbury	10 + ½ inter. in furnace	H. Allen	300	

LAND TRANSACTIONS BY ETHAN ALLEN (*continued*)

Date	Place	Acreage	To	Price	Partner
		Sales (continued)			
1764	Cornwall	72	E. Buell	450	
1765	Salisbury	20	Heber Allen	50	Heman Allen
	Salisbury	95	O. Millard	272	Heman Allen
	Salisbury	⅛ inter. in furnace	G. Caldwell	500	Heman Allen
1769	Salisbury	½ house	H. Allen	200	
1771	Castleton	1 right	I. Holmes	24	
1772	Cornwall	177	E. Reed	23	
	Poultney	1 right	Eben. Allen	12	
1773	Poultney	60	Eben. Allen	?	
	Cornwall	17	S. Whitmore	5	
	Poultney	400	S. Warner	90	
1774	Williston	700	Elihu Allen	?	ORC
1778	Tinmouth	300	T. Russell	300	ORC
1781	Woodbury	25	W. French	22	Mary Allen
	Castleton	1 right	S. Folsom	150	ORC
1783	Middlesex	1 right	?	40	
	New Haven	1 right	?	40	
	Two Heroes	1 right	G. Brownson	0.05	
	Shelburne	1 right	?	50	
1784	Two Heroes	1 right	J. Savage	7.5	
	Two Heroes	1 right	L. Allen	20	
	Two Heroes	1 right	L. Allen	20	
	Sunderland	all interests	I. Allen	300	
	Charlotte	1 right	?	60	
	Charlotte	1 right	?	60	
	Charlotte	300	J. McNeil	300	
	Charlotte	1 right	?	70	
1785	TwoHeroes	?	?	0.25	
	Charlotte	200	T. Chittenden	35	
	GrandIsle	1 right	J. Fay	9	
	Hubbarton	100	S. Huntington	80	
	Shelburne	200	J. Reed	60	
	Charlotte	100	D. Breckenridge	$100	
	Charlotte	200	C. McNeil	£150	
1786	Charlotte	100	A. Barnes	28	

LAND TRANSACTIONS BY ETHAN ALLEN (*continued*)

Date	Place	Acreage	To	Price	Partner
			Sales (continued)		
	Charlotte	1 right	T. Chittenden, etc.	?	
1786	Georgia	1,430	Smith & assoc.	?	
	Two Heroes	1 right	T. Canfield	15	
	Charlotte	173	C. McNeil	100	
1787	Charlotte	½ right	T. Chittenden	35	
1788	Charlotte	50	Wheeler	20	
	Jericho	2 lots	J. Hollenbeck	238	
	Charlotte	50	J. Sawyer	30	

Note: ORC = Onion River Company; CCP = Commission of Confiscated Property (Vermont).

Notes

Abbreviations

AFP   Allen Family Papers, Special Collections, University of Vermont Library, Burlington
AAS   American Antiquarian Society, Worcester, Mass.
CHS   Connecticut Historical Society, Hartford
EAP   Ethan Allen Papers, Henry Stevens Collection, Vermont State Archives, Montpelier
IAP   Ira Allen Papers, Henry Stevens Collection, Vermont State Archives, Montpelier
LAP   Levi Allen Papers, Henry Stevens Collection, Vermont State Archives, Montpelier
LC   Library of Congress, Washington, D.C.
MHS   Massachusetts Historical Society, Boston
PRO   Public Records Office, London
NHHS   New Hampshire Historical Society, Concord
NYHS   New-York Historical Society, New York City
NYPL   New York Public Library, New York City
PAC   Public Archives of Canada, Ottawa, Ontario
PHS   Pennsylvania Historical Society, Philadelphia
VHS   Vermont Historical Society, Montpelier
VSA   Vermont State Archives, Montpelier

INTRODUCTION

1. Epigraph from Allen to the merchants of Montreal, 4 June 1775, EAP. Oliver, *Origin and Progress,* 138.

2. Klein, *Unification of a Slave State;* Taylor, *Liberty Men;* Whittenberg,

"Planters, Merchants, and Lawyers"; Marvin L. M. Kay, "The North Carolina Regulation, 1766–1776: A Class Conflict," in Young, *American Revolution,* 71–124; Rowland Berthoff and John Murrin, "Feudalism, Communalism, and the Yeoman Farmer: The American Revolution as a Social Accident," in Kurtz and Hutson, *Essays on the American Revolution,* 256–88; Countryman, *A People in Revolution;* Mitchell, *Commercialism and Frontier.*

3. Turner, *The Frontier in American History.* For the debate over the meaning of Turner's thesis, see especially Lee, "The Turner Thesis Re-Examined"; Stanley Elkins and Eric McKitrick, "A Meaning for Turner's Frontier," *Political Science Review* 69 (1954), 321–53, 565–602; Dykstra, *Cattle Towns;* Bogue, "Social Theory and the Pioneer"; Hine, *Community on the Frontier.* The frontier definitely served as a population safety valve for the United States. It was not the cities that were swallowing the enormous increase in America's population but the frontier. Darrett Rutman found that New Hampshire's newer towns grew by 6% a year compared with 0.03% in the older towns (Rutman, "The Social Web: A Prospectus for the Study of the Early American Community," in O'Neill, *Insights and Parallels,* 76; Daniel Scott Smith, "A Malthusian-Frontier Interpretation of U.S. Demographic History before 1815," in Borah, *Urbanization in the Americas,* 15–24).

4. Edmund Morgan, "Conflict and Consensus," in *The Challenge of the American Revolution,* 174–95.

5. Turner had himself implied this understanding in "The Problem of the West," in *The Frontier in American History,* 205.

6. Calloway, *The Western Abenakis,* 17–33.

7. See Appendix D.

8. Allen, *Reason,* 212.

CHAPTER ONE

1. Epigraph from "In memory of my dear grand-child Anne Bradstreet," Hutchinson, *Poems of Bradstreet,* 57–58. Ira Allen to Samuel Williams, 6 June 1795, IAP; Gold, *Cornwall,* 449; Hemenway, *Gazetteer* 1:563; Joseph Allen's will, Litchfield Probate Records, vol. 1; J. Allen's death, Cornwall Vital Records, vol. 1; Levi Allen, Autobiography, unpaginated, LAP.

2. See Stannard, *Puritan Way of Death,* ch. 3; Morgan, *Puritan Family,* ch. 3–4; Greven, *Four Generations,* 197–99; Norton, *Liberty's Daughters,* 87–90, 103–4.

3. Epigraph from Allen, *Reason,* 133. Dwight, *Travels* 2:260; Beardsley, *Episcopal Church* 1:201; Gold, *Cornwall,* 19, 45, 121, 375; Starr, *Cornwall,* 36–37, 40, 47, 82. For the opposite view of the economic nature and ideology of

eighteenth-century Connecticut farmers, see Bushman, *Puritan to Yankee.*

4. Each household was rated at £18 per adult male, £3 for a horse or cow, £4 for an ox, and £1 per young cattle. The £18 poll rate has been omitted from the figures in the text as it is regressive and reveals little of a community's economy. Litchfield had a total of fifty-two cows, forty-three horses, forty-one oxen, nine young cattle, and twenty-one swine. Litchfield's total rating was £1,433; Woodbury's was £16,300 (Starr, *Cornwall,* 38–40, 43; Cothren, *Woodbury* 1:775–76). For comparisons of livestock ownership, all of which demonstrate the relative poverty of Cornwall, see Grant, *Kent,* 32–39; Bidwell and Falconer, *History of Agriculture,* 105–6; Judd, *Hadley,* 385.

5. Starr, *Cornwall,* 38–40, 43.

6. The 1748 rating counted seventy families and returned a total evaluation of £3,054, an average of £43. Woodbury was also enjoying an economic boom in this decade, its rating and average increasing by almost 50%, to a total of £24,327 (Gold, *Cornwall,* 14–16; Cothren, *Woodbury,* 1:776; Hemenway, *Gazetteer* 1:766; Starr, *Cornwall,* 45).

7. There is absolutely no evidence that Joseph Allen was a wealthy farmer in either Litchfield or Cornwall, as has been suggested by Ethan Allen's biographers (Kilbourne, *Litchfield,* ch. 1, 3, 10). On the oligarchic structure of most New England towns, see Lockridge, *New England Town,* ch. 3; Tracy, *Edwards,* 38–49; Greven, *Four Generations;* Zemsky, *Merchants, Farmers, and River Gods,* ch. 2–3.

8. Allen, *Allen Memorial,* 27–29; Cornwall Land Records, 1: 28 July 1742; Starr, *Cornwall,* 230–31.

9. Litchfield Probate Records, 1:162; Cornwall Land Records, 1: 30 Dec. 1763, 9 April 1764; Salisbury Land Records, 1: 9 April, 6 Aug. 1764.

10. Woodbury Vital Records, 1: 11 March 1737; Litchfield Probate Records, 1: 9 June 1757, Ethan Allen for Mary Allen, administrator for Joseph Allen's estate, v. Joseph Mather; Levi Allen, Autobiography, LAP. For a different perspective, see Grant, *Kent,* ch. 2–3, 11; Lemon, *Best Poor Man's Country,* ch. 1, 2, 8; Kim, *Landlord and Tenant,* ch. 6; Wolf, *Urban Village,* ch. 2–3.

11. "Capt. Moses Lyman's Co.," CHS *Collections* 9:247. Ethan's orphaned cousin Remember Baker was the only townsman to serve for an extended period in the war. Baker enlisted in 1755, joining Israel Putnam's company, and won distinction for his ferocity in attacking the French at the unsuccessful assault on Fort Ticonderoga in 1758. New England towns typically dealt with such surplus young men by encouraging them to join the military during wars (Baker, "Baker," 598; Hemenway, *Gazetteer* 1:766; Anderson, *A People's Army,* 28–33).

12. Squier to Elihu and Ethan Allen, Cornwall Land Records, 1: 15 Oct. 1761.

13. Samuel and Elisha Forbes to John Hazeltine and Ethan Allen, 12 Jan. 1762; Leonard, Elijah, and Eliphalet Owen to John Hazeltine, Samuel and Elisha Forbes, and Heman and Ethan Allen, 18 Jan. 1762, Salisbury Land Records, vol. 1.

14. Richard H. Schallenberg, "Charcoal Iron: The Coal Mines of the Forest," in Hindle, *Material Culture*, 271–99.

15. Owens to Forbes, Hazeltine, and Allen, Salisbury Land Records, 1: 12 Jan. 1763; WPA, *Connecticut*, 418; Smith, *Housatonic*, 169, 259–60. Several of Ethan's employees at the forge, for example Matthew Lyon, became friends and followed him upriver to the Green Mountains (Austin, *Lyon*, 11–13).

16. Cornwall Land Records, 1: 29, 30 Dec. 1763, 9 April 1764; Salisbury Land Records, 1: 9 April, 2 May, 6 Aug. 1764; Smith, *Housatonic*, 144–62; Taylor, *Colonial Connecticut*, ch. 5.

17. Cothren, *Woodbury* 1:45.

18. Ibid., 1:146, 161. The lot Mary Allen inherited was sold in 1771 to buy land in Vermont (Litchfield County Land Records, 1: Sept. 1771). Biographers of Ethan Allen have emphasized the contrast between Ethan Allen and Mary Brownson. Most have seen her as a shrew lacking a sense of humor, though without offering any evidence. Others have compared her favorably with Ethan: "She was a pious and most excellent woman" (Allen, *Allen Memorial*, 44; see also Pell, *Ethan Allen*, 11; Jellison, *Ethan Allen*, 8). There is no evidence that Mary Brownson ever belonged to a church.

19. Woodbury Vital Records, 1: 23 June 1762. The average age of marriage in eighteenth-century America was 24–25 for men and 21–22 for women. So Allen was right on the average, but Brownson was well beyond the norm (im Potter, "Demographic Development and Family Structure," in Greene and Pole, *Colonial British America*, 141).

20. Barr, *Genealogy of Ethan Allen*, 7–8.

21. Though his mother was still alive and the estate was the product of both their labor, the law defined the estate as terminating with the death of the father. On the gender bias of eighteenth-century law, see Shammas, *Inheritance in America*, ch. 2–3; Ditz, *Property and Kinship*, ch. 7; Salomon, *Women and the Law of Property*, ch. 5.

22. See Norton, *Liberty's Daughters*, ch. 2.

23. Allen, *Allen Memorial*, 19; Larned, *Windham County* 1:187, 191–93; Sheldon, *Deerfield* 1:294–363, 2:8–24.

24. Joseph was born 14 Oct. 1708, in Deerfield (Allen, *Allen Memorial*, 19–20, 27; Wilbur, *Ira Allen*, n.p.).

25. White, *Litchfield*, 18–19; Kilbourne, *Sketches*, 33–36.

26. WPA, *Connecticut*, 194; White, *Litchfield*, 11–13, 17–18; Cothren, *Wood-*

bury 1:248. For an excellent study of town structure in this section of Connecticut, see Grant, *Democracy*, ch. 9–10.

27. Probate Records, Litchfield County, 1: 1 March 1729.

28. Blake, *Dorchester* 1:8; Allen, *Allen Memorial*, 14–16; Windsor County Probate Records, 1: 8 Sept. 1648; Hampshire County Probate Records, 1: 23 July 1684.

29. See, for instance, Greven, *Four Generations*. On patterns of geographic mobility, see Hufton, *Poor of Eighteenth Century France;* Jones, "The Strolling Poor."

30. Epigraph from Allen, *Reason*, app., 42–43; Ira Allen to Williams, 6 June 1795, IAP; Allen, *Reason*, introduction; Smith, *Housatonic*, 145; Gold, *Records of Cornwall*, 18.

31. Dexter, *Biographical Sketches* 1:716–17; Goen, *Revivalism*, 61; Hemenway, *Gazetteer* 1:563; Ira Allen to Williams, 6 June 1795, IAP; Gold, *Cornwall*, 449.

32. Allen, *Reason*, 383–84; Allen to Bradley, 7 Sept. 1785, EAP; Ira Allen to Williams, 6 June 1795, IAP; [Jehiel Johns] to George Benedict, 29 May 1840, AFP.

33. Heimert and Miller, *Great Awakening*, xviii–xxii, xxxix–xliii; Edwards, *Faithful Narrative* (1737) and *Some Thoughts concerning the Revival* (1742), in Goen, *Edwards*, 132, 502–4; Edwards, *History of Redemption*, 398–400, 430–32. On the religious climate of New England at the time of Ethan Allen's birth, see Jones, *Shattered Synthesis*, ch. 6–8; Bonomi, *Under the Cope of Heaven*, ch. 2–4; Middlekauff, *Mathers*, ch. 7; Tracy, *Edwards*, ch. 1; Lucas, *Valley of Discord*, ch. 9; Miller, "Thomas Hooker," 667, 688–89; Bremer, *Puritan Experiment*, 76–77; Ahlstrom, *Religious History*, 152–53; Rutman, *American Puritanism*, 103–5.

34. Edwards, *A Faithful Narrative*, in Goen, *Edwards*, esp. 147–59; Miller, "Edwards and the Great Awakening," *Errand*, 153–66; Tracy, *Edwards*, ch. 5.

35. On the Great Awakening, see Gaustad, *Great Awakening;* Goen, *Revivalism;* Bremer, *Puritan Experiment*, ch. 18; Ahlstrom, *Religious History*, ch. 18 and 19; Bumsted, "Religion, Finance, and Democracy," and "Revivalism and Separatism"; Walsh, "Great Awakening. For eyewitness accounts, see Josiah Smith, "Whitefield's Character and Preaching," and Nathan Cole, "Spiritual Travels," in Heimert and Miller, *Great Awakening*, 62–69, 183–86; Franklin, *Autobiography*, 176–80.

36. Edwards, "Thoughts on the Revival of Religion," in Heimert and Miller, *Great Awakening*, 274; Goen, *Revivalism*, ch. 1–2; Lovejoy, *Religious Enthusiasm*, ch. 9. See also Gilbert Tennent, "The Danger of an Unconverted Ministry," Charles Chauncy, "Enthusiasm Described and Caution'd Against," and "Seasonable Thoughts on the State of Religion," "The Testimony of Harvard

College against George Whitefield," in Heimert and Miller, *Great Awakening*, 72–99, 228–56, 291–304, 340–53; Bushman, *Puritan to Yankee*, ch. 13–14; Nobles, *Divisions*, ch. 2–4; Gaustad, *Great Awakening*, ch. 5–6; Bonomi, *Under the Cope of Heaven*, ch. 5.

37. Miller, *Errand into the Wilderness*, 160.

38. Wright, *Difference between . . . Standing Churches*, 20; Cothren, *Woodbury* 1:115–34, 247, 301–2; Starr, *Cornwall*, 36–43, 50; Gold, *Cornwall*, 10–14; Allen, *Allen Memorial*, 27–29; Litchfield County Land Records, 1: 1742.

39. Starr, *Cornwall*, 43; Gold, *Cornwall*, 47. Some historians have linked religious and economic liberalism and have seen these migrations as the first stirring of Smithian individualism in the New World. Others have found the Great Awakening a rejection of profit maximization and the revivalists harbingers of social change. Cornwall, at least, was not on the frontier of free enterprise. See, for instance, Bailyn, *New England Merchants*, 105–11, 137–42; Heimert, *Religion and the American Mind*, 246–53, 494–509; Bushman, *Puritan to Yankee*, ch. 16.

40. An unfortunate choice on Collins's part. As soon as the liberal group left Litchfield, the evangelical majority first harassed Collins, then refused to pay his salary, ejected him from his house, and finally, in 1750, dismissed him from his pulpit. Collins stayed in Litchfield until his death in 1776, an Arminian thorn in the side of the New Light majority (White, *Litchfield*, 28, 40–41; Kilbourne, *Sketches*, 171–72, 386; Dexter, *Biographical Sketches* 1:182–84; Starr, *Cornwall*, 45). Local historians and previous biographers of Ethan Allen often have confused Collins with Solomon Palmer. See, for instance, Starr, *Cornwall*, 33; Jellison, *Ethan Allen*, 4–5; White, *Litchfield*, 28.

41. Starr, *Cornwall*, 40–42; Gold, *Cornwall*, 46, 50; Dexter, *Biographical Sketches* 1:387–88.

42. The traditional, but unsubstantiated, story is that Palmer was swayed from orthodox Calvinism by the arguments of Joseph Allen (Pell, *Allen*, 3, 6; Beardsley, *Episcopal Church* 1:189–91; Cothren, *Woodbury* 1:247; Starr, *Cornwall*, 40–42, 85; Gold, *Cornwall*, 48–49).

43. Palmer to Bull, 1757, Gold, *Cornwall*, 155; Starr, *Cornwall*, 84; White, *Litchfield*, 197; Dexter, *Biographical Sketches* 1:387n; Beardsley, *Episcopal Church* 1:200–205, 220–23, 228, 237. By 1764 the town records contained the names of nineteen people who were released to "the dissenting collector" for the Episcopalian church. Included in the group were Ethan Allen's mother, aunt, and three cousins. Later Ethan Allen would join with Heman and their cousins to sign an affidavit in behalf of Palmer (Starr, *Cornwall*, 40–42, 49, 84–85, 110, 310; Beardsley, *Episcopal Church* 1:220–24, 237, 293; Dexter, *Biographical Sketches* 1:387). Roughly the same events were replicated in Woodbury and Litchfield (Beardsley, *Episcopal Church* 1:141, 173).

44. Gold, *Cornwall,* 54–57, 121–28, 143, 155–57, 210; Starr, *Cornwall,* 52–53, 83–87, 96–97; Smith, *Housatonic,* 223.

45. Allen, *Reason,* 386, 470–71.

46. Ibid.

47. Epigraph from EAP, 431–34. The prohibition of inoculation was not necessarily a sign of close-minded anti-intellectualism. Inoculating a minority endangered the majority. The most logical policy was to inoculate everyone, but no town was willing to bear such an expense. See Heyrman, *Commerce and Culture,* ch. 9; Henderson, "Smallpox and Patriotism."

48. Tousley v. Heman and Ethan Allen, Salisbury Justice Records 1: 25 Aug. 1764.

49. Ibid., 8 Sept. 1764.

50. Salisbury Land Records, 1: 22 March, 3 Sept., 31 Oct. 1765. At the same time they sold the last of their land in Cornwall, marking the departure of the children of Joseph Allen from that town.

51. Pell, *Ethan Allen,* 19–20; Salisbury Justice Records, 1: 3 Sept. 1765.

52. Salisbury Justice Records, 1: 11, 27 Oct. 1765.

53. Salisbury Vital Records, 1: 25 Nov. 1765; Trumbull, *Northampton* 1: 363; notes of hand, EAP. In the Salisbury Grand List of 1765, Heman and Ethan Allen were evaluated together at £96.18; two-fifths of that amount was their poll rating.

54. Clark, *Antiquities . . . of Northampton,* 160; affidavits of Wood and Clapp, EAP; Allen, *Allen Memorial,* 17, 22–23. There are several references to Edwards in Allen's *Reason.*

55. Northampton Justice Records, 1: 15 July 1767.

56. Warner, Wood, Clapp, and Goodrich affidavits, EAP; Woodbury Justice Records, 1: 6 Oct. 1767; Litchfield County Court Records, 4:73 (7 July 1768); Ira Allen, "Autobiography," in Wilbur, *Ira Allen* 1:27–28.

57. Ira Allen, "Autobiography," in Wilbur, *Ira Allen* 1:8: Levi Allen, Autobiography, LAP.

58. Ira Allen to Williams, 6 June 1795, IAP.

CHAPTER TWO

1. Nobles, "Breaking into the Backcountry," 643.

2. See also Taylor, *Liberty Men,* ch. 2; Slaughter, *Whiskey Rebellion,* ch. 5; Lockridge, *William Byrd,* 136–43; Wyckoff, *Developer's Frontier,* ch. 4–5; Newell, "Culture of Economic Development"; Mark, *Agrarian Conflicts,* ch. 3; Onuf, *Statehood and Union,* ch. 2.

3. Epigraph from Irving, *History of New York,* 228. Levi Allen, Autobiography, LAP; Williams, *Natural and Civil History,* 17–80; *American Husbandry* 1:47; Clark, *Eastern Frontier,* ch. 20.

4. Ira Allen to Samuel Williams, 6 June 1795, IAP, 427–29; Ira Allen, "Autobiography," in Wilbur, *Ira Allen* 1:22–36; Levi Allen, Autobiography; Norton, *Fur Trade in Colonial New York*, ch. 5–7; Phillips, *Fur Trade* ch. 20, 27–30; Calloway, *Western Abenakis*, ch. 7.

5. Levi Allen, Autobiography.

6. Ira Allen, "Autobiography," in Wilbur, *Ira Allen* 1:8–15.

7. Calloway, *Western Abenakis*, ch. 5–8; Williams, *History of Vermont*, ch. 7–8.

8. *Laws of New Hampshire* 2:600, 620–21; Description of the Bounds of New Hampshire, 1749, O'Callaghan, *Documentary History* 4:532–33; Batchellor, *New Hampshire Grants*, 29–34; Belknap, *History of New Hampshire* 1: appendix; Brodhead and O'Callaghan, *Documents* 4:628–30, 5:555–57, 6:121–25; *Colonial Laws of New York* 1:1; Hall, *History of Vermont*, 4–46.

9. Denio, "Massachusetts Land Grants"; Temple and Sheldon, *Northfield*, 99–106; Conant, *Vermont Historical Reader*, 19; Hemenway, *Historical Gazetteer* 5, pt. 2:251, 271–75; Colden to Board of Trade, 14 Feb. 1738, O'Callaghan, *Documentary History* 4:172–79; Hall, *Eastern Vermont*, 13–28, 106; Thompson, "Vermont from Chaos to Statehood"; Hall, *History of Vermont*, app. 3.

10. Acts of the Privy Council, CO, 3:789, PRO; *New Hampshire State Papers* 9:382–83, 491–502, 24:142, 25:51–58, 115–23, 130–38, 363–69; Hall, *Eastern Vermont*, 30–32, 79–80; Attorney and Solicitor General's Report, 14 Aug. 1752, O'Callaghan, *Documentary History* 4:547–48. For the general background on this dispute, see ibid., 4:529–1034; Fox, *Yankees and Yorkers;* Mark, *Agrarian Conflicts*, ch. 6; Handlin, "Eastern Frontier of New York"; Woodard, *Town Proprietors;* Belknap, *History of New Hampshire*, ch. 22–23, 26; Williams, *History of Vermont*, ch. 9–11.

11. Wentworth to Clinton, 17 Nov. 1749, 6 June 1750, O'Callaghan, *Documentary History* 4:531–35.

12. Description of the Bounds of New Hampshire, 3 April 1750, Wentworth to Clinton, 25 April 1750, ibid., 532–34.

13. Wentworth to Clinton, 22 June, 2 Sept. 1750, Clinton to Wentworth, 25 July 1750, Secretary of Board of Trade to Agent for New York, 22 Dec. 1752, ibid., 535–37, 548; Batchellor, *New Hampshire Grants,* 207–11.

14. Wentworth to Board of Trade, 23 March 1751, O'Callaghan, *Documentary History* 4:548–49.

15. Report of Attorney General, September 1751, and Colden to Board of Trade, 14 Oct. 1751, ibid., 545–47; Surveyor General's Observations, Colden to Board of Trade, 28 Feb. 1761, and 11 Feb. 1762, *Colden Letter Books* 9:64–69, 159–61.

16. Report of the Council, 14 Nov. 1753, O'Callaghan, *Documentary His-*

tory 4:550–56. Wentworth's grants are collected in Batchellor, *New Hampshire Grants.*

17. Five council members to Monckton, 25 June 1763, and Colden to Board of Trade, 26 Sept. 1763, *Colden Letter Books* 9:232–45. In fact, most of these grants were sold to New York speculators like Crean Brush, James Duane, and Walter Rutherford.

18. Proclamation of Colden, 28 Dec. 1763, Colden to Board of Trade, 20 Jan., 8 Feb. 1764, O'Callaghan, *Documentary History* 4:558–69.

19. Proclamation of Wentworth, 13 March 1764, ibid., 570–72.

20. Colden to Board of Trade, 12 April 1764, ibid., 572–74.

21. Representation of Board of Trade, 10 July 1764, Jones, *Vermont in the Making,* 402–3.

22. Order in Council Fixing the Boundary, 20 July 1764, O'Callaghan, *Documentary History* 4:574–75.

23. VHS *Collections* 1:153–59; Hall, *History of Vermont,* 79–80, 131–32. The Board of Trade itself remained uncertain of where the border was at least as late as 1773. See Lords of Trade, 6 June 1771, 3 Dec. 1772, Dartmouth to Tryon, 9 Dec. 1772, 10 April 1773, O'Callaghan, *Documentary History* 4:712–20, 803–15, 827–30.

24. Schuyler to Colden, 17 Aug. 1764, O'Callaghan, *Documentary History* 4:575–76.

25. Epigraph from Dwight, *Travels* 2:329. Hall, *Eastern Vermont,* ch. 1–4; Hinden, "White Chief of the St. Francis Abenakis"; McCorison, "Colonial Defence of the Upper Connecticut Valley"; Calloway, "Conquest of Vermont."

26. See Appendix D on population.

27. Young, *Reflections,* 15. On Young, see Hawke, "Dr. Thomas Young"; Edes, "Memoir of Dr. Thomas Young." On the Lydius controversy, see Denio, "Massachusetts Land Grants," 52–59; Brodhead and O'Callaghan, *Documents* 6:569–70, 7:455–58; Goebel and Naughton, *Law Enforcement,* 209–18, 729–30; New York Land Papers, 16:396–405, 34:10–11; Fernow, *Calendar of Council Minutes,* 414, 451–57.

28. Salisbury Land Records, 1:29 Dec. 1763; Cornwall Land Records, 1: 9 April 1764.

29. Poultney Land Records, 1: 29 May 1770; Castleton Land Records, 2:341. See also Connecticut *Gazette,* 7 Feb. 1767; New Hampshire *Gazette,* 11 March 1768.

30. Castleton Land Records 1:122, 2:78; Ira Allen, "Autobiography," in Wilbur, *Ira Allen* 1:8–9, 12.

31. Levi Allen, Autobiography.

32. Ira Allen, "Autobiography," in Wilbur, *Ira Allen* 1:8; Brown to Allen,

30 May 1771, EAP.

33. Levi Allen, Autobiography.

34. Eliot, *Essays*, 23–24; Morrow, *Connecticut Influences;* Ditz, *Property and Kinship;* Henretta, "Families and Farms"; Kross, *Evolution of an American Town.*

35. Starr, *Cornwall,* 43; Belknap, *History of New-Hampshire* 3:196–97. In Newtown, N.Y., which was settled by New Englanders, only 12–16% of all households had more than one adult male((Kross, *Evolution of an American Town,* 103). Timothy Dwight, drawing upon the 1790 census, noted that in Hampshire County there were 9,181 houses and 9,617 families (Dwight, *Travels* 2:185). See Jim Potter, "Demographic Development and Family Structure," in Greene and Pole, *Colonial British America,* 123–156.

36. Henretta, "Families and Farms"; Nobles, *Divisions,* 110–20; Jedrey, *World of Cleaveland,* 74–94. Connecticut's population increased from 87,000 in 1740 to 138,700 in 1760, to 178,000 in 1770, an increase of 28% a decade. New Hampshire's population grew by 60% in the 1760s, Rhode Island's by 30%, while Massachusetts stagnated with a 6% growth rate. In 1774 Benjamin Trumbull estimated that 30,000 people had left Connecticut in the previous decade (Simmons, *American Colonies,* 175; *Connecticut Courant,* 26 April 1774). Greene and Harrington give different figures in *American Population,* 49–50.

37. Calloway, "Conquest of Vermont"; Huden, "Indian Groups in Vermont," 112–15; Jennings, *Invasion of America,* 29; Cook, "Significance of Diseases," 501–3, and "Interracial Warfare and Population Decline."

38. Contemporaries noted the family nature of these migrations. See, for instance, Graham, *Descriptive Sketch,* 16–17, 39, 51, 62, 75; Spaulding, "Retrospect of a Pioneer." See also Riley, "Kinship Patterns," ch. 1–2.

39. Of the remaining twenty-four men, it is possible to locate a family relationship to another member of the company for fifteen of them. The single Rhode Islander in the militia was the one exception. But he had family to the north in Shaftsbury. The names are drawn from the first covenant of Bennington's church, 1767, the militia list, and a petition by Bennington's settlers, 13 Nov. 1767, both in the Bennington Museum. Thirty-one fell between the ages of sixteen and thirty, thirty between thirty-five and seventy-two, and two men were exactly thirty-three. It has been possible to determine the ages of sixty-three of these first adult male settlers at the time of settlement. No claims are made that these figures are in any way indicative of the entire population of Bennington.

40. Names from the first covenant of Bennington's church, the militia list, and petition of Bennnington's settlers, 13 Nov. 1767, all in the Bennington Museum; origins from scattered sources such as local histories, genealogies, and the like. The town in which the settler was living just before migration is taken

as the point of origin. The population estimate of eighty-one adult males in 1765 is Samuel Robinson's.

41. In addition, Freeman's son-in-law persuaded his two brother and his sister and brother-in-law to join the group (Paige, *Hardwick*, 55–57).

42. Hemenway, *Historical Gazetteer* 1:122–23, 136, 232, 239; Shaftsbury Town Records. Based on genealogies in Williams, *History of Danby;* Bigelow and Otis, *Manchester;* Hemenway, *Vermont Gazetteer.*

43. Allen, *History of Vermont*, 183–89; "Schedule of Durham" (Clarendon), 5 Dec. 1770, New York Land Records; Goodhue, *Shoreham*, 7–11. Even when settlers did not come as part of a group, they came in families. John Potter of Rhode Island, one of the first settlers of Pownal, walked across Massachusetts while his pregnant wife rode on their horse (Hemenway, *Historical Gazetteer* 1:214).

44. Genieve Lamson, "Geographic Influences in the Early History of Vermont," in *Essays in Social and Economic History*, 80; Goddard and Partridge, *History of Norwich*, 39; Green, *Centennial Proceedings*, 16; Morrow, *Connecticut Influences*, 15.

45. Roth, "First Radical Abolitionists"; Cowan, *Scottish Covenanters;* Price, "Origin and Distinctive Characteristics."

46. All quotes and the following material from Alexander Harvey's Journal, VHS. James Whitelaw and David Allen followed much the same route two years earlier as representatives of a Scottish cooperative. Curiously, they even took the same boat over to America, looked at much the same land, and reached exactly the same conclusions, buying the southern half of Ryegate in November 1773. Whitelaw, like Harvey, kept a precise journal of his travels, expenses, and opinions. See "Journal of Managers of Scots American Co."; "Journal of Whitelaw"; James Whitelaw Papers, VHS; Fingerhut, "From Scots to Americans"; Bailyn, *Voyagers to the West*, 604–40.

47. Harvey worked on the assumption that nothing, including food, would be available for one year and planned accordingly. He was correct in his estimations. Harvey also sold shares in the United Company to seven Scots he met in New York City.

48. Altogether it had cost the Scot farmers £130 for Harvey to find and prepare their new township.

49. Jack P. Greene, "Independence, Improvement, and Authority: Towards a Framework for Understanding the Histories of the Southern Backcountry during the Era of the American Revolution," in Hoffman, *Uncivil War*, 12–15; Williams, *History of Vermont*, ch. 9, 15; Slaughter, *Whiskey Rebellion*, ch. 2.

50. The exception was Rockingham. But even here, though the settlers did not originate from the same town, they did come from a cluster of neighboring

towns in Worcester County and brought strong family connections with them (based on genealogies in Hayes, *Rockingham*). Families, friends, and congregations were not confined to single townships in the 1760s. Young people wed into nearby communities, establishing family ties across town lines, and churches, especially Separate congregations, often created translocal identifications and connections.

51. Epigraph from Irving, *History of New York*, 224. Slaughter, *Whiskey Rebellion*, ch. 4; Taylor, *Liberty Men*, ch. 3; Szatmary, *Shays' Rebellion*, ch. 1; Marvin L. M. Kay, "The North Carolina Regulation, 1766–1776: A Class Conflict," in Young, *American Revolution*, 71–123; Klein, "Ordering the Backcountry"; Whittenburg, "Planter, Merchants, and Lawyers"; Richard R. Beeman, "The Political Response to Social Conflict in the Southern Backcountry: A Comparative View of Virginia and the Carolinas during the Revolution," in Hoffman, *An Uncivil War*, 213–39; Beeman, *Evolution of Southern Backcountry*, ch. 2.

52. Allan R. Raymond, "Benning Wentworth's Claims in the New Hampshire / New York Border Controversy: A Case of Twenty-Twenty Hindsight?" in Muller and Hand, *In a State of Nature*, 43–53. In 1762 a New York merchant saw a group of New Hampshire surveyors working in the area around Crown Point, measuring out lots for future grants (Brodhead and O'Callaghan, *Documents* 4:557–58). On corrupt land grants in the South, see Gallay, *Formation of a Planter Elite*, ch. 4; Ekrich, *"Poor Carolina"*, ch. 3.

53. Wentworth's grants: 1749: 1, 1750: 1, 1751: 2, 1753: 7, 1754: 3 (16 to this date), 1760: 1, 1761: 63, 1762: 9, 1763: 38, 1764: 2; for a total of 129 grants (Batchellor, *New Hampshire Grants;* Swift, *Vermont Place-Names;* Jones, *Vermont in the Making*, 430–32; Wardner, *Birthplace of Vermont*, 25).

54. Wentworth to Clinton, 17 Nov. 1749, and Willard's deposition, 2 March 1771, O'Callaghan, *Documentary History* 4:531–32, 699–703. Wentworth's commission granted the governor unchecked power: "We do hereby . . . give & grant unto you full Power and authority by & with the advice of out said Council" to issue land titles "under such moderate Quitrents, services & acknowledgments . . . as you . . . shall think fit" (*New Hampshire Provincial Papers* 6:913).

55. Batchellor, *New Hampshire Grants;* Bouten, *Provincial and State Papers* 10:204–7. On the domination of New Hampshire by the Wentworth family and its connections, see Martin, "A Model for the Coming American Revolution."

56. Batchellor, *New Hampshire Grants*, 361–62; Jones, *Vermont in the Making*, 44. Colden also used dummy names when issuing grants, especially when a patent was being given to a government official such as Attorney General Kempe (Mark, *Agrarian Conflict*, 31, 40–46; Smith, *Historical Memoirs*, 103–9).

57. Compiled from Batchellor, *New Hampshire Grants;* Wardner, *Birthplace of Vermont,* 37–38; Hall, *History of Vermont,* 176.

58. Brown, *Colonel John Goffe,* ch. 8–9.

59. Swift, *Place-Names; Laws of New Hampshire* 2:6–7, 340–45, 600–636, 3:274; Batchellor, *New Hampshire Grants,* 566–69.

60. Moore to Shelburne, 9 June 1767, O'Callaghan, *Documentary History* 4:590–605; Crockett, *Vermont* 1:189; Clarke, "Vermont Lands"; Bidwell and Falconer, *History of Agriculture,* 73.

61. Jones, *Vermont in the Making,* 44; Wardner, *Birthplace of Vermont,* ch. 2–4; Wells, *Newbury,* 24.

62. Windsor Land Deeds, 3:18, 33, 39, 47–48; Windsor Proprietors' Records, 15 Dec. 1761; Bennington Proprietors Records and Land Records; Woodard, *Town Proprietors;* Proprietors Records of Shaftsbury.

63. Chester and Arlington Proprietors Records. Cornwall in the Grants followed Chester's lead in 1765 (*Connecticut Courant,* 11 March 1765). See also Alexander Harvey's Journal, VHS; Bennington Land Deeds, 1:1765–66. Once all of the proprietors' shares were finally within a town, the price jumped dramatically. By 1775 the average price of good Bennington land was 10s./acre, two and a half times what it was five years before and twelve and a half times its 1761 price.

64. For instance, by 1765 only three of the original proprietors of Pownall still held their land rights, all of them resident. In Arlington, only one original proprietor, also resident, held title; while Bennington, Manchester, Sunderland, and Shaftsbury had none of their original proprietors by that year (O'Callaghan, *Documentary History* 4:361–62; New York Land Records, 19:28; Batchellor, *New Hampshire Grants,* 14, 31–32, 267–68, 405, 483–84).

65. *New Hampshire Gazette,* 13 Nov. 1761; Williams, *History of Vermont,* 58–65; Windsor Proprietors Records; Windsor Land Deeds, 1; Crockett, *Journals and Proceedings* 1:5–11, 104, 133–35, 350, 354, 501, 521, 528, 543.

66. Dorothy C. Fisher, "The Settlers," *Vermont Quarterly* 21 (1953): 184; William S. Rossiter, "Vermont: An Historical and Statistical Study of the Progress of the State," *American Statistical Association,* n.s., no. 93 (1911): 408; Fox, *Yankees and Yorkers,* 173.

67. Lamson, "Geographic Influences in the Early History of Vermont," in *Essays in Social and Economic History,* 81; Hubbard and Dartt, *Springfield,* 29.

68. Christine L. Heyrman, "Specters of Subversion, Societies of Friends: Dissent and the Devil in Provincial Essex County, Massachusetts," in Hall, *Saints and Revolutionaries,* 38–74; Worrall, *Quakers,* ch. 6–7.

69. Bickford, *Farmington,* 135; Grant, *Democracy,* 14–15; Akagi, *Town Proprietors,* 113–14; Gross, *Minutemen,* 78.

70. Anderson and Woodard, "Agricultural Vermont"; Black, *Rural Economy,* ch. 11; Allen, *In English Ways,* 230–31.

71. Brown, *Middle-Class Democracy,* ch. 2; Lovejoy, *Rhode Island Politics,* 15–17; Labaree, *Patriots and Partisans,* 13; Dinkin, *Voting in Provincial America,* ch. 2; White, *History of Litchfield,* 28–30, 40–41; Starr, *History of Cornwall,* 33–45. Massachusetts and Connecticut required a forty-shilling freehold to vote in provincial elections.

72. Daniels, *The Connecticut Town,* 157; DeForest, *Westborough,* 219; Cothren, *Ancient Woodbury* 1: ch. 8.

73. Lamson, "Geographic Influences in the Early History of Vermont," in *Essays in Social and Economic History,* 80.

74. For the traditional tall tales on Bennington's founding, see Jennings, *Memorials of a Century,* 20; Paige, *Hardwick,* 51–52.

75. Yinger, *Religion, Society, and the Individual;* Goen, *Revivalism;* Gaustad, *The Great Awakening.* For the opposite view, see Niebuhr's study of the "churches of the disinherited" in *Social Sources of Denominationalism;* Heimert, *Religion and the American Mind.*

76. *Vermont Gazette,* 12 July 1825; Jones, *Vermont in the Making,* 22–23; John Spargo, "Bennington Battle Monument and Historical Association Report," 13 Jan. 1926, 3–4; Paige, *Hardwick,* 51–55, 184–85, 226–28; Rand, *Village of Amherst,* 12–13; Jameson, *Records of Amherst,* 6–10; Shipton, *Biographical Sketches* 8:610–15.

77. Jennings, *Memorials of a Century,* 48–49; Bennington Proprietors Records; Caulkins, *History of Norwich,* 193–200; Smith, *Sunderland,* 57–76.

78. Caulkins, *Norwich,* 193–95; Gaustad, *Great Awakening,* ch. 7; Beardsley, *History of the Episcopal Church* 1:141.

79. Newint Church Records, 9–10; Goen, *Revivalism,* 83–85; Larned, *History of Windham County* 1:479–83; Backus, *History of New England* 2:98–99; Denison, *Notes on the Baptists,* 20–36; Caulkins, *History of Norwich,* 193–200.

80. Wardner, *Birthplace of Vermont,* ch. 2–3; Potash, "Welfare of the Regions Beyond"; Roth, *Democratic Dilemma,* ch. 1; Crocker, *History of the Baptists,* 177; Dickerman, *Old Mount Carmel Parish,* 143. The same pattern is evident in several western New Hampshire towns (Goen, *Revivalism,* 252–54). There are examples of entire congregations moving to the western frontier as well. For instance, the Baptist church of Spotsylvania, Virginia, moved to Gilbert's Creek, Kentucky, in 1781 (Sweet, *Story of Religion,* 215).

81. Newint Church Records, 9–22. For similar controversies in Massachusetts, see Goen, *Revivalism,* 201.

82. On cultural diversity not serving as a source of conflict, see Mitchell, *Commercialism and Frontier;* Thorp, *Moravian Communities.*

CHAPTER THREE

1. O'Callaghan, *Documentary History* 4:799–800; Ira Allen, "Autobiography," in Wilbur, *Ira Allen* 1:16–18; Norton, *Fur Trade,* ch. 3; Calloway, *Western Abenakis,* 25–27, 201–3.

2. Epigraph from Irving, *History of New York,* 224. After ten years, every original settler of Ryegate had cleared between fifteen and twenty-five acres, with one large family having succeeded in stripping fifty acres of land for its use. Over in Concord, the most active families had cleared twelve acres in their first five years (Miller Wells, *Ryegate,* 96, 193; Bouton, *Concord,* 128–31; Stilgoe, *Common Landscape,* 170–77).

3. Williams, *History of Vermont,* 121; Belknap, *History of New Hampshire* 3:58–59, 113–19; Eliot, *Essays;* Genieve Lamson, "Geographic Influences in the Early History of Vermont," in *Essays in Social and Economic History,* 21; Dwight, *Travels* 2:226–29; Waselkov and Paul, "Frontiers and Archaeology."

4. Account Book of Jonas Fay, Bennington Museum; Account Book of Timothy Brownson, Arlington Library; Probate Records, Bennington; Hemenway, *Vermont Gazetteer* 1:250; *American Husbandry* 1:47–53; Dwight, *Travels* 1.40; Eliot, *Essays,* 1; Bidwell and Falconer, *History of Agriculture,* 77; Williams, *History of Vermont,* 361–63; La Rochefoucauld-Liancourt, *Travels* 1:385; Graham, *Descriptive Sketch,* 40; Belknap, *History of New-Hampshire* 3:113.

5. Dwight *Travels* 2:238, 325–29; Bidwell and Falconer, *History of Agriculture,* 77; Strickland, *Journal of a Tour,* 95–96; Tocqueville, *Democracy in America,* 551–54.

6. Stilgoe sees frontier methods of clearing the land as "an intelligent and innovative response to a hazardous problem of providing food for family and livestock" (Stilgoe, *Common Landscape,* 174). The eighteenth-century historian Jeremy Belknap would have agreed (Belknap, *History of New-Hampshire* 3:97–98).

7. "Diaries of Rev. Timothy Walker, 1746–1780," NHHS *Collections* 9:139, 169; Chastellux, *Travels,* 34; Bidwell and Falconer, *History of Agriculture,* 9–12, 109; Taylor, *Liberty Men,* ch. 3. Zadock Thompson provided a list of ailments in his *History of Vermont,* pt. 2:220. See also Gallup, *Epidemic Diseases,* 36–50. On the diversity of crops in New England as a response to the fear of agricultural failure, see Stilgoe, *Common Landscape,* 204–7; Jones, "Creative Disruptions"; Loehr, "Self-Sufficiency"; Swift, *History of Middlebury,* 197; Dwight, *Travels* 2:238. The opposite seems to have been the case on the southern frontier, with settlers focusing on crops for market (Ekirch, *"Poor Carolina,"* 178–82; Beeman, *Evolution,* ch. 1–3; Mitchell, *Commercialism and Frontier,* ch. 5–7; Klein, *Unification of a Slave State,* ch. 1–2).

8. Bidwell and Falconer, *History of Agriculture,* 25–26, 35–37, 107, 125, and generally ch. 6 and 8; Deane, *New England Farmer,* 142, 258–60; Harriot, *Struggles through Life* 2:216; La Rochefoucauld-Liancourt, *Travels* 1:516; *American Husbandry* 1:173; NYHS *Collections,* 2d ser., 1:165; Belknap, *History of New-Hampshire* 3:100–102.

9. Wells, *History of Newbury,* 33–34; Dwight, *Travels* 2:326; Arlington Proprietors Records; Lamson, "Geographic Influences in the Early History of Vermont," in *Essays in Social and Economic History,* 118; Hemenway, *Historical Gazetteer* 1:122–23. The practice of voting special incentives to whoever would build these first mills was a long-standing tradition in New England. In his dissertation Charles Grant noted that Kent also subsidized the erection of its first mill; in his book, though, he transformed this action into "nonagricultural" entrepreneurship (Grant, "History of Kent," 43, 57–58; *Kent,* 42, 53).

10. Dwight, *Travels* 2:321–24, 329–30, 404–5; Belknap, *History of New Hampshire* 3:258. See also North, *History of Augusta,* 189; Miller and Wells, *Ryegate,* 94; Stilgoe, *Common Landscape,* 185–88, 204–7; Perkins, *Narrative of a Tour.*

11. Cleaveland inventory, Windham County Probate.

12. While 19% were propertyless, wills indicate that at least one-third of these had already transferred their holdings to heirs. See Appendix B.

13. This figure is equivalent to those in Hampshire County and Worcester County as reported by Jackson T. Main for 1762–70, 1782–88 (Main, *Social Structure,* 22–23). See Appendixes A and B.

14. See Appendixes A and B. Most frontiers experienced similar levels of economic equality, even in the South (Beeman, *Evolution of the Southern Backcountry,* 30–41).

15. Bennington Proprietors Records, 1:1; Brattleboro Town Records, 1; Guilford Town Records, in Gale and Thompson, *History of Guilford;* Hemenway, *Historical Gazetteer* 1:576–600.

16. Proprietors Records of Bennington for 1769–70, 1778–79.

17. It was only in the period of pronounced economic dislocation following the Revolution that warnings out became common. For instance, Bingham and the Horsfords were the only people warned out of Bennington until 1781, when seven people were ordered out; Danby ordered only two families out of town before 1783; Brattleboro ordered no one out before that date; and except for an effort by the pro–New York majority at the mass expulsion of all those holding New Hampshire Grants, Guilford also warned no one out before that date (Bennington Proprietors Records, 99, 102, 115–16; Hemenway, *Historical Gazetteer* 1:576–600; Guilford Town Records in Gale and Thompson, *History of Guilford;* Brattleboro Town Records; Proprietors Records of Windsor; Town Records of Shaftsbury).

18. Stilgoe, *Common Landscape,* 172; Main, *Social Structure,* 75–77; Belknap, *History* 3:261; Bidwell, "Rural Economy."

19. Pruitt, "Self-Sufficiency."

20. Weber, *Economy and Society* 1:86–90; Richard B. Sheridan, "The Domestic Economy," in Greene and Pole, *Colonial British America,* 43–86; Clark, *Roots of Rural Capitalism,* ch. 2–3.

21. Proprietors Records of Windsor, 3 Oct. 1768. See also entries for 27 Aug. 1770, 12 March 1771, 6 April 1774.

22. This continued use of wheat as currency coincided with its disappearance as a primary staple in eastern Massachusetts and the replacement of wheat bread with rye. Only in Litchfield County, Connecticut, the Berkshires, and Vermont did wheat continue as the most important crop (Miller and Wells, *History of Ryegate,* 97; *American Husbandry* 1:52; Dwight, *Travels* 1:376; Bidwell and Falconer, *History of Agriculture,* 90–95).

23. Epigraph from Allen, *Reason the Only Oracle,* app., 70. Rockingham and Guilford Town Records.

24. Bennington Proprietors and Town Records; Jennings, *Memorials,* 24.

25. Bennington Proprietors Records, 12 April 1762, 9 Nov., 17 Dec. 1767.

26. Manchester held its last land division in 1802, thirty-eight years after settlement (Bigelow and Otis, *Manchester,* 1–30; Arlington Proprietors and Land Records; Allen, *History of Vermont,* 79–80, 120–22).

27. Allen, *History of Vermont,* 221, 239.

28. Towns, on the other hand, sued each other often, causing no end of trouble for Vermont in its first years of independence. The following towns were involved in boundary disputes in Vermont's first decade: Addison, Andover, Bennington, Bethel, Braintree, Brownington, Cambridge, Clarendon, Dorset, Enosburgh, Ferrisburg, Hungerford, Hyde Park, Ira, Jamaica, Johnson, Leicester, Manchester, Middlebury, Panton, Randolph, Rochester, Royalton, Salisbury, Sterling, Stratton, Tinmouth, and Whitehall (The town of Leicester v. Proprietors of Salisbury, Manuscript State Papers, 42:40, VSA; Walton, *Records* 1:505–8, 2:108–9, 3:8–89, 126, 129, 131, 147, 156–57, 172, 180, 188, 196, 227; Hoyt, *Petitions,* 19, 23, 48–49, 52–53, 89–90, 108–10, 114–16, 124, 135, 163–66, 214–16, 253–25, 283, 305–6, 310–13, 367–68, 371, 374–76; Williamson, *Vermont in Quandary,* 172; John Johnson to the Green Mountain Repository, VHS; McCarty, "Boundary Controversy").

29. For instance, Proprietors Records of Windsor, 9 Nov. 1767, 3 Oct. 1768, 6 April 1769, 14 Nov. 1771.

30. Dwight, *Travels* 2:327.

31. Town Proprietors Records of Chester, Arlington, Windsor, Bennington, Manchester; Hemenway, *Historical Gazetteer* 1:576–600; Town Records of Brattleboro, Guilford; Kross, *Evolution of an American Town,* 161.

32. Dwight, *Travels* 2:329–31; Lamson, "Geographic Influences in the Early History of Vermont," 75–138.

33. Proprietors Records of Bennington; Shaftsbury Town Records. See also Town Records for Danby, Hemenway, *Historical Gazetteer* 1:598–601; Brattleboro Town Records.

34. Hemenway, *Historical Gazetteer* 1:589–601; Town Records of Brattleboro, Guilford, Windsor; Proprietors Records of Bennington. Participation in town meetings in the Grants remained open to all who took the freeman's oath, which usually meant 90% of the adult males. In contrast, E. Marie Becker found that only a fifth of all adult males in Westchester County, New York, enjoyed full political rights in the 1760s ("The 801 Westchester County Freeholders," 300). See Appendix F.

35. Town Records of Guilford, Bennington, Shaftsbury, Windsor. In 1770 each Bennington town meeting averaged eight items on the agenda; by 1776 the average was ten; by 1783, eighteen, with as many as thirty-one issues to be addressed at a single gathering.

36. From time to time the antiswine faction would crack down and auction off animals, expel their owners from the rights of freemen, and order heavy fines. Usually the majority would forgive the swineherds, and peace would be restored until the following year (Town Records of Brattleboro, Guilford; Proprietors Records of Bennington).

37. Goddard and Partridge, *History of Norwich*, 66. The final cost of the church was £694, though none of this was actually raised as money (ibid., ch. 2). See also Hemenway, *Historical Gazetteer* 1:576–600; Brattleboro Town Records; Hayes, *Old Meeting House;* Peck, *Records of the First Church;* Hall, *Eastern Vermont*, 148, 221, 445, 752.

38. See, for instance, Bennington First Church Records, 1: 30 March 1769, 17 April 1770, 6 Aug., 8, 15, 22, 29 Sept. 1772, 14, 24 Feb., 18 May 1774; Hemenway, *Historical Gazetteer* 1:598–601; Town Meeting Records of Shaftsbury; Proprietors Records of Windsor; Peck, *Vital Records of Rockingham;* Hayes, *The Old Meeting House, Erected 1787*, 15–25 (the title, by the way, is inaccurate in that the meetinghouse was finally built in 1801).

39. On opposition to educated ministers, see William S. Babcock Papers, Account Book of John Haight, and Thomas Fessenden, Manuscript Sermons, 1773–1804, AAS; Walker, "Diaries"; Smith, *Life of Elias Smith,* 30–45; Peak, *Memoirs,* 54–65; Dow, *Dealings of God,* 33–68, 146–54. On questions of ministerial authority, see Scott, *Office to Profession,* ch. 1, 4.

40. Bayle, "Reminiscences," 29; Heyrman, *Commerce and Culture,* ch. 2–3; Jedrey, *World of John Cleaveland,* ch. 2.

41. Crocker, *History of Baptists,* 26–27.

42. Shaftsbury's church records, lost by the Shaftsbury Historical Society,

quoted in Crocker, *History of Baptists,* 16–18, 21–23. For a similar dispute over infant baptism, see Bennington Church Records, 11 April, 30 Sept. 1763.

43. Goen, *Revivalism,* ch. 5.

44. Bennington Church Records, 4 Sept. 1766, 17 April 1770.

45. Larned, *History of Windham County* 1:470; Shaftsbury church records in Crocker, *Baptists.* See also Wright, *History of Baptist Association;* Halifax Church Records; Records of the Second Congregational Church of West Windsor; Records of the Old South Congregational Church of Windsor.

46. Hill, *World Turned Upside Down,* 252.

47. Bennington Church Records, 19 June, 4 Sept. 1766, 24 March, 17 Nov. 1768, 17, 24, 31 Aug., 7, 14 Sept. 1769.

48. Jennings, *Memorials,* 32, 342; Bennington Church Records and Town Records; Goen, *Revivalism,* 184–85.

49. Bennington Church Records, 1770. This solution was essentially that of Solomon Stoddard in the 1720s (Tracy, *Jonathan Edwards,* ch. 1–2).

50. Bennington Church Records, 18 June 1768 to 27 June 1771.

51. Bennington Church Records, 23, 30 Jan. 1772; Jennings, *Memorials,* 32, 342; Goen, *Revivalism,* 184–85. It is possible that the aggrieved brethrens' theological line served as rhetorical cover for an economic issue. Yet the aggrieved did not question the church's legitimacy until the meeting of February 1768, when two nonmembers were elected to church offices. It is unlikely that a specific and coherent group of people would have submitted themselves willingly to such consistent harassment solely to avoid paying thirteen shillings a year in support, especially as Dewey willingly accepted goods in payment. Simpler to have followed the example of Ethan Allen and not attend any church. Instead, the aggrieved brethren consistently resisted what they saw as a fundamental alteration of their covenant.

52. Nobles, *Divisions throughout the Whole,* ch. 2–3; Lucas, *Valley of Discord,* ch. 3–4, 9.

53. Ira Allen, "Autobiography," in Wilbur, *Ira Allen* 1:5–7; *Connecticut Courant,* 27 April, 1 June 1773.

54. Journals of Major Walter Rutherford and James Duane, June and July 1765, James Duane Papers, NYHS; Swift, *Vermont Place-Names,* 591, 778.

55. Epigraph from *Connecticut Courant,* 24 March 1772. Grant, *Memoirs,* 96, 246–47.

56. Grant, *Memoirs,* 249–52, 255.

57. Johnson to Tomlinson, 12 Sept. 1767, Report of Board of Trade, 24 July 1767, VHS.

58. New York Land Papers; Fox, *Yankees and Yorkers,* 18–19; Tryon grant of 4 April 1772, VHS *Collections* 1:156; NYHS *Collections* 7:280–81; Smith, *Historical Memoirs,* 103–4, 107–9, 189–90; Williamson, *Vermont in Quandary,*

11–14; Hillsborough to Tryon, 4 Dec. 1771, VHS. These grants violated not only the Board of Trade's order of 1767 but also Tryon's royal instructions, which specifically limited grants for a single individual to 1,500 acres. Nearly every wealthy family in New York was involved in the purchase of lands in the northeastern part of the state.

59. Affidavit of Stevens, 2 March 1771, O'Callaghan, *Documentary History* 4:691–96; Windsor Proprietors Records, 3 Oct. 1768; Williams, *History of Vermont*, 66–69, 71–72; *Laws of New Hampshire* 2:510–11.

60. Schuyler to Colden, 17 Aug. 1764, Council of 4 Sept. 1764, O'Callaghan, *Documentary History* 4:575–77; Parks, *Pownall*, 35–38.

61. Many historians have seen geography as the decisive factor in Vermont history. It is possible to see the Green Mountains dividing Vermont into two discrete geographic regions, with the west oriented toward New York and Quebec and the east toward New Hampshire and Boston (Williamson, *Vermont in Quandary*, ch. 9–10, 14, 16–17; Mackintosh, "Canada and Vermont"). On the other hand, the Green Mountains gave the Vermonters their identity, and their only exportable crop—timber and its ashes, and acted as their stronghold against outside aggression (see Lamson, "Geographic Influences in the Early History of Vermont," in *Essays in Social and Economic History*, 75a–138). Trade was too localized to speak of an "orientation" toward any place outside of the Green Mountains. Very few individuals had any dealings with Boston, Montreal, or Albany, and the distance and poor roads that lay between the Grants and any of these cities were more of a barrier than the Green Mountains.

62. "Philanthropos," *A Few Observations . . .*, quoted in Bonomi, *A Factious People*, 227; Colden quote in *Journal of the Votes and Proceedings* 2:669. Governor Robert Hunter agreed with Colden on many particulars (Brodhead and O'Callaghan, *Documents Relative to the Colonial History of New-York* 3:394). See also NYHS *Collections*, vols. 4 and 5; Smith, *History of New York* 2:247–48; *Colden Letter Books* 9:149–50, 157, 191, 231; *Letters and Papers of Colden* 5:283–95, 310–19; Bonomi, *A Factious People*, ch. 7; Mark, *Agrarian Conflicts*, 134; Klein, "New York Lawyers," and "Prelude to Revolution"; Greenberg, *Crime and Law Enforcement*, ch. 6; Julius Goebel, Jr., "The Courts and the Law in Colonial New York," in Flaherty, *Essays in Early American Law*, 245–77.

63. Petition for a new county, 22 Oct. 1765, O'Callaghan, *Documentary History* 4:578–83. See also Frank L. Fish, "Vermont Bench and Bar," in Crockett, *Green Mountain State* 5:1–28.

64. Allen, *History of Vermont*, 25–30; Allen, *Vindication*, 445–47; Ethan Allen in the *Connecticut Courant*, 14 July 1772; O'Callaghan, *Documentary History* 4:577–78, 583–84, 586–88, 609–11; Lords of Trade to the King, Brodhead and O'Callaghan, *Documents* 7:918–19. Historians have seen the paucity of radi-

cal political action on the east side as a sign of its greater wealth, its more solid and conservative nature, or the greater number of New England speculators interested in the west side. The first is barely noticeable, the second tautological, and the third clearly incorrect. Of greater significance is the fact that the Green Mountains separated the east side from New York authority. The settlers along the Connecticut River had few contacts with New York except through that province's inefficient courts. They did not experience the direct provocation of New York surveyors on their land, they did not have the immediate example of tenant farmers next door on the Van Renssaeller estate, and New York speculators were concentrating their legal fire on westside landowners.

65. Allen, *History of Vermont,* 21–24; Gloucester County Court Records; Fish, "Vermont Bench and Bar," in Crockett, *Green Mountain State* 5:327–28; Hall, *Eastern Vermont,* 204. In general, see Bellesiles, "Establishment of Legal Structures."

66. In the last two sessions of 1774 the court heard 152 cases, of which 95, or just short of two-thirds, were continued (Cumberland County Court Records).

67. Ibid., 8. See also the cases involving John Taplin, Jr., son of the chief judge of court in the Gloucester County Court Records. For an indication of the New York council's awareness of this corruption, see Smith, *Historical Memoirs,* 22, 188–89.

68. The legitimacy of New York's judges was often denied in the courtroom itself, for instance, in the cases of Elisha Hawley, Ebenezer Hoisington, Sr. and Jr., Andrew Norton, and Elnathan Strong in Cumberland County and the cases of John White and Azariah White in Gloucester County (Cumberland and Gloucester County Court Records; Allen, *History of Vermont,* 31–35; Slade, *Vermont State Papers,* 22–33, 38–39, 49–54; O'Callaghan, *Documentary History* 4:778, 792–93, 824–27, 871–73; VHS *Collections* 1:6; *Connecticut Courant,* 14 July, 22 Sept. 1772, 8, 21 June 1774; Dummerston Town Records 1:19–20; Chester Town Meeting Records, 10 Oct. 1774; Walton, *Records* 1:317–19, 334, 337–38).

69. O'Callaghan, *Documentary History* 4:526, 636–40, 645–47, 748–55, 786–96; Smith, *Historical Memoirs,* 22; Wardner, *Birthplace of Vermont,* 142–58; Hall, *Eastern Vermont,* 146–58.

70. Cumberland County Court Records; O'Callaghan, *Documentary History* 4:759, 777; Fish, "Vermont Bench and Bar," in Crockett, *Green Mountain State* 5:8–9.

71. O'Callaghan, *Documentary History* 4:759; Fish, "Vermont Bench and Bar," in Crockett, *Green Mountain State* 5:8–9; Dwight, *Travels.*

72. Wardner, *Birthplace of Vermont,* ch. 19–20; O'Callaghan, *Documentary History* 4:636–40; Hall, *History of Eastern Vermont,* 146–58.

73. Affidavits of Grout, Wells, William and Willard Dean, Whipple, Fisher, and Duane and complaint of Governor Wentworth, O'Callaghan, *Documentary History* 4:637–60.

74. Affidavit of Wells, 9 Aug. 1770, O'Callaghan, *Documentary History* 4:640–72; Wardner, *Birthplace of Vermont,* 154–65.

75. Brodhead and O'Callaghan, *Documents* 8:252; O'Callaghan, *Documentary History* 4:661–63.

76. Lord to Tryon, 29 Jan. 1772, O'Callaghan, *Documentary History* 4:757–61, 765–66, 770–71; Cumberland County Court Records; Shipton, *Biographical Sketches* 8:69–73.

77. Bonomi, *A Factious People,* ch. 6; Mark, *Agrarian Conflict,* ch. 5; Edward Countryman, "'Out of the Bounds of the Law': Northern Land Rioters in the Eighteenth Century," and Marvin L. Michael Kay, "The North Carolina Regulation, 1766–1776: A Class Conflict," in Young, *American Revolution,* 37–69, 71–123; Taylor, *Liberty Men,* ch. 1.

78. Nathan Stone to William Smith et al., 29 Dec. 1770, James Duane Papers; O'Callaghan, *Documentary History* 4:672–75; Jones, *Vermont in the Making,* 262; Wardner, *Birthplace of Vermont,* 361–62, 412–13; Patricia U. Bonomi, "Local Government in Colonial New York: A Base for Republicanism," in Judd and Polishook, *Aspects of Early New York,* 29–50; Guilford Town Records, especially 1772. On local frontier leaders accepting external elite dominance, see Taylor, *Liberty Men,* ch. 6, 8–9.

79. Grant, *Memoirs,* 249, 256, 275; Spencer to Duane, 11 April 1772, James Duane Papers.

80. Levi Allen, Autobiography, n.p., LAP; Ethan Allen to the Caughnawagas, 24 May 1775, Force, *American Archives,* 4th ser., 2:713; Huden, *Indian Place Names,* 26–32. The savagery of European-American traders in comparison to the conduct of the Native Americans disturbed many contemporary observers. See, for instance, Benjamin Franklin, "The Futility of Educating the Indians" (1753) in *The Annals of America* 1:497–98; "Red Jacket and the Missionary" (1809) in Washburn, *Indian and White Man,* 209–14; Heckewelder (1819), *History,* ch. 6 and 23. On Indian traders dealing with native society on its own terms, see Merrell, *Indian's New World,* ch. 1–2; Calloway, *Western Abenakis,* 27–29.

CHAPTER FOUR

1. Quoted in Reid, "In a Defensive Rage," 1052.

2. *Connecticut Courant,* 31 March 1772.

3. Epigraph from "The Vision of Junus, the Benningtonite," *Connecticut Courant,* 22 Sept. 1772, suspected to have been written by Ethan Allen.

O'Callaghan, *Documentary History* 4:615–21; Duane, *Narrative,* 7, 14–15; Hall, *Eastern Vermont,* 117; New York Council Minutes, 26:167; Jones, *Vermont in the Making,* 282–84; *Connecticut Courant,* 19 Feb., 19 March, 4 June 1770.

4. Allen, *History of Vermont,* 24. It was at this same time that Allen bought his first rights in the Green Mountains (Warner to Allen, Poultney Land Records, 1: 29 May 1770; Person to Allen, 6 June 1770, Castleton Land Records, 2:341). Allen listed himself as a yeoman on this deed, Person was a bricklayer.

5. Ira Allen, *History of Vermont,* 23–24; O'Callaghan, *Documentary History* 4:609.

6. Allen, *Vindication,* 445. New York's patent holders insisted that the Grants claimants lacked the courage to appeal to the king. Responding to Allen's complaints, James Duane wrote that "if the New Hampshire Claimants imagined, that they were aggrieved by the Decisions of our Judges, the Means of redress were in their own Power; and, they ought to have sued their Writs of Error; and, in the legal and ordinary Mode, to have referred their Cause to the final Sentence of his Majesty." Allen pointed out that Duane had left out a key fact: writs of error were heard only on individual demands in excess of £500. "The New-York attornies . . . well knew that every action brought against New-Hampshire claimants has been designedly laid below that sum." New York's patriots used the same tactic when suing crown officials, seeking just under £500 so that the case could not be appealed beyond local juries and judges (Duane, *Narrative,* 26; Allen, *Vindication,* 510; Reid, *In a Defiant Stance,* 33).

7. Allen, *History of Vermont,* 24; Duane, *Narrative,* 8–9.

8. Allen, *History of Vermont,* 25; Slade, *Vermont State Papers,* 21.

9. The first five companies and their captains were: Bennington region, Seth Warner; Sunderland, Gideon Warren; Rupert, Robert Cochran; Socialboro, Peleg Sunderland; and Stillwater (the area of the present New York/Vermont state line), Ebenezer Marvin. At least three other companies were organized by the beginning of 1775: Danby, Micah Vail; Poultney, Ebenezer Allen; and Arlington, Remember Baker (Hemenway, *Historical Gazetteer* 1:143; Allen, *History of Vermont,* 26; Hall, *History of Vermont,* 128–37; Walton, *Records* 1:474).

10. Biographical material on rank-and-file Green Mountain Boys is sketchy. See Appendix E.

11. *Connecticut Courant,* 25 May 1772; Ira Allen, "Autobiography," in Wilbur, *Ira Allen* 1:27–43; Rutland Land Records, 1:9, 44; Tinmouth Land Records, 72; Thomas Shepard to E. Allen, 3 Dec. 1772, Ethan and Heman Allen to Thomas Chittenden, J. Spafford, and A. Pratt, 17 May 1773, E. Allen to Isaac Rood, 20 Aug. 1773, EAP; Chittenden et al. to Onion River Co., 17 May 1773, IAP.

12. Allen, *History of Vermont,* 34; Levi Allen, Autobiography, LAP.

13. Allen, *Vindication,* 447; *Connecticut Courant,* 16 Feb. 1770, 31 March 1772, 14 July 1772.

14. *Connecticut Courant,* 31 March 1772; Allen, *Brief Narrative,* 72, 181.

15. *Connecticut Courant,* 31 March 1772; Allen, *Brief Narrative,* 55, 164–65.

16. *New Hampshire Gazette,* no. 915, 1774, rept. in Allen, *Vindication,* 479; *Connecticut Courant,* 31 March 1772; Allen, *Brief Narrative,* 55, 72, 127, 164–65.

17. As Christine Heyrman wrote of the Marblehead anti-inoculation riots of 1731, "Well-disciplined crowds pursued clearly defined objectives and were protected by widespread communal support for their extralegal activities as well as by the concern among protesters to shield comrades from prosecution" (Heyrman, *Commerce and Culture,* 313). See also Nash, *Urban Crucible,* 130–36; Wood, "A Note on Mobs"; Maier, "Popular Uprisings"; Whittenburg, "Planters, Merchants, and Lawyers"; Henderson, "Smallpox and Patriotism"; Nobles, *Divisions,* ch. 5.

18. *Connecticut Courant,* 31 March 1772; Allen, *Brief Narrative,* 166.

19. *Connecticut Courant,* 28 April, 14 July 1772. See also ibid., 31 March 1772. These views were present in several earlier land disputes. For instance, in 1730 a group of Scotch-Irish settled in a "disorderly manner" on 15,000 acres belonging to the Penn family. They justified their action to London by arguing that "it was against the laws of God and nature that so much land should be idle when so many Christians wanted it to labor on and to raise their bread" (quoted in Botein, *Early American Law,* 14). See also Gardiner, "History of the Kennebec Purchase"; Barbara Karsky, "Agrarian Radicalism in the Late Revolutionary Period," in Angermann, *New Wine in Old Skins,* 87–114; Paine, *Common Sense,* in Foner, *Complete Works of Paine* 1:4–5; Paine, *Rights of Man,* ibid., 406.

20. Loraine Allen was born in 1763, Joseph in 1765, Lucy in 1768, and Mary Ann in 1772; Mary Allen would give birth to a fifth child, Pamelia, in 1779 (Barr, *Genealogy of Ethan Allen,* 8).

21. Allen, "Remarks, &c.," *New Hampshire Gazette,* no. 915 (1774), in Allen, *Vindication,* 477–78.

22. *Connecticut Courant,* 31 March 1772; Allen, "Remarks, &c.," *New Hampshire Gazette,* no. 915 (1774), in Allen, *Vindication,* 478; Allen, *Brief Narrative,* 44, 47. See also Slade, *Vermont State Papers,* 49–54; *Connecticut Courant,* 8 June 1774, supplement; Allen, *Brief Narrative,* 36–48; O'Callaghan, *Documentary History* 4:871–73.

23. *Connecticut Courant,* 31 March 1772.

24. James Lemon, "Spatial Order: Households in Local Communities and Regions," in Greene and Pole, *Colonial British America,* 86–122; Allen, *Brief Narrative,* 160. See also *Connecticut Courant,* 21 and 28 June 1774.

25. Munro to Duane, 17 Aug. 1772, James Duane Papers, NYHS; Hough to Colden, September 1774, O'Callaghan, *Documentary History* 4:875–77; *Connecticut Courant,* 21 June 1774.

26. Allen, *Vindication* 1:452–55; Allen and Fay, *Concise Refutation,* 13, 27. Allen's views are in line with the general Whig perception that the need to maintain order could justify even revolution—though a a well-ordered revolution, of course. Maier, *From Resistance to Revolution,* especially ch. 1–2; Wood, *Creation of the American Republic,* especially pt. 1; Dirk Hoerder, "Boston Leaders and Boston Crowds, 1765–1776," in Young, *American Revolution,* 233–71; Peterson, *Adams and Jefferson,* ch. 1; Bailyn, *Ideological Origins,* 272–301.

27. Epigraph from Allen, "Remarks, &c.," New Hampshire *Gazette,* no. 915 (1774), in Allen, *Vindication,* 479; Maier, *Resistance to Revolution;* Heyrman, *Commerce and Culture,* ch. 9; Wood, "A Note on Mobs."

28. Reid, *In a Defiant Stance,* 77–78, 92–99, 162–63.

29. Cockburn to Duane, 10 Sept. 1771, Duane Papers, NYHS. See also Hall, *History of Vermont,* 130; Jones, *Vermont in the Making,* 289.

30. Jones, *Vermont in the Making,* 284.

31. Duane, *Narrative,* 7; O'Callaghan, *Documentary History* 4:685–91. On New York's land policies, see, for instance, Bidwell and Falconer, *History of Agriculture,* 72–75; Mark, *Agrarian Conflict,* ch. 1–2; Kim, *Landlord and Tenant,* ch. 2–4.

32. Yates to Duane and Kempe, 20 July 1771, Duane Papers, NYHS. See also Allen, *History of Vermont,* 29–31; Hall, *History of Vermont,* 124; O'Callaghan, *Documentary History* 4:732 47.

33. Yates to Duane and Kempe, 20 July 1771, Duane Papers, NYHS; O'Callaghan, *Documentary History* 4:735.

34. Allen, *Brief Narrative,* 8, 166; see also Allen, *Vindication,* 446.

35. Munro to Duane, 15 July 1772, see also Munro to Duane 28 March, 20 April, 9 July, 10 Aug., 12 Nov. 1772, Spencer to Duane, 11 April, 22 May 1772, Walworth to Duane, 18 Aug. 1772, Embary to Duane, 18 June 1772, Duane Papers, O'Callaghan, *Documentary History* 4:486, 529–30, 800–801, 843–52, 859–66, 880–84; Allen, *History of Vermont,* 46–47.

36. Allen, *Natural and Political History,* 26–28; certificate of Ethan Allen and Seth Warner to Benjamin Hough, 30 Jan. 1775, EAP, 1:46–47. See also the depositions of Jonathan Wheate, John Cameron, James Henderson, Angus McBean, Benjamin Spencer, Jacob Marsh, Nathan Rice, Benjamin Hough, Anna Button, Sandy Trueby, and Daniel Walker in O'Callaghan, *Documentary History* 4:764–65, 846–54, 859–69, 893–903. Allen saw a poetic justice in these whippings, as they "chastised" the Yorkers "with the whips of the wilderness, the growth of the land which they coveted" (Allen, *Vindication,* 446–47).

37. See, for instance, T. Rowlee to J. Duane, 21 Sept. 1772, J. Blanchard to Duane, 20 Nov. 1772, C. Button to N. Stone, 30 Nov. 1773, EAP.

38. New York Land Papers, 27:132, 31:73, 39:10, 14; New York Land Patents, 16:112, 17:5, Jones, *Vermont in the Making*, 145–46, 317–18; New York Council Minutes, 27:447 (22 April 1771); Duane's notes on this meeting, Duane Papers, NYHS.

39. Jones, *Vermont in the Making*, 318–19; Hall, *History of Vermont*, 175–76; Emmett Papers, no. 4501, NYHS; Affidavit of C. Button, 24 Nov. 1773, Duane Papers, NYHS; B. Spencer to Goldsborough, 14 Dec. 1773, EAP.

40. Petition of Spencer and Colvin, 17 Oct. 1777, O'Callaghan, *Documentary History* 4:956–57; Thompson, *History of Vermont*, pt. 3:55; Slade, *Vermont State Papers*, 500. The controversy was not resolved until the Vermont General Assembly intervened in 1785.

41. Affidavits of Benjamin Hough and others, O'Callaghan, *Documentary History* 4:866–71.

42. Ibid., 859–60, 865–66.

43. Ibid., 861. Pell has a different version, source unspecified, with the roof being taken off and put on again, after Spencer acknowledged that it was put on under New Hampshire authority (Pell, *Ethan Allen*, 63–65).

44. Affidavit of Hough, O'Callaghan, *Documentary History* 4:523; Pell, *Ethan Allen*, 65; letter of Ethan Allen to the town of Durham, Emmett Papers, NYHS; Spencer to Duane, 11 April, 22 May 1772, Duane Papers, NYHS.

45. Affidavit of Capt. Wooster, 20 Feb. 1773, O'Callaghan, *Documentary History* 4:824–27; Hemenway, *Historical Gazetteer* 1:77–80.

46. Hemenway, *Historical Gazetteer* 1:77. See also VHS *Collections* 1:5–6; Allen, *History of Vermont*, 26, 35, 51–53; Hall, *History of Vermont*, 127, 130; O'Callaghan, *Documentary History* 4:712, 762. On the ease with which Allen organized companies of Green Mountain Boys, see the testimony of Benjamin Gardner, 20 Feb. 1772, Rowlee to Duane, 21 Sept. 1772, Duane Papers, NYHS; Hemenway, *Historical Gazetteer* 1:582–85.

47. *Connecticut Courant* 28 April 1772; Allen, "Remarks, &c.," New Hampshire *Gazette*, no. 915 (1774), in Allen, *Vindication*, 478; Allen, *Brief Narrative*, 163.

48. Allen, *History of Vermont*, 35–37, 43–44, 46–47; Cockburn to Duane, 10 Sept. 1771, Stevens to Munro, 4 Jan. 1772, Munro to Duane, 28 March, 10 Aug. 1772, Duane Papers, NYHS.

49. Duane, *Narrative*, 15; Affidavit of Charles Hutcheson, 12 Nov. 1771, O'Callaghan, *Documentary History* 4:745–46; New York Land Papers, 18:160.

50. O'Callaghan, *Documentary History* 4:748–55.

51. McNaughton to Fanning, 12 Nov. 1771, O'Callaghan, *Documentary History* 4:747. Governor Tryon admitted to the council that "the number of the

New Hampshire rioters and their situation in the mountains was such that no sheriff or constable would apprehend them" (quoted in Master's Report, Supreme Court Records, Vermont State Archives, 259).

52. Duane, *Narrative,* 12; "Report of the Convention of the West-Side Towns," Ethan Allen on Tryon's reward, *Connecticut Courant,* 21, 28 June 1774; Hall, *History of Vermont,* 134; Jones, *Vermont in the Making,* 291; the original reward poster, dated 5 Feb. 1772, in AFP. Peter Yates sent Duane a copy of this poster which had been left in an Albany tavern, reporting that Allen's reward offer was the subject of much humor in the area (Yates to Duane, 7 April 1772, Duane Papers).

53. O'Callaghan, *Documentary History* 4:685–91, 710–12, 720, 723–24, 744–45, 762–63; Allen, *History of Vermont,* 27–28; Grant, *Memoirs* 2:255–57, 274–75.

54. "Account of the Temper of the Rioters," 15 April 1772, Munro to Tryon, 15 April 1772, O'Callaghan, *Documentary History* 4:776–78, 800–801; Allen, *History of Vermont,* 31–32; Baker, "Baker," 606.

55. *Connecticut Courant,* 28 April, 2, 9 June 1772.

56. Ibid., 31 March 1772. See also Allen, *History of Vermont,* 33n; Allen, *Brief Narrative,* 44, 47; Slade, *Vermont State Papers,* 22–33; O'Callaghan, *Documentary History* 4:778; VHS *Collections* 1:6; Allen, *Miscellaneous Remarks,* 141–42. On the Hudson River tenant uprisings of 1766, see Countryman, *A People in Revolution,* ch. 2; Botein, *Early American Law,* 123–24.

57. Ira Allen, "Autobiography," in Wilbur, *Ira Allen* 1:13; Allen, *Vindication,* 471; Allen, *History of Vermont,* 32–35; O'Callaghan, *Documentary History* 4:778; *Connecticut Courant,* 31 March 1772.

58. Tryon to Inhabitants of Bennington, 19 May 1772, O'Callaghan, *Documentary History* 4:777–79. According to William Smith, the real reason for Tryon's proclamation was a stern letter from Hillsborough ordering Tryon to stick to the letter of his instructions and not to interfere in the Grants (Smith, *Memoirs* 1:124–27; Hillsborough to Tryon, 18 April 1772, Brodhead and O'Callaghan, *Documents* 8:294).

59. Allen, *Brief Narrative,* 51–67; *Connecticut Courant,* 14 July 1772.

60. Dartmouth to Tryon, 2 June 1773, O'Callaghan, *Documentary History* 4:856–59; Hillsborough to Tryon, 18 April 1772, Brodhead and O'Callaghan, *Documents* 8:294.

61. Report of the Council on the Disorders at Bennington, 1 July 1772, O'Callaghan, *Documentary History* 4:786–92; Stephen and Jonas Fay, Manuscript Journal, Bennington Museum.

62. Allen, *Brief Narrative,* 68; *Connecticut Courant,* 22 Sept. 1772; "Report of a Public Meeting at Bennington," 15 July 1772, O'Callaghan, *Documentary History* 4:792–93; Munro to Duane, 15 July 1772, Duane Papers.

63. Allen, *Brief Narrative,* 71; Duane, *Narrative,* 22; Jones, *Vermont in the Making,* 304–7; affidavit of Colonel John Reid, CO 5/1103:759–62, PRO; Hemenway, *Vermont Gazetteer* 1:79; O'Callaghan, *Documentary History* 4:799–800; Ira Allen, "Autobiography," in Wilbur, *Ira Allen* 1:16–18.

64. Tryon to the Inhabitants of Bennington, 11 Aug. 1772, O'Callaghan, *Documentary History* 4:793–94; Manchester Convention and Allen to Tryon, Aug. 1772, Slade *Vermont State Papers,* 30–33.

65. Minutes of the Council, 29 Sept. 1772, O'Callaghan, *Documentary History* 4:795–97.

66. Tryon to Hillsborough, 7 Oct. 1772, ibid., 798.

67. Deposition of James Henderson, Allen, *Brief Narrative,* 152–55; Henderson to Mackintosh, Cameron's deposition, O'Callaghan, *Documentary History* 4:842–43, 846–54.

68. Henderson deposition, Allen, *Brief Narrative,* 152–55; Council Minutes, 31 Aug. 1773, O'Callaghan, *Documentary History* 4:280–81, 843–44.

69. Haldimand to Tryon, 1 Sept. 1773, O'Callaghan, *Documentary History* 4:844–45. See also Dartmouth to Colden, 10 Dec. 1774, *Colden Papers* 7:256–57.

70. Report to the New York Assembly, 4 Feb. 1774, O'Callaghan, *Documentary History* 4:526, 891; *New York Colony Laws,* 33–38; B. Hough depositions, January and 7 March 1775, EAP.

71. Allen, *Vindication,* 479.

72. Slade, *Vermont State Papers,* 38–39; Allen, *Brief Narrative,* 14–23; *Connecticut Courant,* 21 June 1774, supplement; Hemenway, *Vermont Gazetteer* 1:121–35; Austin, *Matthew Lyon,* 23; Nye, *Sequestration,* 7–17.

73. Epigraph from Genieve Lamson, "Geographic Influences in Early Vermont," in *Essays in Social and Economic History,* 100. New York Land Papers, 13:132, 155, 30:100–101, 31:15–17; *New York Gazette,* 13, 20, 27 April, 4 May 1772; Paine and Morris v. Smead, Chipman, *Reports,* 99; Nathan Stone Papers, VHS. For similar events, see Hartland Proprietors and Town Records, 1766–71; Bail, "Zadock Wright," 187–89.

74. Munro to Duane, 20 April, 10 Aug. 1772, Duane Papers.

75. Allen, *Connecticut Courant,* 31 March 1772; Allen, *Vindication,* 452, 461–62, 465–67, 479; Allen, *History of Vermont,* 88.

76. Chester Town Meeting Records, 10 Oct. 1774.

77. Cumberland County Court Records; Dummerston Town Records, 1:18–20; Gale and Thompson, *Guilford,* 26. For similar actions in Manchester, see O'Callaghan, *Documentary History* 4:881.

78. Chester Town Meeting Records, 10 Oct. 1774.

79. Noah Sabin et al., "State of the Facts," 14 March 1775, Walton, *Records* 1:337–38.

80. Records of the First Cumberland County Convention, Oct. 19, 1774, ibid., 1:317–19.

81. Ibid., 1:314–19, 321–33; Hall, *Eastern Vermont,* 197–98.

82. Hall, *Eastern Vermont,* 218; O'Callaghan, *Documentary History* 4:905–6; Jones, *Vermont in the Making,* 270.

83. William French of Brattleboro died the next morning of wounds he received in the first fusillade. Daniel Houghton of Dummerston died nine days later. It is unlikely that any gunfire had been returned, for the defenders appear not to have been armed. The only Yorkers injured were those struck by Philip Safford, who charged into the mob swinging a large club, knocking down eight or ten men. See O'Callaghan, *Documentary History* 4: 906, 912–14; *New York Journal,* 23 March 1775; Reuben Jones, "Relation of Proceedings," Noah Sabin et al. "State of the Facts," March 1775, Walton, *Records* 1:332–38; Bradley, *Vermont's Appeal;* Hall, *Eastern Vermont,* 232–33, 746–55; Jones, *Vermont in the Making,* 271.

84. Hall, *Eastern Vermont,* 223; "State of the Facts," Walton, *Records* 1:337–38; Cumberland County Court Records.

85. Jones, "A Relation of the Proceedings," Walton, *Records* 1:332–36; Hall, *Eastern Vermont,* 236.

86. The exact number and names of these new justices of the peace is unknown (O'Callaghan, *Documentary History* 4:914–18).

87. Allen's emphasis, "Remarks, &c.," *New Hampshire Gazette,* no. 915 (1774), in Allen, *Vindication,* 479; Allen, *Brief Narrative,* 176–83.

88. Records of the Second Cumberland County Convention, 30 Nov. 1774, Walton, *Records* 1:320–22; Dummerston Town Records, 1:28, 37–40.

89. Hall, *Eastern Vermont,* 237–38.

90. Walton, *Records* 1:338–39; Allen to Wolcott, March 1775, EAP.

91. Allen, *Brief Narrative,* 168–69. In another place Allen said the New York government's "notions of justice and equity seem to be unnatural and unjust" (Allen, *Vindication,* 459); while their laws "correspond with the depravedness of their minds and morals" (Allen, "Remarks, &c.," ibid., 478).

92. "The Bennington Mob," O'Callaghan, *Documentary History* 4:861.

93. Reid, *In a Defiant Stance;* Reid, "The Irrelevance of the Declaration," in Hartog, *Law in the American Revolution,* 46–89; Reid, "In a Defensive Rage"; Wills, *Inventing America;* Gross, *Minutemen.* Nelson, *Americanization of the Common Law,* and Horwitz, *Transformation of American Law,* find a conflict between localized, agrarian, communitarian law and the law of a more centralized and centralizing capitalist state.

94. Jones, "A Relation of the Proceedings," 23 March 1775, Walton, *Records* 1:334.

95. Hine, *Community on the Frontier,* 88–89.

96. Allen, *Brief Narrative,* 181.

97. Affidavit of Charles Phelps, Misc. MSS, Henry Stevens Collections, VSA. See also Williamson, *Vermont in Quandary,* ch. 1–2.

CHAPTER FIVE

1. Allen to the New York Provincial Congress, 2 June 1775, EAP.

2. Adams, "Notes for an Oration at Braintree," 1772, Adams, *Diary* 1:59. See also Allen to the Massachusetts Provincial Congress, 9 June 1775, AAS; Allen and Warner to Continental Congress, 4 July 1775, EAP; John Adams to Abigail Adams, 3 July 1776, Butterfield, *Adams Family Correspondence* 2:30–31; Adams to Trumbull, 5 Nov. 1775, to Osgood, 15 Nov. 1775, to Tudor, 14 Nov. 1775, 10 July 1776, 24 Aug. 1776, Taylor, *Papers of John Adams* 3:278–79, 310, 4:376–77, 490–92; Wills, *Cincinnatus,* ch. 8; Adair, "Fame and the Founding Fathers"; Shy, *Toward Lexington,* 143–48.

3. Epigraph from Allen, *Vindication,* 453. Ethan Allen record book, AFP; Minutes of the Convention, 11 April 1775, Slade, *Vermont State Papers,* 60.

4. Allen, *Vindication,* 447–48; Allen, *History of Vermont,* 42; Murdoch, "A French Report on Vermont," 223.

5. Allen, *Vindication,* 447–48.

6. For contemporary descriptions, see Grant, *Memoirs,* ch. 9; John Montressor's report to General Gage, May 13, 1774, Gage Papers, box 1775, PRO, quoted at length in French, *Taking of Ticonderoga,* 7–12. The British planned to rebuild Ticonderoga and Crown Point to keep the Americans in line. Lt. Jocelyn Feltham arrived with reinforcements in March with more to follow within a few months (ibid., 12–17, 38, 53, 59).

7. Brown to Boston Committee of Correspondence, Chittenden, *Capture of Ticonderoga,* 97; Jeffry, "Journal Kept in Quebec," 105; Arnold to Massachusetts Committee of Safety, 30 April 1775, Force, *American Archives,* 4th ser., 2:450.

8. Mott, "Journal," Parsons to Trumbull, 2 June 1775, Phelps to Connecticut General Assembly, 16 May 1775, Petition of Col. Parsons, 30 May 1775, CHS *Collections* 1:165–69, 175, 181–86; Parsons to ?, 2 June 2 1775, *Pennsylvania Magazine of History and Biography* 8 (1884): 363–64; Massachusetts Committee of Safety to New York Committee, 30 April 1775, "Extract of a Letter from a Gentleman in Pittsfield," 4 May 1775, Force, *American Archives,* 4th ser., 2:450, 507; Hartford Committee of Correspondence to Heman Allen, Papers Relating to the Revolutionary War, 3:26ab, Connecticut State Library. Others who discussed attacking Fort Ticonderoga included Silas Deane, Samuel Wyllys, Edward Mott, Samuel H. Parsons, and the Massachusetts Committee of Safety.

9. Hemenway, *Vermont Gazetteer* 1:143; Allen, *History of Vermont*, 26; Hall, *History of Vermont*, 128–37.

10. Mott, "Journal," 170–71; Hemenway, *Vermont Gazetteer* 3:510; Goodhue, *Shoreham*, 13.

11. Jeffry, "Journal," 109–10; Mott, "Journal," Phelps to Connecticut General Assembly, 16 May 1775, CHS *Collections* 1:166–69, 174–77; Thomas Allen to General Pomeroy, 9 May 1775, Chittenden, *Capture of Ticonderoga*, 116–17; "Extract of a Letter from a Gentleman at Pittsfield," 9 May 1775, Force, *American Archives*, 4th ser., 2:546; Hemenway, *Vermont Gazetteer* 3:943; Goodhue, *Shoreham*, 12–13; Papers Relating to the Revolutionary War, 26:219, Connecticut State Library; Gordon, *History of the United States* 1:344–48. Carleton ordered Delaplace to keep a careful eye on affairs in his "neighbourhood." But the Americans did an excellent job of keeping information about Lexington and Concord from reaching Delaplace (French, *Taking of Ticonderoga*, 36–38).

12. Arnold, "Regimental Book," 364; Mott, "Journal," 171–72; Lossing, *Field-Book* 1:124; Sparks, *Life of Arnold*, 15–17; Allen, *History of Vermont*, 43. For an argument supporting Arnold's right to command, see Arnold, *Life of Arnold*, 39–41. See also the account of Major Noah Callender in Goodhue, *Shoreham*, 12–15; Mott to Massachusetts Congress, 11 May 1775, Force, *American Archives*, 4th ser., 2:557–60.

13. Allen, *Narrative of Allen's Captivity*, 6–7; Goodhue, *Shoreham*, 13–16; Thompson, *Gazeteer*, pt. 2:33, 73; French, *Taking of Ticonderoga*, 79.

14. *Vermont Antiquarian* 3 (1905): 138–43; Goodhue, *Shoreham*, 14; Allen, *Narrative of Allen's Captivity*, 6–7; French, *Taking of Ticonderoga*, 80–82; Allen, *History of Vermont*, 43.

15. Feltham to Gage, 11 June 1775, French, *Taking of Ticonderoga*, 42–55; Allen, *Narrative of Allen's Captivity*, 7–8; Proceedings of Continental Congress, 20 May 1775, Force, *American Archives*, 4th ser., 2:623–24; Goodhue, *Shoreham*, 15.

16. Scholars have spilled much ink over Allen's exact words. Eyewitnesses agreed on the general tone of those words, disagreeing on a word or two. One added the believable expletive "by God!" to Allen's call for surrender (Lossing, *Field-Book* 1:125n; French, *First Year*, 151–52; Allen, *Narrative of Allen's Captivity*, 8; Goodhue, *Shoreham*, 14; Allen, *History of Vermont*, 58–59; Warner and Sunderland to Connecticut General Assembly, 12 May 1775, Chittenden, *Capture of Ticonderoga*, 109; Worcester *Spy*, 17 May 1775). For a completely different version, see Williamson, *Vermont in Quandary*, ch. 5. Williamson claimed that "the Allens" took the fort by trickery after making a truce with Delaplace, using as evidence a letter from Lord Dartmouth in London to General Gage, 1 July 1775, which says nothing of the kind (Carter, *Correspondence of Gage* 2:199–202).

17. Allen, *Narrative of Allen's Captivity,* 9. Easton and Arnold each tried to claim credit for the capture (Arnold to Massachusetts Committee of Safety, 11 May 1775, "Veritas" to Holt, 25 June 1775, Proceedings of Massachusetts Provincial Congress, 18 May 1775, *Oracle of Liberty, Worcester Spy,* 24 May 1775, Force, *American Archives,* 4th ser., 2:557, 624, 1085–88; *Connecticut Courant,* 28 July 1775; CHS *Collections* 1:181–84; French, *Taking of Ticonderoga,* 28, 86–90; Chittenden, *Capture of Ticonderoga,* 71–74). Delaplace, who should have known, told the Connecticut General Assembly (24 May 1775) that he surrendered to Ethan Allen, though he was "ignorant by what authority said Allen thus took them" (Force, *American Archives,* 4th ser., 2:698–99. See also French, *Taking of Ticonderoga,* 44–45; CHS *Collections* 1:182; Delaplace to *Connecticut Courant,* 28 July 1775; and Mott to Massachusetts Congress, 11 May 1775, Force, *American Archives,* 4th ser., 2:557–60.

18. Allen to Massachusetts Congress, 11 May 1775, Force, *American Archives,* 4th ser., 2:556.

19. Allen to Albany Committee of Safety, 11 May 1775, EAP. See also Jones, *History of New York* 1:47; *Journals of Albany Committee of Correspondence* 6:31.

20. Committee of War to Massachusetts Congress, 10 May 1775, Arnold to Massachusetts Committee of Safety, 11, 14, 19, 23, 29 May 1775, and to Continental Congress, 29 May 1775, Force, *American Archives,* 4th ser., 2:556–57, 584–85, 645–46, 693–94, 734–35; Mott, "Journal," 172; Arnold, "Memorandum Book," 364–66; Papers Relating to the Revolutionary War, 3:34, 356, 32:325a; Arnold, *Life of Arnold,* 41; Starr, *History of Cornwall,* 309, 329; Chittenden, *Capture of Ticonderoga,* 44, 109; Phelps to Connecticut General Assembly, 16 May 1775, General Account of Money's Expended, 18 Nov. 1775, Barnabus Deane to Silas Deane, 1 June 1775, CHS *Collections* 1:175, 186–88, 2:247; Council of War to Provincial Congress of Connecticut, 11 May 1775, Henry Stevens Collection, 1:75, 87, 100, VSA. Allen issued Delaplace a receipt for the rum, which the British captain collected on (Allen to Delaplace, 10 May 1775, EAP; Revolutionary War Papers, Connecticut State Library, 1–3:356; French, *Taking of Ticonderoga,* 45).

21. Phelps to Connecticut General Assembly, 16 May 1775, Allen to Trumbull, 12 May 1775, CHS *Collections* 1:175–79; Allen to Albany Committee of Safety, 12 May 1775, Albany Committee of Safety to New York Committee of Safety, 12 May 1775, New York Congress to Trumbull, 29 May 1775, Force, *American Archives,* 4th ser., 2:605–6, 728. Fifty soldiers and twenty-four women and children were taken at Ticonderoga, with one British private joining the Green Mountain Boys. The Americans also seized more than one hundred cannon and wagons full of munitions at Ticonderoga and another hundred cannon, most in need of repair, at Crown Point. Arnold wanted to give the

officers their swords and guns back, but Allen refused (French, *Taking of Ticonderoga*, 45, 55; Arnold to Massachusetts Committee of Safety [with Romans's ordinance list], 19 May 1775, petition of Delaplace to Connecticut General Assembly, 24 May 1775, Force, *American Archives*, 4th ser., 2:645–46, 698–99; Ordnance list from Crown Point, Stevens Collection, 1:81–85; Delaplace to Schuyler, 1 Dec. 1775, NYPL; Papers Relating to the Revolutionary War, 3:633.

22. Arnold, "Memorandum Book," 367–68; Allen, *Narrative of Allen's Captivity*, 10–11; Arnold to the Massachusetts Committee of Safety, 14 May 1775, Force, *Archives*, 4th ser., 2:584–85; Arnold, *Arnold*, 17–29; *Connecticut Courant*, 29 May 1775.

23. Arnold, "Memorandum Book," 367–68, 372, 375; Carleton to Dartmouth, 7 June 1775, CO, Q: 11, PAC; Allen to Lee, 21 May 1775, *Historical Magazine* 3 (1859): 347; Journals of Sanguinet and Berthelot, Verreau, *Invasion du Canada*, 29, 227; Barnabus Deane to Silas Deane, 1 June 1775, CHS *Collections* 2:246; letter from Ticonderoga to a gentleman in Hartford, 23 May 1775, Stevens Collection, 1:234–36; letter of General Warren, Frothingham, *Life of Warren*, 494; Arnold to Massachusetts Committee of Safety, 23 May 1775, Allen to Merchants of Montreal, 18 May 1775, Force, *American Archives*, 4th ser., 2:639, 693–94.

24. Allen to Caughnawagas, 24 May 1775, Allen to Lee, 21 May 1775, Allen and Easton to merchants of Montreal, 4 June 1775, Allen and Warner to Dyer and Deane, 3 July 1775, EAP; Allen to Continental Congress, 29 May 1775, Force, *American Archives*, 4th ser., 2:713–14, 732–34; deposition of Pierre Charlan, 6 Aug. 1775, Historical Section, *War of the American Revolution*, 65–66.

25. Worcester *Spy*, 17 May 1775; Warren to Scholly, 17 May 1775, Bancroft Collection, NYPL, 229. See also New York *Journal*, 18 May 1775; Philadelphia *Journal*, 20 May 1775; Walcott and others to Massachusetts Congress, 16 May 1775, Gilliland to Continental Congress, 29 May 1775, Force, *American Archives*, 4th ser., 2:618–19, 731–32; Irving, *Life of Washington* 1:248; Callaghan, *Henry Knox*, ch. 3.

26. Ford, *Journals of Congress* 2:24–25, 52, 56, 68–70, 75; Congress to the Canadian People, 29 May 1775, Chittenden, *Capture of Ticonderoga*, 113; Allen, *History of Vermont*, 44. New York obeyed these orders and halted preparations for an invasion of Canada (Proceedings of Provincial Congress of New York, 25 May 1775, Force, *American Archives*, 4th ser., 2:1251–53; *Journals of the Provincial Congress* 1:9).

27. Gilliland to Continental Congress, 29 May 1775, Easton to Massachusetts Congress, 6 June 1775, Hawley to Warren, 9 June 1775, Arnold to Continental Congress, 13 June 1775, Force, *American Archives*, 4th ser., 2:731–

35, 877–78, 895–96, 919, 944–45, 976–77; Allen and Warner to Connecticut Delegates to Congress, 4 July 1775, Stevens Collection, 1:383–84; Phelps to Connecticut General Assembly, 16 May 1775, CHS *Collections* 1:176.

28. Arnold, "Memorandum Book," 365, 373; Elmore to President of Continental Congress, 10 June 1775, Massachusetts Provincial Congress to Arnold, 22 May 1775, Force, *American Archives*, 4th ser., 2:957, 1382–83; Massachusetts Committee of Safety to Arnold, 28 May 1775, Chittenden, *Capture of Ticonderoga*, 121; Rossie, *Politics of Command*, ch. 3–4.

29. Arnold, "Memorandum Book," 373; "Veritas" to Holt, 25 June 1775, Schuyler to Continental Congress, 11 July 1775, Force, *American Archives*, 4th ser., 2:1086–87, 1645–46.

30. Ford, *Journals of Congress* 2:109–10; Hancock to New York Congress, 24 June 1775, Proceedings of Congress, 27 June 1775, Force, *American Archives*, 4th ser., 2:1076, 1855–56; Continental Congress Papers for 23 June 1775, in Stevens Collection. Christopher Ward gave Allen credit for helping to shift Congress's resolve to invade Canada (Ward, *War of Revolution* 1:140). On the invasion of Canada, see Smith, *Struggle for the Fourteenth Colony;* Wrong, *Canada and the American Revolution,* ch. 14; Hatch, *Thrust for Canada;* Stanley, *Canada Invaded.*

31. Minutes of New York Provincial Congress, 4, 20 July 1775, EAP; *Journals of the Provincial Congress* 1:65–66, 107; Schuyler to Continental Congress, 3 July 1775, Allen to Trumbull, 6 July 1775, Force, *American Archives*, 4th ser., 2:1536, 3:1593. New York even accepted the name of their former opponents, voting to "Provision the Green Mountain Boys."

32. Allen and Warner to Connecticut Delegates, 4 July 1775, Stevens Collection, 1:383–84. See also Force, *American Archives*, 4th ser., 2:716, 723–24, 728, 808–9, 847, 850–51, 916, 986–88, 1596–1600, 1645–47; CHS *Collections* 2:247; Chittenden, *Capture of Ticonderoga*, 121–24; Sparks, *Life of Arnold*, 22; Arnold, "Memorandum Book," 374–75.

33. Allen, *Narrative of Allen's Captivity*, 9.

34. Epigraph from ibid., 5. Though they did not know it, seizing Ticonderoga also prevented a planned attack on the Green Mountain Boys by British regulars (Gage to Carleton, 19 April 1775, French, *Taking of Ticonderoga*, 16–17).

35. Allen to Trumbull, 12 July 1775, EAP; Higginbotham, "Military Leadership," 89. See also Higginbotham, *Washington*, 33–38, 46–51; Richard H. Kohn, "American Generals of the Revolution: Subordination and Restraint," in Higginbotham, *Reconsiderations*, 104–23; Bailyn, *Ideological Origins*, 61–66, 112–16; Royster, *Revolutionary People*, 35–36, 260–66; Kohn, *Eagle and Sword*, 2–6, 282–83; Reid, *In Defiance of the Law;* Jefferson, *Notes on the State of Virginia*, in *Thomas Jefferson, Writings*, 252–55; Wills, *Cincinnatus*, 17–23.

36. There is no information as to who was present at this convention other than its chair, Nathan Clark, and clerk, John Fassett. Both men were among the leading Separatists of Bennington. The vote for Warner was 41–5 (Dorset Convention, 26 July 1775, Walton, *Records* 1:6–10; Wilbur, *Ira Allen* 1:67–68).

37. Allen to Trumbull, 3 Aug. 1775, Force, *American Archives*, 4th ser., 3:17–18; State of Vermont, *Rolls of the Soldiers*, 816. As Edward Shils has written, "The military bureaucracy at higher staff levels does not find it easy to accommodate within its own circles the charismatically inclined soldier who tries to attain to new principles of warfare or who, as a hero, arouses the devotion of ordinary soldiers" (Shils, "Charisma," in Sills, *Encyclopedia of Social Sciences* 2:388).

38. Allen, *Narrative of Allen's Captivity*, 12–13. Schuyler and Congress both were surprised by Warner's selection. Schuyler had already given instructions to his paymaster to advance Allen £200 as colonel of the new regiment (Walton, *Records* 1:9–10; Lossing, *Life of Schuyler* 1:365–66; Affidavit of Peter Griffin, 25 Aug. 1775, Force, *American Archives*, 4th ser., 3:670–71; Jeffry, "Journal," 131; Allen, *History of Vermont*, 62–63; *Journals of the Provincial Congress* 1:106–7, 129–30).

39. Halsey to Schuyler, 1 Aug. 1775, Allen to Trumbull, 3 Aug. 1775, Jonathan Trumbull Papers, 4:142ab and 144a-d, CHS; Schuyler to Hancock, 5 Oct. 1775, Stevens Collection; Mott to Trumbull, 6 Oct. 1775, Force, *American Archives*, 4th ser., 3:972–74; Ainslie, *Canada Preserved*, 18–20; Bellemere, *Histoire de Nicolet*, ch. 10; Everest, *Moses Hazen*, ch. 3; Verreau, *Invasion du Canada*; Arnold "Memorandum Book," 369.

40. Schuyler to Hancock, 8 Sept. 1775, "To the Inhabitants of Canada," 5 Sept. 1775, Allen to New York Congress, to Massachusetts Congress, to Schuyler, 2, 9 June, 6 Sept. 1775, Schuyler to Continental Congress, 19 Sept. 1775, Easton to Massachusetts Congress, 6 June 1775, Trumbull to Schuyler, 24 July 1775, Force, *American Archives*, 4th ser., 2:891–93, 919, 939–40, 1721, 3:669–72, 738–39, 742–43; Allen, *Narrative of Allen's Captivity*, 12–13; Allen to Schuyler, 14 Sept. 1775, *Continental Congress Papers* 1:158; Smith, *Struggle for Fourteenth Colony* 1:324; Allen and Warner to Connecticut's Delegates, 4 July 1775, Bancroft Collection, NYPL.

41. Force, *American Archives*, 4th ser., 3:459, 796, 1093–98, 1107–8; Ward, *War of Revolution* 1:155–56; Smith, *Struggle for the Fourteenth Colony* 1:343–44, 418.

42. Allen to Montgomery, 20 Sept. 1775, Force, *American Archives*, 4th ser., 3:754; Allen, *Narrative of Allen's Captivity*, 13–14; John Brown's Certificate, 22 July 1776, Force, *American Archives* 1:498; "Benjamin Trumbull's Journal of 1775," CHS *Collections* 7:145; journals of Sanguinet and Badeaux, Verreau, *Invasion du Canada*, 28, 45, 165; Jeffry, "Journal," 136.

43. Hey to the Lord Chancellor, Shortt and Doughty, *Documents,* 672; Watson to Faneuil, 16 Oct. 1775, Force, *American Archives,* 4th ser., 3:1599–1600. See also ibid., 954, 2:891–93; Hatch, *Thrust for Canada,* 41, 55; Smith, *Struggle for Fourteenth Colony* 1:380, 407, 410; Ward, *Revolution* 1:155–56; Jeffry, "Journal," 116–18, 124, 132–41; Ainslie, *Canada Preserved,* 20. John Adams, among others, faulted the excessive caution of General Schuyler and Congress for losing this unique opportunity to seize Montreal (Adams, *Diary* 3:324–25; Rossie, *Politics of Command,* ch. 4–5).

44. Allen, *Narrative of Allen's Captivity,* 14–15; Irving, *Life of Washington* 2: ch. 5.

45. Allen to the New York Provincial Congress, 2 June 1775, EAP; Allen to the New York Provincial Congress, 2 June 1775, EAP; Allen, *Narrative of Allen's Captivity,* 7, 17; Hatch, *Thrust for Canada,* 57; journals of Sanguinet, Lorimier, and Lanaudière, Verreau, *Invasion,* 50, 255–56, 315; Smith, *Struggle for Fourteenth Colony* 1:380–94; *Quebec Gazette,* 1 Dec. 1775; *Connecticut Gazette,* 20 Nov. 1775; *London Gazette,* 4 Nov. 1775; Watson to Franklin, 19 Oct. 1775, Force, *American Archives,* 4th ser., 3:1601.

46. Allen, *Narrative of Allen's Captivity,* 17–22; Papers Relating to the Revolutionary War 4:396; "Extract of a Letter from a Gentleman in Quebeck," 30 Sept. 1775, "Substance of Letters from America," 4 Nov. 1775, Force, *American Archives,* 4th ser., 3:798–99, 845; Ainslie, *Canada Preserved,* 20; Jeffry, "Journal," 139–41; Lanaudière to Baby, 28 Sept. 1775, Verreau, *Invasion du Canada,* 315–16; Carleton to Dartmouth, 21 Sept. 1775, Cruikshank, *History of the Military Forces of Canada* 2:79.

47. Schuyler to President of Congress, 5 Oct. 1775, Bedel to Montgomery, 28 Sept. 1775, Force, *American Archives,* 4th ser., 3:951–54; Washington quoted, Irving, *Life of Washington* 1:322. For other responses to Allen's attack and captivity, see Mott to Trumbull, 6 Oct. 1775, Force, *American Archives,* 4th ser., 3:800–801, 972–74, 1095–97, 1341–42, 1373–75, 1600–1602; Hatch, *Thrust for Canada,* 58; Allen, *History of Vermont,* 46; Smith, *Struggle for Fourteenth Colony* 1:410; Johnson to Dartmouth, 12 Oct. 1775, Cramahe to Dartmouth, 30 Sept. 1775, Carleton to Dartmouth, 25 Oct. 1775, CO5/76:169, CO42/13:185–89, 34:206–11, PRO; Snyder Affidavit, 19 Jan. 1776, Force, *American Archives,* 4th ser., 4:872; *Quebec Gazette,* 19 Oct. 1775; journals of Sanguinet, Badeaux, Lanaudière, Verreau, *Invasion,* 53–57, 169–70, 315; Hatch, *Thrust for Canada,* 59–61; Ainslie, *Canada Preserved,* 20–21; Jeffry, "Journal," 134–39, 141.

48. Allen, *Narrative of Allen's Captivity,* 23, 28–31; Allen to Prescott, 25 Sept. 1775, Force, *American Archives,* 4th ser., 3:801–2; Jeffry, "Journal," 142. For validations of Allen's account of his early captivity, see letters from Quebec, 25 Oct. 1775, Montgomery to Stopford, 20 Oct. 1775, to Carle-

ton, 22 Oct. 1775, and to Schuyler, 24 Nov. 1775, Washington to Schuyler, 18 Dec. 1775, to President of Congress, 14, 18, 31 Dec. 1775, and to Howe, 18 Dec. 1775, Howe to Washington, 21 Dec. 1775, Affidavits of Rammon and Snyder, 19 Jan. 1776, Bruyerede Belair, 27 Feb. 1776, Thomas Walker, 26 April 1776, William Bradley, Levi Solomon, and James Morrison, 14 Feb. 1776, "Memorandum of what passed at the interview . . .," 20 July 1776, Force, *American Archives,* 4th ser., 3:1185–87, 801–2, 1134, 1138, 1694, 4:262–63, 310–11, 314–15, 454, 485–86, 871–72, 1175–79, 5:149, 5th ser., 1:500–1; "A Diary of the Invasion of Canada," *New Hampshire Antiquarian Society Collections,* no. 2(1876): 37–54; Smith, *Struggle for Fourteenth Colony* 1:395–99; Hunt, *Biographical Notes,* 15.

49. House of Lords, 5 March 1776, Wedderburn to Eden, 27 Dec. 1775, EAP; Cruger to Palfrey, 16 Feb. 1776, Force, *American Archives,* 4th ser., 6:294–96, 508; Bowman, *Captive Americans,* 10–11. On the treatment of American prisoners of war, see ibid.; Armbruster, *Wallabout Prison Ships;* Metzger, *Prisoner in the American Revolution.*

50. Allen, *Narrative of Allen's Captivity,* 66, 79–81, 107; Allen, *History of Vermont,* 65–67. Thomas McKean reported that John Wilkes procured Allen's writ of habeas corpus (McKean to John Adams, 19 Sept. 1777, Taylor, *Papers of John Adams* 5:288). See also Boudinot, *Journal,* 14–17; Fell, "Memorandum Book," Onderdonck, *Revolutionary Incidents,* 207–10, 224, 245–47; Stirling, "Prisoners of War," 380; Force, *American Archives,* 4th ser., 3:1133–34, 1185, 1342–44, 1391–95, 1597, 1603, 4:1234; 5th ser., 1:233, 238, 390, 445, 450, 559, 650, 794, 3:1054–58; Board of War Report, Ford, *Journals of Congress* 10:74; Ward, *War of Revolution* 1:160, 196–201; "Reminiscences of Frye Bayley," 32–45; Digby, *British Invasion,* 83–184; Middlekauff, *Glorious Cause,* ch. 13–15.

51. Fitch, *Diary,* 84, 122, 131, 179–80, 187.

52. Allen later insisted that he feigned his delirium; as on other occasions "my extreme circumstances . . . rendered it political to act in some measure the madman." But there is every indication that the British estimation of Allen's mental health was partially accurate (Allen, *Narrative of Allen's Captivity,* 77–78; Fitch, *Diary,* 110, 159, 166–67, 209; Ethan to Levi Allen, 27 July 1777, to Heman Allen, 4 June 1777, to General Assembly of Connecticut, 30 June 1777, EAP; Allen to Connecticut Assembly, 30 April, 3 June 1777, Papers Relating to the Revolutionary War 7:169, 12:133; Fitch's "Narrative," in the Vermont Historical Society; Minutes of Connecticut State Assembly, May 1777, *Public Records of Connecticut* 1:257; Graydon, *Memoirs,* 243, 245, 247, 252–55, 524–25).

53. Ethan to Heman Allen, 4 June 1777, EAP; Ethan to Levi Allen, 27 July 1777, *Connecticut Courant,* 30 March 1779.

54. Webb to Trumbull, 19 Dec. 1777, Webb, *Correspondence and Journals* 1:403–4; Fitch, *Diary,* 122, 179, 203–4, 208–9; Graydon, *Memoirs,* 245; Allen, *Narrative of Allen's Captivity,* 77–78, 104. For a different version of Allen's arrest, see Huguenin, "Ethan Allen, Parolee," 118; Manhattan Company, *Manna-hatin,* 101.

CHAPTER SIX

1. For the most succinct statement of this view, see Onuf, "State-Making in Revolutionary America." See also Wardner, *Birthplace of Vermont,* ch. 28–29; Williamson, *Vermont in Quandary,* ch. 5–6; Van de Water, *Reluctant Republic,* ch. 5–6, 10.

2. Epigraph from Allen, *Vindication,* 463–64. On the efforts of New York's elite to use the war to enhance their power, see Countryman, *A People in Revolution,* ch. 5, 6, and 9.

3. Allen to New York Provincial Congress, 20 July 1775, EAP. See also Journal of New York Provincial Congress, 15 Aug. 1775, Force, *American Archives,* 4th ser., 3:530–31.

4. Allen to New York Provincial Congress, 20 July 1775, EAP; *Journal of the Provincial Congress of New York* 1:106–8; Sullivan, *Minutes of Albany County Committee* 1:27, 212, 227–28, 589, 605; Paltsits, *Minutes of Commissioners for Detecting Conspiracies* 1:92, 97–98, 726–28; Walton, *Records* 1:195–96, 200, 339–41; Force, *American Archives,* 5th ser., 3:267, 525, 590–91, 1237; Spargo, *David Redding.*

5. John Taylor to Pierre Van Cortlandt, 3 Nov. 1776, Force, *American Archives,* 5th ser., 3:503–4.

6. *Journals of New York Provincial Congress* 1:82, 199, 228, 237–38, 242; Walton, *Records* 1:347–48; Allen, *History of Vermont,* 72, 74–76. On the timidity of New York's government in the years 1775–77, see Mason, *Road to Independence,* ch. 3–5; Becker, *History of Political Parties,* ch. 9–11; Dillon, *New York Triumvirate,* ch. 7–8; Douglass, *Rebels and Democrats,* ch. 5; Nettles, *George Washington,* 285–87; *Journal of New York Provincial Congress* 1:57, 76; Rossie, *Politics of Command,* 41–49.

7. Digby, *British Invasion,* 119–84; Mahan, *Major Operations,* 17–19; Ward, *War of Revolution* 1: ch. 35; Allen, *History of Vermont,* 72; Jones, *History of the Campaign,* 105–12, 143–44; VHS *Collections* 1:34; "Report of the Committee of Proceedings," Walton, *Records* 1:37–38.

8. Proceedings of the Convention, Walton, *Records* 2:493; Allen, *History of Vermont,* 72–75; *Connecticut Courant,* 14 April 1777.

9. *Journals of Congress* 4:405, 416; Proctor, *Records of the Conventions,* 32.

10. Walton, *Records* 1:21–22. See also ibid., 16–26, 33; Proctor, *Records of Conventions,* 34, 37, 42–44; Ethan Allen, "Reply to Clinton's Proclamation," 1778, quoted in Allen, *Vindication,* 452.

11. James Clay's statement, 20 Nov. 1776, Clay to Session, 26 Sept. 1776, O'Callaghan, *Documentary History* 4:555–56; Marlborough Notification, 4 Oct. 1776, Wardner, *Birthplace of Vermont,* 316–17; Hartford Committee to Clay, 29 Oct. 1776, Force, *American Archives,* 5th ser., 3:941; Hall, *History of Eastern Vermont,* 268–96; *Journals of the New York Provincial Congress* 2:214, 3:210–14, 272–73, 420–21.

12. Walton, *Records* 1:38–51, 2:244–45, 5:527–28, 542; Proctor, *Records of Conventions,* 63. At least seven Connecticut River valley towns called specifically for statehood.

13. There are several versions of the declaration, each altered slightly to suit the audience being addressed. I have quoted from the original declaration of 15 Jan. (Walton, *Records* 1:40–44). The Vermont declaration erred in assigning the date of 15 May to this congressional resolution, which passed 10 May 1776 (*Journals of Congress* 2:342). See also Walton, *Records* 1:46–52, 357–60, 394–96; *Connecticut Courant,* 17 March 1777; Allen, *Miscellaneous Remarks;* Allen, *History of Vermont,* 78–85; Proctor, *Records of Conventions,* 65; Ford, *Journals of Congress* 2:158, 166; Adams, *First Constitutions,* ch. 2.

14. Walton, *Records* 1:394–96; *Journals of Congress* 4:342, 357–58, 7:239; Allen, *History of Vermont,* 77, 86. Willi Adams gave Young credit for inventing the phrase "constituent power" (Adams, *First American Constitutions,* 65).

15. VHS *Collections* 1:72, 100; the Windsor Convention, 2–8 July 1777, Walton, *Records* 1:62–75; Allen, *History of Vermont,* 92–93. Hutchinson was surprised that the convention met at all. Two months later he wrote, "I had expected the Convention would not sit at that time, by reason of the dark cloud then coming over us, and which overwhelmed us the week after" (VHS *Collections* 1:170).

16. For Vermont's constitution see Walton, *Records* 1:90–103; for Pennsylvania's, see Selsam, *Pennsylvania Constitution of 1776;* Force, *American Archives,* 5th ser., 2:1–62. Daniel Chipman first saw the two constitutions as virtually identical, and most authors on the subject have followed his lead (Chipman, *Memoir,* 81, 114–15, 142–43). There are also similarities to several local models, such as the Cumberland County Committee of Safety's 1776 petition to New York and Ethan Allen's *Brief Narrative* of 1774 (Wilbur photostat no. 3102, Wilbur Collection, Special Collections, University of Vermont; Thompson, *History of Vermont* 2:107; Walton, *Records* 1:348–50). On democracy as a pejorative in these years, see Bailyn, *Ideological Origins,* ch. 6; Daniell, *Experiment in Republicanism,* ch. 5 and 7.

17. Walton, *Records* 1:90–92. Compare with Ethan Allen, *Brief Narrative*, 126–28, and "Remarks, &c.," *New Hampshire Gazette,* no. 915 (1774), in Allen, *Vindication,* 477–81.

18. For the opposite point of view, see Shaeffer, "A Comparison of the First Constitutions." Shaeffer maintained that Vermont's constitution not only was less democratic than Pennsylvania's but was actually a conservative document. He based this judgment on the Allens' continued rule. Shaeffer's understanding of conservatism is based on the holding of power; the political persistence of even a radical group is thus conservative.

19. Article three of the Declaration of Rights proclaimed that "all men have a natural and unalienable right to worship *Almighty God,* according to the dictates of their own consciences," but then limited full civil rights to those "who profess the protestant religion." Though never enforced, article three marked the constitution's one great inconsistency and met much resistance and modification over the ensuing thirty years before being eliminated (Walton, *Records* 1:93–94, 97–98, 400–402; Allen, *History of Vermont,* 109).

20. Walton, *Records* 1:94–95.

21. Before 1825, twenty-six of Windsor County's twenty-eight judges and twenty-one of Chittenden County's judges served simultaneously in the legislature and/or on the governor's council. As Donald Lutz pointed out, "The distinction between legislative and judicial matters was a relatively new one" (Lutz, *Popular Consent,* 166, 205–7).

22. Walton, *Records* 1:94, 96–97, 99–100; Dwight, *Travels* 2:405. The assembly represented the towns, while the council, which was elected on a statewide basis, was seen to serve the greater interests of the state. In this sense the council filled the role of an upper house. See Morgan, *Inventing the People,* ch. 10; John Adams in the *Boston Gazette,* 27 Jan. 1766; Drayton, *A Letter from the Freemen,* 10; Bailyn, *Pamphlets,* 66–69, 249–55; Wood, *Creation of the American Republic,* 16–61, 291–95, 298–304, 452–56, 462, 549, 552, 598; Wardner, *Birthplace of Vermont,* 159–61.

23. Walton, *Records* 1:100–101.

24. Walton, *Records* 1:94, 5:508–9; Rozwenc, "Agriculture and Politics," 93. On the centrality of the town in New England political tradition, see Brown, *Revolutionary Politics,* 29–30; Grant, *Democracy in Kent,* ch. 9. Compare Becker, *History of Political Parties,* 200–204.

25. Walton, *Records* 1:152–54, 247, 366; *Journal of the New York Congress* 1:995; Goodrich, *Rolls of the Soldiers,* 798–99; Thompson, *History of Vermont,* pt. 2:107.

26. Horwitz, *Transformation of American Law,* 63–74.

27. Walton, *Records* 1:99–102. Vermont continued to administer its own naturalization even after it joined the Union, maintaining that right until

1828 (Kettner, *Development of American Citizenship*, 239, 267–69. On New York voting practices, see Lynd, "Who Shall Rule at Home?"

28. A contrary argument holds that since so many adult males owned property, there was no need to establish property qualifications. This position fails to explain the absence from Vermont's constitution of the extensive hairsplitting of property qualifications present in every other state. It also does not account for the absence of the linkage of property and liberty which dominated the debate elsewhere. In Vermont each person was a member of a free community first, a landowner second (Adams, *First Constitutions;* Kettner, *American Citizenship*, ch. 8; Upton, *Revolutionary New Hampshire*, 176–84; Daniell, *Experiment in Republicanism*, 53–62; Taylor, *Massachusetts, Colony and Commonwealth*, 16–29, 42–47, 59–72, 93–101, 106–10, 117–23, 151–59).

29. Slade, *Vermont State Papers*, 505. For the finest treatment of the issue of comity in the new nation, see Finkleman, *An Imperfect Union*. On popular support within Vermont for the prohibition of slavery, see the grant of freedom from Captain Ebenezer Allen's militia company to Dinah Mattis and her baby, November 1777, Walton, *Records* 1:93, and "An Act to Prevent the Sale and Transportation of Negroes & Mulattoes out of this State," 30 Oct. 1786, Williams, *Laws of Vermont, 1785–1791*, 100.

30. Vermont fit traditional notions of a unified state's reliance on homogeneity. Pennsylvania more closely matched the judgments of the framers of the American Constitution on the existence and value of diversity. See Madison's *Federalist Papers* nos. 10 and 51, in Hamilton, *Federalist*, 41–48, 263–67; Jefferson, *Notes on Virginia*, 83, 113–24, 142–43, 150–54.

31. No one knows who wrote Vermont's constitution. E. P. Walton plausibly has suggested that Jonas Fay, Thomas Chittenden, and Heman Allen, all members of the Council of Safety and Vermont's agents to Congress, joined with Ira Allen in "compiling" the constitution (Walton, *Records* 1:64, 67–78, 83–84, 201; Proceedings of the Council of Safety, 6 Feb. 1778, Slade, *Vermont State Papers*, 81; Allen, *History of Vermont*, 93).

32. Epigraph from Allen, *History of Vermont*, 102. For contemporary accounts of Burgoyne's invasion, see Burgoyne, *State of the Expedition;* Fonblanque, *Political and Military Episodes;* Stone, *Memoirs of Riedesel;* narrative of Samuel Woodruff in Neilson, *Account of Burgoyne's Campaign*, 249–59; Stone, *Journal of Pausch;* Rogers, *Hadden's Journal*. The attitudes of most historians are revealed in their titles: Huddleston, *Gentleman Johnny Burgoyne: Misadventures of an English Gentleman in the Revolution;* Glover, *General Burgoyne in Canada and America: Scapegoat for a System;* Lewis, *The Man Who Lost America*.

33. Higginbotham, "Military Leadership," and "Daniel Morgan: Guerrilla Fighter."

34. From Capt. Paul Bringham's orderly book, VHS. On the community

of the front line, see Robert Middlekauf, "Why Men Fought in the American Revolution," in Hall, *Saints and Revolutionaries*, 318–31. The numbers of Vermont troops were drawn from Goodrich, *Revolutionary Rolls*. Cornish, N.H., for a time part of Vermont, had a population of 309 in 1775. Over the next eight years 111 residents of that town served with the Continental army, 19 for periods of greater than six months (drawn from Child, *History of Cornish* 1:70–74, 188).

35. Frye Bayley described efforts by prisoners of war to make money from their captivity, most with little success (Bayley, "Reminiscences," 30–33, 76–78). Vermont's involvement in the war was based on local initiative. Col. Timothy Bedel kept 200 men under arms in the Coos country during 1778 and 1779, stockpiled arms for an American invasion of Canada, and built barracks and guardhouses, all at his own expense (Bedel to General Clinton, 6 Jan. 1779, to Schuyler, 11 Jan. 1779, to Gates, 12 Jan. 1779, to Hazen, 8 Feb. 1779, 4 Dec. 1780, *New Hampshire State Papers* 17:310–17, 884–85; Powers, *Historical Sketches of Coos Country*, 190–220). See also Bringham, Orderly Book, VHS; Wells, *History of Barnet*, 300; Everest, *Moses Hazen*, 49.

36. Shy, *People Numerous and Armed*, 177, 217–20; narrative of David Welch, Dann, *Revolution Remembered*, 274–77.

37. Fonblanque, *Life of Burgoyne*, 484; Burgoyne, *State of the Expedition*, 10, 12–19, 96–97, 102, 111–13, 133–36, app.: 13, 21–25, 46; Jones, *History of the Campaign*, 158, 181; Ward, *War of Revolution* 1:402–5; Stone, *Memoirs of Riedesel*, 89–92, 96–108; Stone, *Campaign of Burgoyne*, 275–76; Digby, *British Invasion*, 201, 355; Flick, *Revolution in New York*, 339–40; Anburey, *With Burgoyne*, 122–26, 133–34; Toynbee, *Letters of Walpole* 10:188; Carleton to Germain, 28 Sept., 17 Nov. 1776, CO42/35: 171–77, 213–14, PRO; Lamb, *Memoirs* 1:153; Burns, "Mad Jack M'Alpine"; M'Alpine, *Genuine Narratives*.

38. Burgoyne, *State of the Expedition*, app.: 37. Burgoyne's proclamations inspired numerous satires, including one by William Livingston, the governor of New Jersey. See Stone, *Campaign of Burgoyne*, 413–14, 420–22; Digby, *British Invasion*, 192, 229–33; Allen, *Vindication*, 464; Huddleston, *Burgoyne*, 148–51; *Providence Gazette*, 16 Aug. 1777. One burlesque, sent from "we the reptiles of America" to the "Most Puissant and Sublime General," welcomed his invading army in saving the Americans from their liberties (Flick, *Revolution in New York*, 341–42).

39. Ward, *War of Revolution* 1:407–8; Digby, *British Invasion*, 200–209; Hadden, *Journal*, 54, 82; Lamb, *Memoirs*, 135; Anburey, *With Burgoyne*, 134–43; Samuel Stevens, Journal, VHS; Burgoyne, *State of the Expedition*, app.: 24–31.

40. Burgoyne, *State of the Expedition*, app.: 31–33; Stone, *Memoirs of Riedesel*, 113–19; Anburey, *With Burgoyne*, 143–46; Wilkinson, *Memoirs* 1:186–88;

Digby, *British Invasion,* 209–13; Hadden, *Journal,* 85–86, 92; Journal of Moses Greenleaf, Military Papers, MHS.

41. Wilkinson, *Memoirs* 1:186–89; Hadden, *Journal,* 88, app.: 15; Burgoyne, *State of the Expedition,* app.: 25, 31–34; Lamb, *Memoirs,* 89, 142.

42. Digby, *British Invasion,* 227–28, 233; Hadden, *Journal,* app. 1. Oddly, Burgoyne perceived the disadvantages of the southern route back in London but seems to have forgotten these dangers once in America ("Thoughts for Conducting the War," Burgoyne, *State of the Expedition,* 17, app.: 9). For Burgoyne's contradictions on the causes of the Bennington raid, see Burgoyne, *State of the Expedition,* 18–19, 22, 60–61, 137.

43. Hadden, *Journal,* 91–100, 109; Burgoyne, *State of the Expedition,* app.: 39–40; Digby, *British Invasion,* 215–43; Wilkinson, *Memoirs* 1:192, 200; Sparks, *Correspondence of the Revolution* 1:397–99; narrative of David Holbrook in Dann, *Revolution Remembered,* 88.

44. Hadden, *Journal,* 95–97; Wilkinson, *Memoirs,* app. B.

45. *Journal of the Continental Congress* 8:604, 9:787; Samuel Stevens Journal; Stone, *Campaign of Burgoyne,* 287–88; Allen, *History of Vermont,* 102, 106; *Journal of Provincial Congress* 1:988, 992, 994, 997.

46. Howe to Burgoyne, 17 July 1777, Burgoyne to Carleton, to Harvey, and to Germain, 11, 29 July, 20 Aug. 1777, Burgoyne's instructions to Skene, Baum's orders, Burgoyne, *State of the Expedition,* 51, 76, app.: 38–39, 41–49, 62, 71–76, 101, 137; Allen, *History of Vermont,* 102–3; *Journal of Provincial Congress* 1:1044–45; Stone, *Memoirs of Riedesel,* 127–33, 238–39, 247–48, 252–54; Stone, *Campaign of Burgoyne,* 277–85; Lamb, *Memoirs,* 151; Hadden, *Journal,* 111–17.

47. Coburn, *Centennial History,* 22–31, 42; Dann, *Revolution Remembered,* 88–90; Stone, *Campaign of Burgoyne,* 286–87, 301–2; Allen, *History of Vermont,* 94, 98–99.

48. Coburn, *Centennial History,* 31; Sparks, *Correspondence* 1:397, 423; *Journals of the Continental Congress* 8:656–57. The Vermont Council of Safety specifically ordered Col. Herrick "not to put himself under the command of General Schuyler" (Allen, *History of Vermont,* 97).

49. Canning's narrative, Stone, *Campaign of Burgoyne,* 302; Baum to Burgoyne, 13, 14 Aug. 1777, Burgoyne, *State of the Expedition,* app.: 69–71; Dawson, *Battles of the United States* 1:260.

50. Dawson, *Battles* 1:260; Coburn, *Centennial History,* 40.

51. Dawson, *Battles* 1:260; Lamb, *Memoirs* 1:153; Stone, *Memoirs of Riedesel,* 131; Dann, *Revolution Remembered,* 89–90; Stone, *Campaign of Burgoyne,* 286–97; Digby, *British Invasion,* 248–51.

52. Holbrook narrative, Dann, *Revolution Remembered,* 90–91; Narrative of

Jacob Safford, and Report of General Stark, 13 Aug. 1777, Coburn, *Centennial History*, 56–57, 62–64.

53. Quotes from Balcarras and Money, Burgoyne, *State of the Expedition,* app.: 46, 61. See also ibid., 135–40, 144, 248–49, 259–64; app.: 42–46, 50, 61, 70, 98, 138, 142; Hadden, *Journal,* 118; Dawson, *Battles* 1:260–64; Stone, *Memoirs of Riedesel,* 129–31, 255–58; Anburey, *With Burgoyne,* 164–67; *Journals of the Continental Congress* 9:770; Ward, *War of Revolution* 2: ch. 37.

54. Burgoyne to Germain, 20 Aug. 1777, Burgoyne, *State of the Expedition,* app.: 40, 46; see ibid., also 160.

55. Burgoyne's long delay at Fort Miller is difficult to explain and caused the most anger in Parliament during its investigation. See especially Burgoyne, *State of the Expedition,* 63–64, 76–77, 80–81. For Burgoyne's lame explanation, see ibid., 146–54; for his debilitating feelings of isolation and desertion, see ibid., 22–23, 166; Hadden, *Journal,* 119; Ward, *War of Revolution* 2: ch. 38 and 39; Stone, *Memoirs of Riedesel,* 159–63; Digby, *British Invasion,* 226, 245–48, 255–56, 265–67; Wilkinson, *Memoirs* 1:223–29, 234–38; Allen, *History of Vermont,* 106.

56. Allen, *History of Vermont,* 95–97.

57. Burgoyne, *State of the Expedition,* 26, 60, 73–75, 175, app.: 83–106; Ward, *War of Revolution* 2: ch. 42 and 43; Bowler, *Logistics of the British Army,* 225–30; "Col. Thomas Johnson's Letters and Documents, 1775–1807," VHS *Proceedings* 1926: 87–140; Dann, *Revolution Remembered,* 91–100; Walton, *Records* 3:498; Digby, *British Invasion,* 259–324; Stone, *Campaign of Burgoyne,* 346–52; M'Alpine, *Genuine Narratives,* 22–42; Bayley, "Reminiscences," 46–55; Allen, *History of Vermont,* 103–6.

58. Allen, *Vindication,* 464.

59. Walton, *Records* 1:396–97; *Journals of the Continental Congress* 8:491, 508–13, 9:770; Slade, *Vermont State Papers,* 73–75; Flick, *Revolution in New York,* 77–78, 327.

60. Allen, *Narrative of Allen's Captivity,* 124.

61. Epigraph from Washington to the President of Congress, 12 May 1778, Fitzpatrick, *Writings of Washington* 11:379–80. Allen to Connecticut Assembly, 8 Aug. 1776, Force, *American Archives,* 5th ser., 1:860–61. On Allen's condition and perceptions in the days immediately after his release from captivity, see Allen to Congress, 9 May 1778, Papers of the Continental Congress, LC, 6:35; Allen, *Narrative of Allen's Captivity,* 97, 122–24; Burnett, *Letters of Congress* 3:427; Fitzpatrick, *Writings of Washington* 11:379–81, 415–17; Force, *American Archives,* 5th ser., 1:928–29; Allen to Gates, 28 May 1778, Soldiers of the Revolution Collection, PHS; Hemenway, *Vermont Gazetteer* 1:562; Allen, *Allen Memorial,* 50.

62. Washington to McKay, 11 April 1776, Allen to Connecticut Assembly,

8, 12 Aug. 1776, Force, *Archives,* 4th ser., 5:858, 5th ser., 1:860–61, 928–29; Allen to Washington, 2 Nov. 1776, to Massachusetts Board of War, 19 July 1777, EAP; Moore, *Diary of the Revolution* 1:190.

63. On the events of late 1777, see Thomas Paine, "The American Crisis," in Conway, *Writings of Paine,* vol. 1; Martin and Lender, *A Respectable Army,* ch. 4.

64. Allen, *Narrative of Allen's Captivity,* 94–95; Axtell, "The White Indians of Colonial America," in *European and Indian,* 168–206. The accuracy of Allen's memories have been questioned many times. Yet his two accounts of the Lake Champlain campaign and his captivity (the *Narrative* and *Vindication*) match each other in detail and were published when most of the participants were still alive and able to contradict any falsehoods. Not even Benedict Arnold, still a U.S. officer in good standing, offered any corrections to Allen's relation of the facts. Over the years the publication of other narratives and letters about both the campaign and Allen's captivity have supported his versions of these events. In contrast, Arnold's accounts were full of contradictions and barefaced lies. See, for instance, Arnold to the Massachusetts Committee of Safety, 19 May 1775, Force, *American Archives,* 4th ser., 2:645–46. For documents supportive of Allen's *Narrative,* see Graydon, *Memoirs;* Fitch, *Diary;* John Fell, "Memorandum Book," in Onderdonk, *Revolutionary Incidents,* 219–26; Chittenden, *Ticonderoga;* Force, *American Archives,* 4th ser., 4:836, 871–72.

65. Allen noted the humanity of his captors when he saw it but found it too rarely (Allen, *Narrative of Allen's Captivity,* 37–38, 54–64, 79). See also Dring, *Recollections;* Thatcher, *Military Journal;* Herbert, *Relic of the Revolution;* Stirling, "Prisoners of War"; Stiles, *Letters from Prisons;* Bowman, *Captive Americans,* 20–22. Elias Boudinot, the American commissary general of prisoners, writing years later, gave Allen full credit for drawing his attention to Cunningham, effecting the British captain's transfer, and generally improving the treatment of prisoners at the provost's jail (Boudinot, *Journal,* 14–17). See also Fell, "Memorandum Book," Onderdonk, *Revolutionary Incidents,* 207–10, 224, 245–47; Stirling, "Prisoners of War," 380; Allen, *Narrative of Allen's Captivity,* 79–81.

66. Allen, *Narrative of Allen's Captivity,* 67–68. See also ibid., 97–103; Onderdonk, *Revolutionary Incidents,* 65, 224–25; Boudinot, *Journal,* 14.

67. Allen, *Narrative of Allen's Captivity,* 48–53, 67–73. Allen's entire account is confirmed in all its particulars, including the very contents of the basket he was given by a resident of Cork in an "Extract of a Letter from Cork," January 1776, Force, *American Archives,* 4th ser., 4:836. See also ibid., 6:508; Thatcher, *Military Journal,* 89–91; Onderdonk, *Revolutionary Incidents,* 220–25; Fitch, *Diary,* 185–88; Boudinot, *Journal,* 58–59. On English support of American prisoners of war, see Alexander, "Forton Prison," 378–79; "Diary

of George Thompson," 232–33, 241–42; Anderson, "The Treatment of Prisoners of War," 80–81; "Journal of Samuel Cutler," 187, 397; *Annual Register for 1778,* 78–79. On the American belief that the English people would rise to the defense of liberty, see Maier, *Resistance to Revolution,* ch. 7 and 8.

68. Allen, *Narrative of Allen's Captivity,* 40–42.

69. Ibid., 28–29, 43–44. See also ibid., 65–67; Force, *American Archives,* 4th ser., 3:245–47, 6:508, 5th ser., 1:860–61; Graydon, *Memoirs,* 253; Bowman, *Captive Americans,* ch. 1; Metzger, *The Prisoner in the Revolution,* ch. 1; Fitzpatrick, *Writings of Washington* 6:359.

70. Allen, *Narrative of Allen's Captivity,* 23–24, 42; *Connecticut Courant,* 20 Nov. 1775; Smith, *Struggle for Fourteenth Colony* 1:394.

71. Allen, *Narrative of Allen's Captivity,* 60–61; Force, *American Archives,* 4th ser., 4:314–15, 5th ser., 1:860–61; Allen to Washington, 2 Nov. 1776, EAP; *Connecticut Courant,* 25 Nov. 1776. Col. Archibald Campbell wrote John Adams that Tryon was indeed blocking Allen's exchange (18 Dec. 1777, Taylor, *Papers of John Adams* 5:357–59).

72. Allen, *Narrative of Allen's Captivity,* 62, 65–66.

73. Ibid., 82–83; Johnson to Dartmouth, 12 Oct. 1775, CO5/76:169, PRO. On the dedication of common prisoners of war to the American cause, see Lemisch, "Listen to the 'Inarticulate.' "

74. Allen, *Narrative of Allen's Captivity,* 82, 89–90.

75. Ibid., 119–20.

CHAPTER SEVEN

1. Slade, *Vermont State Papers,* 269; Walton, *Records* 1:120, 261, 263–64; Crockett, *Assembly Journals* 1:22–23.

2. Slade, *Vermont State Papers,* 269; Hemenway, *Vermont Gazetteer* 1:161–62; Pell, *Ethan Allen,* 139–41; Jennings, *Memorials of a Century* 222; Spargo, *Story of David Redding.*

3. Paltsits, *Minutes of Commissioners for Detecting Conspiracies* 1:92, 97–98.

4. Epigraph from Allen, *Vindication,* 464. *Connecticut Courant,* 17 March 1777; Allen, *Some Miscellaneous Remarks,* 379–81; Walton, *Records* 1:379, 381, 383, 390–91; Allen, "Remarks, &c.," *New Hampshire Gazette,* no. 915 (1774), in Allen, *Vindication,* 477–82; the Manchester Covenant of 1775, in Walton, *Records* 2:489–97; Allen, *Brief Narrative.* Ira Allen's state of nature argument bears a striking resemblance to that of the Pittsfield petition of May 1776, which called for a constitutional convention in Massachusetts, and to Rev. Thomas Allen's "Vindication" (1778) of that petition (Taylor, *Western Massachusetts,* 27–28; Hammett, "Revolutionary Ideology in Massachusetts").

5. Jefferson to Randolph, 15 Feb. 1783, Boyd, *Papers of Jefferson* 6:247–

48; Congressional Resolutions, 30 June 1777, 23 May 1780, Ford, *Journals of Congress* 5:508–13, 17:452; Allen and Fay, *Concise Refutation,* 228–29, 232–34.

6. Duane, "State of the Evidence" (1784), 12–13. For similar contradictions, see pp. 30–34, 38–39, 49, 58. For his earlier presentation of the case, see [Duane], *Narrative of the Proceedings* (1773).

7. Cumberland County towns to New York Council of Safety, 26 June 1777, Gale and Thompson, *Official History,* 33–35, 40.

8. Ibid., 40; Remonstrance against Congress, Report of the New York Convention, 20 Jan. 1777, Ten Broeck to President of Congress, 20 Jan. 1777, O'Callaghan, *Documentary History* 4:924–30; Instructions to congressional representatives, 7 April 1777, Livingston et al. to Provincial Congress, 2 July 1777, Duane to New York Council of Safety, 10 July 1777, *Journal of Provincial Congress* 1:869, 998–1000; Force, *American Archives,* 5th ser., 3:1455–56; Allen, *History of Vermont,* 88–90. Gouverneur Morris continually objected to these actions by his state as counterproductive (Morris to the Council of Safety, 21 July 1777, *Journal of Provincial Congress* 1:1011–12).

9. Schuyler to Washington, 17 July 1777, Morris to Van Cortlandt, 21 July 1777, *Journal of Provincial Congress* 1:999, 1005–12.

10. Walton, *Records* 1:397–99.

11. Allen, *Vindication,* 465; Walton, *Records* 1:25, 29–30; Proctor, *Records of Conventions,* 47–48; Force, *American Archives,* 5th ser., 3:503–4; *Journal of Provincial Congress* 1:554, 912–13. Ironically, the New York government was unsuccessful in collecting quitrents anywhere in the state (Cochran, "New York in the Confederation," 45, 87, 105–8, 157–58).

12. Flick, *Revolution in New York,* 77–92, 326–39. Some historians have seen this constitution establishing a weak executive, comparing it to its royal predecessor rather than to the more democratic alternatives (see, for instance, Mason, *Road to Independence,* 239–40). Of more importance, different incomes brought different rights under New York's constitution. Only an estimated 10% of the adult male population could vote for the senate and governor. Many of those who wrote New York's constitution owned land in the disputed northeast. On the conservative nature of this document, see Adams, "The Spirit of Commerce"; Flick, *Revolution in New York,* 83; Klein, "New York Lawyers."

13. Hoisington to Cumberland Committee, n.d., Bayley to New York Council of Safety, 14 June 1777, and to President of New York Convention, 19 Feb. 1777, Walton, *Records* 1:30–31, 368, 373–75; see also ibid., 361–70. On similar shifts of opinion in Charlotte County, see *Journal of Provincial Congress* 1:775–76, 977, 2:465; O'Callaghan, *Documentary History* 4:942.

14. Allen, *Vindication,* 463–65; Allen, *History of Vermont,* 76; Force, *American Archives,* 5th ser., 3:503–4; VHS *Collections* 1:130–31.

15. Slade, *Vermont State Papers,* 287–88; Walton, *Records* 1:425, 2:160,

3:133, 4:118; Wardner, *Birthplace of Vermont*, 391; Town Records of Bennington, Rockingham, Chester, Halifax, Marlboro, Windsor, Guilford, and Brattleboro; VHS *Collections* 2:279; Allen, *History of Vermont*, 108–9; Deming, *Catalogue of Principal Officers*, 17, 19.

16. *Connecticut Courant*, 18 Aug. 1777; Allen, *Vindication*, 465; Walton, *Records* 1:130–39, 143–229; Slade, *Vermont State Papers*, 80; Allen, *History of Vermont*, 94–97.

17. On the influence of the early committees of safety on constitutionalism in New York and New Hampshire, see Adams, *First Constitutions*, 43–44; Becker, *Political Parties*, 211; Daniell, *Experiment in Republicanism*, ch. 5.

18. Allen, *Some Miscellaneous Remarks*, 141. Daniel Chipman held the opposite view, that the framers of the Vermont Constitution had no concept of fundamental law, placing legislation above constitutionality (*Memoir of Chittenden*, 100–113). See also Walton, *Records* 1:425, 3:133; VHS *Collections* 1:64–65. The presence of the Council of Censors calls Chipman's opinion into question.

19. See Crockett, *Assembly Journals;* Walton, *Records*, vols. 1 and 2. In its first decade, the legislature largely deferred to the governor's council, requesting that it write the first treasury bill, decide on adjournment, and set the place and time for the assembly's next sitting (Crockett, *Assembly Journals* 1:16–18, 2:126).

20. Allen, *Vindication*, 446, 452–53; Bradley, *Vermont's Appeal*, 214; Ira Allen, *To the Inhabitants*, 487.

21. Force, *American Archives*, 5th ser., 3:525, 590–91, 947–48, 1237; Allen, *Proceedings of the Convention*, 491–97; Goodrich, *Rolls of Soldiers*.

22. Allen's bills, August, October 1779, EAP; Clinton, *Public Papers* 5:175; Walton, *Records* 1:305; Crockett, *Assembly Journals* 1:56; Burlington Land Records, 1:607.

23. Lansing to Schuyler, 26 July 1780, VHS; Hemenway, *Vermont Gazetteer* 1:240. Another indication of Allen's impact is the number of close friends, such as Jonas Fay and Edward Vail, who named their sons Ethan Allen.

24. Slade, *Vermont State Papers*, 293–94; Walton, *Records* 1:15–30, 136, 248–49; Crockett, *Assembly Journals* 1:53, 56, 91; Pemberton, "Justus Sherwood," 313–14. As both Ethan and Ira Allen pointed out, the Loyalists had built no structures through which they could defend Britain except the state, a state which the overwhelming majority of their neighbors rejected and invalidated (Allen, *Some Miscellaneous Remarks*, 378–79; Ethan Allen, *Vindication*, 454–55).

25. Bayley, "An Address on Jacob Bayley"; Wells, *History of Newbury*, 96–100.

26. Chipman, *Life of Chipman*, ch. 1, 3; Kalinoski, "Sequestration, Confiscation, and the 'Tory,'" 237; Williams, *History of Vermont*, ch. 9–11; Hayes, *History of Rockingham*, 205; Wardner, *Birthplace of Vermont*, 242, 445; Wells,

History of Newbury, 79, 86, 657; E. Payne to R. Sherman, 28 Oct. 1778, Payne Papers, Dartmouth College Library; *Vermont Gazette,* 18, 25 Sept., 2 Oct. 1783.

27. *Vermont Gazette,* 28 Aug. 1786, 2 Nov. 1789, 18 Oct. 1790; *Vermont Journal,* 4 Sept., 18, 25 Nov. 1786; Austin, "Vermont Politics in the 1780's"; Hemenway, *Historical Gazetteer* 3:1154–59; Knowlton to Haldimand, 10 Jan. 1783, B, 178:22, PAC. For a contrary view, see Samuel B. Hand and P. Jeffrey Potash, "Nathaniel Chipman: Vermont's Forgotten Founder," in Sherman, *A More Perfect Union,* 52–78; Slade, *Vermont State Papers,* 511–16, 531–44; Wilbur, *Ira Allen* 1:493–96.

28. Walton, *Records* 1:134–35; *Journals of the Provincial Congress* 1:826.

29. Crockett, *Assembly Journals* 1:26, 29; Allen, *History of Vermont,* 253; Allen to Payne, 11 July 1778, Minutes of Committee to deal with enemies of the state, 23 April, 16, 25 June 1778, EAP; Clinton, *Public Papers* 3:552–53; Fitzpatrick, *Writings of Washington* 12:194–95, 197, 217n; Allen to Gates, 15 June 1778, James Duane Papers, NYHS.

30. Allen, *History of Vermont,* 111. Connecticut, like Vermont, called up its militia every year during the Revolution. That state suffered inflation, hoarding, high taxes, price controls, and impressment, all of which undermined popular support of the Revolution and called the very legitimacy of the state's government into question (Buel, *Dear Liberty*). Most of Vermont's income between 1777 and 1786 came from land sales: £190,433 from the sale of confiscated lands; £66,815 from the sale of land grants; and £44,948 from taxes (these are assigned values, as payments were generally made in wheat and notes). In comparison, in 1794 £11,081 of the state's total receipts of £12,920 came from taxes (VHS *Proceedings* 2:466; Williams, *Public Papers of Chittenden,* 26–28, 138–41, 162–65, 177, 196; Walton, *Records* 1:61, 136, 304, 2:64, 76; Allen, *History of Vermont,* 232; *Vermont Gazette,* 19 June 1783; Crockett, *Assembly Journals* 1:103; Nye, *Sequestration,* 54, 209–12, 267).

31. Nye, *Sequestration,* 15–17, 37–39; Williamson, *Vermont in Quandary,* 79–84; Walton, *Records* 1:283–87, 518–25, 2:62–63; Slade, *Vermont State Papers,* 272, 305–12; Crockett, *Assembly Journals* 1:107–9; Stilwell, *Migration from Vermont,* 79.

32. Slade, *Vermont State Papers,* 268–75; Allen to Wheelock, 14 June 1778, MSS, Dartmouth College Library; Allen to Laurens, 17 June 1778, U.S. Revolutionary War Papers, LC; Ford, *Journals of Continental Congress* 11:676; Dorset Town Records, 17 June 1778; Allen's account to the state, July 1782, EAP; Transcripts of Loyalist Claims, 2:266–67, 11:25–52, 20:511; 21:53–55, 57, 44:397, 607–31, 46:383–84, NYPL. Sherwood did not lose all his land in Vermont, thanks to the personal intervention of his friend Ethan Allen (Pemberton, "Justus Sherwood," 313–14).

33. Walton, *Records* 1:196. See also ibid., 1:150–56, 164, 188–89, 197–

98, 208, 226, 281, 285; Nye, *Sequestration*, 67–69; Crockett, *Assembly Journals* 1:25, 61–62; Wells, *Newbury*, 119, 736; Porter to Haldimand, 5 March 1784, B, 75–2: 38, PAC; Fisher, "Loyalists in Strafford"; Castleton Town Records, 1784; Roberts, "An Unknown Vermonter"; Cruikshank, "Adventures of Roger Stevens"; Caverly, *History of Pittsford*, 175; Hemenway, *Historical Gazetteer* 3:505–6; Bellesiles, "Establishment of Legal Structures."

34. Butler to J. Iredell, 5 April 1782, A. Lee to J. Warren, 8 April 1782, Burnett, *Letters of the Members of Congress* 6:326–27; Woodard, *Town Proprietors*, 114–16, 123, 130–32; Hammond, *Documents Relating to Towns*, 765–66; VHS *Collections* 2:324–26; Clinton, *Public Papers* 6:741–45. Among the various representatives Connecticut sent to Congress, eleven held title to Vermont lands: Andrew Adams, Eliphalet Dyer, Pierrepont Edwards, Benjamin and Samuel Huntington, William S. Johnson, Stephen M. Mitchell, William Pitkin, Roger Sherman, Joseph Spencer, and Oliver Wolcott (Gerlach, "Connecticut, Congress, and Independence," 189; Collier, "Roger Sherman").

35. Williams, *Chittenden Papers*, 162, 177–79, 186; Nye, *Sequestration;* Kalinoski, "Sequestration." Towns welcomed this opportunity, using these seized lands as a reserve source of capital through the rest of the 1780s. See, for example, Somerset Deeds 1:24–27; Shaftsbury Town Records, 1783–86.

36. Hall, *Eastern Vermont*, 720; Soule, *Laws of Vermont, 1777–1780*, 25–26, 29; Crockett, *Assembly Journals* 1:10, 17, 36–38, 53, 56, 69, 72, 94; Nye, *Sequestration;* Windham County Court Records; Walton, *Records* 1:304, 8:298–300; *Minutes of Commissioners for Detecting Conspiracies* 1:312–13, 343–44, 2:453, 478, 482; VHS *Proceedings* 1923–25: 134–38; Maguire, "British Secret Service," 158–60.

37. Crockett, *Assembly Journals* 1:107–9, 144; Dewart, *Charters Granted by Vermont*, 108–11, 309. On the enormous confusion of land grants in early Vermont, see McCarty, "Boundary Controversy."

38. Allen, *History of Vermont*, 112; Ethan Allen to the General Assembly, 26 Oct. 1779, VHS; *Connecticut Courant*, 22 June 1779; Bayley, "Reminiscences"; VHS *Collections* 2:324–26; Woodard, *Town Proprietors*, 123; Fitch, *Diary*, 259–60; Manuscript State Papers, vol. 46, Petitions, VSA; Capt. Paul Bringham, Orderly Book, VHS; Kalinoski, "Sequestration," 241; Aldrich and Holmes, *History of Windsor County*, 367; Crockett, *Assembly Journals* 3:99; Lynd, *Class Conflict*, 33–34; Countryman, "Consolidating Power," 667–69.

39. Freemen v. Williams, Supreme Court Records; Nye, *Sequestration*, 264.

40. Nye, *Sequestration*, 59; Misc. MSS, no. 3608, New York State Library.

41. John Mebus, 1779, Transcripts of Loyalist Claims, 27:386–87, NYPL.

42. Epigraph from Allen, *History*, 108. Allen, *Brief Narrative*, 134. See also Clifford K. Shipton, "The Locus of Authority in Colonial Massachusetts,"

in Billias, *Law and Authority*, 136–48; Nelson, *Dispute and Conflict Resolution;* Konig, *Law and Society;* Julius Goebel, Jr., "King's Law and Local Custom in 17th Century New England," in Flaherty, *Essays in Early American Law,* 83–120; Allen, *In English Ways.*

43. Colden, *Letters and Papers* 56:71. See also ibid., 68–78, 68:205–6; Colden, *Letter Books* 9:421–25, 444–45, 455, 462, 10:70; *Report of an Action;* "Sentinel" series, *New York Gazette,* 28 Feb.–18 July 1765; Klein, *Politics of Diversity,* 166–72; Julius Goebel, Jr., "The Courts and the Law in Colonial New York," in Flick, *History of New York* 3:3–43; Miller, *Case for Liberty,* ch. 8; Botein, *Early American Law,* 26–35; Smith, *Appeals to the Privy Council,* 390–412.

44. In fact, no lawyer sat in the first Vermont legislature, which owned only a single lawbook to guide its deliberations: a Connecticut statute book (Walton, "The First Legislature," 41).

45. On the expropriation of Levi Allen's Vermont lands, see Bellesiles, "Anticipating America," 86–89; Ethan and Ira Allen v. Levi Allen, 1779, Rutland Court Records, 98, and Vermont Superior Court Records, 1:4; *Connecticut Courant,* 15 Dec. 1778. Levi Allen was not the only Loyalist dispossessed by his own family. Members of Roger Stevens's family brought charges against him as a Loyalist, and his own father signed the liquidation order for his estate (Nye, *Sequestration,* 257, 275; Cruikshank, "Adventures of Roger Stevens," 11–12).

46. Allen, *Vindication,* 479, 515–17; Walton, *Records* 1:338–39, 356; VHS *Collections* 1:5–6; Allen, *History of Vermont,* 345–47; Hall, *History of Vermont,* 127, 130; O'Callaghan, *Documentary History* 4:523, 712, 762–64, 848–54, 893–903, 914–16; Pell, *Ethan Allen,* 35, 65; Allen to town of Durham, November 1773, Emmett Papers, NYPL.

47. Jacob to Stiles, 7 July 1780, Misc. Documents, Manuscript State Papers, 17:169, VSA; Deming, *Catalogue of Principal Officers;* Fish, "Vermont Bench and Bar," in Crockett, *Green Mountain State* 5:59; *Vermont Gazette,* 7 Feb. 1784, 28 Aug. 1786; Matthew Lyon, "Twelve Reasons," *Rutland Farmer's Library,* 19 Aug. 1794. Most towns did not have lawyers until the turn of the century. For instance, in its first forty years Pittsford enjoyed the services of an attorney for just four months (Gaverly, *History of Pittsford,* 602–3). On the New England tradition of lay judges and the lack of concern for the separation of the branches of government, see Haskins, "Lay Judges."

48. Old Supreme Court Files, Sept. 1784; Bennington County Court Dockets, 1:2; Fish, "Vermont Bench and Bar," in Crockett, *Green Mountain State* 5:364. Vermonters resorted to legal technicalities when it served their purposes. See, for instance, Scott v. Johnston, 1784, Old Superior Court Files.

49. Fish, "Vermont Bench and Bar," in Crockett, *Green Mountain State*

5:77–78; Old Superior Court Files, 2: n.p., September 1784; Allen, *Reason,* 190–91. On the continuing American suspicion of lawyers, see Miller, *Life of the Mind,* 99–116; Bloomfield, *American Lawyers,* 32–58.

50. On the frontier economy of northern New England, see Bidwell and Falconer, *History of Agriculture;* Clark, "Household Economy"; Merrill, "Cash Is Good to Eat"; Shammas, "How Self-Sufficient?"

51. Treasurer's Records, VSA; Ira Allen's Accounts, VHS. On this economic structure, see Clark, *Roots of Rural Capitalism.*

52. Brissot, *New Travels,* 269.

53. I.e., Adams v. Fuller, 1780, Burnham v. Willson, 1782, Sargant v. Willson, 1782, Richardson v. Fletcher, Barney v. Pratt, 1783, Windham County Court Records.

54. Bird v. Allen, 1783, Bennington County Court Records.

55. I.e., Grenell v. Williams, 1777–79, Knapp v. Field, 1784, Windham County Court Records; Somerset Deeds, 1:47–48. See also Smith v. Smith, 1776, Swan v. Stearn, 1781, Wood v. Chilzon, Spencer v. Nichols, and Priest v. Hitchcock, 1783, Windham County Court Records; Freemen v. Gardiner, Ethan and Ira Allen v. Levi Allen, 1779, Superior Court Records, 20, 31; Harmon v. Loggan, 1781, Old Supreme Court Files, 1: n.p.; Foot v. Bennet, 1779, Bennington County Court Records and Old Supreme Court Files.

56. See, for instance, Freemen v. Blakeley (failure to warn town of danger), 1781, Freemen v. Matthews ("tumultous carriage"), 1779, Freemen v. Willoughby (failure to attend town meetings), 1780, Freemen v. Porter (bigamy), 1781, Superior Court Records, 22, 51, 61, 64, 89; Freeman v. Eastman (selling strong liquor without approval), 1781, Bennington County Court records, 2: n.p.; Freemen v. Root (disrupting town meetings), 1782, Windham County Court Records; Freemen v. Bink (profanity), 1783, Freemen v. Shepardson (lying), 1784, in Old Supreme Court Files; Freemen v. Reed, Lovell, and Evans (insulting conduct), and Windsor County v. Stone (scandalous words), 1779, Old Supreme Court Files and Superior Court Records; and the case of the Quakers Samuel Sleeper and Benoni Wright in Hall, *Eastern Vermont,* 125. See Appendix C.

57. Freemen v. Smith, 1781, Smith v. Smith, 1776, 1781, Windham County Court Records; Hall, *Eastern Vermont,* 703; *Journal of Provincial Congress* 1:82, 199, 228, 3:122, 420–21, 431.

58. See Appendixes C and D.

59. David Brydie v. Nehemiah French, 1782, Strong, Justice Records, Wilbur Collection. On the smallness of lawsuits, see, for example, Ethan and Ira Allen v. Tupper and E. and I. Allen v. John Pudney, Salisbury Justice Records, each of which involved a debt of £1.

60. Nelson, *Americanization of Common Law,* 77–88; Nelson, "The Ameri-

can Revolution and the Emergence of Modern Doctrines"; John P. Reid, "The Irrelevance of the Declaration," in Hartog, *Law in the American Revolution.*

61. In the political conflicts of the late eighteenth and early nineteenth centuries, support for an independent judiciary was seen as distrust of democracy and popular rule. An independent judiciary operated as a "guardian class," to employ the Federalist phrase (Ellis, *Jeffersonian Crisis,* 111–22; Miller, *Life of the Mind,* 105–16, 239–54; Thomas, "*The Pioneers,* or the Sources of American Legal History"; Livermore, *Twilight of Federalism;* Horton, *James Kent;* Chipman, *Reports of Cases;* Horwitz, *Transformation of American Law*).

62. Williams, *Papers of Chittenden,* 162, 177–79, 186; Nye, *Sequestration;* Hall, *Eastern Vermont,* 720; Audit Office Transcripts, ser. 12, 24:305, PAC; Windham County Court Records; Kalinoski, "Sequestration," 241; Aldrich and Holmes, *History of Windsor County,* 367; Crockett, *Assembly Journals* 1:99.

63. New York's Governor Clinton tried to get first troops and then artillery from Washington (O'Callaghan, *Documentary History* 4:975–76). Allen noted that this step was necessary as "their own militia seem not inclined to undertake" the task (Allen, *Vindication,* 462). See also Cumberland Committee to Clinton, 8 June 1779, George Clinton Papers, 8: doc. 2394, New York State Library; O'Callaghan, *Documentary History* 4:875–77, 957–60, 964–67, 981–95, 1010–14; *Colden Papers* 7:280–81; Countryman, *A People in Revolution,* ch. 2; Smith, *Historical Memoirs* 1:221; Becker, *Political Parties,* 255–65; Onuf, *Origins of the Federal Republic,* 103–25.

64. Walton, *Records* 1:94, 442–43, 528, 2:169–92; Allen, *Vindication,* 459; Allen, *History of Vermont,* 405; Slade, *Vermont State Papers,* 556–57; Kettner, *American Citizenship.*

65. Windham County Court Records, vol. 2; Windham County Court Files, 1782; Bennington County Court Records, 1782; Rutland County Court Records, 1782; Strong, Justice Records. Older accounts of the Vermont government have argued that the Allen faction lacked popular support and maintained its power through coercion and deception. While the Allens certainly were not strangers to such tactics, it is apparent that their use of the courts won them substantial support within a democratic system. The Allens combined intimidation and political theater with an effective legal structure to gain adherents. For the opposite view, see, especially, Williamson, *Vermont in Quandary,* 68–164; and more recently, Samuel B. Hand and P. Jeffrey Potash, "Nathaniel Chipman: Vermont's Forgotten Founder," in Sherman, *A More Perfect Union,* 52–78.

66. I.e., Zuckerman, *Peaceable Kingdom,* 88–94; Grant, *Kent,* ch. 5; Boorstin, *The Americans,* 196–98.

67. Countryman, *A People in Revolution,* 195–220; Kammen, *Colonial New York,* 364–69, 373–75.

68. See, for instance, Cross and Hand, *English Legal System;* Llewellyn, *Common Law Tradition;* Joseph Smith, "New Light on the Doctrine of Judicial Precedent in Early America," in Hazard and Wagner, *Legal Thought in the United States,* 9–39; Allen, *In English Ways;* Reid, *Law for the Elephant.* One notable exception is Dykstra, *Cattle Towns.*

69. Allen, *Vindication,* 512–17; O'Callaghan, *Documentary History,* 4:861; John P. Reid, "The Irrelevance of the Declaration," in Hartog, *Law in the American Revolution,* 46–89; Reid, "In a Defensive Rage"; Isaac, *Transformation of Virginia,* 93–94.

70. Epigraph from Allen, *Vindication,* 460. Ibid., 462.

71. Hall, *Eastern Vermont,* 756. Towns usually identified as pro–New York were fairly evenly divided. Guilford reported 53 votes for New York and refused to give the number supporting Vermont, only noting that it was "not so many." In Halifax the vote was New York 63, Vermont 36, neutral 20. Wilmington, which should have reported twice as many votes as Halifax, came in with 12 for New York, 15 for Vermont, and 8 neutral, indicating that most freemen failed to participate. Westminster, Springfield, and Weathersfield were all equally divided, reporting 40, 20, and 12 each, respectively. One-third of New York's votes came from Brattleboro, which reported 165 for New York, no neutrals, and only one vote for Vermont (Town Records of Brattleboro; Wilbur, *Ira Allen* 2:484–91).

72. Clinton to Fitch, 7 July 1778, quoted in Allen, *History of Vermont,* 123; O'Callaghan, *Documentary History* 4:960–64; Hall, *Eastern Vermont,* 332–62; Clinton, *Public Papers* 5:54–57, 59–61, 64–65.

73. Allen, *History of Vermont,* 129.

74. O'Callaghan, *Documentary History* 4:965–66; Walton, *Records* 1:338, 519–25; Affidavit of Charles Phelps, Stevens Collection, 2:105–9, VSA; Chittenden to Jay, 5 Aug. 1779, Hall, *Eastern Vermont,* 362–63; Windham County Court Records, 1779; Allen, *History of Vermont,* 126–29; Gale and Thompson, *History of Guilford,* 46–47.

75. Allen, *History of Vermont,* 129; Walton, *Records* 1:300, 519; Hall, *Eastern Vermont,* 339.

76. Allen, *History of Vermont,* 129.

77. Supreme Court Records. See also Slade, *Vermont State Papers,* 305–12; O'Callaghan, *Documentary History* 4:957–66; Hall, *Eastern Vermont,* 332–45; Hall, *History of Vermont,* 298–303, 307–9, 442–43, 518–25; Gale and Thompson, *History of Guilford,* 49–50.

78. Clinton *Public Papers* 5:63–65; O'Callaghan, *Documentary History* 4:957–60, 975–76, 981–87; Allen, *Vindication,* 462.

79. Soule, *Laws of Vermont,* 176–77; Crockett, *Assembly Journals* 1:69–71; Walton, *Records* 1:302–3.

80. Slade, *Vermont State Papers*, 389–90; Walton, *Records* 1:442–43; Clinton, *Public Papers* 4:696–700, 815, 5:172; Duane, "State of the Evidence," 33, 49, 58.

81. For instance, all three of Cumberland County's representatives in the New York assembly—Micah Townshend, John Sessions, and Elkanah Day—whom Allen arrested in 1779 held positions in the Vermont government by 1783 (Clinton, *Public Papers* 5:67–68, 175; Allen, *Vindication*, 462).

82. Allen, *History of Vermont*, 127. See also Allen to Benjamin Bellows, quoted in Hall, *Eastern Vermont*, 345.

83. Allen, *Vindication*, 456, 462–64; Allen, *Andimadversory Address*.

84. Crockett, *Assembly Journals* 1:91, 127–28; Pemberton, "Justus Sherwood," 313–14; Walton, *Records* 1:15–30, 61, 134–36, 283, 287, 518–25, 2:62–63; Kalinoski, "Sequestration, Confiscation, and the 'Tory,'" 237; Williams, *History of Vermont*, 210–310; Hayes, *History of Rockingham*, 205; Wardner, *Birthplace of Vermont*, 242, 445; Wells, *History of Newbury*, 79, 86, 657; *Journal of Provincial Congress* 1:826; Nye, *Sequestration*, 15–17, 37–39, 54; Williams, *Public Papers of Chittenden*, 162–65, 177, 196; Williamson, *Vermont in Quandary*, 79–84; Slade, *Vermont State Papers*, 272, 305–12.

85. Higginbotham, *War and Society*, 119.

CHAPTER EIGHT

1. Allen to Caughnawagas, 24 May 1775, to Lee, 21 May 1775, to Dyer and Deane, 3 July 1775, EAP; Allen to Continental Congress, 29 May 1775, Force, *American Archives*, 4th ser., 2:713–14, 732–34; Levi Allen, Autobiography, LAP.

2. Townshend to ?, 13 June 1779, Townshend Papers, boxed with Windham County Court Records; Levi Allen, Autobiography, LAP; Kelsay, *Joseph Brant;* Wallace, *Death and Rebirth of the Seneca*.

3. Epigraph from Walton, *Records* 2:326. In the early 1780s Ira Allen issued £21,155 worth of bills of credit which gained broad credibility as legal tender. After 1785 Vermont minted copper coins which circulated widely (Edmund F. Slater, "The Vermont Coinage," VHS *Collections* 1:289–318).

4. Manchester Land Records, 1:8.

5. Chittenden to Stevens, 17 June 1779, to Pearl, 19 June 1779, Commissioners' Report, 23 March 1779, Fassett's bill, 19 June 1780, Smith's bill, July 1781, Allen's bill, 12 Aug. 1784, Nicholson's bill, 11 July, 14 Aug. 1778, Misc. Documents, Manuscript State Papers, 8:140–41, 256–57, 10:64, 37:58, VSA; Crockett, *Assembly Journals* 2:91.

6. Ira Allen to Elderkin, 1780, Misc. Documents, Manuscript State Papers, 8:256–57, VSA. See also *Vermont Gazette*, 19 June 1782.

7. Slade, *Vermont State Papers,* 396. See also ibid., 295, 424, 440, 511–16, 531–44; Williams, *Chittenden Papers,* 364–65.

8. The only bill rejected concerned the regulation of highways (Crockett, *Assembly Journals* 1:9). See also ibid., 91–97; Walton, *Records* 2:14.

9. Hammond, *Documents,* 760–64; Belknap, *History of New Hampshire* 2:338; *Connecticut Courant,* 17 March 1777; Saunderson, *History of Charlestown,* ch. 7–8; Wardner, *Birthplace of Vermont,* 142, 282–83, 455–58, 465–74; Town Records of Windsor, Brattleboro, and Guilford for 1778; Walton, *Records* 1:427.

10. Bouton, *Miscellaneous Documents,* 239–40. On the exclusion of the western towns from the government of both colonial and revolutionary New Hampshire, see ibid., 126–27; Wentworth to Shelburne, 3 June 1767, Wentworth Transcripts, NHHS; Letteiri, "New Hampshire Committees of Safety," 253–55; Upton, *Revolutionary New Hampshire,* ch. 13–14; Turner, *The Ninth State,* ch. 2; Daniell, *Experiment in Republicanism,* 145–62; Saunderson, *Charlestown,* ch. 8; Chase, *History of Dartmouth College* 1: ch. 7.

11. Hammond, *Documents,* 760–65; Crockett, *Assembly Journals* 1:5, 9, 24; Belknap, *History* 2:339–41; Allen, *History of Vermont,* 112–14. On Vermont's flexibility toward the Connecticut River towns, see Walton, *Records* 1:243–44, 264–65; Burnett, *Letters of Members of Congress* 3:423.

12. Walton, *Records* 1:413–14.

13. Ibid., 1:415–17, 429; Crockett, *Assembly Journals* 1:35–37; Allen, *History of Vermont,* 115; Belknap, *History of New Hampshire* 2:342.

14. Clinton, *Public Papers* 4:100, 5:17–19; *Journals of Congress* 12:947; Ethan Allen's bill, 1778, EAP; Burnett, *Letters* 3:427.

15. Walton, *Records* 1:415–16; Ethan Allen's appendix to Ira Allen, *Vindication of the Assembly,* 47–48; Ira Allen, ibid., 23, 38–43; Ethan Allen's report to the assembly 10 Oct. 1778, EAP. Individuals who were not members of the assembly continued to served on committees until 1791.

16. Walton, *Records* 1:416–26, 430–33; Crockett, *Assembly Journals* 1:33–34, 42, 45–46, 51–53; Slade, *Vermont State Papers,* 96–97, 285; Allen, *History of Vermont,* 116–18; Belknap, *History of New Hampshire* 2:344.

17. Walton, *Records* 1:426–27, 431–32; Belknap, *History of New Hampshire* 2:342; VHS *Proceedings* 1 (1930): 184–85.

18. Lincklaen, *Travels,* 82, 87–88; Crockett, *Assembly Journals* 1:48; Allen's petition, 22 Oct. 1778, EAP.

19. Clinton, *Public Papers* 5:63–65; *Journals of Congress* 14:741.

20. Clinton, *Public Papers* 4:100; Allen's account of trip to Philadelphia, November 1778, EAP; Ethan Allen's appendix to Ira Allen, *Vindication of the Assembly,* 47–48; Burnett, *Letters* 3:513–14; Walton, *Records* 2:170–74.

21. O'Callaghan, *Documentary History* 4:992–95.

22. Crockett, *Assembly Journals* 1:51–56; Allen's petition, 10 Feb. 1779, EAP; Walton, *Records* 1:290, 431–36, 2:45–49; Allen, *History of Vermont,* 118–23, 132; Belknap, *History of New Hampshire* 2:343; Ira Allen to Inhabitants of Vermont, 13 July 1779, Wilbur, *Ira Allen* 2:484–91; Allen, "Defence of Vermont in Uniting with portions of New York and New Hampshire," 1782, EAP, 359; Allen, *Vindication of the Assembly,* 459; O'Callaghan, *Documentary History* 4:964–67, 987–92, 1010–14. The "Defence of Vermont" appears to be a rough draft of Allen, *Present State of the Controversy.* As there are substantial differences and as Allen circulated his drafts widely, I have treated them as separate works.

23. Allen, *History of Vermont,* 134; Slade, *Vermont State Papers,* 556–57; Walton, *Records* 1:442–43. Ira Allen also passed out copies of Ethan's *Vindication* to members of the Assemblies of New Jersey, Maryland, Delaware, and Pennsylvania, as well as members of Congress (Ira Allen, memo, November 1779, IAP).

24. Walton, *Records* 1:524.

25. Allen, *History of Vermont,* 123; Walton, *Records* 2:169; *Journals of Congress* 14:794; Crockett, *Assembly Journals* 1:84–86. Clinton understood Allen's tactics, as he revealed in a discouraged letter to John Jay: "It is clearly the Interest of the Revolters to procrastinate, as while they continue to exercise the Powers of Govern't they are gain'g Strength & Stability at our Expence" (Clinton, *Public Papers* 5:93).

26. Epigraph from Crowfoot to Sherwood, 1781, B, 160:182, PAC. Washington proposed invasions of Canada in 1777, 1778, 1781, and 1782, while other officers, primarily Lafayette, favored invasions in 1779 and 1780. France consistently opposed these efforts (Smith, *Our Struggle* 2: ch. 36–39).

27. Ira Allen, Treasurer's Account, 14, 21 Feb., 1 March 1780, Manuscript State Papers, VSA; Walton, *Records* 2:22, 33; Crockett, *Assembly Journals* 1:102–4, 122.

28. Hall, *Eastern Vermont,* 383–99; Thompson, *History of Vermont,* pt. 2:68–69; Steele, *The Indian Captive;* Anderson, "Jonathan Carpenter," 88–89; Williams, *History of Vermont,* pt. 2:235–42. On the general fear of Indian raids, see Underwood, "Indian and Tory Raids"; Cruikshank, "The Adventures of Roger Stevens."

29. Walton, *Records* 1:295–96, 2:28–31, 60; Allen, "Defence of Vermont," 1782, Allen to Towner, 26 March 1780, EAP; Brandon Town Records, vol. 1; Crockett, *Assembly Journals* 1:122, 138, 142–44; *Vermont Gazette,* 11 Sept. 1783.

30. Germain to Clinton, 27 Sept. 1779, Papers of Sir Henry Clinton, Clements Library; VHS *Collections* 2:93; Whitson Affidavit, George Wash-

ington Papers, LC; Walton, *Records* 2:405–6. In general, see Ira D. Gruber, "British Strategy: The Theory and Practice of Eighteenth-Century Warfare," in Higginbotham, *Reconsiderations,* 14–31.

31. Sherwood to Powell, 12 Aug. 1780, Haldimand to Clinton, 13 Aug. 1780, Marsh to Haldimand, 10 Oct. 1780, Sherwood to Matthews, 11 May 1781, B, 161:107–10, 150–52, 47:85, 176:78, PAC; Walton, *Records* 2:397.

32. Lansing to Schuyler, 26 July 1780, VHS; Fitzpatrick, *Writings of Washington* 20:304–6; VHS *Collections* 2:76–78. The treasurer's records reveal that Allen was indeed in Connecticut buying powder in May (Manuscript State Papers, VSA). Interestingly, the British were also debating whether they should kidnap Ethan Allen (E. Jessup to Haldimand, 8 Aug. 1780, Sherwood to Powell, 24 Aug. 1780, B, 161:306–7, 182:245–47, PAC).

33. Clinton, *Public Papers* 6:39–43; Walton, *Records* 2:35–36, 39, 397–98; VHS *Collections* 2:32–33; Allen, *History of Vermont,* 150. At this same time New York and New Hampshire discussed dividing Vermont along the Green Mountains, and Washington withdrew Warner's regiment from the northern frontier (Allen and Fay, *Concise Refutation,* 223; Hall, *History of Vermont,* 272, 307–9, 415; Walton, *Records* 2:224n).

34. Allen to Washington, 12 Aug. 1780, PHS; Fitzpatrick, *Writings of Washington* 19:473–75; VHS *Collections* 2:91–92.

35. Fitzpatrick, *Writings of Washington* 19:475–76; Allen's bill, September 1780, EAP; Justus Sherwood, "Journal," 103–6.

36. Clinton, *Public Papers* 6:305–7, 351–56, 358; VHS *Collections* 2:51, 66, 76.

37. VHS *Collections* 2:51; Clinton, *Public Papers* 6:358.

38. VHS *Collections* 2:70–71; Sherwood, "Journal," 102–6.

39. VHS *Collections* 2:87–91; Sherwood, "Journal," 218–20; Clinton to Gloucester, 14 Dec. 1780, Papers of Sir Henry Clinton; Clinton to Cornwallis, 5 March 1781, quoted in Wilbur, *Ira Allen* 1:204; Clinton to Germain, 25 Jan. 1781, Germain to Clinton, 2 May 1781, CO5/101:114, 311, PRO.

40. VHS *Collections* 2:71.

41. Ethan's cousin Major Ebenezer Allen wrote Webster that he could not believe that the British would adhere to the cartel and feared that "the enemy has out-generaled Ethan." Major Allen soon realized, much to his surprise, that cousin Ethan had actually succeeded (VHS *Collections* 2:73; Ethan Allen to Carleton, 4 Nov. 1780, B, 175:61, PAC; Clinton, *Public Papers* 6:364–65; Crockett, *Assembly Journals* 1:142–44).

42. Sherwood, "Journal," 218–19; Crockett, *Assembly Journals* 1:138, 145–46; Allen to Carleton, 4 Nov. 1780, B, 175:61, PAC; VHS *Collections* 2:72; Allen, *History of Vermont,* 151–53.

43. Crockett, *Assembly Journals* 1:170–71; Allen, *History of Vermont,* 155.

44. Clinton, *Public Papers* 6:890–91; VHS *Collections* 2:131; Fitzpatrick, *Writings of Washington* 22:81–82; J. McKenstry to Schuyler, 5 Aug. 1781, Schuyler Papers, NYPL.

45. Schuyler to Washington, 24 May 1780, EAP; VHS *Collections* 2:84; Allen to Carleton, 4 Nov. 1780, Carleton to Allen, 15 Nov. 1780, B, 133:175, PAC; Allen, *History of Vermont,* 153.

46. VHS *Collections* 2:32–33, 83–85; Walton, *Records* 2:175–76; Wilbur, *Ira Allen* 2:488–89.

47. VHS *Collections* 2:86–87, 91–92, 275–76.

48. Ibid., 2:82; Smith to Schuyler, 8 May 1780, included in letter from Schuyler to Washington, 24 May 1780, EAP.

49. Sherwood, "Journal," 220; Beckwith to Clinton, 13 Feb. 1781, and Clinton manuscript 9C-128, Papers of Sir Henry Clinton; VHS *Collections* 2:81–82.

50. Clinton, *Public Papers* 6:777; VHS *Collections* 2:104–5. Washington employed a double agent, Capt. David Gray, who had been with Allen at Ticonderoga and in Canada to watch events in Vermont. In June 1781 Gray exaggerated Allen's dealings with British to Sir Henry Clinton, raising the British commander's hopes and keeping him in New York instead of moving South to aid Cornwallis (Bakeless, *Turncoats,* 244–47).

51. VHS *Collections* 2:104–5.

52. Townshend to Clinton, 10 April 1781, CO5/102:75–82, PRO; Allen to Clinton, 14 April 1781, Soldiers of the Revolution, PHS.

53. The contention of these towns that New York was unable to defend them was supported by generals Clinton and Schuyler and Governor Clinton (Clinton, *Public Papers* 6:840–44, 885, 890–91). All but a few adult males in each of these towns signed the petitions for annexation (Hoyt, *General Petitions,* 30–37; Crockett, *Assembly Journals* 1:193–97).

54. Allen, *History of Vermont,* 155.

55. Walton, *Records* 8:424; Slade, *Vermont State Papers,* 132–36; Crockett, *Assembly Journals* 1:197–210; Allen, *History of Vermont,* 156–60; Allen, *Present State,* 363. Ethan Allen favored adding Berkshire County to his list of annexations as they were "very anxious to join and make a part of Vermont" but was persuaded by Ira that Massachusetts was still a friendly government (*The Vermonter* [White River Junction, Vt.], 28 [1923]: 79; Crockett, *Assembly Journals* 1:185–97; Walton, *Records* 2:280–87; Allen, *History of Vermont,* 146–49).

56. "People the Best Governor," in Chase, *Dartmouth* 1:654–63; Rice, "Dartmouth College"; Ira Allen, *Vindication of the Assembly; New Hampshire State Papers* 10 (1877): 259–70, 296–324.

57. Haldimand to Germain, 8 July 1781, CO42/41:105, PRO; Crockett, *Assembly Journals* 1:213–17.

58. Allen, *Present State,* 12, 361; Walton, *Records* 2:133; Ethan Allen's account, 1785, EAP.

59. VHS *Collections* 2:83n; Walton, *Records* 2:266–67, 296; Crockett, *Assembly Journals* 1:200, 207; Clinton, *Public Papers* 6:742–45.

60. Crockett, *Assembly Journals* 1:214–35. This reintegration of Loyalists into public life produced a flurry of debate in the Vermont press. See, for instance, *Vermont Gazette,* 17, 24 July, 7, 21, 28 Aug., 11 Nov. 1783.

61. Windsor and Brattleboro Town Records; *Centennial Proceedings and Facts Relating to Newfane,* 34–35; Walton, *Records* 1:23n, 2: 259–60, 280; Duane, "State of the Evidence," 36, 43–44, 48–49. Chittenden even offered Vermont Loyalists certificates of confiscation so that they could prove that their land had been seized and receive restitution from the British. The committee considered sixty-three claims from former Vermonters, dismissing seven as still living in Vermont, and allowing fifty-one claims for an average of £156 (Loyalist Claims, B, 27:318–27, 435, AO 12:53, 69, PAC).

62. Haldimand to Germain, 8 July 1781, with Journal of conference with Ira Allen, 8–25 May, CO42/41:104–43, PRO; Shelburne to Haldimand, 20 April 1782, Haldimand to Shelburne, 17 July 1782, Q18:204, 207, PAC; Sherwood, "Journal," 218–20.

63. VHS *Collections* 2:142–43; Allen, *History of Vermont,* 175; Allen to Outman, 4 July 1781, EAP. Schuyler was of the opinion that Allen had successfully "duped" the British into not attacking (Clinton, *Public Papers* 7:318).

64. Sherwood to Haldimand, CO, B, 177–1:155–67, PAC; Haldimand to Germain, 8 July 1781, with Journal of conference with Ira Allen, 8–25 May, CO42/41:104–43, PRO. See also Allen, *History of Vermont,* 184–89; VHS *Collections* 2:161–63, 174–77, 179–80. The British emissaries did not trust the Vermonters. After all, "the majority of [their] leaders were men of low character and no consequence in the country until they made themselves popular in the present rebellion by actions at which a man of honor and integrity would revolt." They were all little more than "mad rebels." Another Loyalist described Vermont as "a receptical for the scum of rebellion" (VHS *Collections* 2:148–53, 158–59; Clinton to Germain, May 13, 1781, CO 5/102:149, PRO; Bail, "Letter to Lord Germain," 230). While the British and most other contemporaries did not believe that the Allens were sincere, a great number of historians, following Chilton Williamson's lead, have persisted in seeing that family as sincere Loyalists (*Vermont in Quandary,* 104–5).

65. Allen, *History of Vermont,* 189–93; VHS *Collections* 2:181–82, 189–91, 194–96.

66. Samuel Robinson wrote a marvelously sarcastic letter to General Stark suggesting he find "some other employment" for the Albany militia. Stark

was furious with the New Yorkers and ordered them home (VHS *Collections* 2:184–85; Walton, *Records* 2:332–34).

67. Bleecker, *Posthumous Works,* 151–53; Clinton, *Public Papers* 7:611–20, 623–25; Walton, *Records* 2:121–22; Crockett, *Assembly Journals* 2:20.

68. Epigraph from affidavit of T. Baker and D. Lamb, 9 Sept. 1782, VHS *Collections* 2:299. O'Callaghan, *Documentary History* 4:1012–14; affidavit of Timothy Phelps, 1782, EAP; Walton, *Records* 2:353–55; Onuf, *Federal Republic,* ch. 9; Ford, *Journals of Congress* 20:770–71, 829–31, 838, 923–25, 21:887, 22:157; Duane to Clinton, with notes on debate, 9 Aug. 1781, Clinton to New York delegates, 27 Aug. 1781, New York delegates to Clinton, 15 March 1782, James Duane Papers, NYHS.

69. Walton, *Records* 2:381–85; VHS *Collections* 2:57; Crockett, *Assembly Journals* 2:44–45, 57–68, 79–81, 90–92. The New Hampshire towns had little trouble attaining the forgiveness of the Portsmouth government and were in a strong negotiating position, forming the largest part of the state. The New York towns were less fortunate, having to submit formal petitions of submission to Gov. Clinton, who jailed a great number of people anyway (O'Callaghan, *Documentary History* 4:1007–10; Saunderson, *Charlestown,* 199–205; Chase, *Dartmouth* 1:503–27; Bouton, *Miscellaneous Documents,* 486–98).

70. Walton, *Records* 2:394; Murdoch, "A French Report," 234. See also Walton, *Records* 2:356–58, 385–95; Clinton to Duane, 8 Aug. 1782, James Duane Papers, NYHS; Sherman to Payne, 1 Nov. 1778, Payne Papers, Dartmouth College Library; *Journals of the Continental Congress* 8:510; 14:675, 818, 20:770–72, 21:837–38, 25:888; Burnett, *Letters* 6:220, 312, 340–41, 543–44.

71. [Ethan Allen] to Haldimand, unsigned, B, 177–1:25, 264, PAC; Wilbur, *Ira Allen* 1:379–80; VHS *Collections* 2:283–86, 311–13.

72. Allen's account of April 1782, EAP; Allen, *History of Vermont,* 231; Wilbur, *Ira Allen* 1:386; Wells to Sherwood, 13 June 1782, B, 177–1:337, PAC; VHS *Collections* 2:81–82, 119–21; VHS *Proceedings* 2 (1931): 929. Some British agents were remarkably inept and highly competitive with one another. One, George Smyth, used to send coded messages which no one at Haldimand's headquarter could decipher, (e.g., "Orient intelligence is of no weight, and Black Birds spray upon my branches in the South," Pemberton, "British Secret Service," 134–40).

73. Ira Allen (or perhaps Jacob Lansing, see Wilbur, *Ira Allen* 1:392) to Haldimand, 11 July 1782, Wright's affidavit, June 1782, B, 179–2:40, 182:554–55, PAC; VHS *Collections* 2:275–76, 280–81; Ira Allen to Haldimand, 10 July 1781, CO42/42:43–47, PRO.

74. VHS *Collections* 2:273–74, 288–91; Pemberton, "Justus Sherwood,"

ch. 4. At the same time, Halidmand feared that Vermont might push north into Canada on its own, spreading its "damnable inheritance" of republicanism (Haldimand to Lord North 24 October 1783, CO42/45:51–53, PRO).

75. Allen to Sherwood, 22 Nov. 1782, Smythe to Matthews, 8 Jan. 1783, B, 177–2:508, 178:15–16, PAC.

76. Allen to Sherwood, 22 Nov. 1782, ibid., 177–2:508; Allen to Governor Clinton, 14 April 1781, EAP; VHS *Collections* 2:104–5, 131; Clinton, *Public Papers* 7:11–13. On Vermont's finances, see Treasurer's Papers, Manuscript State Papers, VSA.

77. VHS *Collections* 2:289. See also ibid., 283–93; Wilbur, *Ira Allen* 1:418–20; Allen, *History of Vermont,* 244–46.

78. Allen, *History of Vermont,* 244; Sherwood to Haldimand, 16 Jan. 1783, B, 178:35 (see also 88, 112, 122, 151–52), PAC; Wilbur, *Ira Allen* 1:430.

79. Allen, *History of Vermont,* 244–46; Haldimand to Allen, 29 Nov. 1782, Allen to Haldimand, 20 Dec. 1782, Ira Allen to Sherwood and Knowlton, 25 March 1783, B, 175:300–303, 178:11, 62, PAC; Wilbur, *Ira Allen* 1:418–20; VHS *Collections* 2:293–94. On British officers seeking a profit through contacts with the Allens, see B, 175:82, 174, 185, 177–2:673, 681, PAC; Wilbur, *Ira Allen* 1:411–12; Levi Allen, Autobiography, LAP.

80. Ira Allen's Accounts, Treasurer's Papers, Manuscript State Papers, VSA. Vermont was not the only frontier region to enter into separatist negotiations with the British in the 1780s. See Taylor, *Western Massachusetts,* 104–5; Onuf, *Federal Republic,* ch. 3–5; Slaughter, *Whiskey Rebellion,* ch. 2. Charles Jellison convicted Ethan Allen of treason for his role in these negotiations since Vermont did not exist and was still part of New York; as Edward Brynn so succinctly put it, the "Allens' 'defiance' of history was treasonous" (Jellison, *Ethan Allen,* 248–50; Brynn, "Vermont and the British Emporium," 28).

81. Clinton, *Public Papers* 4:289. Ethan Allen's way of war does not match John Ferling's description of the "American way of war" which maximizes cruelty or destruction (Ferling, *A Wilderness of Misery*). On colonial patterns of warfare, see also Leach, *Arms for Empire;* Peckham, *Colonial Wars;* Sosin, *Revolutionary Frontier.*

82. Town Records of Guilford and Brattleboro.

83. Windham County Court Records, May 1782; Walton, *Records* 1:441; VHS *Collections* 2:277.

84. VHS *Collections* 2:286; O'Callaghan, *Documentary History* 4:1010–13; Clinton, *Public Papers* 8:6–12.

85. Walton, *Records* 2:161–63.

86. VHS *Collections* 2:297–302.

87. Freemen v. Phelps et al., 1782, Superior Court Records; Walton, *Records*

2:22, 239–40; Affidavit of Timothy Phelps, EAP; VHS *Collections* 2:301; O'Callaghan, *Documentary History* 4:1012–14.

88. *Vermont Gazette,* 27 Nov., 8 Dec. 1783; Walton, *Records* 1:117–18, 3:19, 22, 30, 239–40, 253, 268n, 270, 279–80, 299–302, 313–14; Crockett, *Assembly Journals* 2:21, 162–71, 212; Gale and Thompson, *History of Guilford,* 73, 82–83.

89. Crockett, *Assembly Journals* 2:190, 195–96, 200, 208–12; Slade, *Vermont State Papers,* 476; *Vermont Gazette,* 1 Jan. 1784; Walton, *Records* 3:301–4.

90. Sergeant Fisk took nine months to die of his wounds, living long enough to sue the more prominent Yorkers present at the Battle of Guilford and attaching their real estate for the use of his heirs (Windham County Court Records; Hall, *Eastern Vermont,* 509–13; *Vermont Journal,* 18 Feb. 1784).

91. Bradley to the editor, *Vermont Journal,* 18 Feb. 1784; Hall, *Eastern Vermont,* 514–18; Yorker trials, February, March 1784, Superior Court Records; Crockett, *Assembly Journals* 3:23–24, 27, 41, 51–52, 88, 92–93, 97–98; Walton, *Records* 3:311; Hoyt, *General Petitions,* 291–92. In Philadelphia the Green Mountain Boys were seen as restoring order (*Independent Gazetteer,* 10 Jan., 21 Feb. 1784).

92. *Vermont Gazette,* 3, 10 April 1784; Walton, *Records* 3:315–26; *Vermont Journal,* 11 Aug. 1784. On growing support for Vermont statehood in other states, see *Vermont Gazette* 5 June 1783; *Independent Gazetteer,* 10 Jan., 8 and 22 May 1784.

93. Petitions took up over half the business conducted by the assembly. See, for instance, Hoyt, *General Petitions,* xviii–xix, 13–17, 22–29, 32, 38–42, 58–59, 66–69, 79–81, 103, 132. The figure of 1,000 petitions, which bear more than twice that number of different signatures, does not include petitions for land, dealing directly with legislation, or concerning sequestration. These are to be found in vols. 3, 5, and 6 of *Vermont State Papers* and account for more than another thousand petitions. Also not included are petitions addressed to the governor and council, most of which have been lost. Washington's spies reported that even those hostile to the government of Vermont were equally suspicious of New York's claims to the soil of the Green Mountains (Lansing to Schuyler, 26 July 1780, VHS).

94. VHS *Collections* 2:311–12, 324–26. For a similar assessment from a British perspective, see Bail, "Letter to Lord Germain," 230; Pemberton, "British Secret Service," 129–32, 140.

95. See Sharp, *Making Europe Unconquerable.*

96. Allen, "Defence of Vermont."

CHAPTER NINE

1. Hatch, *Democratization of American Christianity.*

2. For examples within Vermont, see Shaftsbury Baptist Church Records for March 23, 1774, Crocker, *Baptists,* 20, 25; Wright, *Shaftsbury Association,* 17; Benedict, *History of the Baptist Denomination* 1:551. In general, see Bonomi, *Under the Cope of Heaven,* ch. 6. For the opposite view, see Heimert, *Religion and the American Mind,* 500–509; May, *Enlightenment in America,* 159–64.

3. Epigraph from Melville, *Pierre, or, the Ambiguities* (Chicago, 1971), 339. Perkins, *Narrative of a Tour,* 26.

4. Perkins, *Narrative of a Tour,* 19–21.

5. Ibid., 10, 13–14, 12–17, 19–21, 26–28.

6. Ibid., 30. Rev. Thomas Robbins had similar frustrations in 1799 (Robbins, *Diary* 1:83–87).

7. See Perkins, *Narrative of a Tour* 16–17, 83–92; Dwight, *Travels* 2:30–356; Timothy Walker, "Diaries, 1746–1780," Bouton, *Town Papers,* 123–91; Smith, *Life of Elias Smith,* 30–45; Peak, *Memoirs,* 54–65; Dow, *Dealings of God,* 33–68, 146–54.

8. Onuf, *Origins,* ch. 7–8.

9. Purcell, *Connecticut in Transition,* ch. 1–2; Hatch, *Sacred Cause of Liberty,* ch. 3.

10. Archer, "Quaker's Attitude towards the Revolution"; Brock, *Pacifism,* ch. 5–6; Graham, *Descriptive Sketch.* All other states, even Rhode Island and Pennsylvania, limited religious freedom. Both states denied full civil rights to Jews, Rhode Island until 1842. Until 1790 Pennsylvania required all officeholders to affirm the divinity of the Bible as well as their belief in heaven and hell (see Stokes, *Church and State* 1: ch. 13).

11. Sermon dated 17 March 1776, Thomas Fessenden, Manuscript Sermons, 1773–1804, AAS. For the contrary view, see Fessenden's sermon of 22 June 1777, which calls on the state to pass a law requiring everyone to pray for victory. On opposition to establishment, see "Integrity" and "Fidelity," *Vermont Gazette,* 19 June, 24 July 1783.

12. Slade, *Vermont State Papers,* 396. See also ibid., 313–15, 355–56, 396, 440, 472–73; Fish, "Vermont Bench and Bar," in Crockett, *Green Mountain State* 5:474; Hoyt, *Petitions,* 83–84, 173–74, 293–95, 349–51; Bennington, Brattleboro, and Grafton Town Records.

13. Slade, *Vermont State Papers,* 472–73; Goodrich, "Immigration to Vermont," 75; Crocker, *History of the Baptists,* 20–26.

14. "Fidelity," *Vermont Gazette,* 24 July 1783; see also ibid., 19 June, 28 Aug. 1783; Slade, *Vermont State Papers,* 245; Hoyt, *Petitions,* 83–84, 293–95, 322, 349–51; *Acts and Laws of Vermont* (1783), 180; *Acts and Laws of Vermont* (1797),

201–2; Williams, *Laws of Vermont, 1785–1791,* 292–93, 348–50; Tolman, *Laws of Vermont* 2:178–80; Superior Court Records, 1783; Hemenway, *Vermont Gazetteer* 1:620.

15. Graham, *Descriptive Sketch,* 181–82.

16. Marini, *Radical Sects,* 53–54; Lee, *Uncommon Vermont,* 196. Other religious exhorters who made Vermont unsafe for normalcy in the last decades of the eighteenth century included the dismissed predestinarian Baptist minister William Grow; Abner Jones, founder of the Christian Church; the self-proclaimed prophet William Bullard who led his pilgrims into the Green Mountains; the Annihilationists, a.k.a. Nothingarians, who held that the souls of the damned cease at death and only the elect live on; Nathaniel Wood and his New Israelites, an authoritarian sect which collapsed when they discovered their messiah, Wingate the Diviner, was a convicted counterfeiter, its members drifting off to try their hand at philosophers' stones and Mormonism; and the former Tory regular, Zadock Wright, converted by Mother Ann to Shakerism in an Albany jail (Marini, *Radical Sects,* ch. 3; Delano, *Miscellaneous Thoughts;* Lee, *Uncommon Vermont,* 190–99; Bullard, *Union Prescribed;* Ellsworth, *Solemn Predictions,* 7–8; Frisbee, *History of Middletown,* 57–61). Joseph Smith, Sr., was a member of the New Israelite sect.

17. Marini, *Radical Sects,* 68–75, 83–86, 106–9, 122–27, 144–48; Winch, "Reverend Joel Winch."

18. Shipton, *Biographical Sketches* 14:258; Fessenden, *Luminous Shinig Character,* 13–14; Fessenden, sermons dated September 1775, 22 June 1777, 22 Nov. 1778, Manuscript Sermons, AAS. See also Fessenden, *Theoretic Explanation; New-Hampshire Gazette,* 7 Sept. 1764; Ebenezer Parkman, diary entry for 16 Dec. 1766, AAS; Carmichael, *Self-Defensive War;* Bentley, *A Sermon;* Bonomi, *Under the Cope of Heaven,* 208–13; Morais, *Deism,* ch. 4; Hart, *The Popular Book,* 35–37.

19. For other examples of natural religion, see Whitaker, "Antidote against Toryism," Moore, *Patriot Preachers,* 206; Howard, *A Sermon,* 14; Elsworth, *Astronomical Diary;* Perry, *Vermont Almanack;* Elsworth, *Solemn Predictions; Christian Oeconomy;* Dodsley *Economy of Human Life.*

20. Epigraph from Smith, *American Poems,* 142. Allen to Crèvecoeur, 31 May 1785, EAP; Allen to Bradley, 7 Sept. 1785, AFP; Sherwood, "Journal," 220; Sunderland Land Records, 3:23 (10 Aug. 1784); Shaftsbury Land Records, 1: n.p., 129, 183 (3 May 1784, 8 March, 5 May 1785); Charlotte Land Records, 1: n.p., 30 (24 Nov., 4, 10, 21 Dec. 1784, 1 May 1785); Hubbardton Land Records, 1:101 (7 May 1785); Rutland Land Records, 4:331 (30 June 1785; Allen v. Hunt, August 1785, Superior Court Records; Allen to Van Schaick, 5 Aug. 1784, Allen's receipt for commuting his pay, 25 May 1785, EAP; Allen to Caldwell, 7 Feb. 1785, *Magazine of American History* 14 (1885): 320; introduc-

tion to Allen, *Reason,* edited by "A Free Thinker" (New York and Philadelphia, 1836), n.p.

21. Few historians have devoted much space to a close examination of Allen's theology. One exception is Dennis, "Deistic Trio."

22. Allen, *Reason,* 285–92, 359–63. See also May, *Enlightenment in America,* 112, 174, 217, 353–54.

23. Allen, *Reason,* 309.

24. Ibid., 346–47, 352–53.

25. Ibid., 377–78; see also ibid., 364, 367, 383, 415. Among many others who felt original sin inconsistent with a just god, see Whitby, *Discourse.* Charles Chauncey of Boston was telling his congregation almost the same thing (Griffin, *Old Brick,* 170–76). See also Smith, *Conceptions of Original Sin,* ch. 3–5; Walker, *Decline of Hell,* ch. 10.

26. Allen, *Reason,* 398–400.

27. Ibid., 387–89, 395, 397, 399.

28. Ibid., 279–80, 346–47, 455; see also ibid., 200, 207, 352. Much of Allen's attack on superstition was drawn from David Hume, "The Natural History of Religion," *Four Dissertations* (1757).

29. Allen, *Reason,* 96–97. Most scholars have seen deism as a negative critique of Christianity rather than the grounds for an alternative faith. See, for instance, Turner, *Without Creed, Without God,* 53.

30. Robert Boyle in his *Christian Virtuoso* of 1690 first put forth the notion that the observation of nature proved the existence of a benevolent deity.

31. Allen, *Reason,* 91; see also ibid., 83–90, 324, 333–34.

32. Ibid., 91–96, 158, 186–87; Kames, *Elements of Criticism* (1762).

33. Allen roundly rejected religious justifications of war, either in the Bible or his own times. "Every one who dares to exercise his reason, free from bias, will readily discern, that the inhumanities exercised towards the Canaanites and Amorites, Mexicans and Peruvians, were detestibly wicked, and could not be approbated by God, or by rational and good men. Undoubtedly avarice and domination were the causes of those unbounded cruelties, in which religion had as little to do as in the crusades to the holy lands (so called)" (*Reason,* 311–12).

34. Cousins, *Republic of Reason,* 141–44, 279–81; Morais, *Deism,* ch. 4; Hart, *Popular Book in America,* 35–37; Mecklin, *Story of American Dissent,* 349–54; Post, *Popular Free Thought,* ch. 1; Winch, "Reverend Joel Winch"; Allen and Eddy, *History of Unitarians and Universalists,* ch. 4–6; Buckley, *History of Methodists,* ch. 8.

35. Allen, *Reason,* 86–87, 472–77.

36. Ibid., 194–96, 200; see also ibid., 142–43, 147, 207, 225, 254, 453.

37. Ibid., 402.

38. Ibid., 31, 50; see also ibid., 32–33, 249, 271–72, 277–78. Allen's

conception of the deity was especially influenced by John Tillotson, an arch-bishop of Canterbury, who wrote of an omnipotent but reasonable God (May, *Enlightenment,* 17, 21).

39. Allen, *Reason,* 337–38; see also ibid., 150–54, 259–62, 335–36, 339–42, 471–75.

40. See Huntley, "Jefferson's Religion." Allen anticipated later interest in comparative religion, though, unlike later commentators, did not hesitate in stating that one religion was as good as another. The first popular work on comparative religion was Joseph Priestley, *Comparison of the Institutions of Moses with Those of the Hindoos* (1799). See Reynold, *Faith in Fiction,* ch. 1–2; Jackson, *Oriental Religions,* ch. 1–4.

41. Allen, *Reason,* 77–78.

42. Ibid., 212–17.

43. Ibid., 188, 222; see also ibid., 226–32. Many once Calvinist ministers came to share the Enlightenment view that nature was itself a source of divine knowledge. Salem's Rev. William Bentley wrote in 1790 that "the will of God" is made apparent in both nature and the Bible (Bentley, *A Sermon*). See also Carmichael, *Self-Defensive War;* Bonomi, *Under the Cope of Heaven,* 208–13.

44. Allen, *Reason,* 255–56, 258. "The Clergy have been combined against the devil" for seventeen hundred years, "and it is the constant cry that he had been all this time gaining ground on them, seducing more souls to hell, than they have savingly converted to Heaven; so that we are told, the former is much more popular than the latter" (ibid., 379–80).

45. Ibid., 31, 81–82. Allen seems to have been influenced by Anthony Ashley Cooper (earl of Shaftsbury), *A Letter concerning Enthusiasm* (1708).

46. Jonathan Edwards exerted the greatest intellectual influence on Allen's theology. Like Edwards, Allen based his epistemology on the observation of nature; both saw God's hand in the world around them. Borrowing from Locke, Allen and Edwards argued that the mind knows by experiencing the external world, not through inherent qualities. But Edwards thought people could experience God directly, through a sixth sense, while Allen thought this experience, in Locke's term, a secondary quality, an emotion. A knowledge of God, in Allen's cosmology, required the mediation of nature. Allen rejected natural depravity but found the rest amenable; Edwards's vague "Being in general" is the very image of Allen's deity (Edwards, "Dissertation concerning the Nature of True Virtue," *Works* 1:299; Elwood, *Philosophical Theology of Edwards,* ch. 4–5; Hopkins, *Inquiry into the Nature of Holiness;* Conforti, "Samuel Hopkins and the New Divinity"; Allen, *Reason,* 177–85).

47. As Christopher Hill has written of events in seventeenth-century England, radical religion gave common people more control over their lives, and congregations gave themselves more freedom (*World Turned Upside Down*). On

American religion responding to social change, see Bonomi, *Cope of Heaven,* ch. 8; Mead, *The Lively Experiment,* ch. 7; Oscar Handlin, "The Significance of the Seventeenth Century," in Smith, *Seventeenth-Century America,* 3–12.

48. Hammond, *Documents,* 55–58; Dexter, *Literary Diary of Stiles* 2:406.

49. Crocker, *Baptists,* 177–83; Hall, *Eastern Vermont,* 125–26; Jamaica Town Records, 1; Hemenway, *Vermont Gazetteer* 2:920–22, 931–34; Vail, *Pomfret* 1:212–14; Peck, *Records of Rockingham,* iv–v; Haynes, *Old Meeting House,* 26–51, 77–89.

50. Wallingford Town Records, 1 (1787–93).

51. Robbins, *Diary,* 90; Babcock, Journal, especially Babcock to Mrs. E. Smith, 1801, William S. Babcock Papers, AAS. Jacob Cram preached 168 sermons in thirty-eight towns within twenty-six weeks, riding nearly 1,000 miles in 1808 (Cram, *Journal*). See also Robbins, *Diary,* 83–92; Peach, "Rev. Joel Winch," 247–60; Mudge, *History of the New England Conference,* ch. 1; Goen, *Revivalism,* 110, 143–47, 255–57; Wright, *Shaftsbury Association,* 317–19; Marshall "Memoir," 193–99. James Fenimore Cooper's *The Pioneers* expresses this frontier religious democracy well; see ch. 8–11. See also Crèvecoeur, *Letters,* 54–56.

52. Crocker, *Baptists,* 177–83; Goen, *Revivalism,* 252–53. As James Oblekevich, *Religion and Rural Society,* discovered in England, evangelists were most successful in those communities which had no regular contact with ministers.

53. Lyman to White, 1798, Misc. MSS, Stevens Collection, VSA; Babcock, Journal, entry for 25 April 1801, Babcock Papers. See also Vermont Church History, Methodism, Rutland, 3, VHS; Babcock, "Notes on Religion" (1802), Babcock Papers; Peach, "Reverend Joel Winch," 243, 252–53, 260; Cram, *Journal.*

54. Babcock, Journal, entries for 18 Feb. 1801, Jan. 1802, Babcock Papers; Wallingford Church Records, Crocker, *Baptists,* 20–26.

55. Dexter, *Literary Diary of Stiles* 3:148.

56. From Shaftsbury's First Baptist Church Records, lost by the Shaftsbury Historical Society, quoted in Crocker, *Baptists,* 19, 21–23; Bottum Family Album, 32, Shaftsbury Historical Society. See also Stewart, *History of Freewill Baptists,* ch. 1.

57. Babcock, Journal, entries for 7 Feb., 25 April 1801, Babcock, "Notes on Religion," Babcock Papers. See also Halifax Church Records, Special Collections, University of Vermont Library; Wallingford Church Records, Crocker, *Baptists,* 20, 26.

58. "Memoir of Asa Burton," *American Quarterly Register* 10 (Boston, May 1838): 324; Dexter, *Graduates of Yale* 3:151–53; Hemenway, *Vermont Gazetteer* 1:161, 2:134; Jennings, *Memorials of a Century,* 92–99; *Connecticut Evangelical Magazine* 2 (Hartford, 1809): 341–42; Swift, *Discourses.*

59. Allen, *Reason,* app.: 69; Batchelder, *Documentary History,* 41. On the Church of England in Vermont, see Rothwell, *A Goodly Heritage.*

60. Marshall, "Memoir," 204; Crocker, *Baptists,* 25–27, 177–83; Wright, *Shaftsbury Association,* 17–18; Winch, "Reverend Joel Winch," 260–70; Comstock, *Congregational Churches of Vermont,* 13, 151; Bayley, "Reminiscences," 29; Hemenway, *Vermont Gazetteer* 1:604–52; Hall, *Eastern Vermont,* 125–26. On the often contradictory Puritan conception of the ministry, see Hall, *Faithful Shepherd,* ch. 6; Scott, *From Office to Profession.*

61. Goen, *Revivalism,* 254; Bennington First Church Records, 1; Jennings, *Memorials of a Century,* 58–60.

62. Bennington Church Records, n.p., 27 Jan. 1779–3 March 1780; Jennings, *Memorials,* 60–63, 88–92; Dexter, *Biographical Sketches* 3:305–10; Hemenway, *Vermont Gazetteer* 1:160–61; Avery, *Narrative,* 16–17; Avery, *Nature and Evil,* 27–31. The titles of Avery's published works say a great deal about his attitudes: *A Narrative of the Rise and Progress of the Difficulties Which Have Issued in a Separation between the Minister and People of Bennington* and *On the Nature and Evil of Professors of Religion Not Bridling the Tongue.*

63. Bennington Church Records, 3 May 1780; Avery, *Narrative,* 6–11, 37–40, 43; Avery, *Nature and Evil,* 8–9, 22.

64. Avery, *Narrative,* 52–54.

65. *Vermont Gazette,* 9 Oct. 1783; Avery, *Narrative,* 13–15; Bennington Church Records, 1781–82.

66. Avery, *Narrative,* 25–30; Bennington Church Records, 26 May 1783; *Vermont Gazette,* 9 Oct. 1783.

67. Avery, *Narrative,* 36–40, 43–46, 50–52. Avery was dismissed from his next ministry in 1794 for "his overbearing manner in the pulpit and imprudence of speech." Appealing to the courts, Avery was lectured by the judge on the irrational and arbitrary nature of church government. As if to prove that point, Avery organized a Separate church in his house. The following year, Avery was dismissed even from this pulpit, as he was from three more over the next decade. This perfect evangelist, known for his eloquence and style, was an utter failure as a minister, spending a life in controversy and being dismissed from all six positions he held (Dexter, *Graduates of Yale* 3:308–10; Jennings, *Memorials,* 91–92; Hemenway, *Vermont Gazetteer* 1:161).

68. Avery, *Nature and Evil,* 34, 45, 52, 56–62; Emmon, *Office of Ministry the Best,* 25.

69. Avery, *Narrative,* 31–35; *Vermont Gazette,* 9 Oct. 1783.

70. Marini, *Radical Sects,* 45–46; Crocker, *Baptists,* 20–22, 621; Bennington Church Records; Goen, *Revivalism,* 143–48; Smith, *Life of Elias Smith,* 21–24; Wright, *History of Shaftsbury Association,* 15–20. See also Mathews, "Second Great Awakening as Organizing"; Gregory Singleton, "Protestant Voluntary

Organizations and the Shaping of Victorian American," in Howe, *Victorian America,* 47–58; Duffy and Muller, "Jedidiah Burchard."

71. On the view that a multiplicity of religious views within a town does not preclude community, see Cook, *Fathers of the Towns,* 134–41; Steiner, "Anglican Officeholding in Pre-Revolutionary Connecticut."

72. John E. Goodrich, "Immigration to Vermont," in *Essays in the Social and Economic History of Vermont,* 251–52; Allen, "Autobiography," in Wilbur, *Ira Allen* 1:13; Locke, *Letter concerning Toleration,* ed. Thompson, iii–iv.

73. Shaftsbury Church Records in Crocker, *Baptists;* Bennington Church Records; Halifax Church Records; Babcock, Journal; Records of Second Congregational Church of West Windsor; Records of Old South Congregational Church of Windsor.

74. Epigraph from Allen, *Reason,* 340. Marini, *Radical Sects,* 144–48; Ballou, *Treatise on Atonement;* Ferris, *Five Sermons.* Hosea Ballou and Walter Ferris were Vermonters. The Ferris and Allen families were close friends, and Ballou, like the Adventist leader William Miller, stated that Allen's *Reason* exerted a strong influence on the development of his theology. One of the twenty-five known remaining copies of *Reason* comes from Jefferson's library (*Vermont History* 53 [1985]: 134).

75. Allen, *Reason,* 37, 45–46; Hatch, *Democratization of American Christianity,* ch. 4; Turner, *Without God,* ch. 2–3; Brooks, *Flowering of New England.*

76. Goen, *Revivalism,* 146; Jennings, *Memorials of a Century,* 118–19.

77. Allen to Crèvecoeur, 2 March 1786, EAP; Allen, *Reason,* 90–91.

78. Allen to Crèvecoeur, 2 March 1786, Starr to Allen, 2 Feb. 1786, EAP.

79. Hopkins in Smith, *American Poems,* 142; Dwight, *Triumph of Infidelity,* iii; *American Museum* 2 (1787): 171, 408–10. Dwight wrote two hundred sermons attacking deism and natural religion, delivering a series every year to the students of Yale. See, for instance, *Theology Explained and Defended* (1795) and *The Nature and Danger of Infidel Philosophy* (1798) (Morais, *Deism,* ch. 6; Gabriel, *Religion at Yale,* ch. 4).

80. Henry, *Account of Arnold's Campaign,* 120. For other contemporary responses, see "Ethan Nomatterwho" letter, EAP; *Vermont Gazette,* 15 June, 19 Sept. 1786; *New-Haven Gazette,* 19 April 1787; Sherman, *Oracles of Reason* and *A Sermon to Swine.*

81. *Vermont Gazette,* 10 July 1783; Allen to Brownson, South Hero Land Records, 1:83. At this time Allen purchased and sold rights on the Two Heroes for prices from £1.10 to £40 (ibid., 1:114, 129, 200, 4:229, 231, 234; North Hero Land Records, 1:265–67).

82. Allen, *Reason,* 164.

83. Ibid., 159, 164–65, 168, 171–75, 466.

84. Ibid., 118–21.

85. Ibid., 128, 137–39; see also ibid., 123–33, 164–75.

86. Ibid., 128–29, 136.

87. Hall, *Eastern Vermont,* 628–30. Margaret Wall was an adventurous woman who helped Crean Brush escape from the Boston jail in 1777 by exchanging clothes with him (ibid., 624; *Boston Gazette,* 21 May 1778).

88. Hall, *Eastern Vermont,* 630.

89. Ibid., 631; DePuy, *Ethan Allen,* 425. The source for this story was Stephen Bradley's son William, who claimed to have been present for the ceremony. Most works repeat his version almost word for word. Supposedly the only snag in the ceremony came when Robinson asked Allen if he promised to live with Buchanan "agreeable to the law of God." Allen said, "The law of God as written in the great book of Nature? Yes!" (DePuy, *Ethan Allen,* 425–26; Hall, *Eastern Vermont,* 630–31, 633n; Ullery, *Men of Vermont,* 32–33; Allen, *Allen Memorial,* 49).

90. Pell, *Ethan Allen,* 252.

91. Allen, *Reason,* 257–58.

CHAPTER TEN

1. Ethan to Ira Allen, 31 Aug. 1784, EAP; *Vermont Gazette,* 11 Nov. 1785.

2. Epigraph from Smith, *American Poems,* 142. The decade of the 1780s may have been period of greatest population growth in U.S. history (J. Potter, "The Growth of Population in America, 1700–1860," in Glass and Eversley, *Population in History,* 631–88). See Appendix D on the population of frontier Vermont; *Boston Chronicle,* 16 Aug. 1787; Stilwell, *Migration from Vermont,* ch. 1–2; D'Agostino, *History of Public Welfare,* 31; Holbrook, *Vermont 1771 Census,* xii–xxii.

3. Slade, *Vermont State Papers,* 316–19, 475–82; *Vermont Gazette,* 31 Jan. 1784; Williams, *Laws of Vermont,* 83, 322–23; Windham County Court Records, 1783–85.

4. *Vermont Gazette,* 28 Feb., 6 March 1786; *Vermont Journal,* 24 March 1786; Walton, *Records* 3:357–66.

5. Allen to Bradley, 2 June 1786, to Ira Allen, 18 Aug. 1786, EAP; Lossing, "Ethan Allen," 743; Pell, *Ethan Allen,* 255–57.

6. *Vermont Gazette,* 28, 31 Aug. 1786; *Vermont Journal,* 4 Sept. 1786; *New York Gazetteer,* 6 Nov., 13 Dec. 1786; *Pennsylvania Packet,* 27 Dec. 1786; Walton, *Records* 3:362–63; Thompson, *History of Vermont,* pt. 2:79.

7. *Vermont Gazette,* 27 Nov., 11 Dec. 1786; Caverly, *History of Pittsford,* 252–58; Hollister, *Pawlet,* 220–21; Hall, *Eastern Vermont,* 548–51.

8. Szatmary, *Shays' Rebellion;* Starkey, *A Little Rebellion;* Minot, *History of the Insurrections.*

9. Onuf, *Origins of the Federal Republic,* 59; Boyd and Taylor, *Susquehannah Company Papers* 1:88, 106, 197, 263. Ira and Levi Allen each purchased a share in the Susquehannah Co. in August 1773.

10. Boyd and Taylor, *Susquehannah Company* 7:256, 328, 8:213–14, 372, 376–77; Robert Taylor's introduction to vol. 8 of ibid.; Kettner, *Development of American Citizenship,* ch. 8–9; *Pennsylvania Packet,* 21 March 1786; Onuf, *Origins,* 61–71; Boyd, "Attempts to Form New States"; Brady, "Wyoming," 212–33.

11. Letter to Allen, 4 Aug. 1785, Boyd and Taylor, *Susquehannah Company* 8:254; *Connecticut Courant,* 6 March 1786. See also Boyd and Taylor, *Susquehannah Company* 8:271, 310, 357–58, 9:182–83, 206–7.

12. Allen's receipt, 19 Aug. 1785, VHS, MSS 785469; Boyd and Taylor, *Susquehannah Company* 8:270–71.

13. Hamilton to Franklin, 24 March 1786, Boyd and Taylor, *Susquehannah Company* 8:313. A glister pipe was used to give enemas, a treatment Hamilton seemed to believe the Pennsylvanians in need of. This letter inspired a marvelous parody from "a Doctor without Glyster Pipe" to John Franklin, entreating him to save Pennsylvania from Allen: "The news of the future arrival of Ethan Allen with his glyster pipe, had penetrated the people in general with suche panik that one halff is already Standing on all [fours] with their breeches hanging on their [h]eels in order to receive the glyster" (Boyd and Taylor, *Susquehannah Company* 8:312–13, 388; Connecticut Settlers' Papers, 1:181–92, American Philosophical Society.

14. Allen to Johnson, 15 Aug. 1785, Boyd and Taylor, *Susquehannah Company* 8:255–56. See also xxvii, 315, 326.

15. Shaw to Franklin, 18 May 1786, Grant to Franklin, 20 May 1786 Boyd and Taylor, *Susquehannah Company* 8:332, 335–36. See also ibid., 8:xxxvi, 326–30, 356–57, 388, 9:254–55; *Connecticut Courant,* 19 June 1786; *Hudson Valley Gazette,* 8 Nov. 1787.

16. Allen to Johnson, 15 Aug. 1785, Boyd and Taylor, *Susquehannah Company* 8:256. See also ibid., 8:271, 331, 9:38.

17. Julian P. Boyd, "A Rare Broadside by Ethan Allen," in Lawler, *To Doctor R.,* 39; Boyd and Taylor, *Susquehannah Company* 8:363–64; *Connecticut Courant,* 6 March 1786.

18. Boyd, "A Rare Broadside by Ethan Allen," in Lawler, *To Doctor R.,* 41; Boyd and Taylor, *Susquehannah Company* 9:523–45; Boyd, "Attempts to Form New States," 265–70; *Hudson Valley Gazette,* 8 Nov. 1787. Ira Allen remained involved in the affairs of the Susquehannah Company until 1802 (Boyd and Taylor, *Susquehannah Company* 9:330–33).

19. Hopkins in Smith, *American Poems,* 142; *Connecticut Courant,* 19 June

1786, 10 Sept. 1787; Boyd and Taylor, *Susquehannah Company* 7:97–98, 8:197, 10:172–73, 189.

20. *Pennsylvania Packet,* 3 July 1786; Debate on the Repeal of the Confirming Acct, 18 March 1790, Pickering's representation to the assembly, 2 March 1790, Boyd and Taylor, *Susquehannah Company* 10:58, 88. See also ibid., 56–58, 67–68, 118; Onuf, *Origins,* 70. On Allen's influence, see *Connecticut Courant,* June 19, 1786; Boyd and Taylor, *Susquehannah Company* 8:332–33, 336–38, 356–57, 423–24, 9:8; *Pennsylvania Packet,* 18 Sept. 1786.

21. Boyd and Taylor, *Susquehannah Company* 11:182; Carmer, *The Susquehanna,* 190.

22. Epigraph from Allen to Crèvecoeur, 2 March 1786, EAP. Washington to Madison, 5 Nov. 1786, Fitzpatrick, *Writings of Washington* 29:50–52, see ibid., also 26–28, 33–35; Syrett, *Papers of Hamilton* 4:112–18; Boyd, *Papers of Jefferson* 10:13–14, 596–97, 11:221–23.

23. Bowdoin to King and Dane, 11 March 1787, to the Governors of New York, Connecticut, and Vermont, 16 May 1787, MHS *Collections* 6:169, 185–86; Clinton to Lincoln, 6 March 1787, NYHS; Spaulding, *New York in the Critical Period,* 150–51, 184–85; Tyler to Lincoln, 18 Feb. 1787, MSS Collection, Massachusetts Archives.

24. Tyler's report to Lincoln, March 1787, Royall Tyler Papers, VHS; Hall, *Eastern Vermont,* 709; Walton, *Records* 3:375–79; *Vermont Gazette,* 5 March 1787.

25. Tyler's report to Lincoln, March 1787, Tyler Papers.

26. Walton, *Records* 3:423–24. See also ibid., 379–80, 425–38; *Vermont Gazette,* 26 Feb., 5 March, 16 April, 7 May, 16, 30 July 1787.

27. *Vermont Gazette,* 5 March, 7, 30 May 1787; Tyler's report to Lincoln, March 1787, Tyler Papers; Hall, *Eastern Vermont,* 709; Walton, *Records* 3:375–79.

28. Walton, *Records* 3:372–80.

29. Allen to Simmons, 3 May 1787, Walton, *Records* 3:379–80. See also ibid., 438–63; Allen to Tyler, 28 Aug. 1787, Tyler, "Memoirs," 57–58, Tyler Papers; *Vermont Gazette,* 9 April, 16 July 1787; Crockett, *Green Mountain State* 2:421; *Independent Chronicle,* 8 March 1787.

30. *Boston Gazette,* 8 March 1787.

31. Ethan and Ira Allen contract, 1 May 1787, EAP; papers on Ethan Allen's estate in IAP.

32. Ethan to Levi Allen, 3 June 1787, VHS; Ira Allen to Williams, 6 June 1795, Misc. MSS, Stevens Collection, VSA; Gold, *Cornwall,* 449; Hemenway, *Vermont Gazetteer* 1:563.

33. Allen to Bradley, 6 Nov. 1787, EAP.

34. Wilbur goes into enormous detail in *Ira Allen,* vol. 2.

35. Allen tried without success to borrow £20 from Royall Tyler in order to publish the "Appendix." It was not published until 1873 in the *Historical Magazine* (Allen to Tyler, 28 Aug. 1786, quoted in Pell, *Ethan Allen,* 263; Allen, *Memorial,* 49; Ethan to Levi Allen, 3 June 1787, VHS).

36. Ira Allen to Williams, 6 June 1795, Misc. MSS, Stevens Collection, VSA; Ira to Levi Allen, 5 June 1789, IAP. Allen left an estate valued at $70,000 (Burlington Probate Records, vol. 1). It took until 1802 to straighten out Allen's landholdings (Joseph Fay to Ira Allen, 15 Nov. 1802, IAP). Ethan Allen's two surviving sons, Hannibal Montresor and Ethan Voltaire, attended West Point and became regular army officers.

37. Levi to Ira Allen, 3 May, 21 Nov. 1789, IAP; *Vermont Gazette,* 23 Feb. 1789; Joseph to John Fay, 12 April 1798, VHS *Proceedings* 24 (1956): 253.

38. *Vermont Gazette,* 23 Feb. 1789; Graham, *Descriptive Sketch of Vermont,* 143; Dexter, *Literary Diary of Stiles* 3:345; Joseph to John Fay, 12 April 1798, VHS *Proceedings* 24 (1956): 253; Levi to Ira Allen, 3 May, 21 Nov. 1789, IAP. See also Ogden, *Antidote to Deism* 1:vii (note).

39. Wood, *Creation of the American Republic,* 322–28, 396–413.

40. For the competing views, see especially, Allen, *Vindication;* James Duane, legal brief, 1784, James Duane Papers, NYHS.

41. Wills, *Cincinnatus,* ch. 1–2.

42. Epigraph from Perkins, *Narrative of a Tour,* 24. Wecter, *The Hero in America.*

43. Fisher, *Vermont in Tradition,* 153; Fox, *Yankees and Yorkers,* 168. See also the judgments of the Italian traveler Luigi Viaggio, *Travels,* 337; the Vermont politician Deane C. Davis, VHS *Proceedings* 10 (1942): 147; historians Leon W. Dean, *Admission of Vermont,* 5; John Spargo, *Vermont Quarterly* 12 (1944): 102; Arthur W. Peach, *Vermont History* 22 (1954): 150; Codman Hislop, ibid., 38 (1970): 80; and high school student John Lajoie, ibid., 34 (1966): 236.

44. Gerth and Mills, *From Weber,* ch. 3, 9, 10.

45. My understanding of charisma is drawn from Edward Shils, "Charisma," in Sills, *International Encyclopedia of the Social Sciences* 2:386–90, and from conversations with Robert Smith of Montana State University.

46. Weber, *Theory of Social Organization,* 358–73, 386–92.

47. Morgan, *Inventing the People,* 169. Morgan, Richard Morris, and many other historians are incorrect in stating that Massachusetts was the first state to hold such a convention in 1780 (ibid., 258, 261; Morris, *Forging the Union,* 121). The Handlins present the Massachusetts convention as responding to popular will rather than elite desires (*Popular Sources,* 23–25, 51–52).

48. Robinson, *Jeffersonian Democracy in New England,* 10, 166; Spargo, *Haswell;* Paullin, *Atlas of Historical Geography,* plate 102. The *Vermont Journal,* 18 Nov. 1796, noted six Democratic societies in the state, all on the west side.

49. Williams, *Laws of Vermont,* 60; Conant, "Imprisonment for Debt," 68–69; Coleman, *Debtors and Creditors,* 68–73; Wilbur, *Ira Allen* 2:311.

50. Chipman, *Reports of Cases in the Supreme Court,* 9–10, 15, 29.

51. See Duffy and Muller, *Anxious Democracy;* Taylor, *Freedom's Ferment;* Crocker, *History of the Baptists;* Ludlum, *Social Ferment;* Morrissey, *Allen's Daughter.*

52. McWilliams, "The Faces of Ethan Allen"; Bellesiles, "Works of Historical Faith."

53. On symbolic worth exceeding real value, see McDonald, *Presidency of Washington.*

54. McWilliams, "The Faces of Ethan Allen," 270.

55. Flitcroft, *Novelist in Vermont,* 93. Allen is akin also to the "alligator horse" riverboatmen of the Mississippi described in Allen, *Western Rivermen.*

56. Sullivan, *Benedict Arnold,* 63–64; Davis, "Great Jehovah," 66, 77; Lajoie, "History of the Green Mountain Boys," 236; Holbrook, *Ethan Allen,* viii. The biographer was Stewart Holbrook. John Clement, *"Ethan Allen:* A Review," VHS *Proceedings* 8 (1940): 352–53. Holbrook, like Daniel Thompson, Benjamin Hall, and Frederic Van de Water, invented conversations. Thompson was an honest novelist; the rest claimed to be historians.

57. Dorson, *America in Legend,* 170. Catherine Albanese has said that Crockett became what he sought to extinguish, "a wild man" ("Davy Crockett and the Wild Man," in Lofaro, *Davy Crockett,* 85). See also John Seelye, "A Well-Wrought Crockett," ibid., 21–45; Slotkin, *Regeneration through Violence.*

58. Smith-Rosenberg, "Davy Crockett as Trickster"; Wills, *Cincinnatus;* Alan Dundes, "Metafolklore and Oral Literary Criticism," in Brunvand, *Readings in American Folklore,* 404–15.

59. Zall, *Lincoln Laughing,* 60. For the continued life of Ethan Allen stories into this century, see Fisher, *Vermont Tradition,* 134–53.

60. Much of this discussion is inspired by Ward, *Jackson.* See also Bancroft, "Progress of Civilization"; Allen, *Western Rivermen;* Smith-Rosenberg, "Crockett as Trickster."

61. An unsigned article from the 1850s in *Vermont Quarterly* 21 (1953): 136–39.

62. Chacko and Kulscar, "Israel Potter."

63. Melville, *Potter,* 6 (first published in *Putnam's Monthly Magazine*). The best study of this book is Rampersad, *Melville's Israel Potter.*

64. Melville, *Potter,* 38–39.

65. Ibid., 62–63, 120. Melville asked, "Is civilization a thing distinct, or is it an advanced stage of barbarism?" (p. 130).

66. Ibid., 142–51.

67. Ibid., 149, 159, 166.

68. Now that materialism has won, it is appropriate that Ethan Allen has largely vanished from the public imagination. The *Encyclopedia of American Biography* (New York, 1975), for instance, does not include Ethan Allen. The editors, John A. Garraty and Jerome L. Sternstein, held him to be neither significant nor famous, neither notorious nor typical—their standards for inclusion.

69. Allen, "Brief Narrative," Walton, *Records* 1:492–93. See Crowley, *This Sheba, Self*. On the significance of the family as a social institution in colonial America, see Peter D. Hall, "Farm Structure and Economic Organization: Massachusetts Merchants, 1700–1850," in Haraven, *Family and Kin*, 38–64; Greven, *Four Generations;* Jim Potter, "Demographic Development and Family Structure," in Greene and Pole, *Colonial British America*, 123–56.

70. On this theme in other areas of New England and England, see Heyrman, *Commerce and Culture*, esp. ch. 9; Whittenberg, "Planters, Merchants, and Lawyers"; Cal Winslow, "Sussex Smugglers," and John G. Rule, "Wrecking and Coastal Plunder," in Thompson, *Albion's Fatal Tree*, 119–88.

71. Fox, *Yankees and Yorkers;* Szatmary, *Shays' Rebellion;* Mark, *Agrarian Conflicts;* Kim, *Landlord and Tenant;* Countryman, *People in Revolution;* Taylor, *Liberty Men and Great Proprietors;* Slaughter, *Whiskey Rebellion*.

72. Allen, *Brief Narrative*, 79–84, 125–28, 157–60; Klein, *Politics of Diversity*, 156–61, 166–72; Smith, *Appeals to the Privy Council*, 390–412; *Colden Papers* 7:1–7, 9, 205–6; *Colden Letter Books* 9:421–25, 444–45, 455, 462, 10:70–71; Miller, *Case for Liberty*, 185–202; *The Report of an Action of Assault* (New York, 1764); "Sentinel" series, *New York Gazette*, 28 Feb.–18 July 1765; Goebel, "Courts and the Law"; Allen, *Vindication*, 466.

Bibliography

Primary Sources

Larger collections of documents are listed by name; miscellaneous manuscript sources in these repositories were also consulted.

MANUSCRIPT COLLECTIONS

American Antiquarian Society, Worcester, Mass.
    William S. Babcock Papers
    Fay Family Papers
    Thomas Fessenden Papers
    Seth Packard Papers
    Samuel Williams Papers
American Philosophical Society, Philadelphia
    Connecticut Settlers' Papers
Arlington Library, Arlington, Vt.
    Dorothy Canfield Fisher Collection
Bennington Museum, Bennington, Vt.
William L. Clements Library, University of Michigan, Ann Arbor
    Papers of Sir Henry Clinton
Connecticut Historical Society, Hartford
    Jonathon Trumbull Papers
Connecticut State Library, Hartford
    Papers Relating to the Revolutionary War
Dartmouth College Library, Hanover, N.H.
Library of Congress, Washington, D.C.
    Papers of the Continental Congress
    United States Revolutionary War Papers

Massachusetts Archives, Boston
Massachusetts Historical Society, Boston
    Military Papers
    Wentworth Family Papers
Newfane Jailhouse, Newfane, Vt.
    Townshend Legal Papers
New Hampshire Historical Society, Concord
    Wentworth Family Papers
New-York Historical Society, New York
    James Duane Papers
    Horatio Gates Papers
    Transcripts of Loyalist Claims
New York Public Library, New York
    American Loyalist Transcripts
    Bancroft Collection
    John Emmett Papers
    Philys Schuyler Papers
    Horatio Gates Papers
New York State Library, Albany
    George Clinton Papers
    New York Council Minutes, 1668–1783. 28 vols.
Pennsylvania Historical Society, Philadelphia
    Soldiers of the Revolution Collection
Public Archives of Canada, Ottawa
    Colonial Office Transcripts (Series Q)
    Haldimand Collection (Series B)
    Loyalist Claims
    Military Papers (Series C)
Public Records Office, London
    Audit Office Series
    Colonial Office Series
    Colonial Correspondence
    Thomas Gage Papers
Shaftsbury Historical Society, Shaftsbury, Vt.
University of Vermont Library, Burlington
    Special Collections
        Allen Family Papers
        Wilbur Collection

Vermont Historical Society Library, Montpelier
    David Hall Papers
    Alexander Harvey Papers
    Nathan Stone Papers
    Samuel Thrall Papers
    James Whitelaw Papers
Vermont Public Records Office, Montpelier
Vermont State Archives, Montpelier
    Manuscript State Papers
    Henry Stevens Collection
        Ethan Allen Papers
        Ira Allen Papers
        Levi Allen Papers
        Miscellaneous Manuscripts
    Tax files
    Town Manuscripts
    Treasurer's Records

TOWN AND LAND RECORDS
(in town clerk's offices, unless otherwise noted)

Land Records
    Arlington
    Bennington, Bennington Museum
    Bradford, Vermont Public Records Office
    Burlington
    Castleton
    Charlotte
    Cornwall, Conn.
    Grafton
    Hubbardton
    Jamaica
    Litchfield County Land Records, Litchfield Courthouse
    Manchester
    New York Land Papers and Original Letters Patent, Secretary of
        State's Office, Albany
    North Hero

   Poultney
   Rutland, Rutland County Courthouse
   Salisbury, Conn.
   Shaftsbury
   Somerset Deeds, Windham County Courthouse, Newfane
   South Hero
   Sunderland
   Rutland
   Tinmouth
   Windsor
Town Meeting Records
   Barnet
   Bennington, Bennington Museum
   Brattleboro
   Brandon
   Brattleboro
   Castleton
   Chester
   Dorset
   Dummerston
   Grafton Town Records, vol. 1 of Deeds and Land Records, and
     Selectmen's Records
   Guilford
   Halifax, Vermont Public Records Office
   Hardwich, in Mount Tabor Town Clerk's Office
   Jamaica
   Marlboro
   Rockingham, in Bellows Falls Town Clerk's Office
   Shaftsbury
   Tinmouth
   Wallingford, in Town of Wallingford Field Book
   Windsor
Town Proprietors' Records
   Arlington
   Bennington, Bennington Museum
   Chester
   Danby, Vermont Public Records Office
   Hartland

Jamaica
Manchester
New Haven
Pownal
Shaftsbury
Tinmouth, in Charter Book
Wallingford, in Town of Wallingford Field Book
Windsor
Vital Records
Woodbury, Conn.
Cornwall, Conn.

CHURCH RECORDS

Bennington First Church Records, Bennington Historical Museum
Halifax Church Records, Special Collections, University of Vermont
Newint Church Records, Bennington Historical Museum
Tinmouth Church Records, Town Clerk's Office
Vermont Church History Papers, Vermont Historical Society
Second Congregational Church of West Windsor, in church
Old South Congregational Church of Windsor, in church

COURT RECORDS
(in county courthouse unless otherwise noted)

Bennington County Court Records
Bennington County Probate Records
Cumberland County Court Records, bound in with Windham County
    Court Records, vol. 2, Windham County Courthouse, Newfane, Vt.
Gloucester County Court Records, Orange County Clerk's Office,
    Chelsea
Hampshire County Probate Records
Inferior Court of Common Pleas for the County of Albany
Litchfield County Court Records
Litchfield County Probate Records
Manchester District Probate Records
Miscellaneous Justice Records, Vermont State Archives

Northampton Justice Records, Town Clerk's Office

Old Supreme Court Files, Rutland County Courthouse

Rutland County Probate Records

Salisbury Justice Records, Town Clerk's Office

John Strong Justice Records, Wilbur Collection, Special Collections,
   University of Vermont Library

Superior Court Records, vol. 98 of the Rutland County Records,
   Rutland County Courthouse

Supreme Court Records, Rutland

Windham County Court Records, Newfane, Vt.

Windham County Probate Records, Newfane, Vt.

Windsor County Probate Records

Woodbury Justice Records, Town Clerk's Office

PUBLISHED CONTEMPORARY DOCUMENTS

"A Journal of the Managers of the Scots American Company of Farmers."
   Proceedings of the Vermont Historical Society 1926–28:184–203.

Adams, John. *Diary and Autobiography of John Adams.* Ed. L.H. Butterfield
   4 vols. Cambridge, Mass., 1962.

Adler, Mortimer J., ed. *The Annals of America.* 20 vols. Chicago, 1976.

Ainslie, Thomas. *Canada Preserved: The Journal of Captain Thomas Ainslie.* New
   York, 1968.

Allen, Ethan. *A Brief Narrative of the Proceedings of the Government of New York
   Relative to Their Obtaining the Jurisdiction of That Large District of Land West-
   ward from Connecticut River.* Hartford, 1774.

——. *The Proceedings of the Convention of the New Hampshire Settlers.* Hartford,
   1775. Rept. in Walton, *Records of the Governor and Council* 2:491–500.

——. *Andimadversory Address to the Inhabitants of the State of Vermont.* Hartford, 1778.

——. *A Vindication of the Opposition of the Inhabitants of Vermont to the Government of New-York.* Bennington, Vt., 1779. Rept. in Walton, *Records of the
   Governor and Council* 1:444–517.

——. *The Narrative of Colonel Ethan Allen's Captivity.* New York, 1968.

——. *Reason the Only Oracle of Man.* New York, 1940.

——, and Jonas Fay. *A Concise Refutation of the Claims of New-Hampshire and
   Massachusetts-Bay to the Territory of Vermont.* Hartford, 1780.

——, et al. *Present State of the Controversy between the States of New-York and New-
   Hampshire on the One Part, and the State of Vermont on the Other.* Hartford, 1782.

Allen, Ira. *Some Miscellaneous Remarks*. Hartford, 2nd. ed. 1777. Rept. in Walton, *Records of the Governor and Council* 1:376–89.

———. *Vindication of the Conduct of the General Assembly of the State of Vermont*. Dresden, N.H., 1779.

———. *To the Inhabitants of the State of Vermont*. Dresden, N.H., 1779. Rept. in Wilbur, *Ira Allen* 2:484–91.

———. *The Natural and Political History of the State of Vermont*. London, 1798.

Anburey, Thomas. *With Burgoyne from Quebec*. 1789. Rept. Toronto, 1963.

Annual Register for 1778. London, 1779.

Arnold, Benedict. "Benedict Arnold's Regimental Memorandum Book." *Pennsylvania Magazine of History and Biography* 8 (1884): 363–76.

Avery, David. *A Narrative of the Rise and Progress of the Difficulties Which Have Issued in a Separation between the Minister and People of Bennington*. Bennington, Vt., 1783.

———. *On the Nature and Evil of Professors of Religion Not Bridling the Tongue*. Boston, 1791.

Bail, Hamilton V. "A Letter to Lord Germain about Vermont." *Vermont History* 34 (1966): 226–34.

Bailyn, Bernard, ed. *Pamphlets of the American Revolution*. Cambridge, Mass., 1965.

Baldwin, Thomas W., ed. *Vital Records of Deerfield, Massachusetts, to the Year 1850*. Boston, 1920.

Ballou, Hosea. *A Treatise on Atonement*. Randolph, Vt., 1805.

Batchelder, Calvin, ed. *Documentary History of the Protestant Episcopal Church in the Diocese of Vermont*. Claremont, N.H., 1876.

Batchellor, Albert S., ed. *The New Hampshire Grants*. Vol. 26 of *New Hampshire Provincial and State Papers*. Concord, N.H., 1895.

Bayley, Frye. "Reminiscences of Col. Frye Bayley." *Proceedings of the Vermont Historical Society* 1923–25:22–86.

Bentley, William. *A Sermon, Preached at the Stone Chapel in Boston*. Boston, 1790.

Blake, J. *Annals of the Town of Dorchester*. 2 vols. Boston, 1846.

Bleecker, Ann. *The Posthumous Works of Ann Elize Bleecker*. New York, 1793.

Boudinot, Elias. *Journal or Historical Recollections of American Events during the Revolutionary War*. Philadelphia, 1894.

Bouton, Nathaniel, ed. *Town Papers: Documents Relating to Towns in New Hampshire*. Vol. 9 of *Collections of the New Hampshire Historical Society*. Concord, N.H., 1875.

———, ed. *Miscellaneous Documents and Records Relating to New Hampshire at Different Periods*. Vol. 10 of *State Papers of New Hampshire*. Concord, N.H., 1877.

Boyd, Julian P., et al., eds. *The Papers of Thomas Jefferson*. 22 vols. to date. Princeton, N.J., 1950- .

——, and Robert J. Taylor, eds. *The Susquehannah Company Papers.* 11 vols. Ithaca, N.Y., 1930–71.

Bradley, Stephen. *Vermont's Appeal to the Candid and Impartial World.* Hartford, 1779. Rept. in Walton, *Records of the Governor and Council* 2:200–222.

Brissot, Jacques-Pierre. *New Travels in the United States of America, 1788.* Ed. Durand Echeverria. Cambridge, Mass., 1964.

Brodhead, J. R., and E. B. O'Callaghan, eds. *Documents Relative to the Colonial History of the State of New-York.* 11 vols. Albany, 1855–61.

Bullard, William. *A Union Prescribed and Recommended.* Windsor, Vt., 1804.

Burgoyne, John. *A State of the Expedition from Canada.* 2d ed. London, 1780.

Burnett, E. C., ed. *Letters of the Members of the Continental Congress.* 8 vols. Washington, D.C., 1921–36.

Butterfield, L.H. *Adams Family Correspondence.* 4 vols. Cambridge, Mass., 1963–73.

Carmichael, John. *A Self-Defensive War Lawful.* Lancaster, Pa., 1775.

Carter, Clarence E., ed. *The Correspondence of General Thomas Gage.* 2 vols. London, 1933.

Chastellux, François J. *Travels in North America, in the Years 1780, 1781, and 1782.* Trans. Howard C. Rice, Jr. 2 vols. Chapel Hill, N.C., 1963.

Chipman, Daniel. *Reports of Cases Argued and Determined in the Supreme Court of the State of Vermont.* Middlebury, Vt., 1824.

Clinton, George. *Public Papers of George Clinton, First Governor of New York.* 10 vols. Albany, 1899–1914.

Colden, Cadwallader. *The Colden Letter Books, 1760–75.* Vols. 9–10 of *Collections of the New-York Historical Society.* New York, 1876–77.

——. *The Letters and Papers of Cadwallader Colden.* 9 vols. New York, 1917–23, 1934–35.

Connecticut Historical Society. *Collections of the Connecticut Historical Society.* Vols. 1 and 2. Hartford, 1860.

Conway, Moncure D., ed. *The Writings of Thomas Paine.* 4 vols. New York, 1894–96.

Cooper, James Fenimore *The Pioneers.* Ed. Lance Schachterle and Kenneth Anderson. Albany, 1980.

Cram, Jacob. *Journal of a Missionary Tour in 1808.* Rochester, N.Y., 1909.

Crèvecoeur, St. John. *Letters from an American Farmer.* Garden City, N.Y., n.d.

Crockett, Walter H., ed. *Journals and Proceedings of the General Assembly of the State of Vermont, 1778–1781.* Vol. 3 of *The State Papers of Vermont.* 8 vols. Bellows Falls, Vt., 1924–78.

Cruikshank, Ernest, ed. *A History of the Organization, Development, and Services of the Military and Naval Forces of Canada.*

Cutler, Samuel. "Journal of Samuel Cutler." *New-England Historical and Gene-*

alogical Register 32 (1878): 42–44, 184–88, 305–8, 395–98.

Dann, John C., ed. *The Revolution Remembered: Eyewitness Accounts of the War for Independence.* Chicago, 1980.

Deane, Samuel. *The New England Farmer: or Georgical Dictionary.* Worcester, Mass., 1797.

Delano, Stephen. *Miscellaneous Thoughts on the Doctrine of Limited Election and Reprobation, As It Stands Contrasted with Scripture and Reason.* Windsor, Vt., 1798.

Dewart, Franklin H., ed. *Charters Granted by the State of Vermont.* Vol. 2 of *State Papers of Vermont.* Montpelier, Vt., 1922.

Dexter, Franklin B., ed. *The Literary Diary of Ezra Stiles.* 3 vols. New York, 1901.

Dodsley, Robert. *The Economy of Human Life.* Bennington, Vt., 1788.

Dow, Lorenzo. *The Dealings of God, Man, and the Devil, as Exemplified in the Life, Experiences, and Travels of Lorenzo Dow.* Norwich, Conn., 1833.

Drayton, William H. *A Letter from the Freemen of South-Carolina* Charleston, S.C., 1774.

Dring, Thomas. *Recollections of the Jersey Prison-Ship.* Providence, R.I., 1829.

[Duane, James.] *A Narrative of the Proceedings Subsequent to the Royal Adjudication.* New York, 1773.

———. "State of the Evidence and Argument in Support of the Territorial Rights of New York against the Government of New Hampshire and the Claimant under It." *Collections of the New-York Historical Society* 3 (1871): 1–144.

Dwight, Timothy. *Travels in New England and New York.* Ed. Barbara M. Solomon. 4 Vols. Cambridge, Mass., 1969.

———. *The Triumph of Infidelity.* n.p., 1788.

Edwards, Jonathan. *A History of the Work of Redemption.* Ed. John F. Wilson. New Haven, 1989.

———. *Jonathan Edwards: The Great Awakening.* Ed. C. C. Goen. New Haven, 1972.

———. *A Faithful Narrative of the Surprising Work of God.* London, 1737.

———. *Works of Jonathan Edwards.* Ed. E. Hickman. 2 Vols. New York, 1843.

Eliot, Jared. *Essays upon Field-Husbandry in New-England, As It Is or May Be Ordered.* Boston, 1760.

Elsworth, Samuel. *An Astronomical Diary, or Almanack.* Bennington, Vt., 1784.

———. *Solemn Predictions.* Bennington, Vt., 1787.

Emmon, Nathaniel. *The Office of the Ministry the Best Office.* Providence, R.I., 1786.

Fernow, Berthold, comp. *Calendar of Council Minutes, 1669–1783.* Harrison, N.Y., 1987.

Ferris, Walter. *Five Sermons.* Randolph, Vt., 1807.

Fessenden, Thomas. *A Luminous Shining Character*. Keene, N.H., 1789.
——. *A Theoretic Explanation of the Science of Sanctity*. Brattleboro, Vt., 1804.
Fitch, Jabez. *The New York Diary of Lieutenant Jabez Fitch*. Ed. W. H. W. Sabine. New York, 1954.
Fitzpatrick, John C., ed. *The Writings of George Washington*. 39 vols. Rept. Westport, Conn., 1970.
Foner, Philip S., ed. *The Complete Works of Thomas Paine*. 2 vols. New York, 1945.
Force, Peter, ed. *American Archives*. 9 vols. Washington, D.C., 1837–53.
Ford, Worthington C., ed. *Journals of the Continental Congress, 1774–1789*. 34 vols. Washington, D.C., 1904–37.
Franklin, Benjamin. *Autobiography of Benjamin Franklin*. Ed. Leonard W. Labaree. New Haven, 1964.
Goodrich, John E., ed. *Rolls of the Soldiers in the Revolutionary War, 1775–1783*. Rutland, Vt., 1904.
Gordon, William. *History of the Rise, Progress, and Establishment of the Independence of the United States of America*. 2 vols. London, 1788.
Graham, John A. *A Descriptive Sketch of the Present State of Vermont*. London, 1797.
Grant, Anne M. *Memoirs of an American Lady*. Philadelphia, 1846.
Graydon, Alexander. *Memoirs of a Life, Chiefly Passed in Pennsylvania, within the Last Sixty Years*. Edinburgh, 1822.
Hamilton, Alexander, John Jay, and James Madison. *The Federalist or the New Constitution*. New York, 1922.
Hammond, Isaac W., ed. *Documents Relating to Towns in New Hampshire*. Vol. 13 of *Provincial and State Papers of New Hampshire*. Concord, N.H., 1884.
Harriot, John. *Struggles through Life*. 2 vols. London, 1808.
Heckewelder, John. *History, Manners, and Customs of the Indian Nations*. New York, 1971.
Heimert, Alan, and Perry Miller, eds. *The Great Awakening*. Indianapolis, 1967.
Henry, John J. *Account of Arnold's Campaign against Quebec*. Albany, 1877.
Herbert, Charles. *A Relic of the Revolution*. Boston, 1847.
Hopkins, Samuel. *An Inquiry into the Nature of True Holiness*. Newport, R.I., 1773.
Howard, Simeon. *A Sermon Preached to the Ancient and Honorable Artillery-Company of Boston*. Boston, 1773.
Hoyt, Edward A., ed. *General Petitions, 1778–1787*. Vol. 8 of *State Papers of Vermont*. Montpelier, Vt., 1952.
Hutchinson, Robert, ed. *Poems of Anne Bradstreet*. New York, 1969.
Jefferson, Thomas. *Notes on the State of Virginia*. New York, 1964.
——. *Thomas Jefferson, Writings*. New York, 1984.

Jeffry, James. "Journal Kept in Quebec in 1775," *Historical Collections of the Essex Institute* 50 (1914):97–150.

Journal of the Votes and Proceedings of the General Assembly of the Colony of New York. New York, 1764–66.

Journals of the Albany Committee of Correspondence. Albany, 1923.

Lamb, R. *Memoirs of His Own Life.* 2 vols. Dublin, 1809.

La Rouchefoucauld-Liancourt, François A. F. *Travels through the United States of North America, in the Country of the Iroquois, and Upper Canada, in the Years 1795, 1796, and 1797.* 2 vols. London, 1800.

Lincklaen, John. *Travels in the Years 1791 and 1792 in Pennsylvania, New York, and Vermont.* New York, 1897.

Locke, John. *Letter concerning Toleration.* Ed. Joseph Thompson. Windsor, Vt., 1788.

M'Alpine, Jack. *Genuine Narratives.* Edinburgh, 1883.

Marshall, Joseph. "Memoir of Rev. Joseph Marshall." *Advisor, or Vermont Evangelical Magazine* 7 (1815):193–207.

Melville, Herman. *Israel Potter: His Fifty Years of Exile.* Ed. Evanston and Harrison Hayford, Hershel Parker, and G. Thomas Tanselle. Chicago, 1982.

Moore, Frank, ed. *The Patriot Preachers of the American Revolution.* New York, 1860.

Mott, Edward. "Journal of Capt. Edward Mott." *Collections of the Connecticut Historical Society* 1 (1860): 163–88.

Neilson, Charles. *An Original, Compiled, and Corrected Account of Burgoyne's Campaign, and the Memorable Battles of Bemis's Heights.* Albany, 1844.

New York Colony Laws for 1774 and 1775. Albany, 1775.

New Hampshire Provincial and State Papers. 34 vols. Concord, N.H., 1867–1919.

Nye, Mary. *Sequestration, Confiscation, and Sale of Estates.* Vol. 6 of *State Papers of Vermont.* Montpelier, Vt., 1941.

O'Callaghan, E. B., ed. *Documentary History of New York.* 4 vols. Albany, 1850–51.

Ogden, Uzel. *Antidote to Deism.* 2 vols. Newark, N.J., 1795.

Oliver, Peter. *Peter Oliver's Origin and Progress of the American Rebellion: A Tory View.* Ed. Douglass Adair and John A. Schutz. Stanford, Calif., 1967.

Paltsits, V. H., ed. *Minutes of the Commissioners for Detecting and Defeating Conspiracies in the State of New York: Albany County Sessions.* 3 vols. Albany, 1909–10.

Peak, John. *Memoirs of Elder John Peak, Written by Himself.* Boston, 1832.

Peck, Thomas B., ed. *Records of the First Church of Rockingham, Vermont.* Boston, 1902.

———. *Vital Records of Rockingham, Vermont.* Boston, 1908.

Perkins, Nathan. *A Narrative of a Tour through Vermont.* Woodstock, Vt., 1937.

Perry, Eliakim. *The Vermont Almanack for the Year 1785.* Bennington, Vt., 1784.

Priestly, Joseph. *A Comparison of the Institutions of Moses with those of the Hindoos.* Northumberland, Pa., 1799.

Proctor, Redfield, ed. *Records of the Conventions of the New Hampshire Grants for the Independence of Vermont, 1776–1777.* Washington, D.C., 1904.

Public Records of the State of Connecticut. Hartford, 1894.

Robbins, Thomas. *Diary of Thomas Robbins, D.D.* 2 vols. Boston, 1886.

Rogers, Horatio, ed. *Hadden's Journal and Orderly Book: As Kept in Canada and upon Burgoyne's Campaign in 1776 and 1777, by Leiut. James M. Hadden, Royal Artillery.* Albany, 1884.

Sherman, Josiah. *Oracles of Reason: As Found by the Deists, are Husks for Deistical and Heathen Swine.* Litchfield, Conn., 1787.

———. *A Sermon to Swine: From Luke XV.16.* Litchfield, Conn., 1787.

Shortt, Adam, and Arthur G. Doughty, eds. *Documents Relating to the Constitutional History of Canada, 1759–91.* Ottawa, 1918.

Slade, William, ed. *Vermont State Papers.* Middlebury, Vt., 1823.

Smith, Elias. *The Life of Elias Smith.* Portsmouth, N.H., 1816.

———, ed. *American Poems Selected and Original.* Litchfield, Conn., 1793.

Smith, William. *Historical Memoirs from 16 March 1763 to 9 July 1776.* Ed. William H. W. Sabine. 2 vols. New York, 1956.

Soule, Allen, ed. *Laws of Vermont, 1777–1780.* Vol. 12 of *State Papers of Vermont.* Montpelier, Vt., 1964.

Sparks, Jared, ed. *Correspondence of the American Revolution.* 4 vols. Boston, 1853.

State of New Hampshire. *Laws of New Hampshire.* 10 vols. Manchester, N.H., 1904–5.

State of New York. *Journals of the Provincial Congress, Constitutional Convention, Committee of Safety, and Council of Safety of the State of New-York, 1775–1777.* 2 vols. Albany, 1842.

State of Vermont. *Acts and Laws, Passed by the General Assembly of the State of Vermont.* Windsor, Vt., 1783.

———. *Acts and Laws, Passed by the Legislature of the State of Vermont.* Bennington, Vt., 1797.

———. *Acts and Laws Passed by the Legislature of the State of Vermont.* Rutland, Vt., 1797.

———. *State Papers of Vermont.* 14 vols. Bellows Falls, Vt., 1918–65.

Steele, Zadock. *The Indian Captive: or A Narrative of the Captivity and Sufferings of Zadock Steele.* Montpelier, Vt., 1818.

Sterling, David L., ed. "American Prisoners of War in New York: A Report by Elias Boudinot." *William and Mary Quarterly* 13 (1956): 376–93.

Stiles, Henry, ed. *Letters from the Prisons and Prison-Ships.* New York, 1865.

Stone, William, ed. *Journal of Captain Pausch, Chief of the Hanan Artillery during the Burgoyne Campaign.* Albany, 1886.

——, ed. *Memoirs, and Life and Journals, of Major General Riedesel, during His Residence in America.* Albany, 1868.

Strickland, William. *Journal of a Tour in the United States of North America.* Ed. J. E. Strickland. New York, 1971.

Sullivan, James, ed. *Minutes of the Albany County Committee of Correspondence, 1775–78.* 2 vols. Albany, 1923–26.

Swift, Job. *Discourses on Religious Subjects.* Ed. Lemuel Haynes. Middlebury, Vt., 1805.

Syrett, Harold C., ed. *The Papers of Alexander Hamilton.* 27 vols. New York, 1961–87.

Taylor, Robert J., ed. *Papers of John Adams.* 8 vols. Cambridge, Mass., 1977–89.

——, ed. *Massachusetts, Colony and Commonwealth: Documents on the Formation of Its Constitution.* Chapel Hill, N.C., 1961.

Tennent, Gilbert. *The Dangers of an Unconverted Ministry.* Philadelphia, 1741.

Thatcher, John. *A Military Journal during the American Revolutionary War.* Boston, 1823.

The Christian Oeconomy. Bennington, Vt., 1788.

The Report of an Action of Assault. New York, 1764.

The Colonial Laws of New York. Albany, 1894.

Thompson, Zadock. *A Gazeteer of the State of Vermont.* Montpelier, Vt., 1824.

——. *History of Vermont, Natural, Civil, and Statistical.* Burlington, Vt., 1842.

Thompson, George. "Diary of George Thompson of Newburyport." *Essex Institute Historical Collections* 76 (1940): 221–42.

Tolman, Thomas, ed. *The Laws of the State of Vermont, Digested and Compiled.* 2 vols. Randolph, Vt., 1808.

Toynbee, Paget, ed. *The Letters of Horace Walpole.* 19 vols. Oxford, 1903–25.

Vermont Historical Society. *Collections of the Vermont Historical Society.* 12 vols. Montpelier, Vt., 1870–1946.

Verreau, H. A., ed. *Invasion du Canada: Collection de Mémoires, Recueillis et Annotés.* Montreal, 1873.

Viaggio, Luigi C. *Travels in the United States of North America, 1785–1787.* Trans. and ed. Antonio Page. Syracuse, N.Y., 1983.

Walton, E. P., ed. *Records of the Council of Safety and Governor and Council of the State of Vermont.* 8 vols. Montpelier, Vt., 1873–80.

Washburn, Wilcomb, ed. *The Indian and the White Man.* Garden City, N.Y., 1964.

Webb, Samuel B. *Correspondence and Journals of Samuel Blachley Webb.* Ed. Worthington C. Ford. 3 vols. Lancaster, Pa., 1893–94.

Whitelaw, James. "Journal of General James Whitelaw, Surveyor General of Vermont." *Proceedings of the Vermont Historical Society* 1905–6:121–55.

Wilkinson, James. *Memoirs of My Own Times.* 3 vols. Philadelphia, 1816.

Williams, John A., ed. *Laws of Vermont, 1785–1791.* Vol. 14 of *Vermont State Papers.* Montpelier, Vt., 1966.

———, ed. *The Public Papers of Governor Thomas Chittenden, 1778–1797.* Vol. 17 of *State Papers of Vermont.* Montpelier, Vt., 1969.

Williams, Samuel. *Natural and Civil History of Vermont.* Walpole, N.H., 1794.

Winch, Joel. "The Reverend Joel Winch—Pioneer Minister." Ed. Arthur W. Peach. *Proceedings of the Vermont Historical Society* 9 (1941): 235–70, 10 (1942): 21–35, 83–103.

Wright, Eliphalet. *The Difference between Those Called Standing Churches and Those Called Strict Congregationalists Illustrated.* Norwich, Conn., 1775.

Young, Thomas. *Some Reflections on the Disputes Between New-York, New-Hampshire, and Col. John Henry Lydius of Albany.* New Haven, 1764.

NEWSPAPERS

American Museum, Philadelphia.

Boston Gazette and Country Journal, Boston.

Connecticut Courant and Hartford Weekly Intelligencer, Hartford.

Connecticut Gazette, New Haven.

Hudson Weekly Gazette, Hudson, Pa.

Independent Chronicle, Boston

Independent Gazetteer, Philadelphia.

London Gazette, London.

Massachusetts Spy, Worcester.

New-Hampshire Gazette, Portsmouth.

New-Haven Gazette, New Haven.

New York Journal, New York.

New York Gazette, New York.

Pennsylvania Journal, Philadelphia.

Pennsylvania Packet, and Daily Advertiser, Philadelphia.

Providence Gazette, Providence, R.I.

The Quebec Gazette—La Gazette de Quebec, Quebec.

Vermont Gazette, or Freeman's Depository, Bennington.

Vermont Journal, and the Universal Advertsier, Windsor.

Secondary Sources

Adair, Douglass. *Fame and the Founding Fathers*. Ed. Edmund P. Willis. Bethlehem, Pa., 1967.

Adams, Willi. *The First American Constitutions: Republican Ideology and the Making of the State Constitutions in the Revolutionary Era*. Chapel Hill, N.C., 1980.

———. " 'The Spirit of Commerce Requires That Property Be Sacred': Gouverneur Morris and the American Revolution." *Amerikastudien* 21 (1976): 309–34.

Ahlstrom, Sidney. *A Religious History of the American People*. New Haven, 1972.

Akagi, Roy. *The Town Proprietors of the New England Colonies: A Study of Their Development, Organization, Activities, and Controversies, 1620–1770*. Philadelphia, 1924.

Albion, Robert G. *Forests and Sea Power: The Timber Problem of the Royal Navy, 1652–1862*. Cambridge. Mass. 1926.

Aldrich, Lewis, and Frank R. Holmes. *History of Windsor County, Vermont*. Syracuse, N.Y., 1891.

Alexander, John K. "Forton Prison during the American Revolution: A Case Study of British Prisoner of War Policy and the American Response to That Policy." *Essex Institute Historical Collections* 103 (1967): 365–89.

Allen, David G. *In English Ways: The Movement of Societies and the Transferral of English Local Law and Custom to Massachusetts Bay in the Seventeenth Century*. Chapel Hill, N.C., 1981.

Allen, Joseph H., and Richard Eddy. *A History of the Unitarians and Universalists in the United States*. New York, 1894.

Allen, Michael. *Western Rivermen, 1763–1861: Ohio and Mississippi Boatmen and the Myth of the Alligator Horse*. Baton Rouge, La., 1990.

Allen, Orrin P. *The Allen Memorial*. Palmer, Mass., 1907.

Anderson, John K. "Jonathan Carpenter and the American Revolution: The Journal of an American Naval Prisoner of War and Vermont Indian Fighter." *Vermont History* 36 (1968): 74–90.

Anderson, Olive. "The Treatment of Prisoners of War in Britain during the American of Independence." *Bulletin of the Institute of Historical Research* 28 (1955): 63–83.

Anderson, Fred. *A People's Army: Mass Soldiers and Society in the Seven Years' War*. Chapel Hill, N.C., 1984.

Anderson, S. Axel, and Florence Woodard. "Agricultural Vermont." *Economic Geography* 8 (1932): 12–42.

Angermann, Erich, et al., eds. *New Wine in Old Skins: A Comparative View of*

Socio-Political Structures and Values Affecting the American Revolution. Stuttgart, 1976.

Archer, Adair. "The Quaker's Attitude towards the Revolution." *William and Mary Quarterly* 1 (1921): 167–82.

Armbruster, Eugene L. *The Wallabout Prison Ships, 1776–1783.* New York, 1920.

Arnold, Isaac N. *The Life of Benedict Arnold: His Patriotism and His Treason.* Chicago, 1880.

Austin, Aleine. *Matthew Lyon: "New Man" of the Democratic Revolution, 1749–1822.* University Park, Pa., 1981.

———. "Vermont Politics in the 1780's: Emergence of Rival Leadership." *Vermont History* 42 (1974): 140–54.

Axtell, James. *The European and the Indian: Essays in the Ethnohistory of Colonial North America.* New York, 1981.

Backus, Isaac. *A History of New England: With Particular Reference to the Denomination of Christians Called Baptists.* 2 vols. Newton, Mass., 1871.

Bail, Hamilton V. "Zadock Wright: That 'Devilish' Tory of Hartland." *Vermont History* 36 (1968): 186–203.

Bailyn, Bernard. *The New England Merchants in the Seventeenth Century.* Cambridge, Mass., 1955.

———. *The Ideological Origins of the American Revolution.* Cambridge, Mass., 1967.

———. *Voyagers to the West: A Passage in the Peopling of America on the Eve of the Revolution.* New York, 1986.

Bakeless, John. *Turncoats, Traitors, and Heroes.* Philadelphia, 1959.

Baker, Ray S. "Remember Baker." *New England Quarterly* 4 (1931): 595–628.

Bancroft, George. "Progress of Civilization." *Boston Quarterly Review* 1 (1838): 390–400.

Barron, Hal. *Those Who Stayed Behind: Rural Society in Nineteenth-Century New England.* New York, 1984.

Bayley, Edwin A. "An Address on the Life and Public Services of Brig.-General Jacob Bayley." *Proceedings of the Vermont Historical Society* 1917–18: 57–92.

Beardsley, Eben E. *The History of the Episcopal Church in Connecticut, from the Settlement of the Colony to the Death of Bishop Seabury.* 2 vols. New York, 1865.

Becker, Carl. *The History of Political Parties in the Province of New York, 1760–1776.* Madison, Wis., 1960.

Becker, E. Marie. "The 801 Westchester County Freeholders of 1763." *New-York Historical Society Quarterly* 35 (1951): 283–321.

Beeman, Richard R. *The Evolution of the Southern Backcountry: A Case Study of Lunenburg County, Virginia, 1746–1832.* Philadelphia, 1984.

Belknap, Jeremy. *The History of New-Hampshire.* 3 vols. Boston, 1792.

Bellemere, J. E. *Histoire de Nicolet, 1669–1924.* Arthabaska, Que., 1924.

Bellesiles, Michael. "The Establishment of Legal Structures on the Frontier: The Case of Revolutionary Vermont." *Journal of American History* 73 (1987): 895–915.

———. "Works of Historical Faith: Or, Who Wrote *Reason the Only Oracle of Man?*" *Vermont History* 57 (1989): 69–83.

Benedict, David. *A General History of the Baptist Denomination in America.* 2 vols. Boston, 1813.

Bickford, Christopher P. *Farmington in Connecticut.* Canaan, N.H., 1982.

Bidwell, Percy W. "Rural Economy in New England at the Beginning of the Nineteenth Century." *Transactions of the Connecticut Academy of Arts and Sciences* 20 (1916):241–399.

——— and John Falconer. *History of Agriculture in the Northern United States, 1620–1860.* New York, 1941.

Bigelow, Edwin, and Nancy Otis. *Manchester, Vermont.* Manchester, Vt., 1961.

Billias, George, ed. *Law and Authority in Colonial America.* Barre, Pa., 1965.

Black, John D. *The Rural Economy of New England: A Regional Study* Cambridge, Mass., 1950.

Bloomfield, Maxwell. *American Lawyers in a Changing Society, 1776–1876.* Cambridge, Mass., 1976.

Bogue, Alan G. "Social Theory and the Pioneer." *Agricultural History* 34 (1960): 21–34.

Bonomi, Patricia U. *Under the Cope of Heaven: Religion, Society, and Politics in Colonial America.* New York, 1986.

———. *A Factious People: Politics and Society in Colonial New York.* New York, 1971.

Boorstin, Daniel. *The Americans: The Colonial Experience.* New York, 1958.

Borah, Woodrow, et al., eds. *Urbanization in the Americas: The Background in Comparative Perspective.* Ottawa, 1980.

Botein, Stephen, ed. *Early American Law and Society.* New York, 1983.

Bouton, Nathaniel. *History of Concord, New Hampshire.* Concord, N.H., 1856.

Bowler, R. Arthur. *Logistics and the Failure of the British Army in America, 1775–1783.* Princeton, N.J., 1975.

Bowman, Larry G. *Captive Americans: Prisoners during the American Revolution.* Athens, Ohio, 1976.

Boyd, Julian P. "Attempts to Form New States in New York and Pennsylvania, 1786–1789." *Quarterly Journal of the New York State Historical Society* 12 (1931): 257–70.

Brady, James E. "Wyoming: A Study of John Franklin and the Connecticut Movement into Pennsylvania." Ph.D. diss., Syracuse University, 1973.

Bremer, Francis. *The Puritan Experiment.* New York, 1976.

Brock, Peter. *Pacifism in the United States: From the Colonial Era to the First World War*. Princeton, N.J., 1968.

Brooks, Van Wyck. *The Flowering of New England*. New York, 1936.

Brown, Robert E. *Middle-Class Democracy and the Revolution in Massachusetts, 1691–1780*. Ithaca, N.Y., 1955.

Brown, William H. *Colonel John Goffe: Eighteenth Century New Hampshire*. Manchester, N.H., 1950.

Brunvand, Jan H., ed. *Readings in American Folklore*. New York, 1979.

Brynn, Edward. "Vermont and the British Emporium, 1765–1865." *Vermont History* 45 (1977): 5–30.

Buckley, J. M. *A History of Methodists in the United States*. New York, 1896.

Buel, Richard, Jr. *Dear Liberty: Connecticut's Mobilization for the Revolutionary War*. Middletown, Conn., 1980.

Bumsted, J. M. "Revivalism and Separatism in New England: The First Society of Norwich, Connecticut, as a Case Study." *William and Mary Quarterly* 24 (1967): 588–612.

——. "Religion, Finance, and Democracy in Massachusetts: The Town of Norton as a Case Study." *Journal of American History* 57 (1971): 817–31.

Burns, Brian. "Mad Jack M'Alpine, A Soldier of the King." *Vermont History* 51 (1983): 158–69.

Bushman, Richard L. *From Puritan to Yankee: Character and the Social Order in Connecticut, 1690–1765*. Cambridge, Mass., 1967.

Callaghan, North. *Henry Knox: George Washington's General*. New York, 1958.

Calloway, Colin G. *The Western Abenakis of Vermont, 1600–1800: War, Migration, and the Survival of an Indian People*. Norman, Okla., 1990.

——. "The Conquest of Vermont: Vermont's Indian Troubles in Context." *Vermont History* 52 (1984): 161–79.

——. *Dawnland Encounters: Indians and Europeans in Northern New England*. Hanover, 1991.

Cameron, Kenneth W. *The Papers of Loyalist Sameul Peters*. Hartford, 1978.

Carmer, Carl. *The Susquehanna*. New York, 1955.

Caulkins, F. M. *History of Norwich, Connecticut*. Norwich, Conn., 1845.

Caverly, Abiel M. *History of the Town of Pittsford, Vermont*. Rutland, Vt., 1872.

Chacko, David, and Alexander Kulscar "Israel Potter: Genesis of a Legend." *William and Mary Quarterly* 41 (1984): 365–89.

Chase, Frederick. *A History of Dartmouth College and the Town of Hanover, New Hampshire*. 2 vols. Cambridge, Mass., 1891.

Child, William H. *History of the Town of Cornish, New Hampshire*. 2 vols. Concord, N.H., n.d.

Chipman, Daniel. *Reports of Cases Argued and Determined in the Supreme Court of the State of Vermont*. Middlebury, Vt., 1824.

——. *Life of Hon. Nathaniel Chipman, LL.D.* Boston, 1846.

——. *Memoir of Thomas Chittenden.* Middlebury, Vt., 1849.

Chittenden, Lucius E. *The Capture of Ticonderoga.* Rutland, Vt., 1872.

Clark, Charles E. *The Eastern Frontier: The Settlement of Northern New England, 1610–1763.* New York, 1970.

Clark, Christopher. *The Roots of Rural Capitalism: Western Massachusetts, 1780–1860.* Ithaca, N.Y., 1990.

——. "Household Economy, Market Exchange, and the Rise of Capitalism in the Connecticut River Valley, 1800–1860." *Journal of Social History* 13 (1979): 168–89.

Clark, Solomon. *Antiquities, Historical, and Graduates of Northampton.* Northampton, Mass., 1882.

Clarke, L. D. "Vermont Lands of the Society for the Propagation of the Gospel." *New England Quarterly* 3 (1930): 279–96.

Coburn, Frank W. *The Centennial History of the Battle of Bennington.* Boston, 1877.

Cochran, Thomas. "New York in the Confederation: An Economic Study." Ph.D. diss., University of Pennsylvania, 1932.

Cohen, Bernard I. "Ethan Allen Hitchcock." *Proceedings of the American Antiquarian Society* 61 (1951): 29–136.

Cole, Arthur H. *Wholesale Commodity Prices in the United States, 1700–1861.* Cambridge, Mass., 1938.

Coleman, Peter J. *Debtors and Creditors in America: Insolvency, Imprisonment for Debt, and Bankruptcy, 1607–1900.* Madison, Wis., 1974.

Collier, Christopher. "Roger Sherman and the New Hampshire Grants." *Vermont History* 30 (1962): 211–19.

Comstock, John M. *The Congregational Churches of Vermont and Their Ministry.* St. Johnsbury, Vt., 1942.

Conant, Edward. *Vermont Historical Reader.* 4th ed. Rutland, Vt., 1907.

Conant, H. J. "Imprisonment for Debt in Vermont: A History." *Vermont History* 19 (1951): 67–80.

Conforti, Joseph A. "Samuel Hopkins and the New Divinity: Theology, Ethics, and Social Reform in Eighteenth-Century New England." *William and Mary Quarterly* 34 (1977): 572–89.

Cook, Edward M., Jr. *Fathers of the Towns: Leadership and Community Structure in Eighteenth Century New England.* Baltimore, 1976.

Cook, Sherburne. "The Significance of Diseases." *Human Biology* 44 (1973): 485–508.

——. "Interracial Warfare and Population Decline among the New England Indians." *Ethnohistory* 20 (1973): 1–24.

Cooley, Timothy M. *Sketches of the Life and Character of the Rev. Lemuel Haynes*. New York, 1839.

Cothren, William. *History of Ancient Woodbury, Connecticut, from the First Indian Deed in 1659*. 3 vols. Waterbury, Conn., 1854–79.

Cousins, Norman, ed. *The Republic of Reason: The Personal Philosophies of the Founding Fathers*. San Francisco, 1988.

Countryman, Edward. *A People in Revolution: The American Revolution and Political Society in New York, 1760–1790*. Baltimore, Md., 1981.

———. "Consolidating Power in Revolutionary America: The Case of New York, 1775–1783." *Journal of Interdisciplinary History* 6 (1976): 645–77.

Cowan, Ian B. *The Scottish Covenanters, 1660–1688*. New York, 1976.

Crocker, Henry. *History of the Baptists in Vermont*. Bellows Falls, Vt., 1913.

Crockett, Walter. *Vermont, the Green Mountain State*. 5 vols. New York, 1923.

Cross, Lord, and G. J. Hand. *The English Legal System*. London, 1971.

Crowley, J. E. *This Sheba, Self: The Conceptualization of Economic Life in Eighteenth-Century America*. Baltimore, 1974.

Cruikshank, E. A. "The Adventures of Roger Stevens: A Forgotten Loyalist Pioneer in Upper Canada." *Proceedings of the Ontario Historical Society* 33 (1939): 11–38.

D'Agostino, Lorenzo. *The History of Public Welfare in Vermont*. Winooski Park, Vt., 1948.

Daniell, Jere R. *Experiment in Republicanism: New Hampshire Politics and the American Revolution, 1741–1794*. Cambridge, Mass., 1970.

Daniels, Bruce C. *The Connecticut Town: Growth and Development, 1635–1790*. Middletown, Conn., 1979.

Davis, Kenneth S. "In the Name of the Great Jehovah and the Continental Congress!" *American Heritage* 14 (Oct. 1963): 66–77.

Dawson, Henry B. *Battles of the United States, By Sea and Land*. 2 vols. New York, 1858.

Day, Clarence A. *A History of Maine Agriculture, 1604–1860*. Orono, Maine., 1954.

Dean, Leon W. *The Admission of Vermont into the Union*. Burlington, Vt., 1941.

DeForest, Heman P. *The History of Westborough, Massachusetts* Westborough, Mass., 1891.

Deming, Leonard. *Catalogue of the Principal Officers of Vermont*. Middlebury, Vt., 1851.

Denio, Herbert W. "Massachusetts Land Grants in Vermont." *Publications of the Colonial Society of Massachusetts* 24 (1920): 35–59.

Denison, Frederick. *Notes on the Baptists, and Their Principles, in Norwich, Connecticut, from the Settlement of the Town to 1850*. Norwich, Conn., 1857.

Dennis, Donald D. "The Deistic Trio: A Study in the Central Religious Beliefs of Ethan Allen, Thomas Paine, and Elihu Palmer." Ph.D. diss., University of Utah, 1978.

DePuy, Henry W. *Ethan Allen and the Green-Mountain Heroes of '76.* Boston, 1853.

Dexter, Franklin B. *Biographical Sketches of the Graduates of Yale College.* 6 vols. New York and New Haven, 1885–1912.

Dickerman, George S. *The Old Mount Carmel Parish, Origins and Outgrowths.* New Haven, 1925.

Digby, William. *The British Invasion from the North.* Albany, 1887.

Dillon, Dorothy R. *The New York Triumvirate: A Study of the Legal and Political Careers of William Livingston, John Morrin Scott, William Smith, Jr.* New York, 1949.

Dinkin, Robert J. *Voting in Provincial America: A Study of Elections in the Thirteen Colonies, 1689–1776.* Westport, Conn., 1977.

Ditz, Toby L. *Property and Kinship: Inheritance in Early Connecticut, 1750–1820.* Princeton, N.J., 1986.

Dorson, Richard. *America in Legend.* New York, 1973.

Douglass, Elisha P. *Rebels and Democrats: The Struggle for Equal Political Rights and Majority Rule during the American Revolution.* Chapel Hill, N.C., 1955.

Duffy, John, and H. Nicholas Muller III. *An Anxious Democracy: Aspects of the 1830s.* Westport, Conn., 1982.

———. "Jedidiah Burchard and Vermont's 'New Measure' Revivals: Social Adjustment and the Quest for Unity." *Vermont History* 46 (1978): 5–20.

Dykstra, Robert S. *The Cattle Towns.* New York, 1965.

Edes, H. H. "Memoir of Dr. Thomas Young." *Transactions of the Colonial Society of Massachusetts* 11 (1906–9): 2–54.

Elkins, Stanley, and Eric McKitrick, "A Meaning for Turner's Frontier," *Political Science Review* 69 (1954): 321–53, 565–602.

Ellis, Richard. *The Jeffersonian Crisis: Courts and Politics in the Young Republic.* New York, 1971.

Elwood, Douglas. *The Philosophical Theology of Jonathan Edwards.* New York, 1960.

Essays in the Social and Economic History of Vermont. Vol. 5 of *Collections of the Vermont Historical Society.* Montpelier, Vt., 1943. Note: pagination seriously in error.

Everest, Allan S. *Moses Hazen and the Canadian Refugees in the American Revolution.* Syracuse, N.Y., 1976.

Fingerhut, Eugene R. "From Scots to Americans: Ryegate's Immigrants in the 1770s." *Vermont History* 35 (1969): 186–207.

Finkleman, Paul. *An Imperfect Union: Slavery, Federalism, and Comity.* Chapel Hill, N.C., 1981.

Fisher, Dorothy C. *Vermont in Tradition: The Biography of an Outlook on Life.* Boston, 1953.

Fisher, Josephine. "Loyalists in Strafford." *Proceedings of the Vermont Historical Society* 5 (1937): 334–44.

Flaherty, David, ed. *Essays in the History of Early American Law.* Chapel Hill, N.C., 1969.

Flick, Alexander C. *The American Revolution in New York: Its Political, Social, and Economic Significance.* Rept. Port Washington, N.Y., 1967.

——, ed. *History of the State of New York.* 3 vols. Rept. Port Washington, N.Y., 1962.

Flitcroft, John E. *The Novelist in Vermont.* Cambridge, Mass., 1929.

Fonblanque, Edward B. de. *Political and Military Episodes in the Latter Half of the Eighteenth Century.* 2 Vols. London, 1876.

——. *Life and Correspondence of John Burgoyne, General, Statesman, Dramatist.* London, 1876.

Fox, Dixon R. *Yankees and Yorkers.* New York, 1963.

French, Allen. *The Taking of Ticonderoga in 1775: The British Story.* Cambridge, Mass., 1928.

——. *The First Year of the American Revolution.* New York, 1968.

Frisbee, James. *History of Middletown, Vermont.* Rutland, Vt., 1867.

Frothingham, Richard. *Life and Times of Joseph Warren.* Boston, 1865.

Gabriel, Ralph H. *Religion and Learning at Yale.* New Haven, 1958.

Gale, John, and Harriet Thompson. *Official History of Guilford, Vermont.* Brattleboro, Vt., 1961.

Gallay, Alan. *The Formation of a Planter Elite: Jonathan Bryan and the Southern Colonial Frontier.* Athens, Ga., 1989.

Gallup, J. A. *Epidemic Diseases in Vermont.* Boston, 1815.

Gardiner, Robert H. "History of the Kennebec Purchase." *Collections of the Maine Historical Society* 2 (1891): 269–94.

Gaustad, Edwin S. *The Great Awakening in New England.* New York, 1957.

Gaverly, A. M. *History of the Town of Pittsford, Vermont.* Middlebury, Vt., 1872.

Gerlach, Larry. "Connecticut, the Continental Congress, and the Independence of Vermont, 1777–1782." *Vermont History* 34 (1966): 188–93.

Gerth, H. H., and C. Wright Mills. *From Max Weber: Essays in Sociology.* New York, 1958.

Gilmore, Robert C. "Connecticut and the Foundation of Vermont." Ph.D. diss., Yale University, 1954.

Gilmore, William. "Elementary Literacy in Rural New England, 1760–1830." *Proceedings of the American Antiquarian Society* 92 (1982): 87–178.

Glass, D. V. and D. E. C. Eversley, eds. *Population in History: Essays in Historical Demography.* London, 1965.

Glover, Michael. *General Burgoyne in Canada and America: Scapegoat for a System.* London, 1976.

Goddard, Merritt, and Henry Partridge. *History of Norwich, Vermont.* Hanover, N.H., 1905.

Goebel, Julius, and T. Raymond Naughton. *Law Enforcement in Colonial New York: A Study in Criminal Procedure, 1664–1776.* New York, 1944.

Goen, C. C. *Revivalism and Separatism in New England, 1740–1800: Strict Congregationalists and Separate Baptists in the Great Awakening.* New Haven, 1962.

Gold, Theodore S. *Historical Records of the Town of Cornwall.* Hartford, 1904.

Goodhue, Josiah F. *History of the Town of Shoreham.* Middlebury, Vt., 1861.

Graffagnino, J. Kevin. " 'Twenty Thousand Muskets!!!': Ira Allen and the *Olive Branch* Affair, 1796–1800." *William and Mary Quarterly* 48 (1991): 409–31.

———. " 'The Country My Soul Delighted In': The Onion River Land Company and the Vermont Frontier." *New England Quarterly* 65 (1992): 24–60.

Grant, Charles. *Democracy in the Connecticut Frontier Town of Kent.* New York, 1961.

———. "A History of Kent, 1738–1796." Ph.D. diss., Columbia University, 1957.

Green, J. J., et al. *Centennial Proceedings and Other Historical Facts and Incidents Relating to Newfane, Vermont.* Brattleboro, Vt., 1877.

Greenberg, Douglas. *Crime and Law Enforcement in the Colony of New York, 1691–1776.* Ithaca, N.Y., 1976.

Greene, Evarts B., and Virginia D. Harrington. *American Population before the Federal Census of 1790.* New York, 1932.

Greene, Jack P., and J. R. Pole, eds. *Colonial British America: Essays in the New History of the Early Modern Era.* Baltimore, 1984.

Greven, Philip J., Jr. *Four Generations: Population, Land, and Family in Colonial Andover, Massachusetts.* Ithaca, N.Y., 1970.

Griffin, Edward M. *Old Brick: Charles Chauncy of Boston, 1707–1787.* Minneapolis, 1980.

Gross, Robert A. *The Minutemen and Their World.* New York, 1976.

Hall, Benjamin. *History of Eastern Vermont.* New York, 1858.

Hall, David D. *The Faithful Shepherd: A History of the New England Ministry in the Seventeenth Century.* Chapel Hill, N.C., 1972.

———, et al., eds. *Saints and Revolutionaries: Essays on Early American History.* New York, 1984.

Hall, Henry. *Ethan Allen: The Robin Hood of Vermont.* New York, 1895.

Hall, Hiland. *The History of Vermont from Its Discovery to Its Admission into the Union in 1791.* Albany, 1868.

Hammett, Theodore M. "Revolutionary Ideology in Massachusetts: Thomas

Allen's 'Vindication' of the Berkshire Constitutionalists, 1778." *William and Mary Quarterly* 33 (1976): 514–27.

Handlin, Oscar. "The Eastern Frontier of New York." *New York History* 18 (1937): 50–75.

Hareven, Tamara K., ed. *Family and Kin in Urban Communities, 1700–1930.* New York, 1977.

Harper, R. Eugene. "The Class Structure of Western Pennsylvania." Ph.D. diss., University of Pittsburgh, 1969.

Hart, James D. *The Popular Book in America.* New York, 1950.

Hartog, Hendrik, ed. *Law in the American Revolution and the Revolution in the Law.* New York, 1981.

Haskins, George L. "Lay Judges: Magistrates and Justices in Early Massachusetts." *Publications of the Colonial Society of Massachusetts* 62 (1984): 39–55.

Hatch, Nathan O. *The Sacred Cause of Liberty: Republican Thought and the Millennium in Revolutionary New Engalnd.* New Haven, 1977.

———. *The Democratization of American Christianity.* New Haven, 1989.

Hatch, Robert M. *Thrust for Canada: the American Attempt on Quebec in 1775–1776.* Boston, 1979.

Hawke, David F. "Dr. Thomas Young—'Eternal Fisher in Troubled Waters': Notes for a Biography." *New-York Historical Society Quarterly* 54 (1970): 7–29.

Hayes, Lyman S. *History of the Town of Rockingham, Vermont.* Bellows Falls, Vt., 1907.

———. *The Old Meeting House, Erected 1787, and the First Church in Rockingham, Vermont, 1773–1840.* Bellows Falls, Vt., 1915.

Hazard, John N., and Wenceslas J. Wagner, eds. *Legal Thought in the United States of America under Contemporary Pressures.* Brussels, 1970.

Heimert, Alan. *Religion and the American Mind: From the Great Awakening to the Revolution.* Cambridge, Mass., 1966.

Hemenway, Abby M., ed. *Vermont Historical Gazetteer.* 5 vols. Burlington, Vt., 1868–91.

Henderson, Patrick. "Smallpox and Patriotism." *Virginia Magazine of History and Biography* 73 (1965): 413–24.

Henderson, Patrick. "Smallpox and Patriotism: The Norfolk Riots, 1768–1769." *Virginia Magazine of History and Biography* 73 (1965): 413–24.

Henretta, James. "Families and Farms: Mentalité in Pre-Industrial America." *William and Mary Quarterly* 35 (1978): 3–32.

Heyrman, Christine L. *Commerce and Culture: The Maritime Communities of Colonial Massachusetts, 1690–1750.* New York, 1984.

Higginbotham, Don. *George Washington and the American Military Tradition.* Athens, Ga., 1985.

——. *War and Society in Revolutionary America: The Wider Dimensions of Conflict.* Columbia, S.C., 1988.

——, ed. *Reconsiderations on the Revolutionary War: Selected Essays.* Westport, Conn., 1978.

Hill, Christopher. *The World Turned Upside Down: Radical Ideas during the English Revolution.* London, 1972.

Hinden, John C. "The White Chief of the St. Francis Abenakis—Some Aspects of Border Warfare: 1690–1790." *Vermont History* 24 (1956): 199–210, 337–55.

Hindle, Brooke, ed. *Material Culture of the Wooden Age.* Tarrytown, N.Y., 1981.

Hine, Robert V. *Community on the American Frontier: Separate but not Alone.* Norman, Okla., 1980.

Historical Section of the [Canadian] General Staff, eds. *A History of the Organization, Development, and Services of the Military and Naval Forces of Canada.* Vol. 2. *The War of the American Revolution.* Ottawa, 1920.

Hoffman, Ronald, Thad Tate, and Peter J. Albert, eds. *An Uncivil War: The Southern Backcountry during the American Revolution.* Charlottesville, Va., 1985.

Holbrook, Jay M. *Vermont 1771 Census.* Oxford, Mass., 1982.

Holbrook, Stewart. *Ethan Allen.* New York, 1940.

Hollister, Hiel. *Pawlet for One Hundred Years.* Albany, 1867.

Horton, John T. *James Kent: A Study in Conservatism.* New York, 1939.

Horwitz, Morton. *The Transformation of American Law, 1780–1860.* Cambridge, Mass., 1977.

Howe, Daniel W., ed. *Victorian America.* University Park, Pa., 1976.

——. *The Unitarian Conscience: Harvard Moral Philosophy, 1805–1861.* Middletown, Conn., 1988.

Hoyt, Edwin P. *The Damndest Yankees: Ethan Allen and His Clan.* Brattleboro, Vt. 1976.

Hubbard, Charles H., and Justus Dartt. *History of the Town of Springfield, Vermont, with a Genealogical Record, 1752 1895.* Boston, 1895.

Huddleston, F. J. *Gentleman Johnny Burgoyne: Misadventures of an English Gentleman in the Revolution.* Indianapolis, 1927.

Huden, John C. *Indian Place Names in Vermont.* Montpelier, Vt., 1957.

——. "Indian Groups in Vermont." *Vermont History* 26 (1958): 112–15.

Hufton, Olwen H. *The Poor of Eighteenth Century France 1750–1789* Oxford, 1974.

Huguenin, Charles A. "Ethan Allen, Parolee on Long Island." *Vermont History* 25 (1957): 103–25.

Hunt, Louise L. *Biographical Notes concerning General Richard Montgomery.* Poughkeepsie, 1876.

Huntley, William B. "Jefferson's Public and Private Religion." *South Atlantic Quarterly* 79 (1980): 286–301.

Hutson, James H. "An Investigation of the Inarticulate: Philadephia's White Oaks." *William and Mary Quarterly* 28 (1971): 3–25.

Irving, Washington. *A History of New York from the Beginning of the World to the End of the Dutch Dynasty.* Philadelphia, 1871.

———. *Life of George Washington.* Boston, 1982.

Isaac, Rhys. *The Transformation of Virginia, 1740–1790.* Chapel Hill, N.C., 1982.

Jackson, Carl T. *The Oriental Religions in American Thought: Nineteenth-Century Explorations.* Westport, Conn., 1981.

Jackson, H. M. *Justus Sherwood: Soldier, Loyalist, and Negotiator.* Ottawa, 1958.

Jameson, John F. *Records of the Town of Amherst, 1725–1788.* Amherst, Mass., 1884.

Jedrey, Christopher M. *The World of John Cleaveland: Family and Community in Eighteenth-Century New England.* New York, 1979.

Jellison, Charles. *Ethan Allen, Frontier Rebel.* Syracuse, N.Y., 1969.

Jennings, Francis. *The Invasion of America: Indians, Colonialism, and the Cant of Conquest.* Chapel Hill, N.C., 1975.

Jennings, Isaac. *Memorials of a Century.* Boston, 1869.

Johnson, Herbert. *Essays on New York Colonial Legal History.* Westport, Conn., 1981.

Jones, Alice H. *American Colonial Wealth.* 3 vols. New York, 1977.

Jones, C. H. *History of the Campaign for the Conquest of Canada.* Philadelphia, 1882.

Jones, Douglas L. "The Strolling Poor: Transiency in Eighteenth-Century Massachusetts." *Journal of Social History* 8 (1975): 28–54.

Jones, E. L. "Creative Disruptions in American Agriculture, 1620–1829." *Agricultural History* 43 (1974): 510–28.

Jones, J. W. *The Shattered Synthesis: New England Puritanism before the Great Awakening.* New Haven, 1973.

Jones, Matt B. *Vermont in the Making, 1750–1777.* Hamden, Conn., 1968.

Jones, Thomas. *History of New York during the Revolution.* 2 vols. New York City, 1879.

Judd, Jacob, and Irwin H. Polishook, eds. *Aspects of Early New York Society and Politics.* Tarrytown, N.Y., 1974.

Judd, Sylvester. *History of Hadley, Massachusetts.* Springfield, Mass., 1905.

Kalinoski, Sarah. "Sequestration, Confiscation, and the 'Tory' in the Vermont Revolution." *Vermont History* 45 (1977): 236–47.

Kammen, Michael. *Colonial New York: A History.* New York, 1975.

Karsted, Peter, ed. *The Military in America: From the Colonial Era to the Present.* New York, 1986.

Kelsay, Isabel T. *Joseph Brant, 1743–1807: Man of Two Worlds.* Syracuse, N.Y., 1984.

Kettner, James H. *The Development of American Citizenship, 1608–1870.* Chapel Hill, N.C., 1978.

Kilbourne, Payne K. *Sketches and Chronicles of the Town of Litchfield, Connecticut.* Hartford, Conn., 1859.

Kim, Sung Bok. *Landlord and Tenant in Colonial New York: Manorial Society, 1664–1775.* Chapel Hill, N.C., 1978.

Klein, Milton. *The Politics of Diversity: Essays in the History of Colonial New York.* Port Washington, N.Y., 1974.

———. "Prelude to Revolution in New York: Jury Trials and Judicial Tenure." *William and Mary Quarterly* 27 (1960): 439–63.

———. "New York Lawyers and the Coming of the American Revolution." *New York History* 55 (1974): 383–407

Klein, Rachel N. *Unification of a Slave State: The Rise of the Planter Class in the South Carolina Backcountry, 1760–1808.* Chapel Hill, N.C., 1990.

———. "Ordering the Backcountry: The South Carolina Regulation." *William and Mary Quarterly* 38 (1981): 661–80.

Kohn, Richard H. *Eagle and Sword: The Federalists and the Creation of the Military Establishment in America, 1783–1802.* New York, 1975.

Konig, David. *Law and Society in Puritan Massachusetts: Essex County, 1629–1692.* Chapel Hill, N.C., 1979.

Kross, Jessica. *The Evolution of an American Town: Newtown, New York, 1642–1775.* Philadelphia, 1983.

Kurtz, Stephen, and James Hutson, eds. *Essays on the American Revolution.* New York, 1973.

Labaree, Benjamin W. *Patriots and Partisans: The Merchants of Newburyport, 1764–1815.* Cambridge, Mass., 1962.

Lajoie, John. "A History of the Green Mountain Boys." *Vermont History* 34 (1966): 235–40.

Larned, Ellen D. *History of Windham County, Connecticut.* 2 vols. Worcester, Mass., 1874.

Laslett, Peter, and Richard Wall, eds. *Household and Family in Past Time.* Cambridge, 1972.

Lawler, Percy E., et al., eds. *To Doctor R.: Essays Here Collected and Published in Honor of the Seventieth Birthday of Dr. A. S. W. Rosenbach.* Philadelphia, 1946.

Leach, Douglas. *The Northern Colonial Frontier, 1607–1765.* New York, 1966.

———. *Arms for Empire: A Military History of the British Colonies in North America, 1607–1763.* New York, 1973.

Lee, Everett S. "The Turner Thesis Re-Examined." *American Quarterly* 13 (1961), 77–83.

Lee, John P. *Uncommon Vermont.* Rutland, Vt., 1926.

Lemisch, Jesse. "Jack Tar in the Streets: Merchant Seamen in the Politics of Revolutionary America." *William and Mary Quarterly* 25 (1968): 371–407.

——— . "Listen to the 'Inarticulate': William Widger's Dream and the Loyalties of American Revolutionary Seamen in British Prisons." *Journal of Social History* 3 (1969): 1–29.

——— and John K. Alexander. "The White Oaks, Jack Tar, and the Concept of the 'Inarticulate,' " with Note by Simeon Crowther and rebuttal by James Hutson. *William and Mary Quarterly* 29 (1972): 109–42.

Lemon, James T. *The Best Poor Man's Country: A Geographical Study of Early Southeastern Pennsylvania.* Baltimore, 1972.

Letteiri, Ronald. "The New Hampshire Committees of Safety and Revolutionary Republicanism, 1775–1784." *Historical New Hampshire* 35 (1980): 241–83.

Lewis, Paul. *The Man Who Lost America.* New York, 1973.

Little, William. *History of Warren, New Hampshire.* Manchester, N.H., 1870.

Livermore, Shaw, Jr. *The Twilight of Federalism.* Princeton, N.J., 1962.

Llewellyn, Karl N. *The Common Law Tradition: Deciding Appeals.* Boston, 1960.

Lockridge, Kenneth A. *A New England Town: The First Hundred Years* New York, 1970.

Loehr, Rodney C. "Self-Sufficiency on the Farm, 1759–1819." *Agricultural History* 26 (1952): 37–52.

Lofaro, Michael A., ed. *Davy Crockett: The Man, the Legend, the Legacy, 1786–1986.* Knoxville, Tenn., 1985.

Lossing, Benson J. *Field-Book of the Revolution.* 2 vols. New York, 1851–52.

——— . *The Life and Times of Philip Schuyler.* New York, 1873.

——— . "Ethan Allen." *Harper's New Monthly Magazine* 17 (1858): 721–43.

Lovejoy, David. *Rhode Island Politics and the American Revolution, 1760–1776.* Providence, R.I., 1958.

——— . *Religious Enthusiasm in the New World: Heresy to Revolution.* Cambridge, Mass., 1985.

Lucas, Paul R. *Valley of Discord: Church and Society along the Connecticut River, 1636–1725.* Hanover, N.H., 1976.

Ludlum, David. *Social Ferment in Vermont, 1791–1850.* Montpelier, Vt., 1948.

Lutz, Donald S. *Popular Consent and Popular Control: Whig Political Theory in the Early State Constitutions.* Baton Rouge, La., 1980.

Lynd, Staunton. *Class Conflict, Slavery, and the Constitution: Ten Essays.* Indianapolis, 1968.

———. "Who Shall Rule at Home? Dutchess County, New York, in the American Revolution," *William and Mary Quarterly* 18 (1961): 330–59.

McCarty, Virgil L. "Boundary Controversy: The Brownington-Johnson Land Problem." *Vermont History* 15 (1947): 157–76.

McCorison, Marcus. "Colonial Defence of the Upper Connecticut Valley." *Vermont History* 30 (1962): 50–62.

McCusker, John J. *Money and Exchange in Europe and America, 1600–1775: A Handbook.* Chapel Hill, N.C., 1978.

McDonald, Forest. *The Presidency of George Washington.* Lawrence, Kans., 1974.

Mackintosh, W. A. "Canada and Vermont: A Study in Historical Geography." *Canadian Historical Review* 7 (1927): 9–30.

McLaughlin, J. Fairfax. *Matthew Lyon: The Hampden of Congress.* New York, 1900.

McWilliams, John. "The Faces of Ethan Allen, 1760–1860." *New England Quarterly* 49 (1976): 257–82.

Mahan, Alfred T. *The Major Operations of the Navies in the War of American Independence.* Boston, 1913.

Maier, Pauline. *From Resistance to Revolution: Colonial Radicals and the Development of American Opposition to Britain, 1765–1776.* New York, 1972.

———. "Popular Uprisings and Civil Authority." *William and Mary Quarterly* 27 (1970): 3–35.

———. "Reason and Revolution: The Radicalism of Dr. Thomas Young." *William and Mary Quarterly* 27 (1970): 3–35.

Main, Jackson T. *The Social Structure of Revolutionary America.* Princeton, N.J., 1965.

Malone, Joseph J. *Pine Trees and Politics: The Naval Stores and Forest Policy in Colonial New England, 1691–1775.* Seattle, Wa., 1964.

Manhattan Company. *Manna-hatin, the Story of New York.* New York, 1929.

Marini, Stephen A. *Radical Sects of Revolutionary New England.* Cambridge, Mass., 1982.

Mark, Irving. *Agrarian Conflicts in Colonial New York, 1711–1775.* New York, 1940.

Martin, James K. "A Model for the Coming American Revolution: The Birth and Death of the Wentworth Oligarchy in New Hampshire, 1741–1776." *Journal of Social History* 4 (1970): 41–60.

——— and Mark E. Lender. *A Respectable Army: The Military Origins of the Republic, 1763–1789.* Arlington Heights, Ill., 1982.

Mason, Bernard. *The Road to Independence: The Revolutionary Movement in New York, 1773–1777.* Lexington, Ky., 1966.

Mathews, Donald. "The Second Great Awakening as an Organizing Process,

1780–1830." *American Quarterly* 21 (1969): 22–43.

May, Henry F. *The Enlightenment in America.* New York, 1976.

Mead, Sidney E. *The Lively Experiment: The Shaping of Christianity in America.* New York, 1963.

Mecklin, John M. *The Story of American Dissent.* New York, 1934.

Merrill, Michael. "Cash Is Good to Eat: Self-Sufficiency and Exchange in the Rural Economy of the United States." *Radical History Review* 4 (1977): 42–71.

Metzger, Charles H. *The Prisoner in the American Revolution.* Chicago, 1971.

Middlekauff, Robert. *The Mathers: Three Generations of Puritan Intellectuals, 1596–1728.* New York, 1971.

——— . *The Glorious Cause: The American Revolution, 1763–1789.* New York, 1982.

Miller, Edward, and Frederick Wells. *History of Ryegate, Vermont, from Its Settlement by the Scotch-American Company of Farmers to Present Time.* St. Johnsbury, Vt., 1913.

Miller, Helen. *The Case for Liberty.* Chapel Hill, N.C., 1965.

Miller, Perry. *Errand into the Wilderness.* Cambridge, Mass., 1956.

——— . *The Life of the Mind in America.* New York, 1965.

——— . "Thomas Hooker and the Democracy of Early Connecticut." *New England Quarterly* 4 (1931): 663–712.

Miner, Charles. *History of the Wyoming Valley.* Philadelphia, 1845.

Minot, George R. *The History of the Insurrections in Massachusetts.* Boston, 1810.

Mitchell, Robert D. *Commercialism and Frontier: Perspectives on the Early Shenandoah Valley.* Charlottesville, Va., 1977.

Moore, Frank. *Diary of the American Revolution.* 2 vols. New York, 1860.

Moore, Hugh. *Memoirs of Col. Ethan Allen.* Philadelphia, 1834.

Morais, Herbert M. *Deism in Eighteenth Century America.* New York, 1934.

Morgan, Edmund S. *Visible Saints: The History of a Puritan Idea.* New York, 1963.

——— . *The Puritan Family: Religion and Domestic Relations in Seventeenth-Century New England.* Rev. ed. New York, 1966.

——— . *The Challenge of the American Revolution.* New York, 1976.

——— . *Inventing the People: The Rise of Popular Sovereignty in England and America.* New York, 1988.

——— , and Helen M. Morgan. *The Stamp Act Crisis: Prologue to Revolution.* New York, 1953.

Morris, Richard. *The Forging of the Union, 1781–1789.* New York, 1987.

Morrison, Kenneth M. *The Enbattled Northeast: The Elusive Ideal of Alliance in Abenaki-European Relations.* Berkeley, Calif., 1984.

Morrissey, Helen. *Ethan Allen's Daughter.* Gardenville, Que., 1940.

Morrow, Rising L. *Connecticut Influences in Western Massachusetts and Vermont*. New Haven, 1936.

Mudge, James. *History of the New England Conference of the Methodist Episcopal Church, 1796–1910*. Boston, 1910.

Muller, H. Nicholas, III and Samuel B. Hand, eds. *In a State of Nature: Readings in Vermont History*. Montpelier, Vt., 1982.

Murdoch, Richard K. "A French Report on Vermont, 1778." *Vermont History* 34 (1966): 217–25.

Nash, Gary. *The Urban Crucibles: Social Change, Political Consciousness, and the Origins of the American Revolution*. Cambridge, Mass., 1979.

Nelson, William E. *The Americanization of the Common Law: The Impact of Legal Changes on Massachusetts Society, 1780–1830*. Cambridge, Mass., 1975.

———. *Dispute and Conflict Resolution in Plymouth County, Massachusetts, 1725–1825*. Chapel Hill, N.C., 1981.

———. "The American Revolution and the Emergence of Modern Doctrines of Federalism and Conflict of Laws." *Publications of the Colonial Society of Massachusetts* 62 (1984): 419–67.

Nettles, Curtis P. *George Washington and American Independence*. Boston, 1951.

Newell, Margaret E. "The Culture of Economic Development in New England, 1783–1799." Paper delivered at SHEAR Conference, 1989.

Niebuhr, H. R. *Social Sources of Denominationalism*. New York, 1957.

Nobles, Gregory H. *Divisions throughout the Whole: Politics and Society in Hampshire County, Massachusetts, 1740–75*. New York, 1983.

———. "Breaking into the Backcountry: New Approaches to the Early American Frontier, 1750–1800." *William and Mary Quarterly* 46 (1989): 641–70.

North, James. *History of Augusta, Maine*. Augusta, Maine., 1870.

Norton, Mary Beth. *Liberty's Daughters: The Revolutionary Experience of American Women, 1750–1800*. Boston, 1980.

Norton, Thomas E. *The Fur Trade in Colonial New York, 1686–1776* Madison, Wis., 1974.

Oblekevich, James. *Religion and Rural Society: South Lindsey, 1825–1875*. Oxford, 1976.

Onderdonk, Henry. *Revolutionary Incidents of Suffolk and King's Counties*. Port Washington, N.Y., 1970.

O'Neill, William L., ed. *Insights and Parallels: Problems and Issues in American Social History*. Minneapolis, 1973.

Onuf, Peter S. *The Origins of the Federal Republic: Jurisdictional Controversies in the United States, 1775–1787*. Philadelphia, 1983.

———. *Statehood and Union: A History of the Northwest Ordinance*. Bloomington, Ind., 1987.

——. "State-Making in Revolutionary America: Independent Vermont as a Case Study." *Journal of American History* 67 (1981): 797–815.

Paige, Lucius. *History of Hardwick, Massachusetts*. New York, 1883.

Parks, Joseph. *Pownall*. Hoosick Falls, N.Y., 1977.

Paullin, Charles O. *Atlas of the Historical Geography of the United States*. Washington, D.C., 1932.

Peckham, Howard. *The Colonial Wars, 1689–1762*. Chicago, 1964.

Pell, John. *Ethan Allen*. Lake George, N.Y., 1929.

Pemberton, Ian V. B. "Justus Sherwood, Vermont Loyalist, 1747–1798." Ph.D. diss., University of West Ontario, 1972.

——. "The British Secret Service in the Champlain Valley during the Haldimand Negotiations, 1780–1783." *Vermont History* 44 (1976): 129–40.

Peterson, Merrill D. *Adams and Jefferson: A Revolutionary Dialogue*. New York, 1976.

Phillips, Paul C. *The Fur Trade*. 2 vols. Norman, Okla., 1961.

Post, Albert. *Popular Free Thought in America, 1825–1850*. New York, 1943.

Potash, Paul J. "Welfare of the Regions Beyond." *Vermont History* 46 (1978): 109–28.

Powers, Grant. *Historical Sketches of the Discovery, Settlement, and Progress of Events in the Coos Country*. Haverhill, N.H., 1841.

Price, James. "Origin and Distinctive Characteristics of the United Presbyterian Church of North America." *Journal of the Presbyterian Historical Society* 1 (1901): 87–110.

Pruitt, Bettye H. "Self-Sufficiency and the Agricultural Economy of Eighteenth-Century Massachusetts." *William and Mary Quarterly* 41 (1984): 333–64.

Purcell, Richard J. *Connecticut in Transition: 1775–1818*. Middletown, Conn., 1963.

Rampersad, Arnold. *Melville's Israel Potter: A Pilgrimage and Progress*. Bowling Green, Ohio, 1969.

Rand, Frank P. *The Village of Amherst, a Landmark of Light*. Amherst, Mass., 1958.

Reid, John Phillip. "In a Defensive Rage: The Uses of the Mob, the Justification in Law, and the Coming of the American Revolution." *New York University Law Review* 49 (1974): 1043–91.

——. *In a Defiant Stance: The Conditions of Law in Massachusetts Bay, the Irish Comparison, and the Coming of the American Revolution*. University Park, Pa., 1977.

——. *Law for the Elephant: Property and Social Behavior on the Overland Trail*. San Marino, Calif., 1980.

――――. *In Defiance of the Law: The Standing-Army Controversy, the Two Constitutions, and the Coming of the American Revolution.* Chapel Hill, N.C., 1981.

Reynold, David S. *Faith in Fiction: The Emergence of Religious Literature in America.* Cambridge, Mass. 1981.

Rice, John L. "Dartmouth College and the State of New Connecticut, 1776–1782." *Papers and Proceedings of the Connecticut Valley Historical Society, 1876–1881* 2 (1881): 152–206.

Riley, Robert A. "Kinship Patterns in Londonderry, Vermont, 1772–1900: An Intergenerational Perspective of Changing Family Relationships." Ph.D. diss., University of Massachusetts, 1980.

Roberts, Gwilym R. "An Unknown Vermonter: Sylvanus Evarts, Governor Chittenden's Tory Brother-in-Law." *Vermont History* 29 (1961): 92–102.

Robinson, William A. *Jeffersonian Democracy in New England.* New Haven, 1916.

Rossie, Jonathan G. *The Politics of Command in the American Revolution.* Syracuse, N.Y. 1975.

Roth, Randolph A. *The Democratic Dilemma: Religion, Reform, and the Social Order in the Connecticut River Valley of Vermont, 1791–1850.* Cambridge, 1987.

――――. "The First Radical Abolitionists: The Reverend James Milligan and the Reformed Presbyterians of Vermont." *New England Quarterly* 55 (1982): 540–63.

Rothwell, Kenneth. *A Goodly Heritage: The Episcopal Church in Vermont.* Burlington, Vt., 1973.

Royster, Charles. *A Revolutionary People at War: The Continental Army and American Character, 1775–1783.* Chapel Hill, N.C., 1979.

Rozwenc, Edwin C. "Agriculture and Politics in the Vermont Tradition." *Vermont Quarterly* 17 (1949): 81–96.

Rutman, Darrett. *American Puritanism.* New York, 1970.

Salmon, Marylynn. *Women and the Law of Property in Early America* Chapel Hill, N.C., 1986.

Saunderson, Henry H. *History of Charlestown, New Hampshire* Claremont, N.H., 1876.

Scott, Donald M. *From Office to Profession: The New England Minister, 1750–1850.* University Park, Pa., 1978.

Selsam, J. Paul. *The Pennsylvania Constitution of 1776: A Study in Revolutionary Democracy.* Philadelphia, 1936.

Shaeffer, John. "A Comparison of the First Constitutions of Vermont and Pennsylvania." *Vermont History* 43 (1975): 33–43.

Shammas, Carole. "How Self-Sufficient Was Early America?" *Journal of Interdisciplinary History* 13 (1982): 247–72.

――――, Marylynn Salmon, and Michael Dahlin. *Inheritance in America from Colo-*

nial Times to the Present. New Brunswick, N.J., 1987.

Sharp, Gene. *Making Europe Unconquerable: The Potential of Civilian-Based Deterrence and Defence.* Cambridge, Mass., 1985.

Sheldon, George. *A History of Deerfield, Massachusetts.* 2 vols. Deerfield, Mass., 1895.

Sherman, Michael, ed. *A More Perfect Union: Vermont Becomes a State, 1777–1816.* Montpelier, Vt., 1991.

Shipton, Clifford K., et al., eds. *Biographical Sketches of Those Who Attended Harvard College in the Classes of 1726–1730.* 17 vols. Cambridge and Boston, 1873–1975.

Shy, John. *Toward Lexington: The Role of the British Army in the Coming of the American Revolution.* Princeton, N.J., 1965.

——— . *A People Numerous and Armed: Reflections on the Military Struggle for American Independence.* New York, 1976.

Sills, David L., ed. *International Encyclopedia of the Social Sciences.* 17 vols. New York, 1968.

Simmons, R. C. *The American Colonies: From Settlement to Independence.* New York, 1981.

Slaughter, Thomas P. *The Whiskey Rebellion: Frontier Epilogue to the American Revolution.* New York, 1986.

Slotkin, Richard. *Regeneration through Violence.* Middletown, Conn., 1973.

Smith, Chard P. *The Housatonic, Puritan River.* New York, 1946.

Smith, H. P., ed. *History of Addison County, Vermont.* Syracuse, N.Y., 1886.

Smith, H. Shelton. *Changing Conceptions of Original Sin: A Study in American Theology since 1750.* New York, 1955.

Smith, James M., ed. *Seventeenth-Century America.* Chapel Hill, N.C., 1959.

Smith, John M. *History of the Town of Sunderland, Massachusetts.* Greenfield, Mass., 1899.

Smith, Joseph H. *Appeals to the Privy Council from the American Plantations.* New York, 1965.

Smith, Justin H. *Our Struggle for the Fourteenth Colony: Canada and the American Revolution.* 2 vols. New York, 1907.

Smith, William, Jr. *The History of the Late Province of New York.* 2 vols. New York, 1829.

Smith-Rosenberg, Carroll. "Davy Crockett as Trickster: Pornography, Liminality, and Symbolic Inversion in Victorian America." *Journal of Contemporary History* 17 (1982): 325–50.

Sosin, Jack M. *The Revolutionary Frontier, 1763–1783.* Albuquerque, N.M., 1974.

Spargo, John. *Anthony Haswell: Printer-Patriot-Ballader.* Rutland, Vt., 1925.

——. *Ethan Allen at Ticonderoga.* Rutland, Vt., 1926.

——. "Bennington Battle Monument and Historical Association Report." Bennington, Vt., 1926. Bennington Museum.

——. *The Story of David Redding Who Was Hanged.* Bennington, Vt., 1945.

——. *Notes on the Ancestors and Immediate Descendants of Ethan and Ira Allen.* Bennington, Vt., 1948.

Sparks, Jared. *Life and Treason of Benedict Arnold.* Boston, 1835.

——. *The Library of American Biography.* 10 vols. New York, 1844–48.

Spaulding, E. Wilder. *New York in the Critical Period, 1783–1789.* New York, 1932.

Spaulding, Reuben. "The Retrospect of a Pioneer in the New Hampshire Grants." *Proceedings of the Vermont Historical Society* 8 (1940): 263–81.

Stanley, George F. G. *Canada Invaded, 1775–1776.* Toronto, 1977.

Stannard, David E. *The Puritan Way of Death: A Study in Religion, Culture, and Social Change.* New York, 1977.

Starkey, Marion L. *A Little Rebellion.* New York, 1955.

Starr, Edward C. *A History of Cornwall, Connecticut.* Cornwall, Conn., 1926.

Steiner, Bruce. "Anglican Officeholding in Pre-Revolutionary Connecticut: The Parameters of New England Community." *William and Mary Quarterly* 31 (1974): 369–406.

Stewart, Isaac D. *The History of the Freewill Baptists for Half a Century.* Dover, N.H., 1862.

Stilgoe, John R. *The Common Landscape of America, 1580 to 1845.* New Haven, 1982.

Stilwell, Lewis D. *Migration from Vermont.* Montpelier, Vt., 1948.

Stokes, Anson P. *Church and State in the United States.* New York, 1950.

Stone, William L. *The Campaign of Lieut. Gen. John Burgoyne, and the Expedition of Lieut. Col. Barry St. Leger.* Albany, 1877.

Sullivan, Edward D. *Benedict Arnold, Military Racketeer.* New York, 1932.

Sweet, William W. *The Story of Religion in America.* Rev. ed. New York, 1950.

Swift, Esther M. *Vermont Place-Names.* Brattleboro, Vt., 1977.

Swift, Samuel. *History of the Town of Middlebury, in the County of Addison, Vermont.* Middlebury, Vt., 1859.

Szatmary, David P. *Shays' Rebellion: The Making of an Agrarian Insurrection.* Amherst, Mass., 1980.

Taylor, Alice F. *Freedom's Ferment: Phases of American Social History from the Colonial Period to the Outbreak of the Civil War.* New York, 1962.

Taylor, Alan. *Liberty Men and Great Proprietors: The Revolutionary Settlement on the Maine Frontier, 1760–1820.* Chapel Hill, N.C., 1990.

Taylor, Robert J. *Western Massachusetts in the Revolution.* Providence, R.I., 1954.

———. *Colonial Connecticut: A History.* Millwood, N.Y., 1976.

Temple, Josiah H., and George Sheldon. *A History of the Town of Northfield, Massachusetts, for 150 Years.* Albany, 1875.

Thomas, Brook. "The Pioneers, or the Sources of American Legal History: A Critical Tale." *American Quarterly* 36 (1984): 86–111.

Thompson, Daniel. *The Green Mountain Boys.* New York, 1839.

Thompson, E. P., et al. *Albion's Fatal Tree: Crime and Society in Eighteenth Century England.* New York, 1975.

Thompson, Francis. "Vermont from Chaos to Statehood: New Hampshire Grants and Connecticut Equivalent Lands." *Proceedings of the Pocumtuck Valley Memorial Association* 6 (1921): 231–71.

Tocqueville, Alexis de. *Democracy in America.* Garden City, N.Y., 1969.

Tracy, Patricia J. *Jonathan Edwards, Pastor: Religion and Society in Eighteenth-Century Northampton.* New York, 1980.

Trumbull, James R. *History of Northampton.* 2 vols. Northampton, Mass., 1898.

Turner, Frederick Jackson. *The Frontier in American History.* New York, 1947.

Turner, Lynn W. *The Ninth State: New Hampshire's Formative Years.* Chapel Hill, N.C., 1983.

Ullery, Jacob G. *Men of Vermont: An Illustrated Biographical History of Vermonters and Sons of Vermont.* Brattleboro, Vt., 1894.

Underwood, Wynn. "Indian and Tory Raids on the Otter Valley, 1777–1782." *Vermont History* 15 (1947): 195–221.

Upton, Richard F. *Revolutionary New Hampshire: An Account of the Social and Political Forces Underlying the Transition from Royal Province to American Commonwealth.* New York, 1971.

Van de Water, Frederic F. *The Reluctant Republic: Vermont, 1724–1791.* Taftsville, Vt., 1974.

Vail, Henry H. *Pomfret, Vermont.* 2 vols. Boston, 1930.

Walker, D. P. *The Decline of Hell: Seventeenth-Century Discussions of Eternal Torment.* Chicago, 1964.

Wallace, Anthony F. C. *The Death and Rebirth of the Seneca.* New York, 1970.

Walsh, James. "The Great Awakening in the First Congregational Church of Woodbury, Connecticut." *William and Mary Quarterly* 28 (1971): 543–62.

Walton, E. P. "The First Legislature of Vermont." *Proceedings of the Vermont Historical Society* (1878): 25–47.

Ward, Christopher. *The War of the Revolution.* 2 vols. New York, 1952.

Wardner, Henry S. *The Birthplace of Vermont: A History of Windsor to 1781.* New York, 1927.

Waselkov, Gregory A., and R. Eli Paul. "Frontiers and Archaeology." *North American Archeologist* 2 (1980–81): 309–29.

Weber, Max. *The Theory of Social and Economic Organization*. Ed. Talcot Parsons. Glencoe, Ill., 1957.

———. *Economy and Society: An Outline of Interpretive Sociology*. Ed. Guenther Roth and Claus Wittich. 2 vols. Berkeley, Calif., 1978.

Wecter, Dixon. *The Hero in America: A Chronicle of Hero-Worship*. New York, 1972.

Weir, Robert M. "Who Shall Rule at Home: The American Revolution as a Crisis of Legitimacy for the Colonial Elite." *Journal of Interdisciplinary History* 6 (1976): 679–700.

Wells, Frederic P. *History of Newbury, Vermont*. St. Johnsbury, Vt., 1902.

———. *History of Barnet, Vermont*. Burlington, Vt., 1923.

White, Alain C. *The History of the Town of Litchfield, Connecticut, 1720–1920*. Litchfield, Conn., 1920.

Whittenberg, James P. "Planters, Merchants, and Lawyers: Social Change and the Origins of the North Carolina Regulation." *William and Mary Quarterly* 34 (1974): 215–38.

Wilbur, James B. *Ira Allen, Founder of Vermont*. 2 vols. Boston, 1928.

Williams, J. C. *The History and Map of Danby, Vermont*. Rutland, Vt., 1869.

Williams, George. *The Radical Reformation*. Philadelphia, 1962.

Williamson, Chilton. *Vermont in Quandary, 1763–1825*. Montpelier, Vt., 1949.

Wills, Garry. *Inventing America: Jefferson's Declaration of Independence*. New York, 1978.

———. *Cincinnatus: George Washington and the Enlightenment*. Garden City, N.Y., 1984.

Wolf, Stephanie G. *Urban Village: Population, Community, and Family Structure in Germantown, Pennsylvania, 1683–1800*. Princeton, N.J., 1976.

Wood, Gordon S. *The Creation of the American Republic, 1776–1787*. New York, 1972.

———. "A Note on Mobs in the American Revolution." *William and Mary Quarterly* 23 (1966): 635–42.

Woodard, Florence M. *The Town Proprietors in Vermont: The New England Proprietorship in Decline*. New York, 1936.

Worrall, Arthur. *Quakers in the Colonial Northeast*. Hanover, N.H., 1980.

WPA, Federal Writers Project. *Connecticut*. Boston, 1938.

Wright, Stephen. *History of the Shaftsbury Baptist Association*. Troy, N.Y., 1853.

Wrong, George. *Canada and the American Revolution*. New York, 1968.

Wyckoff, William. *The Developer's Frontier: The Making of the Western New York Landscape*. New Haven, 1988.

Yinger, J. M. *Religion, Society, and the Individual: An Introduction to the Sociology of Religion*. New York, 1957.

Young, Alfred F., ed. *The American Revolution: Explorations in the History of American Radicalism.* DeKalb, Ill., 1976.

Zall, Paul. *Abe Lincoln Laughing.* Berkeley, Calif., 1982.

Zemsky, Robert. *Merchants, Farmers, and River Gods.* Boston, 1971.

Zuckerman, Michael. *Peaceable Kingdom: New England Towns in the Eighteenth Century.* New York, 1970.

Index

WITHDRAWN

WITHDRAWN

KELLY LIBRARY
Emory & Henry College
Emory, VA 24327

3 1836 0031 7900 4